D0308181

Hadlow College Library
582.16
RUS
JUNE 2012.
Canterbury
00029932
£9.99

NATUREGUIDE

# TREES

DK NATUREGUIDE

# TREES

Tony Russell

LONDON, NEW YORK, MELBOURNE,
MUNICH, AND DELHI

**DORLING KINDERSLEY**

**Senior Editor** Janet Mohun
**Project Art Editor** Anna Hall
**Editor** Miezan van Zyl
**Production Editor** Rebekah Parsons-King
**Production Controller** Erika Pepe
**Database** David Roberts
**New Photography** Gary Ombler
**New Illustrations** Gill Tomblin
**Picture Researcher** Jo Walton
**DK Picture Library** Claire Bowers, Rose Horridge
**Jacket Editor** Manisha Majithia
**Jacket Designers** Laura Brim, Mark Cavanagh
**Managing Editor** Camilla Hallinan
**Managing Art Editor** Michelle Baxter
**Publisher** Sarah Larter
**Art Director** Philip Ormerod
**Associate Publishing Director** Liz Wheeler
**Publishing Director** Jonathan Metcalf

**DK INDIA**

**Editorial Manager** Rohan Sinha
**Consultant Art Director** Shefali Upadhyay
**Deputy Managing Editor** Alka Thakur Hazarika
**Deputy Design Manager** Mitun Banerjee
**Senior Editor** Anita Kakar
**Senior Art Editors** Arup Giri, Ivy Roy
**Editors** Rahul Ganguly, Priyanka Naib, Rupa Rao, Priyaneet Singh
**Art Editors** Vritti Bansal, Sanjay Chauhan, Arijit Ganguly, Rakesh Khundongbam, Pooja Pawwar, Vaibhav Rastogi
**Assistant Editor** Sudeshna Dasgupta
**DTP Manager** Balwant Singh
**DTP Designers** Rajesh Singh Adhikari, Dheeraj Arora, Neeraj Bhatia, Mohammad Usman, Anita Yadav
**Production Manager** Pankaj Sharma

**SPECIAL PHOTOGRAPHY**

The following locations in the UK were used for new photography:
Batsford Arboretum, Gloucestershire, UK
The Forestry Commission at Westonbirt, The National Arboretum, Gloucestershire, UK
The Royal Botanic Gardens, Kew, London, UK

**CONSULTANT**

Rusty Russell, Collections and Informatics,
United States National Herbarium, National Museum of Natural History,
Smithsonian Institution, USA.

First published in Great Britain in 2012
by Dorling Kindersley Limited
80 Strand, London WC2R 0RL
Penguin Group (UK)

2 4 6 8 10 9 7 5 3 1

001 – 183145 – Apr/2012

Copyright © 2012 Dorling Kindersley Limited
All rights reserved

No part of this publication may be reproduced, stored in a retrieval system, or transmitted in any form or by any means, electronic, mechanical, photocopying, recording, or otherwise, without prior written permission of the copyright owner.

A CIP catalogue record for this book is available from the British Library.

ISBN 978-1-4053-7588-7

Reproduced by Bright Arts, China, and MDP, UK
Printed and bound in China by Leo Paper Products

Discover more at **www.dk.com**

# CONTENTS


**INTRODUCTION**

What are Trees? 6

How Trees Work 8

Tree Habitats 10

Identifying Trees 16

**SPECIES GUIDE**

Spore Trees 22

Seed Trees 24

Ginkgos 25

Conifers 27

Flowering Trees 94

Primitive Angiosperms 95

Monocotyledons 113

Eudicotyledons 121

Glossary 336

List of Tree Families 340

Index 341

Acknowledgments 351


## HOW THE SPECIES PROFILES WORK

*main section heading*

*tree group*

*profile information including illustration of form (winter and summer)*

*close-up illustrated details of features such as bark, leaves, flowers, fruits, and seeds*

*species name, with family name in brackets*

*Information on a similar species is given as text alone or with an image of the tree*

### KEY

- Gives the natural height range for the species. Height can vary in cultivation.
- Gives the width of the natural spread of the tree.
- Indicates whether the tree is deciduous (loses its leaves in winter), evergreen, or semi-evergreen.
- Gives information on the leaf type (simple or compound) and leaf arrangement. Simple leaves may be arranged oppostite each other on the stem or alternately; compound leaves may be pinnate or palmate.
- Geographical region where species occurs naturally.
- Similar species: provides information about a related or similar tree.

# WHAT ARE TREES?

**Trees are distinguished from other plants by their upright woody stem, roots, and branches, and by the fact that they do not die back on a regular basis, but continue to grow year upon year. They are the largest plants on Earth.**

## ROLE OF TREES

Trees are essential to all life. They absorb vast amounts of carbon dioxide and other pollutants from the atmosphere, replacing them with oxygen. Forests help regulate excess water flow and can reduce the effects of flooding and soil erosion. Trees influence weather patterns by increasing humidity and generating rainfall. They help to green our cities and towns, and provide a habitat for wildlife.

Despite so many obvious values, large swathes of forest are being lost every year, often for commercial gain or farming. Now, more than 10 per cent of the world's tree species are endangered. More than 8,750 species are threatened with extinction, and across the world at least 40 hectares of trees are felled every minute of every day.

**Rainforest**
There are thousands of different rainforest trees. Madagascar alone supports more than 2,000 different species, and there can be up to 500 different species within a single hectare in the Amazon rainforest.

## EVOLUTION

Trees evolved from early ferns in the Devonian. *Archaeopteris,* was one of the first trees that made up most of the forests on Earth 300 million years ago. Fossil records show it had a woody trunk, up to 40cm (16in) in diameter, with branches and a large root system. It had a vital influence on the planet, removing massive amounts of carbon dioxide from the atmosphere and replacing it with oxygen. As a result, many new organisms evolved. As climate changed, tree species evolved and adapted to take advantage of the conditions. Modern trees are little changed since the Oligocene epoch (34–23MYA) in the Palaeogene.

### TIMELINE

| Geological period | Million years ago | Event |
|---|---|---|
| Devonian | 416–360 MYA | Spore trees emerge. *Archeopteris*, an early tree, dominates. |
| Carboniferous | 360–299 MYA | *Lepidodendron*, the scale tree, flourishes in the warm, humid climate. |
| Permian | 299–251 MYA | First primitive conifers (gymnosperms) emerge. They had protected seeds and an improved reproductive system. |
| Triassic | 251–200 MYA | Conditions not favourable for tree growth but tree ferns, cycads, and conifers survive. Maidenhair tree emerges. |
| Jurassic | 200–146 MYA | Cycads and conifers flourish. |
| Cretaceous | 146–66 MYA | Flowering plants including most modern tree families evolve and begin to exert their dominance over conifers. |
| Palaeogene | 66–23 MYA | Flowering trees dominate and palms first appear. Grassland replaces large amount of forest; modern trees established. |

## TREE CLASSIFICATION

Classification is the grouping and naming of plants, or other living organisms. Scientists have tried to group trees for centuries, but not with great accuracy when compared with what scientists know today. The English oak (*Quercus robur)* and the holm or evergreen oak (*Quercus ilex)*, have always been correctly regarded as being closely related to each other because of the fruit they produce – the acorn. However, the sweet chestnut (*Castanea sativa)* and the horse chestnut (*Aesculus hippocastanum)* were originally grouped together because of their similar fruits. Yet today they are classified as belonging to two quite separate families.

In the 18th century, the Swedish botanist Carl von Linné (Linnaeus ) made the first attempt to link all plants by one specific feature. He classified them by the way they reproduced themselves: their sexual characteristics and the construction of their flowers and reproductive system.

He used two Latin words to name a species. The first word of the name is the generic name (genus) – for example, *Quercus*. This, when combined with the second or specific name (species) – for example, *robur* – becomes a unique identity for that species. Closely related species are all placed in the same genus – plural genera. Closely related genera are then grouped in families, which are in turn grouped in orders. Several orders together form a subclass, and subclasses are then combined under one class – for example, Angiospermae (flowering trees).

In recent years, a system of classification, based on genetic similarities has been introduced. As a result, some family relationships have changed.

**Major divisions**
In this book, chapters are divided into spore trees and seed trees. Seed trees are then are further subdivided into the major divisions: ginkgos, conifers, and flowering trees. Flowering trees are further subdivided into primitive angiosperms, monocotyledons, and eudicotyledons.

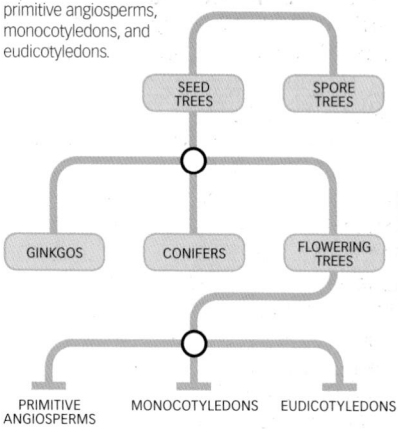


| | |
|---|---|
| **CLASS** | ANGIOSPERMAE |
| **SUBCLASS** | EUDICOTYLEDONEAE |
| **ORDER** | SAPINDALES |
| **FAMILY** | SAPINDACEAE |
| **GENUS** | ACER |
| **SPECIES** | ACER PALMATUM |

**Linnaean system**
In this system, all species are classified by genus, family, and order. The example here shows how Japanese maple (*Acer palmatum*) fits into the order Sapindales.

**ACER PALMATUM**

### CULTIVARS AND HYBRIDS

A hybrid occurs when two species cross-fertilize and produce offspring that display characteristics different to both parents. This can happen naturally in the wild, or be artificially induced. Hybrids are represented by "×" between the genus and species name. With cultivars, a difference in a species' characteristics can only be maintained through horticultural cultivation.

***Quercus rubra* 'Aurea'**
This cultivar of the red oak *(Quercus rubra)* has yellow leaves in contrast to the deep green leaves of the pure species.

# HOW TREES WORK

**There are thousands of different tree species but they all share one feature that distinguishes them from other plants: they produce a woody stem (a trunk) that supports a framework of branches and continues to grow year after year.**

## TREE STRUCTURE

Trees are made up of many different parts, and each part has its own unique function without which the tree could not survive. Some parts, such as the trunk, branches, and leaves, are clearly visible. Others parts are less obvious, for example, the circulatory system, roots, and, in some species, the reproductive organs.

**Parts of a tree**
The main parts of a tree above ground are the trunk and the canopy – the framework of branches bearing leaves, flowers, and seeds.

**Seeds**
The next generation of trees, seeds contain the basic ingredients for creating new trees virtually identical to their parents. Seeds come in various forms and may be contained in fruits, such as berries, nuts, or cones.

**Flowers**
The flowers contain the tree's reproductive organs. Male and female parts may occur within the same flower, or the tree may have separate male and female flowers either on the same or different tree.

**Leaves**
These produce food used by the tree to provide energy for living and growing. This is achieved by photosynthesis (opposite). Leaves are also the site of transpiration (water loss by evaporation).

**Bark**
A waterproof layer that surrounds the trunk and branches and protects the interior of the tree. It has millions of tiny pores (lenticels) that allow oxygen to pass into the living cells inside.

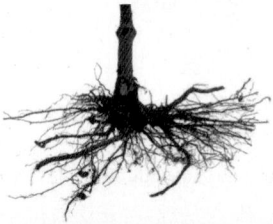

**Roots**
Tree roots provide anchorage and are the means by which the tree obtains water, minerals, and nutrients from the soil. Roots also store food, in the form of starch, for later use.

## MAKING FOOD

Food, in the form of energy-rich sugars, is supplied through a process called photosynthesis that takes place in the leaves. Nutrients are also transported from the soil via the roots. The sugar (sucrose) from photosynthesis provides energy and can be turned into starch and cellulose, which form the tree's cells. Oxygen is a by-product of the process and is released back into the atmosphere.

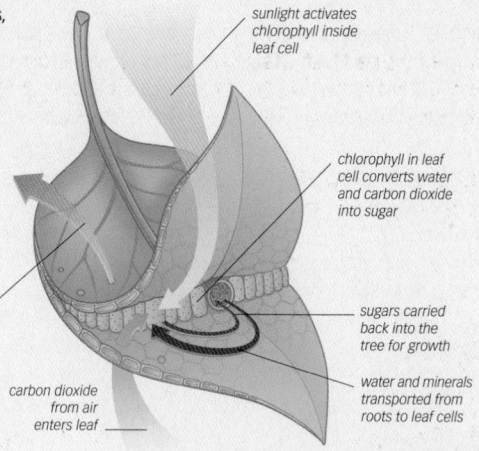


**Photosynthesis**
Chlorophyll, the green pigment in leaves, is activated by light energy from the sun. Tiny pores in the leaf's surface absorb carbon dioxide from the atmosphere. This reacts with water to produce sugar.

## TREE GROWTH AND CIRCULATION

Trees grow from the tips of the previous year's growth. At the tip of each branch are growing cells. As these multiply, the branch grows longer and the tree taller and broader. Cells also divide beneath the bark, making the trunk and branches thicker.

Under the bark is a spongy layer called phloem. This carries the food made in the leaves (above) to the rest of the tree. Under the phloem is a layer of cells called the cambium, which makes phloem cells on the outside and xylem cells on the inside. Xylem transports water and minerals from the roots to the leaves.

**Tree rings**
The bands seen in a cut trunk represent a new layer of xylem, which is deposited during each year's growing season. These bands can be used to tell a tree's age.

**Insect pollination**
Pollen is transferred from the male reproductive structures (stamens) as the insect retrieves sweet nectar from the base of the flower.

## REPRODUCTION

Tree flowers last just long enough to be pollinated by insects, birds, or wind. Once pollinated, and the flower's ovules (female parts) are fertilized, a seed develops from the female flower or part of flower. Depending on tree species, the seed matures within a fruit or cone. Once the seed is mature, it may fall to the ground, or be dispersed by wind or water. Some seeds are eaten by birds or mammals and excreted away from the tree. As long as conditions are suitable, the seed will eventually germinate and a seedling will develop – producing the next tree generation.

# TREE HABITATS

**Across the world, different tree species grow naturally in various locations that suit their specific requirements. These locations are known as their habitat – their natural home. What makes a location exactly right for a species will depend on many factors.**

## ADAPTING TO THE ENVIRONMENT

Over millions of years, each tree species has evolved and adapted to the climate and conditions that surround it. The amount of rainfall, the temperatures they have to endure, and the amount of sunshine they receive have all influenced both the behavioural patterns of trees and their natural distribution across the planet. Other influential factors include soil type, proximity to the oceans, and exposure to predation, disease, and fire. Trees show some remarkable adaptations that allow them to survive in a wide variety of conditions throughout the world. For example, mangrove trees (p.328), which grow close to, or actually in the ocean, have developed an internal desalination process that allows them to extract fresh water from the sea.

### FOREST ZONES

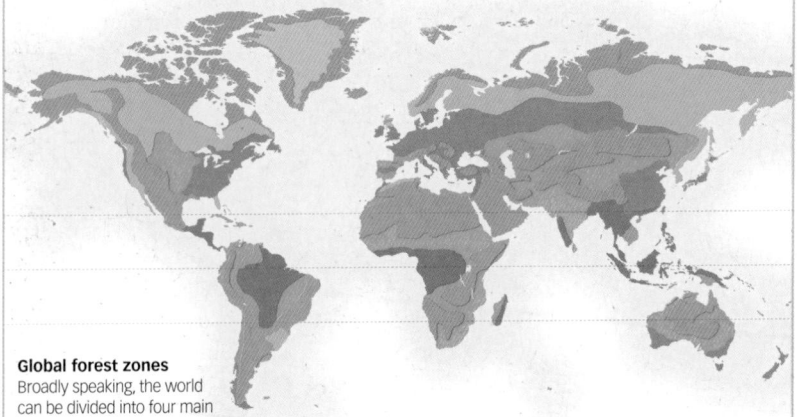

**Global forest zones**
Broadly speaking, the world can be divided into four main forest zones. These zones are interspersed by areas that contain comparatively few trees, such as deserts and high mountain ranges.

**KEY**

- **Coniferous forest**
- **Temperate broadleaf forest**
- **Tropical broadleaf forest**
- **Tropical rainforest**
- **Barren landscapes/deserts**
- **Ice caps**
- **Prairie and savanna**

**Coniferous forest** covers large swathes across the northern hemisphere and some mountain ranges. Conifer trees are well-adapted to harsh winters.

**Tropical broadleaf forest** includes all tropical forest types, except for rainforest. Trees that fit in this category may also thrive in other zones.

**Temperate broadleaf forest** comprises a mix of evergreen and deciduous species, which tolerate the cool conditions that result from seasonal changes.

**Tropical rainforest** is home to plants that thrive only in areas that have very high humidity, such as tropical South America.

## TROPICAL

Tropical trees are located on either side of the equator, in three main regions: Amazonia in South America, Central Africa, and Southeast Asia. Here, rainfall, temperature, and hours of sunlight are relatively constant throughout the year and tree growth is rapid. Consequently, tropical trees reach maturity, flower, set seed, and die much more quickly than trees in other regions. A variety of characteristics help tropical trees grow in this habitat. For example, many trees, such as the weeping fig (p.314), have leathery leaves with pointed "drip tips", which allow them to shed water during tropical rainstorms. As there is little need for protection against frost or water loss, thin bark, as on the rubber tree (p.329), is another common feature. To gain maximum sunlight, while also shading out competing trees, some tropical trees, such as the Brazil nut (p.322), develop a tall trunk with few low branches and a large crown of leaves.

**Dense rainforest**
There is no dry season in areas where tropical rainforests have formed, which means that plant growth is continuous throughout the year. Rainforests are home to a very wide variety of plants.

**Weeping fig leaves**
The leaves of the weeping fig (*Ficus benjamina*) are ovate to elliptic, with a pronounced "drip tip" at the end. During the heavy rainfall that is common in the tropics, this tip allows excess water to run off.

»

## » TEMPERATE

Temperate trees are found between latitudes 40–50 degrees north and south of the equator. Here there are well defined seasons but few extremes in either rainfall patterns or temperature. A temperate climate is suitable for tree growth for approximately six months of the year, when average temperatures are over 10°C (50°F). Although suitable for both deciduous and evergreen trees, including conifers, it is deciduous broad-leaved trees, such as oak (p.165) that predominate in temperate regions. Many trees, such as birch (*Betula* sp., p.173) and hornbeam (p.184), take advantage of the windy conditions that exist within temperate regions and are wind pollinated.

**Autumn colours**
In the autumn, the leaves of deciduous trees undergo a chemical process as they are about to be shed, producing a wide array of colour.

**Winter forest**
Deciduous broad-leaved trees discard their leaves in autumn, growing new ones in the following spring when temperatures and light levels become suitable for growth.

## DESERT

The difficulties facing trees in the desert all relate to a lack of water. Hot sun, desiccating winds, and low rainfall, make it hard for roots to supply enough water to compensate for that lost through leaves. Desert trees have adapted to this harsh habitat in several ways. Some, such as the dragon tree (p.120), have leaves that reduce the transpiration effect. Other trees develop long roots, which allow them to reach moisture near the water table. The baobab (p.319) can store hundreds of litres of water in its broad trunk, which significantly varies its trunk circumference between wet and dry seasons.

**Joshua tree**
The Joshua tree has spike-like, evergreen leaves that occur only at the tips of the branches, reducing the loss of moisture through the leaves.

## MOUNTAINS

In many ways mountains have the same climate as that of the sub-arctic, although this depends on elevation and latitude. They usually have short summers, cold winters, and a mean temperature that rarely rises above 10°C (50°F). Wind speeds also tend to be much greater at high altitudes and the combination of drying winds and shallow soils, which can be frozen for long periods of time, ensure that only the hardiest of trees will survive. The higher the elevation, the slower trees grow and the more stunted they become. The point beyond which no tree will survive is known as the tree line. The narrow needle-like leaves of many conifers are far better able to withstand freezing temperatures than broad leaves. Their narrow conical form, such as on Serbian spruce (p.83) also offers reduced wind resistance and the ability to shed heavy falls of snow.

**Mountain pine**
Mountains tend to be covered with conifers, many from the Pinaceae family – spruce, pine, fir, and hemlock – as they are better adapted to cold conditions.

»

## COASTAL TREES

Exposure to ocean storms and strong salt-laden winds can make it difficult for coastal trees to survive. Salt contact with foliage may cause leaf-burn, branch die-back, and defoliation. This reduces the tree's ability to photosynthesize and produce food, causing stress and possible death. Salt uptake from moisture extracted by tree roots from coastal soils can also poison a tree. It takes only 0.5% of a tree's living tissue to contain salt before it reaches toxic levels. Some trees, such as Monterey cypress (p.51), which grows on the rocky coastline of the Monterey Peninsula in California, USA, are able to absorb higher concentrations of salt without harm.

**Mangrove roots**
Mangroves (*Rhizophora* spp.) produce stilt or prop roots that rise above the water to absorb oxygen. The roots also screen out salt.

**Coastal cypress**
Trees that grow along the coast must be able to withstand harsh conditions caused by strong winds and salt. The Monterey cypress (*Cupressus macrocarpa*) has a higher threshold against salt toxicity than many other trees.

**Urban**
Tree-lined streets and urban parks improve air quality, reduce heat, and help to combat noise and light pollution.

## URBAN TREES

Trees bring many benefits to the urban environment. They reduce air pollution by trapping particle pollutants such as dust, ash, and smoke. They also absorb carbon dioxide and other dangerous gasses, replacing them with clean oxygen. Urban trees help reduce localized flooding by capturing rainwater and increasing soil permeability. They cool the "heat island" effect of cities by absorbing heat and providing shade. Trees reduce wind speed around high-rise buildings, increase humidity in dry city climates, and reduce glare on sunny days. Urban trees also reduce noise and light pollution. Trees such as *Ginkgo biloba* and London plane (*Platanus* x *acerifolia*) are perfect for urban planting because they are extremely tolerant of localized air pollution.

## HEDGEROW

Hedgerows are live barriers consisting of trees (and shrubs) that are used to contain livestock, act as boundary markers, and provide shelter. The best trees for hedgerows are those species that will naturally develop a thick, impenetrable framework of branches, ideally protected by an armoury of thorns or spines. They should be tough, able to withstand exposure, browsing by livestock, and respond well to regular pruning. The most popular trees for planting in hedges are hawthorn, holly, and beech. Hedgerows are valuable to wildlife and provide an ideal nesting habitat for birds.

**Living wall**
The trees growing within hedgerows differ from region to region and reflect the local conditions and the purpose of the hedge.

## WETLAND

The banks of rivers and streams can provide the ideal habitat for many trees. Rivers provide a natural gap in the canopy, which means trees that grow alongside receive plenty of light. Wetland areas are also rich and fertile – flooding and constant fluctuations in water levels ensure regular deposits of minerals and nutrients. However, during prolonged flooding the soil will become waterlogged, preventing oxygen getting to tree roots. Some trees, such as the swamp cypress (p.66), have adapted ways to overcome this. They produce special hollow breathing organs called pneumatophores, or "knees", which rise above the water. These knees have lenticels (breathing pores) in the bark which absorb oxygen and then pipe it back down to the roots beneath the water.

**Swamp cypress**
*Taxodium distichum* can withstand waterlogged conditions for many months. In the Florida Everglades, they form extensive forests where few other trees would survive.

# IDENTIFYING TREES

**Despite the large numbers of different species and varieties, trees offer several clues to their identification. By working through these step-by-step, it should be possible to reach a positive identification.**

## BARK

The great advantage of bark as an identification feature is that it is present all year round. So even in the depths of winter it is possible to identify some trees just by their bark. Colour, flaking, banding, the development of ridges, and the appearance of lenticels (pores) on the bark can all aid identification. However, bark often changes with age, and this is an important factor to take into consideration when identifying a tree.

HORIZONTAL PEELING

VERTICAL PEELING

IRREGULAR PLATES

RIDGED AND FISSURED

SMOOTH IN EARLY YEARS

ROUGH FLAKING

**Types of bark**
The textures and colour of bark are useful aids to identification. Throughout this book, these terms are used to descibe the bark of different species.

## LEAF ARRANGEMENT

After assessing whether leaves are deciduous or evergreen, the way the leaves are arranged on the shoot is a helpful aid to identification. Some trees have large leaves that are divided into smaller leaves, or leaflets. These are compound leaves, and the arrangement of the leaflets provides another clue to identification. Pinnate leaves have leaflets on either side of a central stalk. Palmate leaves have leaflets arranged like fingers on a hand. Leaves that are not divided into leaflets are called simple. Simple leaves may be arranged opposite each other on the stalk or may be alternate.

OPPOSITE

ALTERNATE

PALMATE

PINNATE

**Simple leaves**
Simple leaves do not have leaflets and are arranged in one of two ways: opposite, with leaves paired on either side of the stalk, or alternate, with the leaves in a staggered pattern.

**Compound leaves**
Compound leaves are divided into leaflets, which may branch from the tip of the stalk (palmate) or may be arranged symmetrically along the stalk's length (pinnate).

## LEAF SHAPE

Collectively, trees display scores of different leaf shapes and a wide range of sizes, from just a few millimetres to more than a metre. Broadleaf trees display the greatest variation in shape, but many are either elliptic or obovate. Conifer leaves tend to fall into just a few main categories: scale-like; linear; or needle-like and tapering to a pointed, but not always sharp, end.

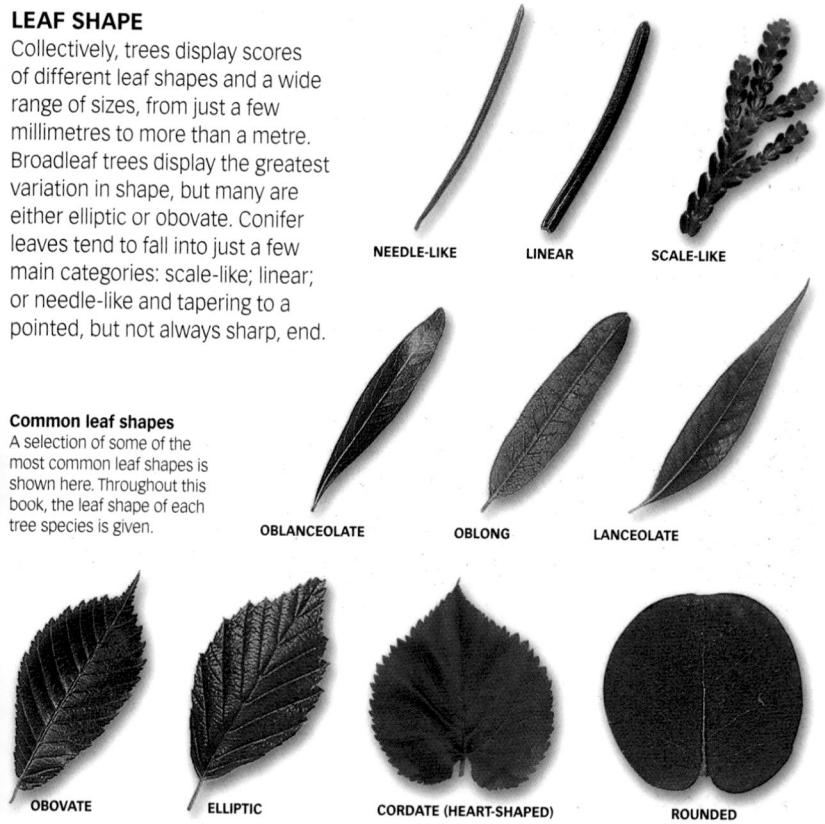


**Common leaf shapes**
A selection of some of the most common leaf shapes is shown here. Throughout this book, the leaf shape of each tree species is given.

## LEAF MARGINS AND TEXTURE

The margins of both compound and simple leaves may be smooth (known as entire) or may have indentations. The leaf margin indentations may be wavy, serrated or toothed (like the teeth of a saw), or lobed. One of the most recognizable leaf margins is that of the common oak (*Quercus robur*), which has regular "bites" along the margin interspersed with rounded lobes. Some leaves are also recognizable by their texture. For example, leaves of the English elm (*Ulmus procera*) have a rough texture, whereas those of the katsura tree (*Cercidiphyllum japonicum*) are velvet-like.

**Types of leaf margin**
Leaf margins may be smooth (entire), wavy, or indented. There are many variations of indentations, some of which are shown here.

»

## FLOWERS

The flowers of many trees have a distinctive appearance and provide valuable clues to identification. In temperate regions the majority of trees flower in the spring, whereas in tropical regions flowers may be produced all year round. The purpose of flowers is to aid reproduction, and flowers tend to be colourful and fragrant in order to attract pollinators such as insects and birds. Some tree species have separate male and female flowers on the same tree; these are known as monoecious. Species in which the male and female flowers are on different trees are known as dioecious.

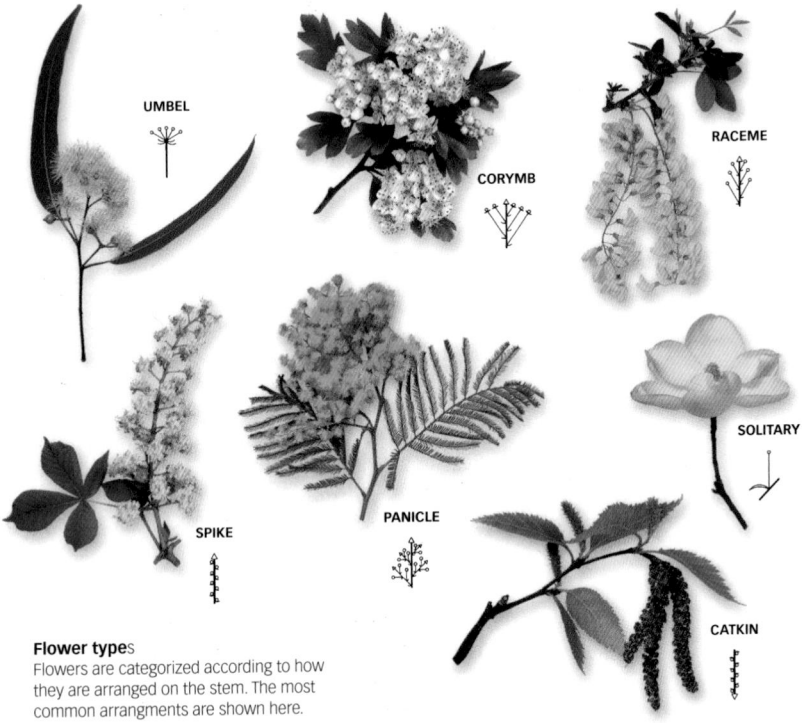


**Flower types**
Flowers are categorized according to how they are arranged on the stem. The most common arrangments are shown here.

### PARTS OF A FLOWER

Most flowers consist of petals, sepals, and reproductive structures. The female parts are the stigma, style, and ovary; the male parts are the anther and filament (together forming the stamen). In most flowers, the sepals and petals are distinct, in primitive angiosperms such as magnolia, they are not.

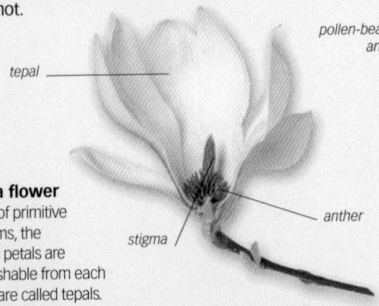


**Magnolia flower**
In flowers of primitive angiosperms, the sepals and petals are indistinguishable from each other and are called tepals.

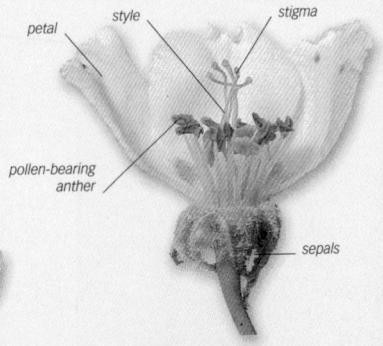


**Normal flower structure**
In most flowers, the sepals and petals are distinct from each other.

## SEEDS AND FRUIT

Nearly all trees begin life as seeds. These seeds are contained within a receptacle, or fruit, of which there are several types, including drupes, berries, pods, and nuts. Observing how a tree carries its seeds can be a useful aid to identification.

Most conifers encase their seeds in a hard, woody conical structure – a cone. Beneath the scales of each cone there may be hundreds of seeds, each attached to a papery wing to aid wind dispersal. Members of the *Acer* (maple) genus also produce seeds that are attached to papery wings, these are called samara.

In some instances, tree seeds are encased in a fruit of soft flesh. Where this flesh surrounds a single hard shell, which in turn encases a single seed, such as in peach, plum, olive, or cherry, the fruit is known as a drupe. When the flesh surrounds multiple seeds the fruit is known as a berry or a pome. Dry fruits that split on maturity to release the seeds inside are commonly called a pod or capsule. Dry fruits that do not automatically split include those fruits commonly known as nuts. Examples of these include hazel, hickory, chestnut, and acorn.

**Types of seeds and fruit**
The form, shape, size , and colour of fruit and seeds can be an aid to tree identification.

## TREE HABIT

The shape of a tree, known as its habit, can be a good clue to identification as some trees have a habit that is easily recognizable, such as the narrow, column-like habit of the Italian cypress (*Cupressus sempervirens*) and the weeping habit of the willow (Salix *babylonica*) A tree's size may also aid identification. However, both habit and size can vary according to factors such as a tree's age, habitat, and climate.

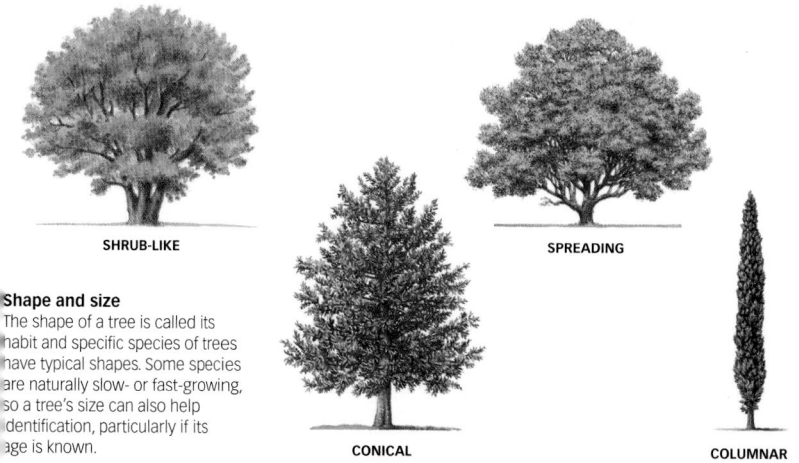


**Shape and size**
The shape of a tree is called its habit and specific species of trees have typical shapes. Some species are naturally slow- or fast-growing, so a tree's size can also help identification, particularly if its age is known.

# SPECIES GUIDE

# SPORE TREES

**The most primitive trees – the tree ferns – do not grow from seeds, but from single cells called spores. This type of life cycle has more in common with lowly mosses than other kinds of trees.**

The very first trees – from around 300 million years ago – were spore trees, such as *Archeopteris* (p.6). Their trunks lifted foliage clear of the prehistoric swamps, giving them more access to sunlight. More light meant more energy to make more food. These primeval forests had many trees unlike anything around today. The only surviving spore-producing trees are tree ferns. Tree ferns have trunks covered in a mantle of aerial roots and a core strengthened by fibre, not wood. They predominate in certain habitats, such as equatorial alpine meadows – but otherwise live in forests dominated by seed trees.

Like all ferns, tree ferns scatter spores from ruptured capsules on the underside of leaves. Spores germinate on wet ground, each growing into a tiny heart-shaped sexual stage called a prothallus. Sperm cells from one prothallus swim to fertilize the egg in another and sprout an embryonic fern plant.

| | |
|---|---|
| **DIVISION** | PTERIDOPHYTA |
| **CLASS** | FILICOPSIDA |
| **ORDER** | CYATHEALES |
| **FAMILIES** | 8 |
| **SPECIES** | c.680 (c.600 SPORE TREES) |

Over many years of growth, a tree fern may come to tower 20 m (65 ft) over neighbouring plants, but the nature of its life cycle means that it will always demand moisture on the ground to reproduce. This kind of spore-dependent reproduction occurs in other plants – such as mosses and liverworts – but none of these has evolved the tree habit.

All ferns belong to the plant division Pteridophyta. Less than 20 per cent of fern species belong to the one tree fern order, which is called Cyatheales. The most primitive Cyatheales are trunkless ferns with creeping stems, but those of the families Dicksoniaceae and Cyatheaceae are tree fern "giants", with tough leathery leaves.

**PROFILE**

- 7 m (22 ft)
- Up to 4 m (12 ft)
- Evergreen
- Compound
- S.E. Australia, Tasmania

**Large, young fronds**
This tree fern has large fronds, up to 4 m (12 ft) long, which grow from the top of the trunk.

*unfurling fern frond*

**FEATURES**

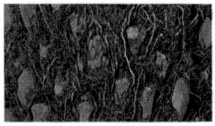

**Bark** Chestnut-brown; fibrous, soft, with black, woody core

**Leaves** Slightly shiny, rich green on upper surface, matt, pale green on underside

*Dicksonia antarctica* (Dicksoniaceae)

# SOFT TREE FERN

**Native to southeastern Australia** and Tasmania, this hardy tree fern has been popular for planting in the warm, wet regions of both Europe and North America since its introduction and cultivation in Europe in 1880. This species is not a tree at all but a true fern; however, its phenomenal popularity lies in the fact that it can reach tree-like proportions.

The trunk is made of the fibrous remains of old roots. Beneath the trunk's surface is a bone-like core. New roots grow down the trunk each year to enable the fern to produce a new set of fronds. Each frond is like a typical fern leaf, but larger in size. The underside of fronds have light brown, rounded spores dispersed at regular intervals. New fronds unfurl from the top of the trunk in spring. In winter, the plant resembles an upright log because in colder climates the fronds die completely.

**Rough tree fern (*Cyathea australis*)** This related tree fern is more cold-hardy, and sheds its fronds each year, even in warm climates, unlike the soft tree fern.

# SEED TREES

**The majority of living trees start their lives bound inside a capsule called a seed. Seeds provide a means of securing the welfare of embryonic trees until they are ready to sprout roots and shoots.**

| SUPERDIVISION | SPERMATOPHYTA |
|---|---|
| DIVISIONS | CYCADOPHYTA |
| | GINKGOPHYTA |
| | GNETOPHYTA |
| | PINOPHYTA |
| | MAGNOLIOPHYTA |

Seed trees are the largest group of trees and include the divisions cycads, ginkgos, gnetophytes, conifers, and the biggest group of all, flowering trees (also called angiosperms). Seed trees combine two key adaptive features: woody trunks and seeds. Wood is built from millions of microscopic hollow struts – called xylem vessels – that carry water and minerals from the roots in the ground to the leaves. The xylem vessels form rings around the core of the trunk, increasing its girth and helping it support more foliage.

The seed is a survival capsule containing a plant embryo (a young plant at an early stage of development). Whereas exposed tree fern (p.23) embryos are vulnerable, embryos inside seeds are protected and are even nourished by a food store – up to the point when conditions are right for them to germinate. Seed trees can reproduce in drier habitats too, as their fertilization happens inside reproductive shoots of the canopy – not on wet ground. Each egg forms inside a female capsule called an ovule. Male cells are delivered in pollen grains from male shoots – carried either on wind, by water, or by animal, such as an insect. A "captured" pollen grain penetrates the ovule with a pollen tube to convey male cells to the egg. The fertilized egg then grows into an embryo and the ovule is now called a seed.

Most seed trees produce their seeds encased in fruit that develops from a flower: these belong to the class Angiospermae within the division Magnoliophyta. Others, such as Ginkgophyta (ginkgos) and Pinophyta (conifers) – collectively called gymnosperms – produce "naked" seeds.

# GINKGOS

**Most non-flowering seed trees alive today are conifers, but a few are remnants of groups that flourished even before the development of conifers. One of these groups is the ginkgos, the sole living representative of which is the maidenhair tree.**

| DIVISION | GINKGOPHYTA |
|---|---|
| CLASS | 1 |
| ORDERS | 1 |
| FAMILIES | 1 |
| SPECIES | 1 |

In contrast to the needle-like leaves of many conifers (p.27), the maidenhair tree has flat leathery leaves that are shed in harsh winters. Ginkgos have extraordinary reproductive behaviour quite unlike any other plant alive today. They produce seed without cones, flowers, or fruits. Each male sex cell (sperm) produced by a pollen grain moves with a tuft of tails – a remnant of primitive fern-like ancestry. Ginkgos are unisexual: each individual carries either male or female structures, but never both. Female ginkgos produce their small egg-containing ovules in exposed pairs. Pollen grains reach them by wind and are "captured" by drops of fluid secreted by the ovules, which also serve to encourage the grains to grow pollen tubes: sperm then swims through the tube to fertilise the egg. Because the ovules are "naked" on the female shoots, ginkgos do not produce true fruits. Instead, their fleshy seeds smell of vomit and rotting flesh – something that humans find nauseating, but might have lured in a long-extinct carnivore to aid dispersal.

**Primitive leaf**
Unlike broadleaved trees, leaves of the ginkgo have veins that spread out like a fan, instead of forming a network.

leaves often deeply notched

leaf up to 8 cm (3 in) wide

leaves spirally arranged on new shoots

shoots form along thin, fawn-grey twigs

veins radiate from base of leaf

**Ginkgo leaves**
The notched, leathery leaves of the maidenhair tree are borne on long, slender stalks and have a distinctive fan shape.

**PROFILE**

- Up to 40 m (130 ft)
- Up to 20 m (70 ft)
- Deciduous
- Fan-shaped
- S.E. China

**FEATURES**

**Bark** Pale grey-brown; vertically fissured when mature

**Seeds** Fleshy, yellow-green seed husk contains kernel

**Leaves**
Golden yellow coloration in autumn

*Ginkgo biloba* (Ginkgoaceae)

# MAIDENHAIR TREE

**Fossil records indicate** that this primitive tree has existed on Earth since the Jurassic period, about 200 million years ago. It is no longer found in the wild, but the presence of ancient cultivated trees in southeast China suggests that the last wild population grew in this area. The tree was introduced in the West in 1730. It produces leaves resembling those of the maidenhair fern (*Adiantum*), hence its common name.

Several leaves emerge, spirally arranged, from each shoot. The yellow-green male and female reproductive organs appear on separate trees. Female trees are seldom grown as the flesh of the seed emits a rancid odour. The leaves have medicinal properties and are used in the treatment of certain circulatory ailments.

**Ornamental tree**
The upright, broadly conical *Ginkgo* is planted as an ornamental tree throughout the northern hemisphere.

# CONIFERS

**Conifers are large woody, sometimes massive, seed trees that have their reproductive parts arranged in shoots called strobili, or cones, instead of flowers. Most are evergreen and have small, but very tough, needle-like leaves that help them survive harsh cold winters or prolonged drought.**

| DIVISION | PINOPHYTA |
|---|---|
| CLASS | 1 |
| ORDERS | 1 |
| FAMILIES | 7 |
| SPECIES | 630 (c. 550 TREES) |

These trees are particularly resilient and many conifers are adapted for unforgiving conditions. Needle leaves, laden with resin and liberally coated in transparent wax, dry out very slowly – so little water is required to keep them alive. This means conifers can stay green when soil is frozen, and the same needle-type leaves helps tropical species survive where land is parched.

Conifers produce seeds in cones. Male cones produce pollen, female ones produce ovules – quite often on the same tree. Lacking the means to attract insects, they rely instead on the wind to carry their pollen. Wind pollination is a hit-and-miss affair, but conifers make up for it by producing their pollen in vast quantities. Ovules, and therefore seeds, arise on scales on female cones. In some conifers, such as junipers and yews, the cones are fleshy and edible to attract animals who disperse seed in their faeces. In others, such as pines, hard woody cones may take years to open to release their seeds.

**Lodgepole pine**
Resinous leaves and cones help this hardy conifer survive in the coldest conditions, such as Tongass National Forest in Alaska.

**PROFILE**

- Up to 30 m (100 ft)
- Up to 15 m (50 ft)
- Evergreen
- Triangular
- S. Chile, S.W. Argentina

*scale tip curved outwards*

*glossy dark green leaves, arranged spirally*

*male cone 7–15 cm (3–6 in) long*

**Monkey puzzle cones**
The male cone remains on the tree for many months. Male and female cones are normally carried on separate trees.

**FEATURES**

**Female cones** Green, ripening to yellow-brown

**Seed cones** Brown; breaking to release up to 200 seeds

*Araucaria araucana* (Araucariaceae)

# MONKEY PUZZLE TREE

**Also known as Chile pine**, this distinctive tree has existed for millions of years. Fossil remains indicate it was abundant in the southern hemisphere during the Mesozoic era. Today, its natural range is exclusive to southern Chile and Argentina. It was introduced into cultivation in the 18th century using seeds collected by Archibald Menzies, the Scottish surgeon aboard the British ship HMS *Discovery*.

Mature trees have cylindrical, gradually tapering trunks, with a light grey bark that is slightly wrinkled. The triangular, stiff leaves terminate in sharp points. Spherical female cones are borne on the top side of branches, high in the crown. They mature over two years, growing up to 15 cm (6 in) wide, and break apart to release the seeds.

**Distinctive shape**
The trunk of the monkey puzzle tree has whorls of horizontal branches emerging at regular intervals.

**Dense foliage**
Leaves of the Norfolk Island pine are densely arranged along light brown branches, which are borne in widely spaced whorls.

*stiff, horizontal to slightly ascending branches*

*leaf 1.2 cm (½ in) long*

**PROFILE**

- 50–70 m (160–230 ft)
- Up to 25 m (80 ft)
- Evergreen
- Needle-like
- Norfolk Island (east of Australia)

**FEATURES**

**Female cones** Green, turning dull brown in 18 months

*Araucaria heterophylla* (Araucariaceae)

# NORFOLK ISLAND PINE

**This ancient tree is endemic** to Norfolk Island, a small island to the east of Australia. Particularly attractive in its juvenile stage, this tree is grown in tropical and subtropical gardens, and is widely grown as a house plant elsewhere. Prone to frost damage, this tree is rarely successful when grown outdoors at latitudes above 45° North.

The scientific name *heterophylla* means "different leaves", referring to the leaf variation between juvenile and adult trees. When young, the tree has light green, drooping, soft, awl-shaped leaves. With maturity, it develops a symmetrical, triangular outline, while the leaves become hard and dark green. Male pollen cones grow to 4 cm (1½ in) long. They are yellowish brown, sometimes reddish in colour and borne in pendulous clusters. Female cones are squat, rounded, 10–12 cm (4–5 in) long and wide.

**Kauri pine (*Agathis australis*)** This tree is easily distinguished from the Norfolk Island pine by its thick, blade-like leaves, and large spreading branches.

**PROFILE**

- 20–40m (70–130ft)
- Up to 10m (30ft)
- Evergreen
- Needle-like
- S.E. Australia

**Leaves and cones**
The leaves of the Wollemi pine are light green at first, turning dark green with age. The male cones are slender and ovoid.

*leaf up to 4cm (1½in) long*

*male cone, up to 7.5cm (3in) long*

**FEATURES**

**Bark** Develops chocolate brown, bubbly texture with age

**Female cones** Small, green; take about two years to mature

*Wollemia nobilis* (Araucariaceae)

# WOLLEMI PINE

**Thought to have been extinct** for at least two million years, this upright conifer was discovered in 1994, growing in a remote canyon in the Blue Mountains of Australia. It is related to the *Araucaria* and *Agathis* genera. Fossilized remains dating back approximately 90 million years indicate that the Wollemi pine was prevalent in the Cretaceous period. Its discovery has been described as the botanical equivalent to finding a living dinosaur. There are fewer than 100 mature trees in the wild, but thousands have been reproduced from them and are being cultivated around the world.

The bark is reddish brown, and peels in thin scales when young. Young leaves are soft and frond-like, while mature ones are linear, pointed, and leathery, and are arranged in four rows. The Wollemi pine produces both male and female cones on the same tree. The cones are initially green and mature to bronze. In winter, the growing tips of the buds are protected by a white, waxy coating and the leaves take on a bronze hue.

**Flattened leaves**
Branches bear flattened and spreading ranks of leaves, glossy green on the upper surface, light matt green on the underside.

*leaf up to 9 cm (3½ in) long*

*purple-brown, ovoid seed*

*blunt-tipped leaf*

**PROFILE**

- 20–26 m (70–85 ft)
- Up to 10 m (30 ft)
- Evergreen
- Needle-like
- C. China

**FEATURES**

**Male cones** Pale yellow, borne in leaf axils

*small female seed cone*

**Female cones** Pale yellow, borne at shoot tips

*Cephalotaxus fortunei* (Cephalotaxaceae)

# CHINESE PLUM YEW

**This small evergreen** was introduced into Europe from central China in 1849 by the Scottish plant collector Robert Fortune – hence the species name *fortunei*. It has a spreading habit, similar in outline to the common yew (p.37). In the wild in China, this tree grows naturally as a woodland species and as such is extremely shade tolerant. It is seldom cultivated in full sun.

The bark is red-brown and flaking, similar to that of the common yew. The Chinese plum yew's stems are erect with distinctive whorls of branches at intervals, each bearing ranks of linear, lanceolate leaves. Both male and female cones are small and pale yellow, and are produced on separate trees in spring. The female seed cone develops into an oval, blue-green, olive-like structure, up to 2–3 cm (¾–1¼ in) long. It matures to become purple-brown and plum-like over a period of two years. The fleshy covering is inedible and contains a single, small, brown nut-like seed.

**PROFILE**

- 8–12 m (25–40 ft)
- Up to 5 m (15 ft)
- Evergreen
- Needle-like
- Japan, Korea

**Leaves and cones**
Male pollen cones of the Japanese plum yew are borne in leaf axils. The leaf undersides are grey-green.

**FEATURES**

**Female cones** Small; develop into fleshy structures

*Cephalotaxus harringtonia* (Cephalotaxaceae)

# JAPANESE PLUM YEW

**As the name suggests**, this small conifer originates from Japan, where it has been cultivated for centuries, both as an ornamental evergreen and for its fruit. It is also native to Korea. It was introduced into the West in 1830 by German physician Philipp Franz von Siebold.

Also known as cow's tail pine because of its elegant drooping branchlets, Japanese plum yew grows as a spreading, bushy, shrublike tree, sometimes broader than tall. It has dense, spirally arranged foliage, which ascends from each branchlet in two planes to form a distinct V-shaped groove, rather like a bird's wings.

The bark is grey and peels in thin strips. Once pollinated, tiny female seed cones turn into light green oval seed structures, which mature to purple. They are fleshy and release a sweet-smelling cloudy resin when squeezed. In Japan, the ripe flesh and the seed inside are eaten, the latter having a pine-like flavour. If eaten before they are mature, they leave a pungent, resinous aftertaste, which may take hours to subside.

**Chilean yew seed**
Plum-like ovoid, edible seeds develop from pollinated female seed cones. Linear leaves are spirally arranged around shoots.

*leaf twisted on branch*

*leaf up to 2.5 cm (1 in) long*

*ovoid seed cone 2 cm (¾ in) long*

**PROFILE**

- 7–25 m (22–80 ft)
- Up to 10 m (30 ft)
- Evergreen
- Needle-like
- Chile, Argentina

*Prumnopitys andina* (Podocarpaceae)

# CHILEAN YEW

**This South American conifer**, also known as plum-fruited yew, is now considered vulnerable in the wild. Native to the Andes mountains of southern Chile and Argentina, it was introduced into cultivation in Europe by English nurserymen Veitch & Sons in 1860. It may reach a height of 30 m (100 ft), with a trunk up to 2 m (6 ft) wide in the wild. However, in cultivation it is a small to medium-sized tree, somewhat resembling the common yew (p.37) in habit.

The bark is graphite-grey. Leaves are bright green on the upper surface and glaucous blue-green on the underside. Each leaf has a distinct midrib. The Chilean yew is dioecious, bearing male and female cones on separate trees. Both male and female cones are small and yellow-green. The yellowish brown seed cone matures to blue-purple, and resembles a small damson. Each seed is borne singly on a slender, scaly stalk. The seed cone is eaten by indigenous Native Americans in Chile, who also make marmalade from it.

**Lush foliage and cones**
Drooping branches bear glossy, dark green leaves. Ovoid green seed cones, either solitary or in pairs, develop on the ends of long stalks.

**PROFILE**

15–20 m (50–70 ft)
Up to 10 m (30 ft)
Evergreen
Needle-like
S. Chile

**FEATURES**

**Bark** Attractive reddish brown in maturity

**Male cones** Greenish yellow; borne in clusters

*Podocarpus salignus* (Podocarpaceae)

# WILLOW-LEAF PODOCARP

**An extensively cultivated** South American conifer, this tree is popular throughout the temperate world as an ornamental tree. However, the wild population in native Chile is now vulnerable due to habitat loss and excessive logging for its durable timber, which is used in construction work. Like a willow, this tree thrives on large amounts of rainfall.

The leaves have a pale underside, with visible bands of stomata (pores). A central ridge runs down each leaf. Greenish yellow male and female cones are borne on separate trees, with male pollen cones borne in clusters on terminal, slender spikes. The seed cone is up to 1 cm (½ in) long.

**Willowy habit**
Its leaf shape and frame, reminiscent of the willow, give willow-leaf podocarp its common name.

**Cone clusters**
Small male pollen cones form amid linear leaves. The leaves are arranged in two ranks along the shoots.

*leaf up to 3cm (1¼in) long*

*tiny male cone cluster*

*slightly curved leaf has sharp tip*

**PROFILE**

- 20–25m (70–80ft)
- Up to 10m (30ft)
- Evergreen
- Linear
- S. Chile, Argentina

**FEATURES**

**Cones** Male (bottom) and female (top) on same shoot

**Seed cones** Small, with fleshy scales

*Saxegothaea conspicua* (Podocarpaceae)

# PRINCE ALBERT'S YEW

**Both the generic and common** names of this tree commemorate Prince Albert of Saxe-Coburg-Gotha, the consort of Britain's Queen Victoria. The genus *Saxegothaea* is monotypic, which means there is only one species in the genus. The tree is native to the temperate rainforests of southern Chile and Argentina, where it grows wild with other forest species such as Coigüe southern beech (p.160), Winter's bark (p.110), and *Podocarpus nubigenus*. All are valued for their timber. Prince Albert's yew was introduced into cultivation by Cornish plant collector William Lobb in 1847.

The linear leaves are similar to members of the *Taxus* (yew) genus, and dark green on the upper surface. Two distinct silvery bands of microscopic pores, or stomata, appear on the underside. Both male and female cones are small, and borne on the same tree. The seed is carried in a small cone with overlapping, pointed, green scales, borne singly at the end of twigs.

**PROFILE**



- 20–30 m (70–100 ft)
- Up to 20 m (70 ft)
- Evergreen
- Linear
- USA (California)

**Male cones**
Numerous rows of yellow, male, pollen-bearing cones are borne in the leaf axils, from spring to early summer.

**FEATURES**

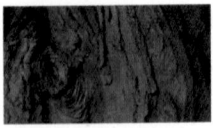

**Bark** Grey to grey-brown, with vertical ridges

**Seed cones** Green, up to 4 cm (1 ½ in) long; encase yellow-brown seeds

*Torreya californica* (Taxaceae)

# CALIFORNIA NUTMEG

**This tree is native to California**, where it occurs sporadically in the Pacific Coast Ranges and the foothills of the Sierra Nevada. The California nutmeg has a conical outline, with a straight stem, and can grow large in the wild. Despite its name, it is not related to the true nutmeg (*Myrisitica fragrans*). It was introduced into western cultivation by plant collector William Lobb in 1851. At first glance, the California nutmeg looks similar to the *Cephalotaxus* genus (plum yews). However, it is easily distinguished by its stiff, sharply pointed leaves.

Mature shoots have a purplish hue. The male cones are about 5–7 mm (¼ in) long and grouped along the underside of each shoot, from where they disperse pollen. The female cones are borne on separate trees and mature into olive-shaped seed cones. The single, large seed found inside tastes like a peanut. The seeds were once a valued food of Native Americans.

## PROFILE

- 15–20m (50–70ft)
- Up to 20m (70ft)
- Evergreen
- Needle-like
- W. Europe, E. Asia

**Fleshy, fruit-like cones**
The berry-like cone, or aril, is open at the top, exposing the seed. It ripens from green to red.

*dark blackish green leaf*

*narrow leaf, up to 3cm (1¼in) long*

*young green aril with seed*

*leaves spread in two rows across shoot*

## FEATURES

**Bark** Rich brown; flaking to reveal pink patches

**Male cones** Small, pale yellow, pollen-bearing; borne beneath shoots

*Taxus baccata* (Taxaceae)

# COMMON YEW

**This evergreen tree** has a natural range extending from western Europe into eastern Asia. In maturity, it develops a dense, dark canopy which gives it a sombre feel. Mature trees are normally multi-stemmed and their spread may be as wide as their height. The common yew may live to a great age and some trees are believed to be several thousand years old. Yew wood is extremely durable and valued for veneer and furniture production.

Its leaves are slightly glossy on the upper surface, with a central groove, and a light green colour on the underside. New growth is bright lime-green. Small male cones shed large amounts of pollen in spring. The soft, fleshy, berry-like cone (aril) encases an olive-green seed. All parts of the common yew are poisonous except for the aril.

**Japanese yew (*Taxus cuspidata*)** This shrubby Asian yew can be distinguished from the common yew by its stiff, spine-tipped leaves, which are gold or brownish yellow on the underside.

**PROFILE**

- 10–20m (30–70ft)
- Up to 10m (30ft)
- Evergreen
- Needle-like
- W. North America

*new leaf growth*

*leaf up to 2.5cm (1in) long*

**Long-lasting foliage**
Borne on shoots in two opposite, horizontally spreading rows, Pacific yew leaves remain on the tree for up to five years.

**FEATURES**

**Bark** Thin, flaking; reddish brown in colour

*Taxus brevifolia* (Taxaceae)

# PACIFIC YEW

**This small conifer** is native to western North America, from British Columbia to California. It grows sporadically in canyons and gullies, often alongside streams. The anti-cancer drug paclitaxel (Taxol) was isolated from this tree's bark in the 1960s, and it has been used in the treatment of lung and breast cancer ever since. However, prolonged felling of the tree for the drug has led to concern among conservationists that it may become endangered in the wild. In recent years, paclitaxel has been produced semi-synthetically from cultivated Pacific yews, ensuring that the wild population is not further endangered.

Juvenile trees tend to be angular, becoming more conical with age. The branches are slender and slightly pendulous. The leaves are dark yellowish green on the upper surface and lighter on the underside. In winter, golden yellow scales cover the buds.

**Chinese yew (*Taxus chinensis*)** Unlike Pacific yew, this tree has sparse foliage and slender, pale yellowish green, needle-like leaves that lie flat on either side of the shoot.

**PROFILE**

- 20–50 m (70–160 ft)
- Up to 15 m (50 ft)
- Evergreen
- Scale-like
- W. USA, Mexico

*flattened spray of leaves*

*mid- to dark green foliage, shiny on top*

*open, woody, brown cone on branch tip*

*seed cone scales open wide*

*longer leaves at base of shoot*

**Foliage and cones**
Dense foliage is carried in flattened sprays of overlapping scales. The seed cones have six scales and ripen to release up to four seeds.

**FEATURES**

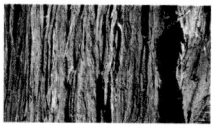

**Bark** Reddish brown; fissured in flaking, coarse plates

**Cones** Small male and female cones borne in small clusters at tips of shoots

*Calocedrus decurrens* (Cupressaceae)

# INCENSE CEDAR

**One of the most easily recognizable** of all evergreen conifers, this tree is native to western North America, from Oregon, USA, to Baja California, Mexico. It has been widely cultivated elsewhere as an ornamental tree since its discovery in 1853. The name refers to the fragrance of the cut timber, which is durable and used for making chests, pencils, and roofing shingles.

The dense foliage extends down to within 2 m (6 ft) of the ground, even on elderly trees. The green shoots turn red-brown in maturity. Each tree carries small golden male and female cones. The seed cones, up to 2 cm (¾ in) long, are sometimes carried in such profusion that the foliage becomes pendulous under their weight.

**Large, columnar tree**
The incense cedar has a distinctive habit, with erect branches and a single, almost columnar form.

**Foliage and cones**
Male and female cones are borne on the same tree. Female cones develop from seed cones, about 7 mm (¼ in) wide.

*dark green to blue-green leaf*

*young globular, green-purple seed cone*

*small, pointed leaf*

**PROFILE**

- Up to 40 m (130 ft)
- 10–15 m (30–50 ft)
- Evergreen
- Scale-like
- USA (S.W. Oregon to N.W. California)

**FEATURES**

**Bark** Shiny grey-brown; vertically fissured in long plates

**Male cones** Produced at leaf tips; grey turning to red

**Mature seed cones** Woody, brown with 8–10 scales

*Chamaecyparis lawsoniana* (Cupressaceae)

# LAWSON CYPRESS

**This popular garden conifer** is a large, conical tree with drooping branches, and makes an excellent hedge or screen. Originally a forest tree from the USA, where it remains an important timber-producing tree, its uses range from boat-building to cabinet-making. The tree is named after Lawson's Nursery in Edinburgh, Scotland, which in 1854 was the first nursery in Europe to receive seeds from America.

The undersides of leaves are marked with white flecks where the scales meet. When crushed, the foliage has a distinctive smell of parsley. Male and female cones are borne in profusion on the same tree. Female cones are slate-blue, and borne on small branchlets away from the tips. Cone scales open as the seeds are shed, but the cone remains on the tree long after seed dispersal.

**Taiwan cypress (*Chamaecyparis formosensis*)** Unlike the Lawson cypress, this tree has a slower growth habit and sharp pointed leaves, which make the sprays rough to the touch.

**PROFILE**



- 15–36 m (50–120 ft)
- Up to 10 m (30 ft)
- Evergreen
- Scale-like
- Cultivated hybrid, not found in the wild

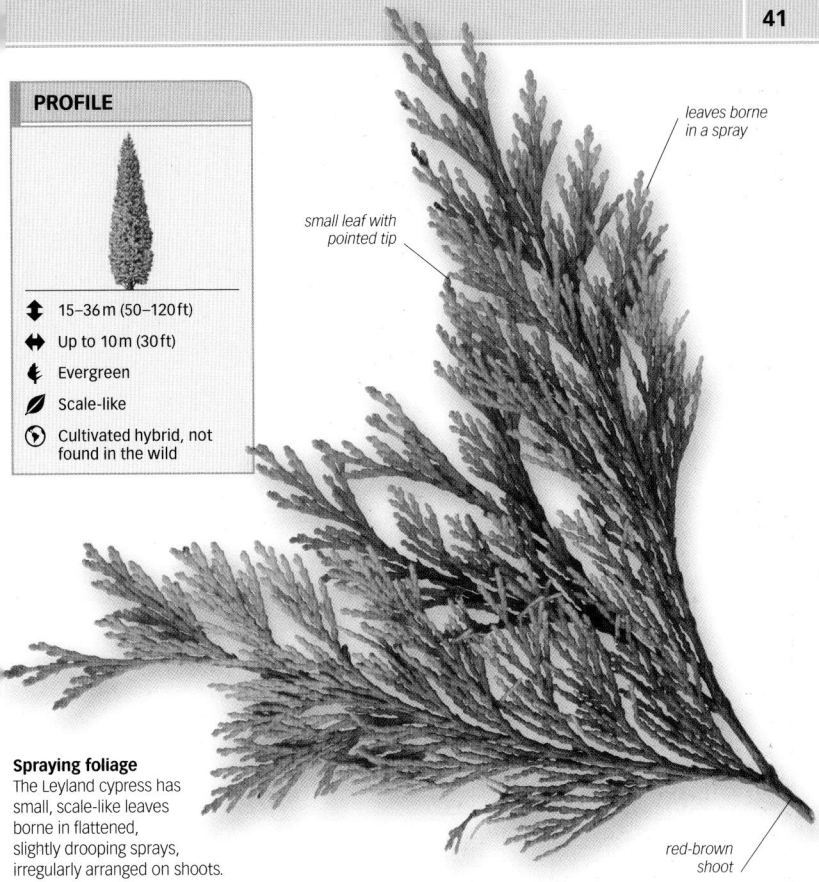


**Spraying foliage**
The Leyland cypress has small, scale-like leaves borne in flattened, slightly drooping sprays, irregularly arranged on shoots.

**FEATURES**

**Bark** Smooth, red-brown; develops shallow fissures in maturity

**Female cones** Angular, globular, up to 2 cm (¾ in) wide

x *Cupressocyparis leylandii* (Cupressaceae)

# LEYLAND CYPRESS

**Perhaps best known** as a hardy, fast-growing conifer, the Leyland cypress is commonly planted as a garden hedge or screen. However, it is only suitable for planting in gardens if regularly trimmed and kept under control. This tree does not occur in the wild, being an intergeneric hybrid between two American species – the Monterey cypress (p.51) and the Nootka cypress (p.44). The original cross pollination between the parent trees took place at Leighton Hall in Wales, UK, in 1888. The tree gets its name from Christopher Leyland, the property owner, who also planted the first seedlings in Britain. Several cultivars of this tree are commercially available.

The leaves have a dark green upper surface and a paler underside. They emit a pungent scent when crushed. Yellow male pollen cones and green female cones appear on the same tree, in clusters at the tips of shoots, in early spring. The mature seed-bearing cone is blue-green, ripening to woody brown. Each cone contains a single seed.

**PROFILE**

- 50–60m (160–200ft)
- Up to 15m (50ft)
- Evergreen
- Needle-like
- Japan, China

**Spiral arrangement**
Growing in spirals on branchlets, the slender, bright green leaves are broad at the base and taper to a soft point.

*leaf up to 1.5cm (½in) long*

*stiff, upright stalk*

*bright green forward-pointing leaf*

*globular cone, up to 2cm (¾in) wide*

**FEATURES**

**Bark** Soft, fibrous, red-brown; peels in long, vertical strips

*female cones in cluster*

**Female cones**
Green rosettes borne on stiff, upright stalks

*Cryptomeria japonica* (Cupressaceae)

# JAPANESE CEDAR

**This fast-growing conifer** originates from Japan but has also been cultivated in China for centuries, where it has become naturalized. It first reached the West in 1842, when its seeds were sent to the Royal Botanic Gardens in Kew, London.

The curving branches of this tree sweep downwards from the trunk, rising towards the tips. They may take root where they touch the ground. The foliage consists of bright green branchlets covered with stiff needles; at the base of each needle is a bulging keel (ridge) that runs down the branchlet. When crushed, the foliage emits an aroma resembling that of orange peel. Male and female cones are borne on the same tree. Yellowish, ovoid male pollen cones are clustered at the tips of branchlets, shedding pollen in early spring. The female seed cones develop into globular woody cones.

***Taiwania cryptomeriodes*** Whip-like branchlets and cylindrical cones, up to 1.2cm (½in) long, help to distinguish this tree from the Japanese cedar.

**PROFILE**

- 30–50 m (100–160 ft)
- Up to 12 m (40 ft)
- Evergreen
- Scale-like
- Japan

*flattened, dark green leaf*

**Fern-like foliage**
This tree's thick, flattened sprays of foliage become pendulous towards the tips. When crushed, they emit a fruity, resinous scent.

**FEATURES**

**Bark** Grey to red-brown, soft, fibrous; vertically fissured, peeling in narrow strips

*Chamaecyparis obtusa* (Cupressaceae)

# HINOKI CYPRESS

**This beautiful, broadly conical tree** is native to Japan, where it is cultivated as an ornamental tree, as well as being important for timber. It is also held sacred by followers of Shinto Buddhism and often used in the construction of Shinto temples. The Hinoki cypress was introduced into the West in 1861.

The branches spread out almost horizontally from the trunk before dividing into purplish orange-brown shoots, which are covered in sprays of foliage. The leaves have a dark green upper surface and a pale yellow underside. Yellow male pollen cones are produced at the tips of each branchlet, releasing clouds of pollen in spring. Female cones are slate-blue, and carried on shorter branchlets on the same tree. They mature over two years into globular, plum-coloured seed cones, up to 1 cm (½ in) long. Each woody cone scale carries a curved spine.

**Sawara cypress (*Chamaecyparis pisifera*)** This tree has sharply pointed leaves, which have distinctive, white markings on the underside, and smaller cones than the Hinoki cypress.

**PROFILE**

- 40–50m (130–160ft)
- Up to 8m (25ft)
- Evergreen
- Scale-like
- N. California to Oregon to Alaska

**Long sprays**
Drooping branches bear scale-like leaves, which make the foliage rough to the touch. The green female cones ripen over a period of two years.

*globular seed cone, up to 1cm (½in) wide*

*flattened, spray of leaves*

*sharp-pointed leaf scale*

**FEATURES**

**Bark** Pink-brown, vertically fissured; sometimes fluted towards the base

*Chamaecyparis nootkatensis* (Cupressaceae)

# NOOTKA CYPRESS

**This hardy North American species** is a large forest tree with a broad, conical outline. It was discovered in 1793 by Scottish physician and naturalist Archibald Menzies, but not introduced into Europe until around 60 years later. It makes a handsome addition to parks, large gardens, and arboreta. Nootka refers to a historical (though inaccurate) European name for many Native American tribes that inhabited the northwest coast.

The leaves have a dark green upper surface and a yellow-green underside. Small male and female cones appear on the same tree from autumn to spring. Male cones are yellow and carried on branch tips; the females are slate-blue.

**White cypress**
This tree (*Chamaecyparis thyoides*) bears erect sprays of aromatic, glaucous-blue foliage and bloomy cones.

**PROFILE**



- Up to 70m (230ft)
- Up to 15m (50ft)
- Evergreen
- Scale-like
- Chile, Argentina

**Oblong, thick leaves**
The leaves of the Patagonian cypress are bluntly pointed, and carried in whorls of three on pendulous shoots.

**FEATURES**

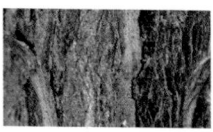

**Bark** Dark red-brown, vertically fissured, peels in shallow strips

*Fitzroya cupressoides* (Cupressaceae)

# PATAGONIAN CYPRESS

**A beautiful, large tree** in its native habitat, the Patagonian cypress is long-lived, with some specimens living for more than 3,000 years. However, it is now endangered in the wild due to forest clearance for agricultural land. Discovered by Europeans travelling with Charles Darwin on his 1834 expedition aboard HMS *Beagle*, it takes its name from the ship's captain, Robert Fitzroy. The plant collector William Lobb introduced it into cultivation in 1849, and the tree is now planted in parks and gardens, where it grows into a small tree with a dense, cypress-like habit.

This tree's trunk forks low to the ground, and the bark peels to reveal pink new bark beneath. The upswept branches end in pendulous sprays of blue-green foliage, which is marked with two white bands of stomata (pores) on each side. The same tree bears both male and female cones in small clusters at the tips of the shoots in spring. The seeds are held within lumpy cones, glossy green ripening to brown, with scales opening wide.

## PROFILE

- 30–40 m (100–130 ft)
- Up to 20 m (70 ft)
- Evergreen
- Needle-like
- N. Africa

**Upright cones**
Pollinated female seed cones develop on the top side of branches, ripening from green to brown.

*barrel-shaped cone, up to 7.5 cm (3 in) long*

*leaves up to 2.5 cm (1 in) long*

*blue-green, needle-like leaf*

*leaves borne in whorls on side shoots*

## FEATURES

**Bark** Slate-grey; develops scaly plates when mature

**Cones** Golden male and green female cones, in separate clusters on same tree

*Cedrus atlantica* (Pinaceae)

# ATLAS CEDAR

**This conifer occurs** naturally in the Atlas Mountains of North Africa, where it grows along the snowline around 2,200 m (7,200 ft) above sea level. Sometimes considered to be a geographical subspecies of the cedar of Lebanon (p.48), it is distinguished by its upswept branches. Its light blue form, *Cedrus atlantica* Glauca Group is often seen in cultivation.

The leaves are borne in dense whorls on side-shoots and singly on leading shoots. The male cones disperse pollen in autumn before falling to the ground. Pollinated female seed cones are green and borne in rows. After two to three years, the cones break apart on the tree, releasing winged seeds.

**High rise**
The Atlas cedar has upswept, ascending branches. The foliage varies from dark green to light grey-blue in the wild.

## PROFILE

- 50–75 m (160–250 ft)
- Up to 15 m (50 ft)
- Evergreen
- Needle-like
- Himalayas

**Deodar cones**
Prominent male cones in clusters turn yellow-brown, and shed large amounts of pollen on maturity.

*young purple-green cone*

*leaves in whorls on short side of shoots*

*leaves in tufts of about 15–20 on shoots*

*male pollen cone, up to 8 cm (3 in) long*

## FEATURES

**Bark** Smooth, dark grey; with age develops pink-grey fissures

**Seed cones** Resinous; growing up to 12 cm (5 in) long

*Cedrus deodara* (Pinaceae)

# DEODAR CEDAR

**Much admired across** the temperate world, the deodar cedar is native to the western Himalayas including northern India. It is sometimes referred to as the Indian cedar. In the days of the British Raj, huge deodars – up to 75 m (250 ft) tall and close to 1,000 years old – could be found on hillsides surrounding the hill station of Simla. Most of these have been felled for their durable, light brown timber, which is highly prized for construction.

This tree is distinguished from other cedars by the drooping tips on its branches. Each shoot bears 4 cm- (1½ in-) long leaves that are blue-green when young, becoming dark green with age. The barrel-shaped seed cones are borne on the top of branches, green ripening to dull brown.

**Distinctive habit**
The graceful deodar tree is narrowly conical when young, broadening as it matures.

**PROFILE**



- 30–40m (100–130ft)
- Up to 20m (70ft)
- Evergreen
- Needle-like
- Middle East

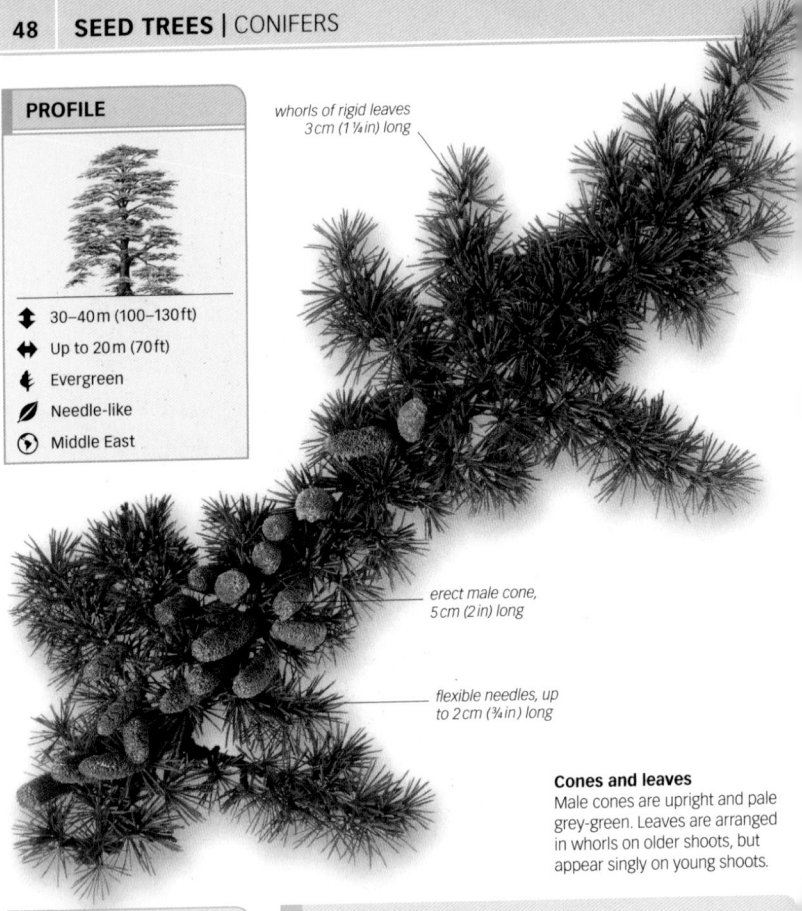


**Cones and leaves**
Male cones are upright and pale grey-green. Leaves are arranged in whorls on older shoots, but appear singly on young shoots.

**FEATURES**

**Female cones** Barrel-shaped; green turning to purple-brown

*Cedrus libani* (Pinaceae)

# CEDAR OF LEBANON

**Among one of the world's** best known trees, the cedar of Lebanon has been revered for thousands of years, and in Biblical times was seen as a symbol of fertility. King Solomon is believed to have built his temple using its timber. On Mount Lebanon, it grows at altitudes of up to 2,140m (7,020ft). It has been widely planted as an ornamental species since the 17th century.

Narrowly conical when young, the tree broadens and develops a flat-topped canopy made up of tiers of long, horizontal branches as it matures. The bark is grey-brown, with shallow, vertical fissures. On young shoots, leaves are flexible and borne singly; older wood has up to 20 rigid leaves arranged in whorls. Leaf colour varies from blue-grey to dark green. Ovoid female cones are pale green, developing a rose-purple tint by early autumn. Young cones have dried, white resin on the scale margins.

**Cyprian cedar (*Cedrus brevifolia*)** Although similar to the cedar of Lebanon in many ways, the Cyprian cedar has greener and shorter needle-like leaves, up to 1.2cm (½in) long.

**PROFILE**

- 30–44 m (100–145 ft)
- Up to 15 m (50 ft)
- Evergreen
- Needle-like
- California, USA

pointed, shiny brown winter bud

leaf up to 5 cm (2 in) long

**Widely spaced leaves** Stiff, pointed leaves of the large-coned Douglas fir are borne widely around the shoots.

**FEATURES**

**Bark** Dull grey and smooth; develops wide, vertical orange fissures when mature

**Cones** Purple-green, cylindrical; ripen to tobacco-brown

*Pseudotsuga macrocarpa* (Pinaceae)

# LARGE-CONED DOUGLAS FIR

**Sometimes known as bigcone fir**, this large conifer is native to southwest California, where some trees are known to be over 600 years old. The overall form of this tree is broadly conical, with frequent whorls of spreading, slightly descending branches. It was introduced into cultivation in Europe in 1910. It has the largest cones in its genus, up to 18 cm (7 in) long and twice as big as its better-known cousin, the Douglas fir (p.50).

The bark develops orange fissures with age. This orange colouring also occurs on the shoots. These are positioned towards the end of each branch, and are covered with stiff needle-like leaves. The large cones have numerous thick, woody scales. From beneath each scale, a paperlike, trident-shaped bract protrudes. The seeds inside each cone are large and heavy. Each seed is attached to a short rounded wing, which is too small to aid wind dispersal.

rich green leaf, up to 3cm (1¼in) long

two white bands on leaf's lower surface

cone up to 10cm (4in) long

three-pronged, papery bract overlying cone scale

**Pendent cone**
Long, hanging cones are a distinctive feature of this tree. The cones, green when young, turn orange-brown with age.

## PROFILE

- 90–100m (300–330ft)
- Up to 20m (70ft)
- Evergreen
- Needle-like
- British Columbia to California

## FEATURES

**Bark** Corky; vertically and deeply furrowed

immature seed cone

**Seed cones** Red, borne in clusters at end of shoot

*Pseudotsuga menziesii* (Pinaceae)

# DOUGLAS FIR

**This fast-growing conifer** has a natural range from British Columbia in Canada to California, USA. However, it has been planted throughout North America, Europe, Australia, and New Zealand for its commercially important timber. Discovered by Scottish physician Archibald Menzies, it was introduced into cultivation by another Scottish plant collector David Douglas. Both are commemorated in the tree's naming.

Mature trees have limited branching for the first 30m (100ft) with a long, straight trunk, which is chestnut-brown in colour. Juvenile trees have smooth, shiny grey bark, marked with resin blisters and regular whorls of light, slightly ascending branches. The needle-like leaves are spirally arranged on shoots. When crushed, they emit a sweet, citrus fragrance. Winter buds are glossy, red-brown, and pointed.

**Japanese Douglas fir (*Pseudotsuga japonica*)** This tree is distinguished from the Douglas fir by its hairless shoots, smaller cones, and shorter, needle-like leaves.

## PROFILE

- Up to 40m (130ft)
- Up to 15m (50ft)
- Evergreen
- Scale-like
- USA (California)

**Changing shape**
Young cones are green and rosette-like, turning into spherical cones in the second autumn after they develop.

*spray of tiny leaves pressed close to shoot*

*scale-like leaf with pointed tips*

*green, rosette-like young cone*

## FEATURES

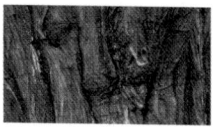

**Bark** Peels in vertical strips when mature to reveal fresh pink-brown bark

*cone up to 3.5cm (1½in) wide*

**Cones** Spherical, shiny purple-brown when ripe

*Cupressus macrocarpa* (Cupressaceae)

# MONTEREY CYPRESS

**This large conifer originates** from the coastal cliffs of the Monterey Peninsula, California, USA. It can withstand exposure to salt-laden winds and has been widely planted to provide shelter in coastal regions in temperate zones. It has a flat-topped, spreading crown of large, heavy, horizontal branches, reminiscent of the cedar of Lebanon (p.48).

Young trees are fast-growing, with a conical or broadly columnar habit. They have lots of upswept branches with spiky shoots and leaves that turn dark green with age. The pale brown bark has fine shallow ridges. When crushed, the foliage emits a lemony fragrance. The male cones release clouds of dust-like pollen in early summer.

**White cedar (*Cupressus lusitanica*)** Smaller and less hardy than the Monterey cypress, this graceful tree has pendulous branches and a brown peeling bark.

**PROFILE**

- Up to 18 m (60 ft)
- Up to 3 m (10 ft)
- Evergreen
- Scale-like
- W. Mediterranean; Tuscany, Italy

**Upward-sweeping shoots**
Closely pressed, scale-like leaves are carried on upward-sweeping, red-brown shoots.

*lumpy, glossy green cone*

*cone up to 4 cm (1½ in) wide*

*dark, dull green leaf*

**FEATURES**

**Bark** Brown-grey; with shallow, scaling ridges visible towards the base of the trunk

*Cupressus sempervirens* (Cupressaceae)

# ITALIAN CYPRESS

**Also called the Mediterranean cypress**, this is one of the most easily recognizable evergreen conifers. It is widely found in the hills, farmland, and roadsides of Tuscany, Italy, and the western Mediterranean region. The tree has a distinctive tight, narrowly columnar form, which it retains all through its life. It has been grown as an ornamental tree, to soften and accentuate architecture, since the rise of the Greek civilization.

Ascending branches covered with dense foliage obscure the stem from around head height. The foliage, unusually for cypresses, has little noticeable scent when crushed. The cones are shiny green, turning dark red-brown, and finally grey, staying on the tree for many years. They are larger than the cones of most other cypresses and found spread across the crown.

**Arizona cypress (*Cupressus arizonica*)** This tree has a densely conical form, unlike the distinctive narrow columnar shape of its Mediterranean cousin.

## PROFILE

- Up to 5 m (15 ft)
- Up to 4 m (12 ft)
- Evergreen
- Needle-like
- North America, Europe, temperate Asia

**Juniper cones**
The berry-like female seed cones, which are initially green, are conspicuously displayed along twigs among the foliage.

*needle up to 1 cm (½ in) long*

*grey-green, awl-shaped leaf*

*leaves arranged in dense whorls of three*

*silver-backed needle with sharp, prickly point*

*female seed cone, up to 6 mm (¼ in) long*

## FEATURES

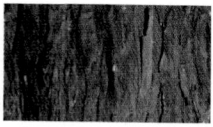

**Bark** Dark red-brown, peeling in vertical papery strips

*frosty, powdery bloom*

**Female cones** Berry-like; ripen to blue-black over two to three years

*Juniperus communis* (Cupressaceae)

# COMMON JUNIPER

**The common juniper is believed** to be the most widespread tree in the world. Its natural range extends from Alaska, Greenland, Iceland, and Siberia southwards through most of Europe, temperate Asia, and North America. It is a small, hardy tree that can tolerate intense cold, high elevations in mountainous terrain, and exposed coastal locations.

New shoots are blue-green with some "blooming", becoming dark red-brown with age. Male and female cones are yellow. They are borne on separate trees in clusters within the leaf axils. Berry-like female seed cones, called juniper berries, are used to give gin its characteristic flavour.

**Alligator juniper**
Unlike the common juniper, this tree (*Juniperus deppeana*) has silver-blue leaves and bark that resembles alligator skin.

**Male cones and leaves**
Pollen-bearing cones are borne from autumn until early spring, when the pollen is shed. Juvenile leaves are awl-shaped.

*mature, scale-like leaf*

*yellow male cone carried at foliage tips*

**PROFILE**

- Up to 20 m (70 ft)
- Up to 5 m (15 ft)
- Evergreen
- Scale-like
- N. and E. China; Japan, Mongolia

**FEATURES**

**Bark** Grey to reddish brown; peeling off in strips

*Juniperus chinensis* (Cupressaceae)

# CHINESE JUNIPER

**Since its introduction in the West** in 1767, many different garden cultivars have arisen from the Chinese juniper. It is also one of the most common conifers used for bonsai (the cultivation of miniature versions). This is an extremely variable species in the wild, growing in north and east China, Mongolia, and coastal regions of Japan.

In its typical form, the tree is compact, erect, columnar, or conical. The bark is sometimes deeply fluted at the base of the trunk. Juvenile leaves are sharp, awl-shaped, up to 1 cm (½ in) long, and rigid. On mature trees, the leaves turn dark green with glaucous blue banding on the underside. When crushed, the foliage emits a "catty" smell. Small male and female cones are scale-like, yellow, and borne on separate trees. The seed cones grow up to 7 mm (¼ in) long, green ripening to bright glaucous white in the second year.

**Drooping juniper (*Juniperus recurva*)** This Himalayan juniper can be distinguished from the Chinese juniper by its shaggy grey bark and its attractive, drooping branchlets.

**Dense foliage**
The leaves are arranged on shoots in six ranks of alternating whorls of three. They range in colour from pale green to a steely blue-green.

**PROFILE**

- 0.15–28m (1–90ft)
- Up to 2.5m (8ft)
- Evergreen
- Needle-like
- Himalayas, China, N.E. Afghanistan to Yunnan

*Juniperus squamata* (Cupressaceae)

# SCALY-LEAVED NEPAL JUNIPER

**Also known as flaky juniper** or Himalayan juniper, this slow-growing tree ranges from a prostrate shrub to a small, bushy tree. Perhaps surprisingly, this untidy-looking species is the parent of many popular garden cultivars, several of which are grown as dwarf conifers. All forms have characteristic nodding tips to the shoots, which is a distinct feature of this species.

The red-brown, papery bark flakes in large scales. Male and female cones are usually borne on separate trees. Yellow-green male cones, up to 4mm (⅛in) long, shed pollen in early spring. Female cones develop into globular to ovoid, berry-like structures, up to 9mm (⅜in) long. Initially reddish brown, they become glossy purple-black when mature. Each cone contains a single seed.

**Prickly juniper (*Juniperus oxycedrus*)** This related tree is distinguished by its open, drooping habit and rigid leaves with two white bands of stomata (pores) on the undersides.

**PROFILE**

- 50–85 m (160–280 ft)
- Up to 15 m (50 ft)
- Evergreen
- Scale-like
- N.W. North America

**Flattened foliage**
The leaves are borne in flattened sprays and have pale green undersides with white streaks.

*thick, blunt, scale-like leaf*

*glossy, bright green upper surface of leaf*

**FEATURES**

**Bark** Red-brown, fibrous; shreds in maturity

**Female cones** Small, ripening from green to brown; open on branchlets

*Thuja plicata* (Cupressaceae)

# WESTERN RED CEDAR

**This large, fast-growing conifer** is found along the northwestern Pacific coastline of North America, where it is a major component of the lowland coniferous forests. In these forests, specimens of western red cedar more than 1,000 years old have been recorded. These have vast, buttressed trunks and multiple stems, which are very often layers from the original tree. The tree produces strong, durable, red timber, which has been used over centuries to build everything from Native American canoes and roofing shingles to garden greenhouses.

Curved, sweeping branches carry large, drooping sprays of foliage. When crushed, the foliage emits a pleasant, fruity aroma, like that of a pineapple. Small, pale yellow male pollen cones are borne at the tips of shoots. Small female cones develop into leathery, erect ovoids with rounded scale tips, 1 cm (½ in) long.

**Pahautea (*Libocedrus bidwillii*)** In addition to its upright, columnar habit, pahautea is distinguished from the western red cedar by its smaller leaves and cones.

**Upright sprays**
The twisting sprays of mid-green foliage are grey-yellow on the underside. They emit the scent of fresh green apples when crushed.

*leaf 2–5 mm (1/16–1/4 in) long*

*flat shoot*

**PROFILE**

- Up to 20 m (70 ft)
- Up to 13 m (43 ft)
- Evergreen
- Scale-like
- E. North America

**FEATURES**

**Seed cones** Yellow; becoming brown and woody when mature

*Thuja occidentalis* (Cupressaceae)

# WHITE CEDAR

**Also known as American arbor-vitae**, this hardy, slow-growing conifer has a columnar habit. Found at high altitudes in forests on rocky outcrops in eastern North America, it is an important source of timber in the USA. It is thought to be the first North American tree to have been introduced into Europe, sometime between 1534 and 1536. Since then it has been widely cultivated in parks and gardens. It has given rise to many cultivars, mostly slow-growing dwarf varieties, which are often grown in ornamental rockeries.

The spreading branches are upcurved at the tips. The reddish brown bark peels in vertical strips. New cones are borne in abundance on the top side of the foliage, giving the whole crown a golden appearance.

**Chilean cedar**
This tree (*Austrocedrus chilensis*) can be recognized by its sea-green, fern-like, flattened foliage.

**Frond-like foliage**
Erect branches bear upright sprays of foliage made up of thick, blunt scales, which are vibrant green on both upper and lower surfaces.

**PROFILE**

- 20–30 m (70–100 ft)
- Up to 5 m (15 ft)
- Evergreen
- Scale-like
- China, Korea

*Platycladus orientalis* (Cupressaceae)

# CHINESE ARBOR-VITAE

**Until recently the botanical name** for this tree was *Thuja orientalis* and some references still name it as such. Originating from China and Korea, this attractive, small tree produces a dense conical or columnar habit, especially when young. Old trees often display bare, upcurved branches high in the crown. The word *arbor-vitae* is Latin for "tree of life". In Buddhist China, the tree is associated with long life and vitality, perhaps due to its unchanging evergreen habit, and the fact that several of the trees planted around Chinese Buddhist temples are more than 1,000 years old.

Chinese arbor-vitae has matt red-brown bark, which shreds in vertical strips. The cones are very small, dull yellow, and borne on the tips of branchlets. Female seed cones are ovoid, borne upright, and a glaucous-green colour ripening to brown. Several garden cultivars have been developed.

**PROFILE**

- 20–30m (70–100ft)
- Up to 10m (30ft)
- Evergreen
- Scale-like
- S. and C. Japan

*leaf bright yellow-green on upper surface*

**Glossy foliage**
Hiba's foliage is so glossy that from a distance it looks artificial, almost like plastic.

*leaf up to 6mm (¼in) long*

**FEATURES**

**Female cones** Ovoid, up to 2cm (¾in) long; green ripening to woody brown

*Thujopsis dolabrata* (Cupressaceae)

# HIBA

**This evergreen tree** is the only species in its genus. It can be distinguished from the similar-looking *Thuja* species by its broader leaves, each with striking and distinctive white banding on the underside. It was introduced into western cultivation in 1853.

A slow-growing tree, hiba takes on a dense, shrublike form in the first 10 years or so. In maturity, it may have a tall, upright, and columnar habit or a low-branching, multi-stemmed, and broadly conical one. The red-brown to grey bark peels off in strips, giving it a shredded appearance. The foliage is made up of hard, scale-like leaves that form large flattened sprays. Their upper surface is bright, glossy yellow-green, while the underside is white, with green margins. Both male and female cones are borne in spring, in separate clusters on the same tree. The blackish green male pollen cones appear at the tips of the branchlets. Blue-grey female seed cones develop into woody, ovoid cones that ripen from green to brown.

**PROFILE**

- 15–40m (50–130ft)
- Up to 10m (30ft)
- Evergreen
- Needle-like
- Tasmania

*sharp-edged leaf curving inwards*

*ovoid cone, approximately 2cm (¾in) wide*

*rigid, triangular, overlapping leaf*

**Leaves and cones**
The foliage is made up of bright green, claw-like, leathery leaves. The cones ripen from bright green to orange-brown.

**FEATURES**

**Bark** Soft, rich red-brown, turning grey-brown with age

*Athrotaxus selaginoides* (Cupressaceae)

# KING WILLIAM PINE

**This medium-sized, evergreen tree** is sometimes called the Tasmanian cedar, or King Billy pine. However, it is neither a cedar nor a pine, being related to cypress instead. It is found in Tasmania, where it grows at an altitude of up to 1,200m (3,940ft) above sea level alongside *Eucalyptus*, in mountain forests that are frequently covered in snow. It is considered to be threatened in the wild, with almost half of its natural range destroyed by bush fires started by loggers clearing debris after felling *Eucalyptus* trees.

From a distance, this sprawling tree could be mistaken for the Japanese cedar (p.42). Up close, the bark, which is soft and fibrous, is sometimes compared to that of the giant redwood (p.63). The foliage is made of short, spike-shaped needles, which curve away from bright apple-green shoots. Cones are bright green at first and ripen to orange-brown. They are borne in pairs on 2.5cm- (1in-) long stalks. The wood is used to make musical instruments and furniture.

**PROFILE**

- 10–20m (30–70ft)
- Up to 10m (30ft)
- Evergreen
- Scale-like
- W. Tasmania

**Leaves and cones**
When young, the shoots and leaves are pale yellow and soft. Yellow-green cones are borne at the end of shoots.

*young leaf, up to 0.5cm (¼in) long*

*bract overlying cone scale*

*tip of leaf curves inwards at the tip*

*deep green, rigid, mature foliage*

*ovoid female cone, up to 2cm (¾in) wide*

**FEATURES**

**Bark** Coppery, becoming deeply fissured with age

*Athrotaxus laxifolia* (Cupressaceae)

# SUMMIT CEDAR

**A small to medium-sized**, hardy tree, the summit cedar differs from the King William pine (p.60) in its more lax habit, leading to its botanical name. Native to western Tasmania, where it grows in high mountain ranges, this tree is able to withstand temperatures of up to –12° C (10.4° F) without damage.

The tree has pale red-brown or coppery bark. Its triangular, pointed, scale-like leaves spread away from the shoots. Yellow-brown male and female cones are borne on the same tree in early spring. Tiny male pollen cones are clustered together at the tips of branchlets, while female seed cones, sometimes solitary, are borne at the ends of shoots. Bright yellow-green, they ripen in autumn.

**Lax habit**
The summit cedar's broadly conical crown develops into a rounded, open top as the tree matures.

**Cones on branches**
Rounded seed cones form on the tips of the branches, against a background of dark green, linear leaves.

*leaf up to 2 cm (¾ in) long*

*leaves in two flat rows on shoots*

*cone 2–3 cm (¾–1¼ in) long*

**PROFILE**

- 40–110 m (130–360 ft)
- Up to 23 m (75 ft)
- Evergreen
- Needle-like
- USA (S.W. Oregon, N.W. California)

**FEATURES**

**Bark** Red-brown, thick, soft, and fibrous

**Seed cones** Pendent, rounded; green ripening to brown

*Sequoia sempervirens* (Cupressaceae)

# COASTAL REDWOOD

**This magnificent species** bears the distinction of producing the tallest tree in the world – currently 115 m (380 ft) tall. It is named after the Cherokee *sequoia*. Its natural range is limited to California and Oregon, USA, where it grows on the coastal side of the Sierra Nevada mountains. From here, it was introduced into Europe in 1840.

Young trees are conical, with widely spaced, slender branches that curve upwards at the tips. The leaves are speckled with two bands of white stomata (pores) on the underside. Yellow-brown male and green female cones appear in separate clusters on the same tree. The female seed cones turn brown and woody when ripe.

**Standing tall**
Mature coastal redwood trees acquire a columnar habit, with flat tops and downswept branches.

**PROFILE**

- 50–95 m (160–310 ft)
- Up to 15 m (50 ft)
- Evergreen
- Scale-like
- USA (California)

**Giant redwood sprig** Male pollen cones develop at the tips of minor shoots and shed clouds of yellow pollen in spring.

**FEATURES**

**Bark** Red-brown, spongy and fibrous, up to 50 cm (20 in) thick

**Seed cones** Long-stalked, ovoid, up to 5 cm (2 in) wide

*Sequoiadendron giganteum* (Cupressaceae)

# GIANT REDWOOD

**The largest living tree** is a giant redwood called "General Sherman", which grows on the western slopes of the Sierra Nevada in California. Giant redwoods are long-lived, with some specimens believed to be 3,500 years old. Introduced into Europe in 1853, it was named "Wellingtonia" to commemorate the British Duke of Wellington, who died in 1852.

The tree has large, downswept branches and a clear trunk of several metres from the ground. The leaves emit a smell of aniseed when crushed. Erect, bright green female cones develop into bunches of drooping, green seed cones. These ripen in two years, becoming brown and woody in the process.

**Tree giant** Weighing up to 2,000 tonnes, giant redwood has a conical crown that turns broadly columnar with age.

## PROFILE

- 50–80 m (160–280 ft)
- Up to 20 m (70 ft)
- Evergreen
- Needle-like
- W. North America

**Foliage and cones**
The dark green leaves are bright lime-green when young. The cones mature from purplish red to deep brown, with papery scales.

*leaf up to 2 cm (¾ in) long*

*purplish red young cone*

## FEATURES

**Female cones** Small, red; grow on shoot tips

**Mature seed cones** Woody, egg-shaped; 2.5 cm (1 in) long

*Tsuga heterophylla* (Pinaceae)

# WESTERN HEMLOCK

**Native to the west coast** of North America, this tall, elegant conifer is characterized by its spreading, arching branches and soft pendulous foliage. This hardy, fast-growing species is shade-tolerant and capable of outgrowing its competitors in dense forests. It produces strong timber, and since its discovery in 1828 by Scottish botanist David Douglas, and introduction into cultivation in 1851, it has been widely grown in plantations as a timber-producing tree in North America and Europe.

This tree has a narrow, conical habit, with a lax leading shoot and thin, ascending branches that arch downwards towards the tip. The bark is reddish purple in young trees, turning dark purple-brown in maturity. The leaves have two blue-white bands of microscopic pores, or stomata, on the underside. The male pollen cones are red and release large amounts of pollen in spring.

**Mountain hemlock (*Tsuga mertensiana*)** This related species is easily distinguished from the western hemlock by its oblong-cylindrical large cones and radially arranged leaves.

**PROFILE**

- Up to 30m (100ft)
- Up to 15m (50ft)
- Evergreen
- Needle-like
- E. North America

*needle-shaped leaf, with blunt tip*

*vibrant green leaf, up to 2cm (¾in) long*

**Eastern hemlock cones** Female cones, up to 1.5cm (½in) long, are borne on the tips of shoots. Green at first, the cones turn coffee-brown when mature.

**FEATURES**

**Bark** Brown-grey; turns scaly and fissured with age

*young seed cone*

**Cones** Small, oval; borne on short stalks

*Tsuga canadensis* (Pinaceae)

# EASTERN HEMLOCK

**This large tree is sometimes called** the Canadian hemlock. Unlike its cousin, the western hemlock (p.64), it may grow either as a multiple-stemmed tree, or with heavy branching from near ground level. It is native to eastern North America where it is currently under threat from an insect known as the hemlock woolly adelgid, a sap-sucking bug accidentally introduced from eastern Asia in 1924.

Branchlets of this tree vary in colour, from yellow-brown to almost cream, and bear small, green-brown, ovoid winter buds at the tips. The leaves are fresh green at first, becoming dark green with age. They have narrow, silvery bands on the lower surface. Yellow-green male pollen cones are borne in clusters along shoots, shedding pollen in spring. Female cones are green and borne in separate clusters from males.

**Japanese hemlock (*Tsuga sieboldii*)** Except for its single-stemmed, spire-like habit and larger cones, up to 3cm (1¼in) long, this tree is similar in most aspects to the eastern hemlock.

## PROFILE

- 30–50 m (100–160 ft)
- Up to 25 m (80 ft)
- Deciduous
- Needle-like
- S.E. USA

**Alternating leaves**
The leaves are arranged alternately along shoots. Bright apple green in late spring, they turn plum-coloured or orange-brown in autumn.

## FEATURES

**Bark** Dull reddish brown, fibrous and frequently fluted

**Aerial roots** Rise above water level to absorb oxygen

*Taxodium distichum* (Cupressaceae)

# SWAMP CYPRESS

**Also known as bald cypress**, this ornamental conifer is native to southeastern USA, where it grows in damp or wet soils. It is widespread in the Florida Everglades. This tree tolerates having its roots submerged in water for several months at a time by developing aerial roots known as "knees" or "pneumatophores".

The crown is conical, becoming slightly domed in maturity with heavy, upswept branches. The base of the trunk may be strongly buttressed. Both male and female cones occur on the same tree. In winter, male pollen cones appear in catkin-like clusters at the end of shoots. They grow up to 10–30 cm (4–12 in) long before shedding pollen in spring. Small, green female seed cones ripen into short-stalked, globular, pale brown cones.

**Pond cypress (*Taxodium distichum* var. *imbricarium*)**
Smaller and slower-growing, this cypress has spreading branches that bear erect shoots and foliage.

## PROFILE

- Up to 25 m (80 ft)
- Up to 7 m (22 ft)
- Deciduous
- Needle-like
- China

**Feathery leaves**
Leaves are soft at first, almost feathery, and are borne in two opposite ranks on the shoot. A pale band runs down each side of the midrib on the leaf underside.

## FEATURES

**Bark** Bright cinnamon-brown; peels in stringy, vertical flakes

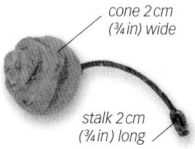


**Seed cones** Cylindrical; green maturing to dark brown

*Metasequoia glyptostroboides* (Cupressaceae)

# DAWN REDWOOD

**Also referred to as** the fossil tree, this conifer was discovered in 1941 by Chinese forester T. Kan in eastern Sichuan province. Until then, it had only been seen as a fossil and was believed to have been extinct for many millennia. It was introduced into western cultivation in 1948. Since then the tree has become a popular species for planting in parks and gardens.

The fibrous bark sometimes has a spiralled appearance. The trunk is fluted with buttressing at the base. The bright green leaves turn pink, sometimes gold, in autumn before falling. Male and female cones are borne on the same tree, with male pollen cones held in prominent clusters.

**Upswept branches**
Conical at first, the crown of the dawn redwood may become broad in maturity, with upswept branches.

leaf up to 6 cm (2 ½ in) long

mature male cones in a cluster

**Spirally set leaves**
Although spirally set, the needle-like leaves twist to lie in two planes on either side of the shoots.

**PROFILE**

- Up to 20 m (70 ft)
- Up to 10 m (30 ft)
- Evergreen
- Needle-like
- S. and W. China

**FEATURES**

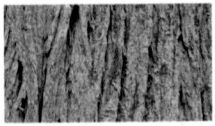

**Bark** Chestnut-brown, with long, parallel, vertical fissures

**Seed cones** Rounded; bright green maturing to brown

*Cunninghamia lanceolata* (Cupressaceae)

# CHINESE FIR

**At first glance, the Chinese fir** may seem similar to the monkey puzzle tree (p.28). However, it is a member of the cypress family and not a true fir as the name suggests. It is a handsome conifer with a domed crown of short, drooping branches made up of distinctive, glossy, dark green foliage. It has become popular as an ornamental tree in parks and gardens.

Widespread branches give this tree an open and somewhat sparse appearance, but this is often masked by its drooping foliage. Its large, prickly leaves are glossy green on the upper surface, with two distinctive bands of white stomata (pores) on the underside. The same tree bears both male and female cones. Male cones are yellow-brown and borne in clusters at the shoot tips, while female cones are yellow-green and held singly on terminal branches. The female cone develops into a squat, rounded seed cone, up to 4 cm (1 ½ in) wide.

**Luanta fir (*Cunninghamia konishii*)** This is a smaller tree than the Chinese fir and has smaller, needle-like leaves and cones.

**Whorled leaves**
The leaves are borne in whorls, which are set 4 cm (1 ½ in) apart, on buff brown shoots. Yellow-green, globular male pollen cones are borne in clusters of 12.

*shiny, rich green, needle-like leaves, up to 12 cm (5 in) long*

*egg-shaped cone, up to 7.5 cm (3 in) wide*

*fused leaves along linear groove*

**PROFILE**

- 20–30 m (70–100 ft)
- Up to 15 m (50 ft)
- Evergreen
- Needle-like
- Japan

**FEATURES**

**Bark** Dark brown to grey; peels in long coarse strips

*Sciadopitys verticillata* (Sciadopityaceae)

# JAPANESE UMBRELLA PINE

**This distinctive tree is not a pine** but the single member of a conifer family known in fossil records for 230 million years. Native to the mountains of central Honshu in Japan, it grows at elevations of up to 1,520 m (5,000 ft) on rocky slopes and ridges.

The leaves are borne in umbrella-like whorls, hence the tree's common name. Immature green female cones develop at the ends of each shoot. Mature seed cones are green, turning to woody brown. They have fleshy grooved scales when young. Needles may sometimes grow out from the centre of the cone.

**Attractive conifer**
Japanese umbrella pine is widely planted because of its unusual leaf formation and regular shape.

**PROFILE**

- Up to 30m (100ft)
- Up to 4m (12ft)
- Deciduous
- Needle-like
- S.E. China

**Delicate foliage**
Leaves are spirally arranged around the shoot but twisted at the base to lie in two horizontal ranks.

*toothed scales on cone*

*female cone up to 3cm (1¼in) long*

*leaf up to 1.5cm (½in)*

**FEATURES**

**Bark** Grey-brown with shallow fissures

*Glyptostrobus pensilis* (Cupressaceae)

# WATER PINE

**This conifer is also known** as the Chinese swamp cypress. It is indigenous to southeastern China, where it grows naturally in swamps and along riverbanks. However, the wild population is now endangered as a result of overcutting for its durable, scented wood. Elsewhere, it has been extensively planted along the banks of rice paddies, where its root system helps to stabilize banks and reduce soil erosion. Despite its common names, it is neither a pine nor a cypress, but a monotypic (single species) genus related to *Taxodium*. Like that genus it produces "knees", or aerial roots, when planted directly in water.

The water pine has sea-green, soft, deciduous leaves. The shoots are grey-green, sometimes angular, and rough to the touch due to "pegs" (raised scars) left by discarded leaves. In autumn, the leaves turn purple-brown before falling. The cones are small and visually insignificant. The female seed cone is rough and pear-shaped. Green at first, it ripens to yellow-brown when each scale opens wide to release winged seeds.

## PROFILE

- Up to 50 m (160 ft)
- Up to 6 m (20 ft)
- Evergreen
- Needle-like
- France, Switzerland, Germany

**Upright cones**
The cones are clustered on the top of branches and disintegrate on the tree after releasing seeds.

*cylindrical red-brown cone, up to 15 cm (6 in) long*

*outward-projecting bract*

*leaf lies horizontally on either side of shoot*

*blunt-tipped leaf, up to 2.5 cm (1 in) long*

## FEATURES

**Leaves** Dark green, two silver bands on the underside

**Male cones** Greenish yellow; grouped on the undersides of shoots

*Abies alba* (Pinaceae)

# EUROPEAN SILVER FIR

**This large, evergreen conifer** is a common species in central Europe, particularly in the alpine mountains of France, Switzerland, and Germany. It is relatively long-lived for a conifer, with some specimens known to be over 300 years old. The silver fir is used as a Christmas tree in many parts of Europe. It is also widely planted for timber, although it needs to be guarded against aphid attacks, which can prove fatal.

Young trees have a narrowly conical and symmetrical form, with slightly ascending branches. When mature, they become forked and more heavily branched, with dead branches covering the trunk for the lower third of its height. The bark is smooth and dull grey on young trees, becoming paler and developing shallow pink-brown fissures as they age. The leaves have white bands on the underside, which make them appear silvery.

**Greek fir (*Abies cephalonica*)** Unlike the European silver fir, this large, handsome tree has stiff, sharp-pointed leaves that are arranged radially around the shoot.

**PROFILE**

- Up to 40m (130ft)
- Up to 5m (15ft)
- Evergreen
- Needle-like
- Caucasus, N.E. Turkey

**Foliage and cones**
The leaves are flat needles with blunt tips, borne more densely on the upper sides of shoots. The seed is contained within a brown, upright, cylindrical cone

*round-tipped leaf, up to 2.5cm (1in) long*

*cone 15–20cm (6–8in) long*

**FEATURES**

*male pollen cone opens yellow*

**Male cones** Red-tinged; borne in clusters below the shoot

*Abies nordmanniana* (Pinaceae)

# CAUCASIAN FIR

**This relatively slow-growing conifer** has dense branches and a uniformly conical outline, which makes it a magnificent specimen in parks, gardens, and arboreta. Since its introduction into western cultivation in 1848, it has been widely planted outside its native regions. It is also a popular Christmas tree and, under the name of Nordmann fir, is marketed as a "non-drop" tree, since it retains its needles for some time after being cut. When crushed, the foliage emits a fruity, resinous aroma.

The bark is grey and smooth, cracking into small, square plates in maturity. Glossy dark green on the upper surface, the leaves have two white bands of stomata (pores) on the underside. Male and female cones are borne on the same tree. The female seed cone, carried above the shoot, is green and turns red-brown as it matures. It has papery bracts, which project beyond each scale.

**Algerian fir (*Abies numidica*)** This tree is distinguished from the Caucasian fir by its more downward-curving branches, as well as its densely set, thick, rounded, needle-like leaves.

**PROFILE**

- Up to 10m (30ft)
- Up to 3.5m (11ft)
- Evergreen
- Needle-like
- South Korea

*cone scale outlined with white resin*

*leaf 1.5cm (½in) long*

*cylindrical, upright cone*

**Korean fir cones**
Dark purple female seed cones develop in clusters on the top of shoots.

**FEATURES**

**Bark** Dark olive-green; develops light, freckle-like pores (lenticels) with age

*Abies koreana* (Pinaceae)

# KOREAN FIR

**This broadly conical conifer originates** from the volcanic island of Quelpeart, South Korea, where it grows on mountain slopes up to 1,000m (3,280ft). One of the smallest firs, the Korean fir has found its place as a much-revered garden tree in Europe and North America since its introduction into cultivation in 1908. In the latter part of the 20th century, several ornamental dwarf cultivars were developed from this species.

The short, stubby, curved leaves are dark green on the upper surface, with two white bands on the underside. The leaves almost obscure the fawn-coloured, pubescent shoots. Male and female cones appear on the same tree. Red-brown male pollen-bearing cones are normally coated in resin and clustered around side shoots. Dark red to purple female seed cones are positioned on the top of shoots.

**Delavay's fir (*Abies delavayi*)** This is a faster growing, larger conifer compared to the Korean fir, and is also distinguished by its larger, barrel-shaped cones.

## PROFILE

- Up to 50m (160ft)
- Up to 6m (20ft)
- Evergreen
- Needle-like
- W. North America

**Noble fir cones** Large green cones, ripening to purple-brown, develop from erect, yellow female cones on the top side of shoots.

*cylindrical, flat-topped cone, up to 25cm (10in) long*

*green, protruding bract on cone*

## FEATURES

**Bark** Smooth silver-grey; develops resin-filled blisters with age

*leaf up to 3.5cm (1½in) long*

**Leaves** Flattened, blunt-tipped, with central groove; with two silver bands on underside

*Abies procera* (Pinaceae)

# NOBLE FIR

**The natural range of this** large, stately conifer extends down the west coast of North America, from northern Washington state to California's Siskiyou Mountains. This evergreen was discovered and introduced in Europe by Scottish plant collector David Douglas in 1825.

The noble fir has a long, straight trunk. Pale reddish brown shoots are obscured by flattened leaves that part below the shoot and sweep upwards at the sides. The leaves have a bluish green upper surface and two narrow bands of stomata (pores) on their underside. When crushed, the leaves emit a pungent, slightly "catty" aroma. Bright crimson male cones are borne along the underside of shoots.

**Colorado white fir** Silver-blue foliage and smaller, narrow, cylindrical cones distinguish this tree (*Abies concolor*).

## PROFILE

- 70–80 m (230–280 ft)
- Up to 6 m (20 ft)
- Evergreen
- Needle-like
- West coast of North America

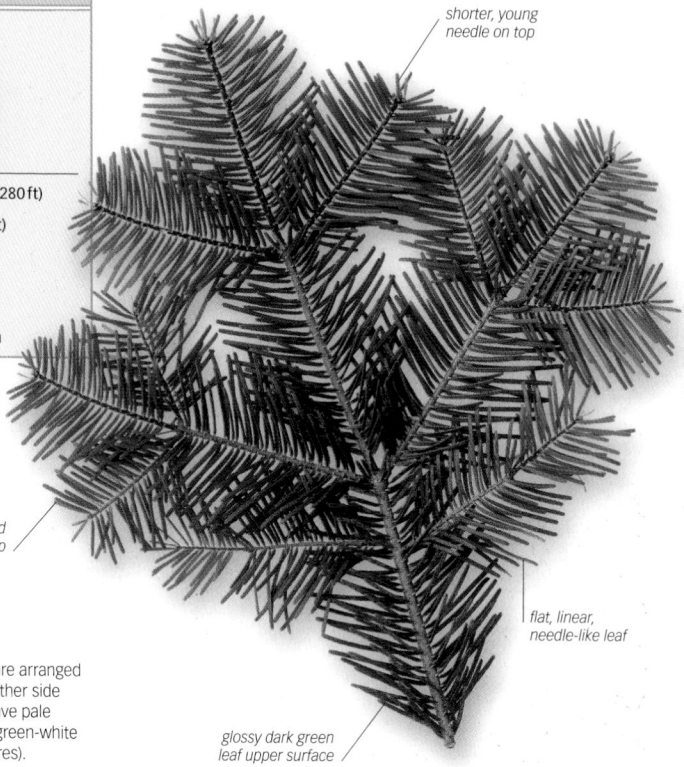


**'lat foliage**
'he flattened leaves are arranged ı a single plane on either side ı f the shoots. They have pale ı ndersides with two green-white ı ands of stomata (pores).

## FEATURES

**Bark** Brownish grey turns purple-grey; cracks into square plates in maturity

**Female cones** Green when young; cylindrical, upright

*Abies grandis* (Pinaceae)

# GRAND FIR

**The grand fir is an extremely** fast-growing conifer reaching a height of 40 m (130 ft) in 50 years. It is native to the Pacific Northwest and northern California regions, where specimens regularly reach up to 80 m (280 ft) in height, with a trunk diameter of 2 m (6 ft). Since its discovery by Scottish botanist David Douglas in 1830, it has been widely cultivated elsewhere.

The bark on young trees is brownish grey with resin blisters. The tree has a conical crown with whorls of branches, becoming broadly columnar in old age. The foliage emits a fruity, orange fragrance when crushed. Small, ovoid, purple male pollen cones, up to 2 mm (1/16 in) long, are borne on the undersides of shoots. The female seed cones are cylindrical and green, up to 10 cm (4 in) long and 4 cm (1 ½ in) wide, becoming red-brown when mature.

**Alpine fir (*Abies lasiocarpa*)** This tree is distinguished from the grand fir by its smaller stature and distinctive, pale, greyish green, needle-like leaves.

**PROFILE**

- Up to 40m (130ft)
- Up to 15m (50ft)
- Deciduous
- Needle-like
- C. Europe

**Larch branchlet**
Leaves grow in dense rosettes on side shoots, while appearing singly on main branches. Green, upright seed cones develop from female cones in spring.

*scale tip turns slightly inwards*

*blunt, ovoid cone, up to 4.5cm (1¾in) long*

*bright green leaf, up to 4cm (1½in) long*

**FEATURES**

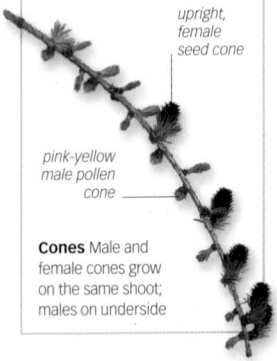


**Cones** Male and female cones grow on the same shoot; males on underside

*Larix decidua* (Pinaceae)

# EUROPEAN LARCH

**This attractive conifer originates** in the Alpine regions of Austria, Switzerland, and Germany, through to the Carpathian mountains of Slovakia and Romania, where it grows up to 2,500m (8,200ft) above sea level. It has been widely planted throughout Europe and North America for forestry and ornamental purposes.

Young trees display a smooth, pale grey bark. In older trees, the bark is grey-pink, with vertical fissures and ridges. Well-spaced whorls of upswept branches produce a narrowly conical outline, which is softened by pendulous, straw-coloured shoots. The leaves are bright green in spring, turning golden yellow in autumn. They are soft at first, but stiffen with age. The female cones appear before the leaves in early spring. The colour of mature female seed cones varies from purple-pink to red.

**Siberian larch (*Larix sibirica*)** Although similar to European larch, this smaller, slower-growing larch can be distinguished by its more conical-shaped, slightly longer cones.

**PROFILE**



- Up to 32 m (105 ft)
- Up to 8 m (25 ft)
- Deciduous
- Needle-like
- Scotland

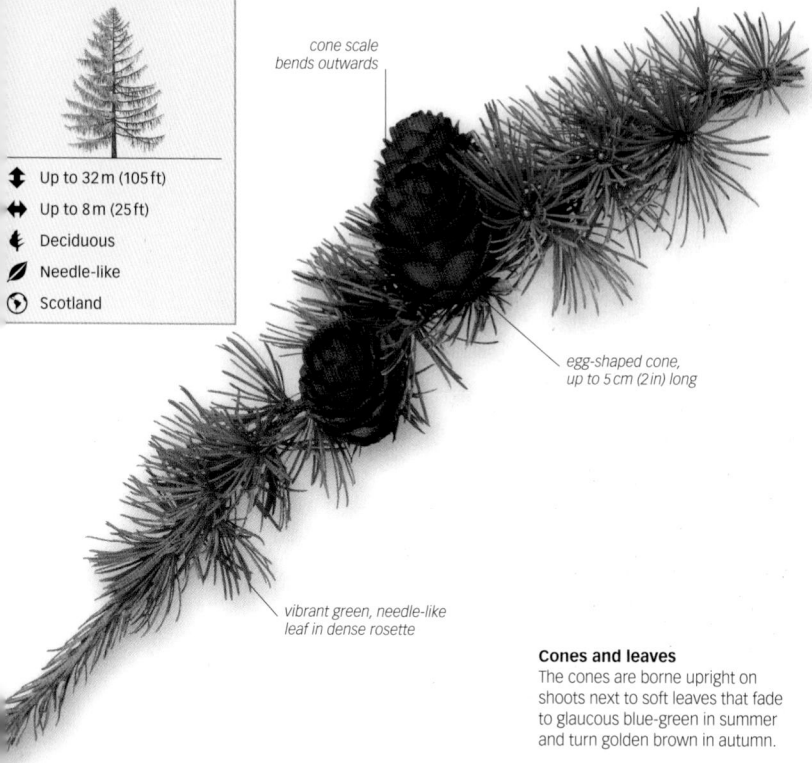


**Cones and leaves**
The cones are borne upright on shoots next to soft leaves that fade to glaucous blue-green in summer and turn golden brown in autumn.

**FEATURES**

**Cones** Cream to pink or red female seed cone; drooping, yellow male pollen cone

*Larix* x *marschlinsii* (Pinaceae)

# HYBRID LARCH

**This broadly conical conifer** is also known as Dunkeld larch, after the Scottish estate where it was created in the late 19th century by cross-pollination between the European larch (p.76) and the Japanese larch (p.78). This tree is now more widely planted than either of its parents. It is particularly widespread in forestry plantations because its vigorous growth enables it to reach timber harvesting size quickly. It is also more resistant to disease than either parent.

The bark is reddish brown and scaly in maturity. The shoots are pendulous, orange-brown to pink-buff, and slightly glaucous. On leading shoots, leaves are borne singly and are up to 8 cm (3 in) long. Elsewhere, leaves occur in dense rosettes and are up to 4 cm (1 ½ in) long. Hybrid larch cones are larger than those of the Japanese larch.

**Tamarack (*Larix laricina*)** This tree is smaller and slower-growing than the hybrid larch. Its needle-like leaves are smaller and thinner, up to 2.5 cm (1 in) long.

seed cone 3 cm (1¼ in) long and wide

seed cone scale turns outwards and downwards

leaf 2 cm (¾ in) long

leaves borne in rosettes on side shoots

**Seed cones and leaves**
The Japanese larch seed cones resemble wooden rose blooms, with scales turned outwards and downwards. The leaves are borne singly on leading shoots and in rosettes on side shoots.

**PROFILE**

- Up to 35 m (120 ft)
- Up to 15 m (50 ft)
- Deciduous
- Needle-like
- Japan

**FEATURES**

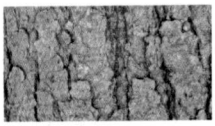

**Bark** Reddish brown; becomes scaly with age

**Female cones** Borne in clusters, pink with cream margins

**Seed cones** Bun-shaped; green maturing to brown

*Larix kaempferi* (Pinaceae)

# JAPANESE LARCH

**Native to Honshu, Japan**, this vigorous tree grows at altitudes of up to 2,750 m (9,020 ft) in the wild. It is also grown in and around Japanese temple gardens, where it may be trained as a bonsai. The Japanese larch was introduced in the West by British nurserymen Veitch & Sons in 1861, and has been planted commercially for its strong, durable timber ever since.

It is broader than the European larch (p.76), with long, upswept branches that become horizontal or even slightly descending in older trees. The leaves are flatter and broader as well. They are bright green at first, dulling to grey-green before turning orange in autumn. Shoots are reddish purple and conspicuous on leafless branches in winter. Yellow male pollen cones appear in rounded clusters on shoots. Female seed cones emerge in early spring before the leaves.

**Himalayan larch (*Larix griffithii*)** Unlike the Japanese larch, this tree has long, pendulous, and down-covered shoots. Its large cylindrical cones grow up to 10 cm (4 in) long.

**PROFILE**

- 35–45 m (120–150 ft)
- Up to 15 m (50 ft)
- Deciduous
- Needle-like
- E. China

**ibrant autumn foliage**
he leaves are borne in dense lusters on older branches. hey turn orange-gold in utumn before falling.

**FEATURES**

**Leaves** Soft, needle-like; spirally arranged around young shoots

*Pseudolarix amabilis* (Pinaceae)

# GOLDEN LARCH

**This beautiful, slow-growing conifer** was introduced into western cultivation by plant collector Robert Fortune in 1852. Despite the name, the golden larch is not a true larch, having cones that disintegrate on the tree, and spurs, or side shoots, which lengthen annually.

This tree has grey-brown bark, smooth at first, becoming deeply fissured into thick, square plates. The shoots are pale yellow to pink-buff. Both male and female cones are yellow and are borne at the end of the shoots on the same tree. Female seed cones only develop into 6 cm- (2½ in-) long mature cones after long, hot summers. Each cone is green, with triangular scales, maturing to golden brown before disintegrating on the tree.

**Curving branches**
The golden larch has a broadly conical habit, with level branches that curve upwards towards the tips.

## PROFILE



- Up to 50 m (160 ft)
- Up to 15 m (50 ft)
- Evergreen
- Needle-like
- N., C., W., and E. Europe

**Cones of the spruce**
Female cones borne across the top half of the tree become cylindrical and pendulous on stout stems.

## FEATURES

**Bark** Coppery-bronze to pink; matures to dark purple-brown

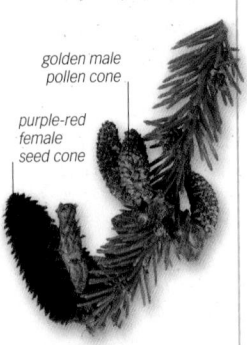


**Cones** Male and female cones borne on the same tree

*Picea abies* (Pinaceae)

# NORWAY SPRUCE

**This common conifer**, recognized as the traditional Christmas tree throughout most of Europe, has a natural range extending from the Pyrenees to western Russia. It is an important timber-producing tree, used in construction and for making the carcasses of violins and other stringed musical instruments.

It has a symmetrical form, with horizontal branches that gradually become upswept towards the top of the tree. The slightly rough bark develops shallow, round or oval plates that lift away from the surface with age. Male pollen cones cluster at shoot tips, releasing clouds of yellow pollen in spring. When crushed, the rich-green leaves emit a citrus-like fragrance.

**Dragon spruce**
This tree (*Picea asperata*) resembles the Norway spruce, but its blue-green leaves are more rigid and sharply pointed.

## PROFILE

- 30–55 m (100–180 ft)
- Up to 15 m (50 ft)
- Evergreen
- Needle-like
- Caucasus region, N.E. Turkey

**Dense foliage**
This tree has a conical form with short, blunt-tipped, needle-like leaves.

*leaf up to 1 cm (½ in) long*

*glossy, rigid, blunt-tipped leaves*

## FEATURES

**Bark** Smooth, pinkish brown; flakes into small irregular plates after 30 years

*patches of sticky resin*

**Cones** Cylindrical, purple; ripening to brown

*Picea orientalis* (Pinaceae)

# ORIENTAL SPRUCE

**Also known as the Caucasian spruce**, this graceful tree is one of the most attractive and best spruces for cultivation, being tolerant of lime-based soils and better able to withstand drier conditions. Native to the Caucasus region and northeast Turkey, where it grows in mountainous regions up to 2,200 m (7,220 ft), it was introduced into cultivation in 1837. It has been widely planted in parks and gardens ever since, especially in the USA.

The blunt leaves are shiny and dark green on the upper surface, paler on the underside, and uniformly point forwards on buff-coloured shoots. Both male and female cones appear in separate clusters on the same tree. The male pollen cones turn from bright red to yellow as they mature. The female cones are also red and develop into drooping cones up to 10 cm (4 in) long.

**Likiang spruce (*Picea likiangensis*)** Unlike the oriental spruce, this related tree has flattened leaves, which are bluish green on the upper surface and blue-white on the underside.

**Leaves and pendulous cones**
The Sitka spruce has blue-green leaves radially arranged around pale brown shoots. Pale brown hanging cones appear on the shoots in summer.

*rigid, sharply pointed leaf, up to 3 cm (1 1/4 in) long*

*thin, papery cone scale*

*pendulous cone, up to 10 cm (4 in) long*

**PROFILE**

- 70–95 m (230–315 ft)
- Up to 15 m (50 ft)
- Evergreen
- Needle-like
- North America

*Picea sitchensis* (Pinaceae)

# SITKA SPRUCE

**Named after Sitka Island** off the Alaskan coast, where it grows in abundance, the Sitka spruce is the largest North American spruce. Valued for its strong, lightweight timber, it was originally used for making aircraft frames, and is now used in the paper industry.

The Sitka spruce has an open, conical habit, with slender, widely spaced, ascending branches. Young trees have a deep purple-brown bark; this lightens on older trees and develops large, curving cracks, which then turn into thin plates of lifting bark. The leaves have two white bands of stomata (pores) on their undersides. Red male and reddish yellow female cones are borne on the same tree in spring.

**White spruce**
Softer, more rounded, lighter-coloured leaves and narrow, cylindrical cones distinguish this tree (*Picea glauca*).

**PROFILE**

- 30–50 m (100–160 ft)
- Up to 10 m (30 ft)
- Evergreen
- Needle-like
- C. Balkans

**Spreading foliage** Slender leaves have a dark glossy green upper surface and two broad bands of stomata (pores) on the underside.

*needle-like leaf, up to 2 cm (¾ in) long*

*blunt leaf tip*

**FEATURES**

**Bark** Orange-brown to copper; breaks into irregular plates

*Picea omorika* (Pinaceae)

# SERBIAN SPRUCE

**Native to the central Balkans**, the Serbian spruce faces increasing threat from deforestation, and is now considered vulnerable in the wild. However, it is commonly cultivated in gardens and arboreta as an ornamental tree. This conifer has a slender, spire-like habit, with branches sweeping downwards before arching upwards at the tips. This form allows the tree to shed snow and so resist damage.

The bark is rarely seen because branching and foliage descends to the ground, obscuring the trunk. Crimson male pollen cones are borne below new shoots, while red female seed cones are confined to the uppermost branches where they become pendulous in shape. Deep purple-brown and shaped like tear drops, each cone is held on a curved stalk, up to 6 cm (2½ in) long.

**Yezo spruce (*Picea jezoensis*)** Also known as the Hondo spruce, this tree is distinguished by a broader conical form, lighter leaf underside, and longer, red cones.

**PROFILE**

- 40–55 m (130–180 ft)
- Up to 10 m (30 ft)
- Evergreen
- Needle-like
- W. North America

**Cones and leaves**
Narrow cylindrical cones form after female cones are pollinated. The leaf undersides are pale green with two white bands.

*soft, black-green leaf, up to 3.5 cm (1½ in) long*

*flat leaf runs to an abrupt fine point*

*seed cone up to 12 cm (5 in) long*

**FEATURES**

**Bark** Dull pinkish grey colour; turns purple-brown with age

**Male cones** Spherical, purple; up to 2 cm (¾ in) wide

*Picea breweriana* (Pinaceae)

# BREWER'S WEEPING SPRUCE

**Possibly the most beautiful** of all spruces, this relatively slow-growing, evergreen tree is popular as an ornamental specimen. It is native to the Siskiyou Mountains of northwest California and southwest Oregon, USA. Brewer's weeping spruce is easily recognized by its weeping foliage, which hangs on branchlets like long verdant curtains – sometimes up to 2 m (6 ft) in length.

The purple-brown bark cracks into hard circular flakes as the tree matures. The soft, flat, needle-like leaves are shiny on the upper surface and paler on the underside. They point forwards along soft pink-brown shoots, which hang downwards like tails. Female seed cones are dark red and clustered on branches near the top of the tree. They become purple as they mature, slightly curving along the length and tapering towards the base. These turn red-grey once the seeds are released.

## PROFILE

- 25–30 m (80–100 ft)
- Up to 15 m (50 ft)
- Evergreen
- Needle-like
- N. Europe, N. Asia

*blue-green leaf, up to 7 cm (3 in) long*

*red, female cone cluster*

*male cones are upright yellow "candles"*

*twisted leaves carried in fascicles of two*

*egg-shaped, woody mature seed cone*

**Stout shoots**
The shoots of the Scots pine bear stout, twisted leaves and male and female cones in separate clusters.

## FEATURES

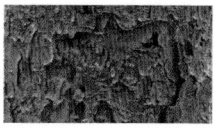

**Bark** Flaking, orange-red in mature trees

*raised "pimple" on scale*

**Seed cones**
Green, ripening to light brown

*Pinus sylvestris* (Pinaceae)

# SCOTS PINE

**This familiar tree** is easily recognized by its characteristic red bark. One of the northern hemisphere's most popular trees, it has long been used as a Christmas tree in North America. Its natural range extends from Ireland, across northern Europe and Asia, to the Pacific coast. It can grow on all types of soil, from dry and sandy to wet and peaty. It produces large quantities of seed and is able to colonize new territory quickly. Mature trees develop broadly domed crowns with large snaking branches.

The bark is sometimes red on young trees, although grey or light red-brown is more common. Stiff leaves are set in a papery, orange-brown sheath known as a fascicle. Male and female cones are borne on young shoots in late spring on the same tree.

**Japanese black pine**
This tree (*Pinus thunbergii*) can be distinguished from the Scots pine by its stout, twisted branches and longer leaves.

**PROFILE**

- 25–30m (80–100ft)
- Up to 20m (70ft)
- Evergreen
- Needle-like
- S. Europe

**Paired foliage**
The slender, needle-like leaves of this pine are forward-pointing and borne in pairs.

*golden male pollen cones in clusters*

*needles point forwards on shoot*

*leaf up to 12cm (5in) long*

*smooth, pale-green shoot*

*grey-green leaves borne in pairs*

**FEATURES**

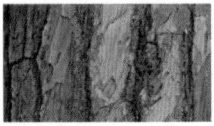

**Bark** Grey, with orange fissure lines down the trunk

*cone up to 10cm (4in) long*

**Seed cones** Spherical, ripen from green to glossy brown

**Seeds** Up to 100 edible seeds released from each cone

*Pinus pinea* (Pinaceae)

# UMBRELLA PINE

**Also known as stone pine**, this large conifer has a natural distribution that extends across the Mediterranean region, from Portugal to Turkey. It is widely cultivated elsewhere for its seeds, commonly known as pine nuts. With its spreading, flat-topped crown, made up of long, horizontal branches and dense foliage, the umbrella pine is a distinctive part of the Mediterranean landscape.

Its trunk is normally short and branches out from relatively low down. The shoots are tipped by chestnut-red buds, fringed with white hairs. The cone is relatively smooth, with a flat base and may weigh up to 400g (14oz). After forming, it remains closed for up to three years before opening to release its seeds.

**Macedonian pine**
Unlike the two-needled umbrella pine, this five-needled tree (*Pinus peuce*) has a narrow conical habit.

## PROFILE

- Up to 40 m (130 ft)
- Up to 15 m (50 ft)
- Evergreen
- Needle-like
- W. Mediterranean mountains

**Corsican pine leaves**
Long, pale grey-green, twisted leaves are borne in pairs, which radiate from the stem.

*leaf up to 18 cm (7 in) long*

*pointed leaf tip*

## FEATURES

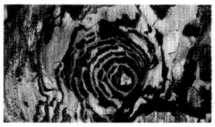

**Bark** Light grey to pink; heavily fissured from an early age

*cone matures to grey-brown*

**Seed cones**
Ovoid to conical, up to 8 cm (3 in) long

*Pinus nigra* subsp. *laricio* (Pinaceae)

# CORSICAN PINE

**This large conifer** is valued for its strong timber, which is widely used in the construction industry. In recent years, the tree has been prone to attack from red-band needle blight disease. The Corsican pine differs from the "parent" species Austrian pine (*Pinus nigra*) in having a more open crown with fewer and shorter branches, which are level rather than ascending.

Stiff yellow-brown shoots bear sharply pointed buds, often covered in white, crystallized resin. The leaves are carried sparsely on the shoots. Golden yellow pollen cones appear at the base of the shoots. These shed dust-like pollen in late spring and early summer. Dull pink seed cones become slightly curved and woody as they mature.

**Arolla pine**
This tree (*Pinus cembra*) has a smaller stature and shorter leaves, borne in groups of five.

**PROFILE**

- Up to 25 m (80 ft)
- Up to 15 m (50 ft)
- Evergreen
- Needle-like
- C. China

*pointed leaf, 5–10 cm (2–4 in) long*

*cone matures to a woody brown colour*

*leaf carried in bundles of three*

**Smooth shoots**
The rigid leaves are carried on young, grey-green shoots, which bear cones in early summer.

**FEATURES**

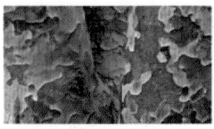

**Bark** Grey-green; peels to reveal a range of colours

**Cones** Small, squat, ovoid; up to 7 cm (3 in) long; each tipped with a spine

*Pinus bungeana* (Pinaceae)

# LACEBARK PINE

**This slow-growing, medium-sized conifer** is native to central China and was first seen by outsiders in 1831, growing in a temple garden near Beijing. It was introduced into western cultivation in 1846. Since then, it has been planted regularly in gardens and parks. It has a rounded top, often developing multi-stems from near the base.

The tree has smooth, silky bark, which is gradually shed to reveal patches of new bark, rather like the London plane (p.204). These patches then turn a succession of colours including cream, pale yellow, green, red, olive-brown, and purple – quite often a patchwork of all. The overall effect can be beautiful and almost reptilian. Male and female cones are borne in separate clusters on shoots.

**Armand pine (*Pinus armandii*)** The bark of this pine is not as attractive as the lacebark pine. However, it has longer and more decorative leaves and cones, both up to 15 cm (6 in) long.

## PROFILE

- 20m (70ft)
- Up to 10m (30ft)
- Evergreen
- Needle-like
- W. North America

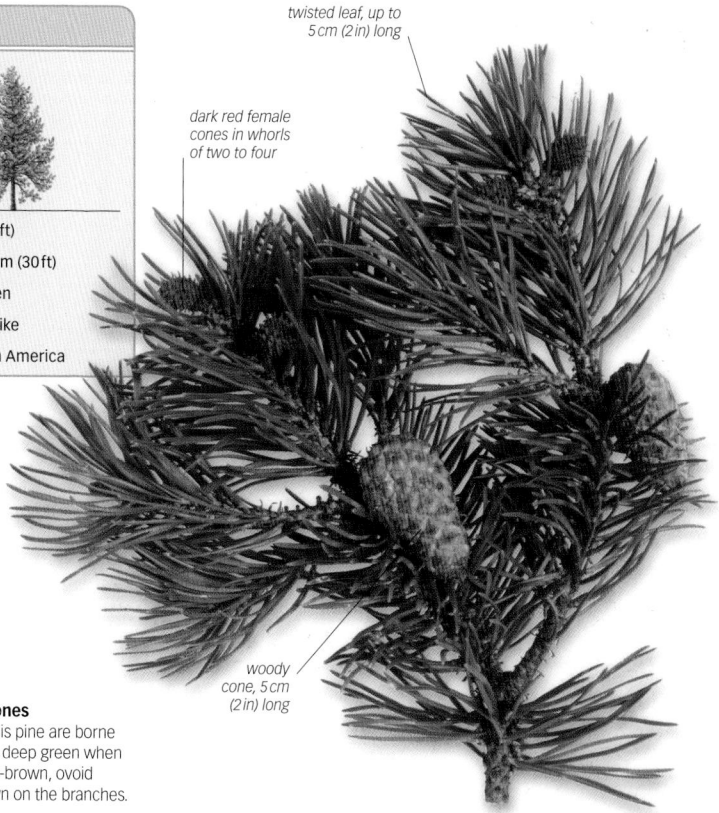


**eaves and cones**
he leaves of this pine are borne
n pairs and are deep green when
oung. The pink-brown, ovoid
ones face down on the branches.

## FEATURES

**Bark** Dark grey, with irregular chestnut-coloured fissures

**Male cones** Yellow; shed pollen in spring

*Pinus contorta* var. *latifolia* (Pinaceae)

# LODGEPOLE PINE

**This hardy conifer gets** its common name from its traditional use by Native Americans for the central pole of their tepees or lodges. Native to the mountains of western North America, the lodgepole pine was introduced into Europe by Scottish botanist David Douglas in 1831. It is able to withstand exposure, cold, and wet soils extremely well.

The tree grows straight with defined whorls of branches, sometimes as much as 1m (3ft) apart. It is broad and bushy near the ground, often with a hockey-stick-like sweep to the base of the trunk. The leaves are borne in dense clusters screening rigid shoots from view, and turn yellow with age.

**Weymouth pine**
Unlike the lodgepole pine, this large, round-headed tree (*Pinus strobus*) bears its glaucous green leaves in groups of five.

**PROFILE**

- 30–40m (100–130ft)
- Up to 15m (50ft)
- Evergreen
- Needle-like
- USA (California)

**Leaves and pollen cones**
Pine shoots have dark green leaves, borne in threes. Male pollen cones, in dense clusters on shoot tips, shed pollen in early spring.

**FEATURES**

**Seed cones**
Borne in clusters on young shoots

**Mature cones** Initially red-brown; up to 10cm (4in) long, roughly oval shape

*Pinus radiata* (Pinaceae)

# MONTEREY PINE

**The natural range** of this fast-growing conifer is limited to Monterey Peninsula, California. Since its discovery in 1833, it has become the most widely planted tree in the world for timber production. In New Zealand alone, it accounts for over 60 per cent of all conifers, covering more than 4,000sq km (2,500sq miles).

In maturity, this tree broadens out to form a large, domed crown. The bark is slate-grey, becoming deeply fissured with age. In spring, the male pollen cones shed large amounts of pollen, while female cones develop into red-brown seed cones, which age to dark grey. They usually take several years to open and release their seeds. They may stay fixed to branches for many years even after seed dispersal.

**Big-cone pine**
This tree (*Pinus coulteri*) has large cones weighing up to 2kg (4½lb) and stiffer, longer needles than the Monterey pine.

**PROFILE**

- 30 m (100 ft)
- Up to 15 m (50 ft)
- Evergreen
- Needle-like
- Canary Islands

**Pollen cones**
Clusters of small, beige, male pollen cones appear as stout "candles" on branch tips.

*individual ripe pollen cone, up to 1 cm (½ in) long*

**FEATURES**

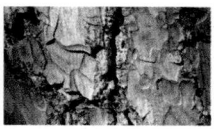

**Bark** Red-brown, thick, fissured, flaking

**Leaves** Slender, lax, up to 30 cm (12 in) long; borne on pendulous shoots in clusters of three

*Pinus canariensis* (Pinaceae)

# CANARY ISLAND PINE

**Widely planted as an ornamental** conifer across warmer regions of Europe, the natural spread of this tree is limited to islands in the Canary archipelago, except Lanzarote and Fuerteventura. It is one of the dominant trees in the Canary Island montane cloud forests, such as those on the western and northern flanks of Mount Teide on Tenerife. Here, the pine's long leaves "comb" low-lying clouds for valuable moisture.

When young the tree is conical in shape. It becomes more widely spreading, with long branches and drooping branchlets, as it matures. Young glaucous leaves turn bright grass-green as they age. The margin of each leaf is finely toothed and feels coarse when run through the fingers. The egg-shaped, cylindrical seed cones, up to 25 cm (10 in) long, with raised stubs on each scale, are rough to the touch.

**Mountain pine (*Pinus mugo*)** This related tree is distinguished by its shrublike sprawling habit, and its short, rigid leaves, up to 4 cm (1½ in) long, which grow in pairs.

**PROFILE**

- 30–40m (100–130ft)
- Up to 15m (50ft)
- Evergreen
- Needle-like
- Himalayas

*pink-purple female seed cone, near tips of new shoots*

**Soft needles**
Although needle-like in form the leaves of the Bhutan pine are slender and flexible. They are held in fascicles (bundles of five by a basal sheath.

*long leaf, up to 20cm (8in) long*

**FEATURES**

**Male cones** Pale yellow; pollen bearing; borne at the base of new shoots

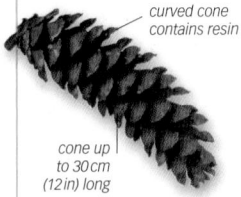


**Seed cones** Pendulous, green ripening to pale brown; release seeds in the second year

*Pinus wallichiana* (Pinaceae)

# BHUTAN PINE

**Also called the Himalayan white pine**, the Bhutan pine is among the most popular pines across the world and is widely planted in parks and gardens. In the Himalayas, this broadly conical tree grows at altitudes of up to 3,800m (12,500ft) and reaches 40m (130ft) in height.

As with many other pines, it is conical when young but develops a "middle-age spread," with lower branches curving downwards from the trunk before sweeping up at the tips. Smooth branches emerge in regularly spaced whorls. The shoots are slate-grey with a purple bloom. The pink-grey bark has some resin blisters, and develops small fissures in maturity. This tree makes good firewood, and is also used to make turpentine.

**Korean pine**
This tree (*Pinus koraiensis*) has a smaller stature and rough, stiff, needle-like leaves

## PROFILE

- 30–50m (100–160ft)
- Up to 15m (50ft)
- Evergreen
- Needle-like
- Mexico, W. Central America

**Graceful, weeping foliage**
This tree has long, drooping leaves, sometimes bent along their length, held in clusters by a papery sheath attached to the shoots.

*slender, spreading foliage*

*blue-green, drooping leaf, up to 15cm (6in) long.*

## FEATURES

**Seed cones** Long, slender, up to 45cm (18in) long, 10cm (4in) wide; large scales

*Pinus ayacahuite* (Pinaceae)

# MEXICAN WHITE PINE

**Native to Mexico** and western Central America, the Mexican white pine grows to more than 40m (130ft) in its homeland; elsewhere it is more likely to grow up to 30m (100ft). It has been cultivated in Australasia, South Africa, northern India, and temperate regions of Europe.

The tree has pale green shoots, with fine hairs along the length. Young trees often produce a sinuous leading shoot, which develops into long, level branching on old trees. The dark purplish brown bark is smooth at first, coarsely flaking into rough, irregular plates later. The needle-like leaves are finely serrated around the margin. Yellow male and red female cones are borne in separate clusters in early summer. The pendulous seed cones are borne on stout stalks, up to 2cm (¾in) long. They are usually covered with sticky, white resin. The scales open to release the seeds inside.

**Holford pine (*Pinus* x *holfordiana*)** A hybrid derived from the Mexican white pine, the Holford pine is a wider spreading tree with longer needles and less-tapering cones.

# FLOWERING TREES

**Also known by the scientific term angiosperms, most trees belong to this class. Flowering trees reproduce by producing flowers and have their seeds within a fleshy casing called an ovary that develops into fruit.**

Flowering trees can be divided into three subclasses: primitive angiosperms (opposite), monocotyledons (p.113), and eudicotyledons (p.121). They evolved over 125 million years ago, and today there is a huge diversity of flowering plant species.

| | |
|---|---|
| **CLASS** | ANGIOSPERMAE |
| **SUBCLASS** | 3 |
| **ORDERS** | 40 |
| **FAMILIES** | 603 |
| **SPECIES** | ABOUT 255,000 (c.60,000 TREES) |

Flowers are reproductive shoots: these may be large and brightly coloured, or small and simple. The basic structure – its male and female parts (p.18) encircled by petals and sepals – is often showy and scented to attract insects and supplies nectar as an incentive. But two more innovations are equally important in flowering trees. Firstly, they exhibit double fertilization: each pollen grain produced by the male anther supplies the female ovule with two male cells at pollination. One fertilizes the egg to make the embryo, while a second fuses with neighbouring tissue to make a seed nutrient store. Secondly, seeds are enclosed in fleshy encasements called fruits. The nutrient store nurtures the embryo, and the fruit lures fruit-eating animals to help scatter seeds.

**Cockspur hawthorn**
This tree produces many flowers, the scent of which is reminiscent of rotting flesh and attracts hungry carrion beetles to pollinate them.

# PRIMITIVE ANGIOSPERMS

**'his group – also known as basal angiosperms – encompass a andful of unrelated plant groups that were the first flowering lants to evolve. Some of these developed the tree habit and few – such as magnolias – are notable for their showy flowers.**

lowering plants used to be lassified into two subclasses: ne monocotyledons (monocots), ontaining mostly non-woody plants such as palms, orchids, and grasses) nd dicotyledons (dicots), containing all ther groups. It is now known that nere are several dicot lineages, some f which – loosely called the "primitive ngiosperms" – were evolutionary ioneers in reproduction by flowers.

| DIVISION | ANGIOSPERMAE |
|---|---|
| GROUP | BASAL ANGIOSPERMS |
| ORDERS | 9 |
| FAMILIES | 29 |
| SPECIES | 7350 (c.3000 TREES) |

## ROAD LEAVES

hese plants produced some of the first owers over 130 million years ago, and nany produced broader leaf blades for nproved photosynthesis (p.9). In the onstantly moist warm tropics these ees could stay evergreen, whereas in emperate and seasonally dry regions ney turned deciduous. But everywhere ne succulent foliage of these first road-leaved forests attracted rowsing animals, such as dinosaurs. hese early flowering plants lacked the stasteful water-proofing resins of onifers, so their leaves evolved an alternative cocktail of chemicals – with tannins and even cyanides – specifically to deter herbivores. The descendants of these bitter-leaved basal angiosperms are still with us today, most belonging to a group collectively known as magnoliids: laurels, avocado, nutmeg and of course the magnolias.

## SIMPLE FLOWERS

Most magnoliids produce flowers with a straightforward arrangement of parts, and some magnoliid trees have large flowers – such as those of magnolia themselves. Their petals are usually indistinguishable from the sepals (so are called tepals), and typically each flower has many male parts (stamens) and female parts (carpels). Many species are pollinated by beetles – an ancient group of insects, whose prehistoric diversification occurred at a time when the magnoliids were coming to prominence. The fruits of basal angiosperms are usually small and dry.

**Magnolia flowers**
The bright large flowers of magnolias, such as these from *Magnolia* x *loebneri* 'Leonard Messer', are made up of tepals rather than petals, and are particularly attractive to pollinating insects.

**PROFILE**

- 18–25 m (60–80 ft)
- Up to 10 m (30 ft)
- Evergreen
- Alternate simple
- US coast (from North Carolina to Florida and east to S.E. Texas)

**Fragrant flower**
The highly fragrant, creamy white flowers of the bull bay carry the scent of citronella.

*creamy white to lemon-coloured sepals*

*flower borne singly at end of shoot*

*flower opens in a saucer shape, up to 30 cm (12 in) wide*

*leaf glossy green on upper surface*

**FEATURES**

**Fruit** Red-brown, cone-like structure with seeds

*Magnolia grandiflora* (Magnoliaceae)

# BULL BAY

**Also known as loblolly magnolia**, bull bay is indigenous to coastal USA. In warm, temperate areas, it develops into a free-standing tree with a broad canopy and short stems, and is a common sight in streets, town squares, parks, and gardens. In cooler regions, it is more often grown as a large wall-shrub, where the combination of glossy, dark green foliage and creamy white flowers is dramatic.

The grey-brown bark is smooth at first, cracking into irregular small plates as it ages. The leaf undersides are sometimes covered in copper-coloured hairs. Flowers, borne through summer and early autumn, provide a late source of nectar for insects, and are followed by erect seed pods displaying red seeds.

**Cucumber magnolia**
This deciduous tree (*Magnolia acuminata*) has ovate leaves, and green and yellow flowers.

**PROFILE**



- Up to 20m (70ft)
- Up to 10m (30ft)
- Deciduous
- Alternate simple
- China

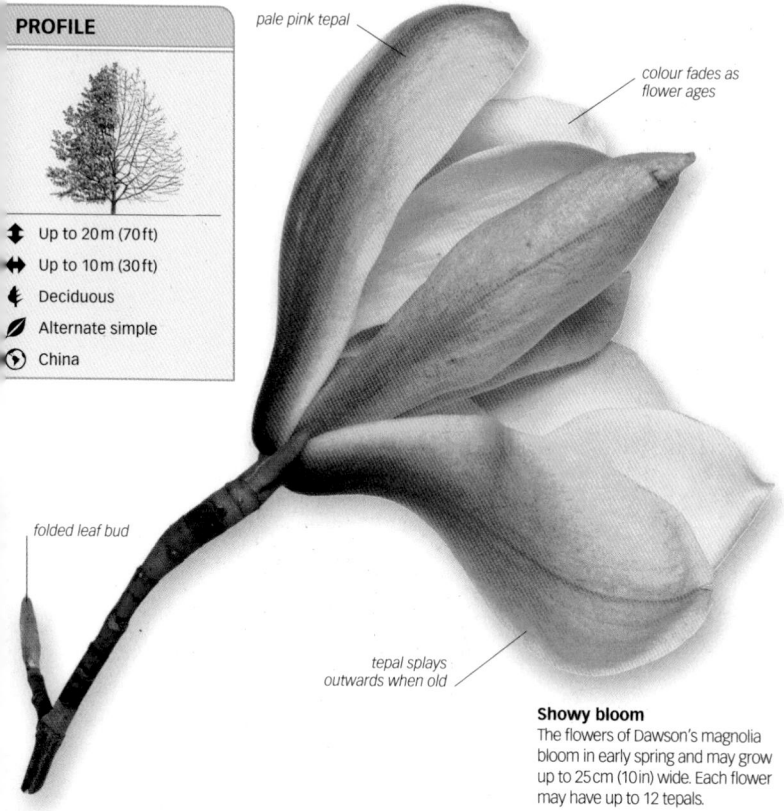


**Showy bloom**
The flowers of Dawson's magnolia bloom in early spring and may grow up to 25cm (10in) wide. Each flower may have up to 12 tepals.

**FEATURES**

**Leaves** Obovate to elliptic, matt with bright green upper surface; 7.5–15cm (3–6in) long

*Magnolia dawsoniana* (Magnoliaceae)

# DAWSON'S MAGNOLIA

**Native to Sichuan and Yunnan** provinces of China, this broadly conical tree grows in mountainous regions at an altitude of around 2,500m (8,200ft). Discovered in 1869 by the French missionary Père Jean Pierre Armand David, it was introduced into western cultivation when English botanist Ernest H. Wilson sent its seeds to the Arnold Arboretum in Jamaica Plain, Massachusetts, USA, in 1908.

A hardy tree, Dawson's magnolia is able to withstand several degrees of frost. The bark is grey-brown and smooth at first, but on older trees develops some shallow cracks and fissures. Leaves are broadest at the middle and taper towards each end, with a blue-silvery green underside. Bright pink buds bloom to produce masses of slightly fragrant, cup-shaped, pale pink flowers. The fruit is an erect, cylindrical pod up to 15cm (6in) long and contains red seeds.

**Lily tree (*Magnolia denudata*)** Unlike the large, pink flowers of the Dawson's magnolia, this tree has smaller, pure white flowers, which bloom in late spring.

## PROFILE

- 8–12 m (25–40 ft)
- Up to 10 m (30 ft)
- Deciduous
- Alternate simple
- Hybrid, originated in Europe

**Early bloom**
Large, goblet-shaped flowers start to open in early spring, often before the leaves emerge.

*flower up to 25 cm (10 in) wide*

*pink-purple staining at base of tepal*

## FEATURES

**Leaves** Smooth, dark green on the upper surface; paler and finely hairy on the underside

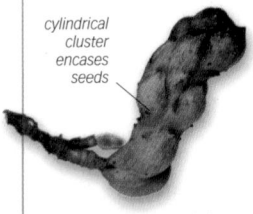


**Fruit** Irregular cylindrical cluster, ripening from green to pink-red

*Magnolia* x *soulangeana* (Magnoliaceae)

# SAUCER MAGNOLIA

**This magnolia was the first** to be hybridized and does not occur in the wild. A cross between *Magnolia denudata* and *M. liliiflora*, it was first raised near Paris in the 1820s by Etienne Soulange-Bodin, a French army officer. Today, it is the world's most widely planted garden magnolia, with many cultivated forms such as 'Alba Superba', 'Brozzonii', 'Lennei', and 'Nigra'.

This tree tends to have multiple stems with low branches. The bark is smooth and grey, while flowers vary in colour, from creamy white to pink or purple-pink. Leaves are elliptic to obovate, tapering to a pointed tip. Seeds form in clusters from late summer to early autumn.

**Loebner's magnolia**
A hybrid of *M. stellata* and *M. kobus*, this tree (*Magnolia* x *loebneri*) flowers later in spring than both parents.

## PROFILE

- Up to 20m (70ft)
- Up to 10m (30ft)
- Deciduous
- Alternate simple
- China

**Large flowers**
The flowers of Sargent's magnolia are among the largest of any magnolia, growing up to 30cm (12in) wide.

*rose-pink inner surface of tepal*

*tepal pale pink inside*

## FEATURES

**Leaves** Thick and leathery; up to 20cm (8in) long and 10cm (4in) wide

**Fruit** Green ripening to pink; open in summer to reveal glossy, bright red seeds

*Magnolia sargentiana* (Magnoliaceae)

# SARGENT'S MAGNOLIA

**This broadly columnar magnolia** is native to the provinces of Yunnan and Sichuan in China, from where it was introduced into western cultivation in 1908 by Ernest H. Wilson. It is named after Charles Sprague Sargent, who was director of the Arnold Arboretum in Jamaica Plain, Massachusetts, USA, at the time of its introduction. As a result of deforestation and habitat destruction, this tree is now considered endangered in the wild.

The grey-brown bark is smooth at first but develops shallow cracks and fissures with age. The leaves are dark green with a slight sheen on the upper surface, and have a pale green underside. The fragrant flowers are rose pink on the outside and pale pink on the inner surface, resembling giant water lilies. They are produced in early spring before the leaves unfurl. The fruit is a rigid, cylindrical pod up to 15cm (6in) long.

**Umbrella tree (*Magnolia tripetala*)** With thin, lax, large, obovate to elliptic leaves, this tree is also distinguished by its fragrant, cream-coloured flowers in early summer.

**PROFILE**

- Up to 4 m (12 ft)
- Up to 5 m (15 ft)
- Deciduous
- Alternate simple
- Japan

**Showy, white blossoms**
Flower buds open in spring to reveal starlike flowers made up of up to 20 narrow, white or pink-blushed tepals.

*narrow, white tepal up to 5 cm (2 in) long*

**FEATURES**

**Bark** Grey, smooth with a slight sheen on trunk; brown on branches

**Leaves** Green, obovate, and narrow; up to 10 cm (4 in) long, 5 cm (2 in) wide

*Magnolia stellata* (Magnoliaceae)

# STAR MAGNOLIA

**This slow-growing, broadly spreading**, small magnolia is native to the mountains of Nagoya, Japan, from where it was introduced into western cultivation in the 1860s. Some suggest that it is a form of *Magnolia tomentosa* or *Magnolia kobus,* and not a true species in its own right; however it does have visual differences to both of these species. The star magnolia is ideal for planting in small gardens and usually flowers from a young age.

This magnolia's chestnut-brown branches are long, thin, and twiglike. It has few large, heavy branches, so the overall effect is more shrublike than treelike. Conical flower buds, evident throughout winter, are covered in silver-grey down. They open gradually in spring, before the leaves appear.

**Northern Japanese magnolia**
This tree (*Magnolia kobus*) is larger, with obovate leaves and creamy white tepals, up to 9 cm (3½ in) long.

**Conspicuous flower**
Large, fragrant flowers open singly from ovoid buds and vary from deep pink to pale pinkish white.

*spreading, pinkish white outer tepal*

*flower up to 30 cm (12 in) wide*

## PROFILE

- 30 m (100 ft)
- Up to 10 m (30 ft)
- Deciduous
- Alternate simple
- Himalayas, S.W. China

## FEATURES

*leaf ends in sharp point*

**Leaf** Grey-green, with slight sheen on upper surface

**Buds** Large, ovoid, covered in short hairs

*Magnolia campbellii* (Magnoliaceae)

# PINK TULIP TREE

**Also known as the giant Himalayan** pink tulip tree or Campbell's magnolia, this majestic, broadly conical tree, grows at heights of up to 3,000 m (9,840 ft) above sea level in its natural range. It is one of the largest magnolias in cultivation, and since the 1860s has been widely planted in parks, large gardens, and arboreta.

This tree has a smooth, mid-grey bark, which it maintains into old age. Obovate leaves grow up to 30 cm (12 in) long, and are pale green, occasionally faintly hairy, on the underside. The flower buds stand out dramatically on bare branches in late winter. The flowers are goblet-shaped at first, opening to a lax cup and saucer shape and have tepals rather than petals and sepals. They open before the leaves and are prone to late frost damage. The tepals fall gradually, and may remain on the ground for some time.

**Veitch's hybrid magnolia (*Magnolia* x *veitchii*)** This smaller related species, up to 16 m (52 ft) tall, is easily distinguished by its compact habit and more goblet-shaped flowers, up to 20 cm (8 in) wide.

**PROFILE**

- Up to 28 m (92 ft)
- Up to 15 m (50 ft)
- Deciduous
- Alternate simple
- C. and W. China

*unripe green fruit, up to 7.5 cm (3 in) long*

*leaf up to 18 cm (7 in) long*

**Fruit and leaves**
The fruit is a rigid pod, which ripens in summer to reveal bright red seeds. The leaves are obovate with a wedge-shaped base.

**FEATURES**

**Bark** Grey; remains smooth in maturity

**Flowers** Rose pink, fading to light pink with lax tepals in maturity; up to 20 cm (8 in) wide

*Magnolia sprengeri* (Magnoliaceae)

# SPRENGER'S MAGNOLIA

**This broadly conical**, medium to large-sized magnolia is native to central and western China, from where it was introduced into western cultivation by plant collector Ernest H. Wilson in 1900. This tree is named after the German Botanist Carl Ludwig Sprenger. It is similar to the pink tulip tree (p.101), although defining features such as overall size, spread, leaves, and flowers are smaller in Sprenger's magnolia.

The leaves are bright green on the upper surface and pale green on the underside. The ovoid flower buds, up to 7.5 cm (3 in) long, are covered with silver-grey down. They remain on the tree throughout late winter, revealing goblet-shaped, fragrant flowers in mid-spring. On maturity, they open out to form water-lily-like flowers.

**Japanese big-leaf magnolia (*Magnolia obovata*)** This tree has very large, obovate leaves, up to 50 cm (20 in) long and 25 cm (10 in) wide, borne in whorls at the ends of shoots.

**PROFILE**

- Up to 8 m (25 ft)
- Up to 5 m (15 ft)
- Deciduous
- Alternate simple
- W. China

*flower up to 10 cm (4 in) wide*

*leaf pale green on underside*

**rooping flowers**
ne flowers hang down from
ching stems in late spring, and
e seen from beneath the tree.

**FEATURES**

**Fruit** Green, cylindrical seed pod; ripening to purple-pink

*Magnolia wilsonii* (Magnoliaceae)

# WILSON'S MAGNOLIA

**This broadly spreading shrublike** tree has become a popular garden plant in recent years. It is named after English plant collector Ernest H. Wilson, who discovered the species in western China in 1908.

The bark is green with a bumpy texture. Leaves are narrowly elliptic, running to a pointed tip. They are up to 20 cm (8 in) long and 10 cm (4 in) wide, with a silk-green upper surface, and a thin, white, felt-like covering on the underside. The flower buds are covered in dense, soft grey hairs and are visible from late winter. Fragrant, cup-shaped, white flowers with crimson-purple stamens emerge after the leaves appear. Over time, the tepals spread and the flower becomes saucer-shaped. A green aggregate fruit, up to 7.5 cm (3 in) long, develops after flowering. It ripens to purple-pink and opens to reveal many bright orange-red, glossy seeds inside.

**Mulan magnolia (*Magnolia liliiflora*)** With its erect, slender, tulip-shaped, purple, or purple-flushed flowers, this related species is unlikely to be mistaken for Wilson's magnolia.

**Multi-petalled flowers**
Blooming in spring, the sweet michelia's cup-shaped, multi-petalled flowers are pale lemon to white in colour.

**PROFILE**

- Up to 20m (70ft)
- Up to 15m (50ft)
- Evergreen
- Alternate simple
- China, Himalayas

*Michelia doltsopa* (Magnoliaceae)

# SWEET MICHELIA

**This broadly spreading tree** is one of the most attractive of all evergreens. It is related to magnolia and was discovered in Yunnan, western China, in 1918 by the Scottish plant collector George Forrest. He sent seeds of the sweet michelia to Caerhays castle in Cornwall, England. These were propagated, producing five seedlings, which were planted in the castle grounds. They flowered for the first time in 1933.

The glossy, dark green, leathery leaves are up to 20cm (8in) long, and covered with a fine coating of rust-coloured hairs on the underside. The flower buds form in autumn and are like erect magnolia buds, but covered in fine cinnamon-coloured hairs rather than the silver hairs typical of magnolia. The buds open in spring to reveal cup-shaped flowers. Each flower is strongly scented, almost pungently so in an enclosed space or on hot spring days.

**Chinese evergreen magnolia (*Magnolia delavayi*)** This tree's leaves are almost twice the size as those of sweet michelia. It also bears flowers that have larger, lax tepals.

## PROFILE

- Up to 50 m (160 ft)
- Up to 20 m (70 ft)
- Deciduous
- Alternate simple
- E. North America

**Tulip tree flower**
Upright, tulip-shaped flowers, 6 cm (2½ in) wide, are produced in summer. Each has six petals and clusters of stamens inside.

*light green to orange-yellow petal*

*orange-yellow stamen*

## FEATURES

**Bark** Smooth, grey-brown; becomes vertically and regularly fissured with age

**Leaves** Bright green; have four pointed lobes with notched tips

*Liriodendron tulipifera* (Magnoliaceae)

# TULIP TREE

**The distinctive tulip tree is native** to eastern North America, from Ontario in the north to Florida in the south. Fossil records show it grew in Europe prior to the last ice age. It was introduced into cultivation in England in the mid-17th century. Since then, this large, long-trunked tree has been widely grown in parks, gardens, and arboreta elsewhere.

The leaves are an unusual shape with four lobes and a cut-off indented leaf tip. They are up to 15 cm (6 in) long and 10 cm (4 in) wide, and pale green on the underside. In autumn they turn butter-yellow before falling. The fruit is cone-shaped and contains seeds with papery wings.

**Broad and columnar**
The tulip tree develops a straight trunk on maturity, with few low branches, topped by a broad canopy.

**PROFILE**

- Up to 20m (70ft)
- Up to 10m (30ft)
- Deciduous
- Alternate simple
- China, Vietnam

*leaf deeply indented between lobes*

*leaf almost straight at the top*

*leaf up to 12cm (5in) long*

**Lobed leaves**
Leaves run to a lobe on either side, with another lobe midway between the leaf tip and the leaf stalk on each side.

**FEATURES**

**Bark** Slate grey, smooth; fissures vertically in maturity

**Flowers** Pale yellow-green outside, orange-yellow banding inside; has orange stamens

*Liriodendron chinense* (Magnoliaceae)

# CHINESE TULIP TREE

**Native to China and Vietnam**, the Chinese tulip tree grows up to around 2,000m (6,560ft) above sea level. It was introduced into western cultivation by English plant collector Ernest H. Wilson in 1901. Some of the first introductions of this species are still growing in the Royal Botanic Gardens at Kew in London, England.

The leaves are dark green on the upper surface, pale blue-green beneath. Between the lobes, the leaves are more deeply cut than on the tulip tree (p.105), giving the impression that the leaf has a waist. The leaves turn a rich golden yellow in autumn. Tulip-like flowers appear singly at the ends of shoots in early to midsummer. The fruit is a pale brown, conical cluster.

**Woodland tree**
This stately, medium-sized, deciduous tree usually grows in mixed woodland in its natural range.

*finely toothed leaf margin*

*pale green leaf underside, with a lighter midrib*

*ounded berry, 1 cm (½ in) wide*

*berry ripens from green to glossy black*

**oliage and fruit**
ne leaves are elliptic to nceolate in shape. Berries form n female trees and turn from een to glossy black when ripe.

**PROFILE**

- 6–18 m (20–60 ft)
- Up to 10 m (30 ft)
- Evergreen
- Alternate simple
- Mediterranean

**FEATURES**

*flower 1 cm (½ in) wide*

**Male flowers** Yellow-green with yellow anthers

**Female flowers** Smaller than male; borne on separate trees

*Laurus nobilis* (Lauraceae)

# BAY LAUREL

**This conical and densely leaved tree** is found across the Mediterranean. It is widely planted elsewhere for ornamental and culinary purposes, as well as for hedging and screening. The Greeks and Romans used it as a symbol of victory, weaving it into crowns to be worn by champions. They also gave acclaimed poets wreaths made of fruiting sprays, hence the term "poet laureate".

Bay laurel is a multi-stemmed tree, with bark that remains smooth even in old age. The elliptic to lanceolate leaves are dark green and leathery, and give off a rich fruity aroma when crushed. Male and female flowers are borne in leaf axils on separate trees in late winter, followed by berries on female trees.

**Spice bush (*Lindera benzoin*)** Unlike the evergreen bay laurel, spice bush has deciduous leaves, which turn bright yellow in autumn, and, on female trees, bright red berries.

**PROFILE**

- Up to 15m (50ft)
- Up to 8m (25ft)
- Evergreen
- Alternate simple
- Azores, Madeira, Canary Islands, Morocco

**Aromatic leaves and flowers**
The elliptic to lanceolate leaves of the Canary Island laurel are very aromatic when crushed. The greenish yellow flowers are also slightly fragrant.

*individual flower up to 1cm (½in) wide*

**FEATURES**

**Bark** Dark grey; remains smooth even in maturity

*Laurus azorica* (Lauraceae)

# CANARY ISLAND LAUREL

**This medium-sized, broadly columnar** tree is an important component of the Laurisilva forests on the northern and western slopes of the Azores, Madeira, an Canary Islands. However, it is now threatened by habita loss in parts of the Canary Islands. It is often cultivated in parks and gardens in warmer regions of Europe. Like its relative the bay laurel (p.107), this tree's foliage emits a pleasant aroma when crushed.

The thick, leathery, dark green leaves feel rigid to the touch. Paler green and hairy on the underside, they displa a wavy-edged margin. The flowers are borne in clusters in the axils of the previous year's leaves. These are followed by the fruit – an ovoid berry, up to 1.5cm (½in) long. Gree at first, the berry ripens to glossy black.

**Japanese spice tree (*Lindera obtusiloba*)** This tree has ovate to obovate, deciduous leaves, with three large, pointed lobes. They turn bright yellow in autumn before falling.

**ight green leaves**
e Chilean laurel bears glossy, ight green leaves, which emit strong aroma when crushed.

*eaf up to 10cm (4in) ng, 4cm (1½in) wide*

*gently serrated leaf margin*

**PROFILE**

- Up to 30m (100ft)
- Up to 15m (50ft)
- Evergreen
- Opposite simple
- Chile

**FEATURES**

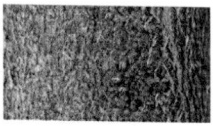

**Bark** Pale yellow-grey, smooth; darkens with age

*Laurelia sempervirens* (Monimiaceae)

# CHILEAN LAUREL

**Also known as Chilean sassafras**, this large, fast-growing, handsome, evergreen tree has long been favoured for its attractive timber, which is strong, durable, and highly scented. This has led to the tree becoming threatened in native Chile due to extensive felling. However, it has been introduced as an ornamental tree in the USA and parts of Europe, including Spain and southwest England. It is not hardy enough to grow in regions much further north than this.

The yellow-grey bark is smooth at first, darkening and cracking into circular plates with age. Its evergreen leaves are glossy and leathery to the touch. Arranged in opposite pairs along the shoot, they are oblong in shape, narrow at the base and tapering to a blunt tip. They are gently serrated around the leaf margin. Clusters of small, slightly fragrant, mustard-yellow flowers appear in the leaf axils in late spring.

**PROFILE**

- 7–15 m (22–50 ft)
- Up to 7 m (22 ft)
- Evergreen
- Alternate simple
- S. Mexico to Chile and Argentina

yellow stamen

rigid terminal stalk

leaf up to 20 cm (8 in) long, 5 cm (2 in) wide

short, individual stalk

**Fragrant flowers** Jasmine-scented flowers are borne on their own short, lax stalks, but are bunched in a cluster.

**FEATURES**

**Leaves** Bright green, with a slight sheen on upper surface; glaucous white underside

*Drimys winteri* (Winteraceae)

# WINTER'S BARK

**With a natural habitat** stretching from southern Mexico to Chile and Argentina, this handsome tree takes its name from Captain William Winter, who sailed with Sir Frances Drake on his famous voyage of discovery in 1577–80. Winter used the bark, high in vitamin C, to treat sailors who were suffering from scurvy. It was first cultivated as an ornamental tree in Europe in 1827.

The bark is relatively soft, brown-grey, and smooth even in old age. The leathery leaves are large, up to 20 cm (8 in) long and 5 cm (2 in) wide. They are widest in the middle and taper to a point at each end. When crushed, they give off a distinctive peppery aroma, as does the bark. The leaves are used in Argentina and Chile as a substitute for pepper. The tree bears ivory-white flowers in late spring, and in late summer and autumn they develop into green fruit, which turn blue-black when ripe.

**Mountain pepper (*Drimys lanceolata*)** Apart from its narrower, smaller leaves, this tree can also be distinguished from the Winter's bark by its purple-red shoots.

leaf up to 45 cm (18 in) long, 15 cm (6 in) wide

pale green leaf underside

glossy, dark green upper surface of leaf

**Deeply veined leaves**
The avocado tree bears elliptic leaves that display pronounced veining on their leathery surface.

## PROFILE

- Up to 20 m (70 ft)
- Up to 10 m (30 ft)
- Evergreen
- Alternate simple
- Mexico, West Indies

## FEATURES

**Bark** Dark grey, smooth; becomes vertically fissured

**Fruit** Pear-shaped; leathery, glossy, green to purple-brown outer skin

*Persea americana* (Lauraceae)

# AVOCADO

**Perhaps one of the best known** of all tropical fruit trees, this medium-sized evergreen is native to Mexico and the West Indies. However, the avocado tree has been extensively cultivated throughout the tropics for its flavoursome and highly nutritious fruit, which is rich in minerals and oils.

The tree has a smooth bark that becomes fissured with age. Small, star-shaped flowers are borne in leaf axils on the ends of erect, open-branched racemes. Individual flowers are fragrant, creamy yellow to white, and up to 1 cm (½ in) wide. The fruit occasionally displays mottled skin, especially on purple-skinned avocado varieties. Its edible inner flesh is light green and surrounds a single seed.

**Short-trunked tree**
Avocado is a fast-growing, broadly spreading tree. It has only a short trunk before it begins to branch.

**Camphor leaves**
In maturity, the leaves are waxy and deep glossy green. They are marked by three distinct veins.

**PROFILE**



- 15–30m (50–100ft)
- Up to 30m (100ft)
- Evergreen
- Alternate simple
- S.E. China, S. Japan, Taiwan

**FEATURES**

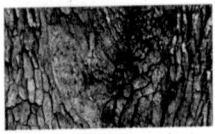

**Bark** Pale and smooth when young, rough and vertically fissured in maturity

*Cinnamomum camphora* (Lauraceae)

# CAMPHOR TREE

**Camphor is a large**, broadly spreading evergreen tree, which develops a distinctive rounded canopy of dense, dark leaves in maturity. It is native to southeast China, Taiwan, and southern Japan. Outside these areas this tree is widely cultivated both for its oil and as an ornamental shade tree in parks, gardens, and streets. Camphor also refers to the white, crystalline substance obtained from the wood, bark, and leaves of the tree. It has been used for centuries as a component of incense, an insect repellent, a culinary spice, and a medicine. Its wood is also sought after for its distinctive red and yellow stripes.

The leaves are coppery pink when young, maturing to bright green, and then becoming deep glossy green. When crushed, they emit the fragrance of camphor. Small, white to creamy green flowers are produced in spring, borne on erect racemes in the leaf axils. They are followed by clusters of black, berry-like, rounded fruit, up to 1cm (½in) wide.

# MONOCOTYLEDONS

**'he non-woody monocotyledons (monocots) generally have ·longated strap-like leaves with parallel veins. They have liversified as ground-hugging plants, such as grasses. But everal families have evolved trees: most notably the palms.**

Most monocotyledon species are low eshy (as opposed to woody) plants and nclude many familiar plants: grasses, rchids, and lilies. They get their name rom the fact that they have a single re-packed seed leaf (cotyledon) inside ne seed before it germinates.

Monocots are generally incapable of roducing woody tissue because their ansport vessels are scattered through ne stem instead of arranged in ood-forming rings (p.9). Yet the tree abit (p.19) has evolved independently n a number of different monocot roups. Yuccas and cordylines produce eafy branches from a central trunk. iant "herbs", such as bananas and ne traveller's palm, *Ravenala nadagascariensis*, strictly have no unk at all and instead are supported y massive leaf stalks growing from the lant base. But most monocot trees elong to a single family: the palms.

| CLASS | ANGIOSPERMAE |
|---|---|
| SUBCLASS | MONOCOTYLEDONEAE |
| ORDERS | 11 |
| FAMILIES | 81 |
| SPECIES | 58,000 (c. 3,000 TREES) |

## TROPICAL GIANTS

The unbranched trunk of a palm is strengthened with fibres reinforced with silica, enabling many to grow to considerable heights. The evergreen fan-like leaves show the familiar compound (palm-leaf) structure, but there is considerable variation and in many species the leaves can grow into giant proportions.

Individually, palm flowers are usually small and inconspicuous, but they may be produced in larger inflorescences (sprays). Most palm species are pollinated by insects, but some are wind-pollinated. Most palms – such as the date palm (p.116) and coconut (p.119) – produce fruits called drupes: here the inner layer of the fruit becomes hardened to form a stone, or shell, which – in turn – encases the true seed. Coconut palms produce large fruits that can float on water, enabling them to colonise oceanic islands. Another member – the Seychelles palm, *Lodoicea maldivica*, – produces the world's largest seed in the largest fruit, which weighs more than 30 kg (66 lb) and is too heavy to float anywhere. Palms reach their greatest diversity in the tropics and, although a few have managed to adapt to temperate climates, most only succeed in warm moist forests.

**European fan palm**
The leaf is typical of the palm family: long with parallel veins, and shaped like a fan. This palm is one of the few that have adapted to temperate climes.

**PROFILE**

- Up to 12 m (40 ft)
- Up to 3 m (10 ft)
- Evergreen
- Palm
- C. China

**Branched flower cluster**
The small, fragrant flowers are clustered together in large, bulbous drooping panicles in summer.

*stout flower stalk emerges from among leaves*

*fruit up to 1.5 cm (½ in) wide*

*creamy yellow male flowers*

**FEATURES**

**Bark** Covered with brown-grey, fibrous hairs; marked with discarded leaf scars

**Leaves** Stiff, leathery, dark green, up to 1.2 m (4 ft) wide

*Trachycarpus fortunei* (Arecaceae)

# CHUSAN PALM

**This exotic species** is also known as windmill palm. Surprisingly, it is not indigenous to the tropics, but originates from the mountains of central China. It is a hardy species and can also grow in warmer regions of Europe and North America. It was introduced into Europe in 1830 by the German physician Philipp Franz von Siebold.

The fan-shaped leaves are divided almost to the base into about 40 linear, pointed strips. The leaves are attached to the slender trunk by a stiff, flattened leaf-stalk, up to 1 m (3 ft) long. Dead leaves may remain on the trunk for years, creating a fringe-like appearance below the new leaves.

**Slender trunk**
This palm has a small hea of clustered leaves at the top of a single trunk, whic is narrower at the base.

## PROFILE

- Up to 2.5 m (8 ft)
- Up to 3 m (10 ft)
- Evergreen
- Whorled compound
- Mediterranean region

**Dense palm leaves**
The European fan palm appears as a dense, semi-circular mass of fan-shaped, stiff, grey-green leaves, borne on a short trunk.

*stiff, pointed leaf segment, up to 45 cm (18 in) long*

## FEATURES

**Bark** Brown, fibrous trunk; bears thick leaf stalks

*Chamaerops humilis* (Arecaceae)

# EUROPEAN FAN PALM

**This tree is the only member** of the palm family native to mainland Europe. In the wild, it grows on coastal mountainsides in Spain, Gibraltar, the Balearics, Sardinia, Italy and Sicily, as well as Algeria and Morocco. It was first cultivated outside this region, in areas such as southwestern Britain, in 1731.

The leaves, up to 90 cm (36 in) wide, are divided near the base into segments or strips. They are attached to the trunk by stalks from the point where the strips converge. The stalks, normally around 30 cm (12 in) long, are covered with sharp, forward-pointing spines. Small, yellow flowers emerge in stiff, upright panicles, up to 15 cm (6 in) long. The fruit, borne in clusters around the leaf base, resemble shiny green olives.

**Small, palm-like tree**
Also known as dwarf fan palm, the European fan palm often has a spreading and shrublike habit.

**PROFILE**

- Up to 12 m (40 ft)
- Up to 10 m (30 ft)
- Evergreen
- Whorled compound
- Canary Islands

*leaflet up to 50 cm (20 in) long*

*dark green, pointed leaflet*

**Comb-like leaves**
The leaves are thick, leathery, comb-like fronds. Individual leaflets are arranged in whorls around the stem.

**FEATURES**

**Fruit** Date-like, borne in bunches, green ripening to purple and then orange

*Phoenix canariensis* (Arecaceae)

# CANARY ISLAND DATE PALM

**This tree is native to the Canary Islands**, and is one of the stateliest palms to thrive outside the tropics. It is surprisingly hardy and can withstand some frost. It has been widely cultivated as an ornamental species in warm, temperate regions throughout the world, particularly along sea fronts and promenades.

The grey-brown bark has prominent scars left from where dead branches have been shed. The trunk may be up to 90 cm (36 in) wide on mature specimens and leaves are up to 5 m (15 ft) long. Golden yellow flower spikes, up to 2 m (6 ft) long, are borne in spring. These are followed by bunches of date-like fruit.

**Stately palm**
This palm has a round crown. Comb-like fronds arch upwards, away from the stout, straight trunk.

## PROFILE

- Up to 8 m (25 ft)
- Up to 4 m (12 ft)
- Evergreen
- Whorled compound
- Argentina, Brazil, Uruguay

*pinnate leaf, up to 3 m (10 ft) long*

**Distinctive leaves**
The large, feathery leaves range in colour from blue-grey to silver. The leaf stems have sharp, hooked spines along both edges.

## FEATURES

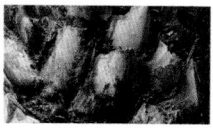

**Bark** Grey-brown; patterned with persistent scars made by bases of previous leaves

**Fruit** Rounded, up to 2.5 cm (1 in) wide; borne in large clusters beneath the foliage

*Butia capitata* (Arecaceae)

# JELLY PALM

**Also known as pindo palm**, this small palm is native to Argentina, Brazil, and Uruguay. However, because of its beauty and ability to withstand subzero temperatures, the jelly palm has been widely cultivated in the warm temperate regions of North America, Europe, and elsewhere. Its fruit is used to make jams, jellies (hence the name), and wine.

The jelly palm has a thick, sturdy trunk. Its small, fragrant flowers are yellow, tinged red to purple, and are carried in sets of threes – two male flowers and one female. These are followed by yellow or orange edible fruit known as pindo dates. They have a flavour like that of apricots, pineapples, and bananas mixed together.

**Attractive crown**
The jelly palm leaves arch upwards and away from the stem, then curve at their tips back towards the trunk.

**PROFILE**

- Up to 10 m (30 ft)
- Up to 5 m (15 ft)
- Evergreen
- Whorled simple
- New Zealand

*flower panicle bears individual flowers, 5–6 mm (¼ in) wide*

**Leaves and flowers**
The branches bear erect leaves, which have a fibrous texture when torn. The long, pendulous flowers appear in spring and early summer.

**FEATURES**

**Bark** Grey, corky, spongy, shallowly fissured

**Leaves** Grey-green; up to 90 cm (36 in) long, 7 cm (3 in) wide

*Cordyline australis* (Asparagaceae)

# CABBAGE PALM

**This slow-growing, palm-like tree** is not a true palm but more closely related to the agaves. The cabbage palm tree is native to New Zealand, where the indigenous Māoris used to eat the tender tips of its shoots, hence its common name "cabbage". Introduced into Europe in 1823, it has been widely cultivated in parks and gardens close to coastal regions.

It is usually a single-trunked tree with sword-like leaves that are striated with many parallel veins, and sometimes display a kink towards their tip. The palm bears masses of fragrant, white flowers in large panicles, 60–100 cm (24–39 in) long. The fruit is a small, pale lilac- to green-coloured berry.

**Ascending branches**
The cabbage palm bears stout, ascending branches which are crowned by a mass of sword-like leaves.

## PROFILE

- 20–30 m (70–100 ft)
- Up to 10 m (30 ft)
- Evergreen
- Compound
- Pacific and Indian Ocean islands, N.W. South America, Australia, India

*fruit up to 30 cm (12 in) long*

**Large fruit**
The fruit is a hard, oval, green sphere, weighing up to 1.5 kg (3 lb). It appears amidst large, slightly arching, pinnate leaves.

## FEATURES

**Bark** Grey, marked with narrow leaf scars

*seed 4–8 cm (1½–3 in) long*

**Seeds** Brown, fibrous shell; containing edible white flesh, coconut milk, and embryo

*Cocos nucifera* (Arecaceae)

# COCONUT

**The origin of this popular palm** remains a mystery. Some believe it is native to the Pacific and Indian Ocean islands; others suggest it was introduced from northwest South America. Fossils from around 40 million years ago place it in Australia and India. However, it is now widely spread across the tropics.

The trunk is long, slender, often curving. At the base, where new roots emerge, it may take on the shape of a hockey-stick hook. The leaves are up to 6 m (20 ft) long and consist of many lax, narrowly lanceolate leaflets, up to 50 cm (20 in) long. Creamy male and female flowers are carried in a 1 m- (3 ft-) long inflorescence with multiple branches.

**"The tree of life"**
The coconut tree is an important source of both food and medicine – hence its popular name.

**PROFILE**

- Up to 15m (50ft)
- Up to 10m (30ft)
- Evergreen
- Whorled simple
- Canary Islands, Cape Verde Islands, Madeira, W. Morocco

**Dense foliage**
Each branch of this short-trunked tree is topped by a rosette of thick, strap-like leaves, each ending in a narrow point.

*blue-green leaf, up to 50cm (20in) long, 5cm (2in) wide*

**FEATURES**

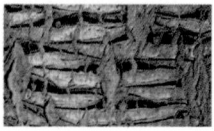

**Bark** Light brown, fades to grey in maturity; horizontally marked with old leaf scars

*Dracaena draco* (Asparagaceae)

# DRAGON TREE

**This widely spreading tree** is indigenous to the Canary Islands, Cape Verde, Madeira, and western Morocco, and has also been planted in the Azores and around the Mediterranean region. The tree is also known as dragon's blood tree, because of its deep red sap, which was once used as a resin to stain wood.

The tree branches where it flowers. Two side shoots are borne at the base of each flower. After flowering, each shoot starts to grow and develops into a branch. The flowers are small, fragrant, greenish white, and borne in panicles (elongated flower clusters). These are followed by fleshy, bright orange berries, up to 1cm (½in) wide, each containing two seeds.

**Wide-branched habit**
The short trunk of the drago tree divides into sturdy branches to form a dense, umbrella-shaped canopy.

# EUDICOTYLEDONS

**ometimes called eudicots, this is the biggest group of lowering plants and trees, encompassing an astonishing ariety of woody seed trees. They are found throughout the vorld, and probably evolved more than 125 million years ago.**

he term eudicotyledon comes from e embryonic seed leaves (called otyledons) found in the seeds before ey germinate. All eudicots have two or ore cotyledons. Apart from this feature, ese trees vary enormously. Some are vergreen, others deciduous; their leaves re simple or pinnate. They are found rtually worldwide: from temperate oodland to tropical rainforest, in arid eserts and at the edges of polar tundra.

Some of the most species-rich enera of trees are eudicots: oaks *Quercus*) produce drab flowers in endulous catkins for wind pollination; um trees (*Eucalyptus)* use pollinating sects, birds or mammals – and have a orrespondingly generous provision of ectar. Some of the most complex and ighly evolved plant–insect interactions ccur among eudicots: in the tropics, undreds of species of fig trees (*Ficus*) se tiny wasps that complete their life ycles inside the fruit.

| CLASS | ANGIOSPERMAE |
|---|---|
| SUBLASS | EUDICOTYLEDONEAE |
| ORDERS | 38 |
| FAMILIES | 307 |
| SPECIES | 182,227 (c.50,000 TREES) |

## MASTERS OF POLLINATION

Genetic similarities indicate that all eudicots evolved from a single common ancestor. The structural features that unite eudicots seem arcane but could have important biological significance. For instance, the pollen grains of all eudicots have three or more pores in their walls – unlike the grains of all other seed plants, which have one.

Female parts of most flowers have special receptive swellings – called stigmas – for catching pollen. Stigmas stimulate pollen tubes to grow through pollen pores, which guide male cells to the egg for fertilization. Stigmas of eudicots enjoy more effective pollination because the additional pores in the pollen make successful pollen tube growth more likely. Since these trees evolved, a combination of intimate flower–insect partnership and efficient pollen growth has led to an explosive diversification of eudicots. Today five in every six tree species are eudicots.

**Gean (wild cherry)**
Bee-pollinated flowers of this tree have both male and female parts; each forms a single seed encased in a stone.

**Bright flowers**
Rata has crimson bottlebrush-type flowers, which emerge from white-bloomed buds. Each flower bears long red stamens.

**PROFILE**

- Up to 20m (70ft)
- Up to 15m (50ft)
- Evergreen
- Alternate simple
- New Zealand

*Metrosideros robusta* (Myrtaceae)

# RATA

**A small to medium-sized**, broadly columnar, evergreen tree, Rata is native to New Zealand where it grows in close proximity to the sea. As well as being tolerant of sea air, it adapts well to wind and drought. This makes it an ideal ornamental tree for mild maritime districts. It was introduced into cultivation in Europe in 1840. Today, some of the finest European specimens of this tree grow on the island of Tresco, part of the Isles of Scilly, situated off the southwest coast of England.

Initially broadly columnar, this tree may become widely spreading in maturity. It has smooth, grey-brown bark. The leaves are initially narrow but become elliptic to almost rounded in maturity. They are dark green on the upper surface with a light green midrib. Thick and leathery in texture, leaves are covered with fine silver-grey hairs on the underside. The flowers appear in terminal clusters in summer, clearly visible in the dark, evergreen foliage.

**PROFILE**

- Up to 25m (80ft)
- Up to 20m (70ft)
- Evergreen
- Alternate simple
- New Zealand

*dark green leaf up to 10cm (4in) long*

*light green leaf midrib*

**hristmas tree foliage**
ne thick, leathery leaves of this ee are narrowly oblong at first, ecoming rounded in maturity. ney have dense white hairs on ne underside.

**FEATURES**

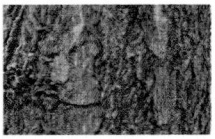

**Bark** Pale brown-grey, smooth; fissures into irregular plates in maturity

**Flowers** Bright crimson, bottlebrush-type in cultivation with long thin red stamens

*Metrosideros excelsa* (Myrtaceae)

# NEW ZEALAND CHRISTMAS TREE

**This dome-like, broadly spreading tree** is native to New Zealand, where it flowers from November to January with a peak in mid-December – hence its common name. It has a natural range along the coastal fringes of New Zealand's North Island and the shores of the lakes in the Rotorua region. In the wild, it normally grows as a multi-stemmed tree, where its stems and branches may be covered in fibrous, aerial roots. This tree was introduced into western cultivation in 1840, but is relatively tender and only thrives in mild, coastal localities in Europe.

The tree flowers over two weeks and carries clusters of hermaphroditic flowers, which emerge from white-bloomed flower buds. In the wild, the flower colour varies from bright crimson-red to pale pink, while in cultivation, the flowers are usually bright crimson. There is also a yellow-flowering cultivar called 'Aurea'.

## PROFILE

- Up to 10m (30ft)
- Up to 7m (22ft)
- Deciduous
- Alternate simple
- China

**Spring time growth**
Arranged alternately along the shoot, young leaves mature by early summer. The flowers are arranged alternately.

*young, rich green, ovate leaf*

*leaf bud*

*male flowers clustered together*

*lime-green young leaf*

## FEATURES

**Bark** Greyish with deep, knobbly, criss-crossed fissures

*long drawn-out leaf tip*

*serrated margin*

**Leaves** Ovate, green, up to 16cm (6in) long

*Eucommia ulmoides* (Eucommiaceae)

# EUCOMMIA

**This attractive, unique species** is the only hardy tree known to produce rubber. It is believed to be closely related to the elm – genus *Ulmus* – hence its species name *ulmoides*. The eucommia is a fast-growing, broadly spreading, deciduous tree and the only member of the Eucommiaceae family. It is thought to have grown wild in China, but no trees have been found outside of cultivation in recent years. It has been cultivated for centuries in China for its bark, which has medicinal properties, and was introduced into western cultivation in 1896. It is also grown as an ornamental or shade tree in temperate regions.

It has rich green leaves that are alternately arranged along the shoots. The leaves, if gently torn in half, will remain held together by thin, silk-like strands of latex. The tree produces small, green-yellow, inconspicuous flowers in spring, and these are followed by oval, winged seeds – 2–3cm (¾–1¼in) long and 2cm (¾in) wide – similar to those produced by elm trees.

pale green underside of leaf

long, orange-red style

flower up to 5 cm (2 in) long

matt, blue-green upper surface

**Tubular flowers**
Red-orange tubular flowers are carried in clusters along the stems. They open into four narrow lobes, which peel back to reveal an orange-red style.

**PROFILE**

- Up to 9 m (28 ft)
- Up to 4 m (12 ft)
- Evergreen
- Alternate simple
- South America

*Embothrium coccineum* (Proteaceae)

# CHILEAN FIRE BUSH

**Originally from South America**, this small, broadly columnar tree is fast becoming a popular species in gardens across the temperate world. It is hardy, and is often found growing in exposed locations in the wild, from the Pacific coast to high in the Andes mountains, both in Chile and Argentina. It was discovered and named from a specimen collected during Captain James Cook's second exploration voyage to this region in 1771 and introduced into cultivation by English plant collector William Lobb in 1846.

The bark is purple-brown, smooth when young, but flaking from the time the tree turns 30 years old. The leaves are elliptic, sometimes oblong to lanceolate, up to 15 cm (6 in) long and 2.5 cm (1 in) wide. The fruit is a woody capsule, up to 2.5 cm (1 in) long, with winged seeds.

**Burning embers**
The flowers of Chilean fire bush resemble burning embers from a distance, hence the name.

**PROFILE**

- Up to 12 m (40 ft)
- Up to 4 m (12 ft)
- Evergreen
- Opposite simple
- Chile, Argentina

*small, rounded flower bud*

*red-brown pedicel (flower stalk), up to 1.5 cm (½ in) long*

*oval to broadly elliptic leaf, up to 2.5 cm (1 in) long*

**Chilean myrtle flowers** The cup-shaped, white flowers are small and fragrant, held singly on stalks. They have four petals and numerous stamens.

**FEATURES**

**Bark** Bright cinnamon-orange, with soft, felt-like texture; peels in patches to reveal cream-coloured surface beneath

*Luma apiculata* (Myrtaceae)

# CHILEAN MYRTLE

**Formerly known by** the botanical name *Myrtus luma* the Chilean myrtle is one of the most interesting trees for bark colour. It has been widely planted in parks and gardens since its introduction in 1844 from the temperate forests of Chile and Argentina. It easily establishes itself in new locations, especially in western Europe, where the North Atlantic drift provides the warm, wet weather it enjoys. In southern Ireland, for example, the tree has become naturalized, reproducing itself with ease.

The tree has a broadly columnar habit. Curiously, its bark feels cold even when in full sunlight. The foliage is dark dull green, and the leaves emit a pleasant aroma when crushed. It bears flowers in profusion in late summer and autumn. The rounded, fleshy fruit is up to 1 cm (½ in) long, and turns purple-black when ripe.

**White Chilean myrtle (*Luma chequen*)** Besides being more shrublike in habit than its larger cousin, the white Chilean myrtle also has grey rather than cinnamon-orange bark.

**PROFILE**

- Up to 25 m (80 ft)
- Up to 15 m (50 ft)
- Deciduous
- Alternate simple
- E. North America

young leaf

flowers borne in drooping, axillary racemes

yellow anthers

small, greenish yellow male flower

**conspicuous bloom**
owers of the sassafras do not ave petals. Male and female owers are borne on separate ees in late spring.

**FEATURES**

leaf up to 15 cm (6 in) long, 10 cm (4 in) wide

**Leaves** Shape varies from unlobed to three-lobed

*Sassafras albidum* (Lauraceae)

# SASSAFRAS

**The natural habitat of this tree** extends from Canada to Florida, and then westwards into Kansas and Texas, USA. Its leaves and bark are strongly aromatic and have been used in the past by both Native Americans and British colonists for their medicinal properties. The bark of the root has been used to make a drink similar to beer.

Sassafras can produce varying leaf shapes on the same tree; from lobed and fig-like, to obovate, without lobes. Its leaves are deep green on the upper surface and blue-green on the underside. In autumn, they turn orange-yellow before falling. Female trees produce a dark blue egg-shaped berry, up to 1 cm (½ in) wide.

**Wide form**
Sassafras is a broadly columnar, medium-sized, suckering tree, with flexible zig-zag branching.

**Foliage and flowers**
The leathery leaves are oblong to oblanceolate, alternately borne along shoots. Small flowers emerg in clusters of 6 to 10 in spring.

**PROFILE**

- 25–30 m (80–100 ft)
- Up to 10 m (30 ft)
- Evergreen
- Alternate simple
- USA (California, Oregon)

*Umbellularia californica* (Lauraceae)

# CALIFORNIA LAUREL

**Also known as the California bay**, California olive, and Oregon myrtle, this is a vigorous, strongly aromatic species. It was introduced into western cultivation by Scottish plant collector David Douglas in 1829. This tree has a dense, leafy habit. The foliage, when crushed, emits a strong odour, which can induce nausea, headaches, and, in extreme cases, unconsciousness. It may also cause skin allergies. Its highly prized timber, known as pepperwood, has a pale brown colour and can be polished to a fine finish.

The bark is dark grey and smooth when young, cracking into small, roughly square plates in maturity. The leaves, which resemble bay leaves, are borne on sage-green shoots. Its leaves are glossy bright green on the upper surface and yellow-green on the underside. Borne in umbels, inconspicuous flowers are held on each stem in the leaf axils. They are followed by small, pear-shaped berries, up to 2.5 cm (1 in) wide, ripening from green to dark purple.

**PROFILE**

- Up to 10m (30ft)
- Up to 8m (25ft)
- Evergreen
- Opposite simple
- Mediterranean region, N. Africa, Middle East, China

**aves and flower clusters**
e olive has tough, leathery, and rrowly obovate leaves and bears nall racemes (stalks) of fragrant hite flowers in summer.

**FEATURES**

**Bark** Grey; fissured in youth

**Fruit** Oval, green, edible; ripening to glossy purple-black

*Olea europaea* (Oleaceae)

# OLIVE

**One of the earliest trees** to be cultivated by man, the olive tree has been highly prized for its fruit and oil for at least 5,000 years. Several specimens in Italy and Greece are more than 1,000 years old. Its natural range extends from the Iberian Peninsula, around the Mediterranean Sea, and eastwards into China. It is cultivated commercially in warm regions elsewhere, including South Africa, Australia, and California, USA. Although the tree survives in cooler climates, it seldom flowers or produces fruit.

The olive is small and evergreen. It has a short trunk, which becomes deformed, thick, and hollow with age. Its broadly spreading crown provides welcome shade in hot climates. Clusters of small flowers bloom in summer and are followed by a berry-like fruit, containing a single seed, or stone, from which olive oil is extracted.

**Chinese fringe tree (*Chionanthus retusus*)** This related species is a deciduous, almost shrublike tree with showy clusters of snow-like flowers.

**Shining privet flowers**
Small, creamy white flowers are borne in large clusters, or panicles, which stand proud above the surrounding foliage.

*flowers borne in large panicle, 20 cm (8 in) long*

*ovate leaf, up to 10 cm (4 in) long, 5 cm (2 in) wide*

*glossy green upper surface on leaf*

*pale green, matt underside of leaf*

**PROFILE**

- Up to 12 m (40 ft)
- Up to 5 m (15 ft)
- Evergreen
- Opposite simple
- C. and W. China

*Ligustrum lucidum* (Oleaceae)

# SHINING PRIVET

**Also known as Chinese privet**, this tree is indigenous to mountains in central and western China, where it grows in hillside woodland above river valleys. It is believed to have been introduced into the West by the botanist Joseph Banks in 1794. It is now commonly planted as a street tree in urban areas because it is able to tolerate atmospheric pollution, compacted dry soils, and regular pruning.

The grey bark is smooth even in maturity, although the trunk may become fluted in old age. The ovate leaves taper to a long, fine point, and are bronze when first produced. The flowers emerge in late summer and early autumn, followed by clusters of small, blue-black, rounded berries in late autumn.

**Lush evergreen tree**
The medium-sized shining privet tree produces a dense canopy of lush, lustrous leaves.

## PROFILE

- Up to 10m (30ft)
- Up to 8m (25ft)
- Evergreen
- Opposite simple
- S. Europe, Canary Islands

**Jasmine flowers**
These fragrant flowers are small, cream or yellowish white, and are produced in clusters in the leaf axils in spring.

*flower has yellow anthers*

*leaf up to 5cm (2in) long*

*bluntly toothed leaf margin*

## FEATURES

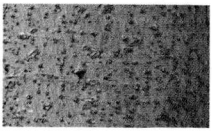

**Bark** Smooth, pewter-grey throughout life, relatively thin

**Fruit** Blue-black, up to 1cm (½in) wide

*Phillyrea latifolia* (Oleaceae)

# JASMINE BOX

**A member of the olive family**, this small, broadly spreading tree is often mistaken for the holm oak (p.167), which originates from the same region. Jasmine box has been in cultivation for at least 400 years, and is widely planted to provide shelter in exposed conditions, especially along the coast. It produces masses of dark green, luxuriant foliage, in some cases causing the branches to bow down under the weight of the leaves, and is often clipped to form a dense hedge, or for topiary.

The thick and leathery leaves are elliptic to ovate, borne opposite each other. They have a glossy dark green upper surface, a pale green underside, and bluntly toothed margins. The flowers bloom in spring and are sometimes followed by berry-like fruit.

**Mayten**
This tree (*Maytenus boaria*) has a graceful habit, slender branches, and narrow, elliptic, finely toothed leaves.

**Glossy green leaves**
The leaves are shiny and slightly waxy with wavy edges. Their shape varies between oblong and elliptic.

**PROFILE**

- Up to 8 m (25 ft)
- Up to 3 m (10 ft)
- Evergreen
- Alternate simple
- New Zealand

*Pittosporum tenuifolium* (Pittosporaceae)

# KOHUHU

**This small, columnar tree** is indigenous to both the North and South islands of New Zealand. It has been widely cultivated in Europe and elsewhere for the last 160 years, even though its foliage is prone to scorch and browning in cold winters. Kohuhu is a Māori name, which roughly translates as "the black one" and refers to the colour of the bark, twigs, and inner wood. The ornamentally placed leaves make this tree's foliage particularly attractive to flower arrangers and florists.

The bright green leaves are alternately placed on thin, dark purple to almost black twigs. The conical leaf bud is pale yellow-green, tipped with crimson-purple, and up to 2 mm (1/16 in) long. The small, dark flowers are cup-shaped and bear five petals with out-curved tips. They appear in the leaf axils from late spring to early summer, and are particularly fragrant at night.

**Karo (*Pittosporum crassifolium*)** This tree bears large, leathery, oval-shaped leaves, and purple flowers that are larger and more showy than that of the kohuhu.

**PROFILE**

- Up to 30m (100ft)
- Up to 20m (70ft)
- Deciduous
- Alternate simple
- W. Europe

**Dutch elm foliage**
The leaves are rough and unequal at the base, with hairs on the underside. A pink stalk attaches the leaves to the shoot.

*fruit up to 2.5cm (1in) long*

*leaf up to 12.5cm (5in) long, 7.5cm (3in) wide*

*irregularly serrated leaf margin*

*oval to ovate-acuminate, green-grey leaf*

**FEATURES**

**Bark** Grey-brown; smooth at first, becomes vertically cracked in maturity

*Ulmus* x *hollandica* (Ulmaceae)

# DUTCH ELM

**This broadly columnar tree**, also known as the European hybrid elm, is a natural hybrid between the smooth-leaved elm (*Ulmus minor*) and the wych elm (p.136). It is found throughout western Europe, including Britain, and is widespread in France, Belgium, Germany, and the Netherlands.

The spreading canopy of the Dutch elm is open and thin, with relatively few branches ascending steeply away from the trunk. The base of the tree's trunk may be fluted, and its twigs may have corky ridges. Dark red flowers are produced in large clusters on stout shoots in early spring. The fruit is an oval, winged seed; it is pale green turning to gold and, finally, brown in early summer.

**Smooth-leaved elm**
Related to the Dutch elm, this tree (*Ulmus minor*) has smaller leaves with a smooth upper surface.

**Elm leaves**
The leaves of the European white elm are obovate and distinctly oblique at the base, with double-toothed margins.

*leaf 11 cm (4½ in) long, 6 cm (2½ in) wide*

*double-toothed leaf margin*

## PROFILE

- Up to 30 m (100 ft)
- Up to 20 m (70 ft)
- Deciduous
- Alternate simple
- C. and E. Europe, W. Asia

## FEATURES

**Bark** Remains smooth, ridged, even in old age

**Fruit** Oval-shaped, paper-like samara; contain single seed, green ripening to brown

*Ulmus laevis* (Ulmaceae)

# EUROPEAN WHITE ELM

**This large, widely spreading** tree is native to central and eastern Europe and western Asia. It has been widely cultivated for many years, particularly in Russia, where it is planted alongside roads and railway lines to protect them from snowdrifts. The other name for this majestic tree is fluttering elm, which refers to the fact that the long-stalked flowers and fruit flutter in the slightest breeze.

Whereas most other elms develop a rough, fissured bark, the bark of this tree remains smooth, even in maturity. This gives this tree its species name *laevis*, which translates as "smooth". The leaves are mid-green on the upper surface, with soft, grey down on the underside. There may be up to 17 veins on the long side of the leaf and only 14 on the short side. Small, purple flowers emerge in clusters in early spring. In summer, fruit are borne in bunches on long, pendulous stalks.

**Siberian elm (*Ulmus pumila*)** This tree, up to 10 m (30 ft) tall, is distinguished by its smaller size, multi-stemmed often shrubby habit, and small, ovate to lanceolate leaves, up to 5 cm (2 in) long.

**parse leaves**
e ovate leaves are pointed at the , unequal at the base, and rough the touch. The fruit are small, d oval-shaped structures ntaining the seed.

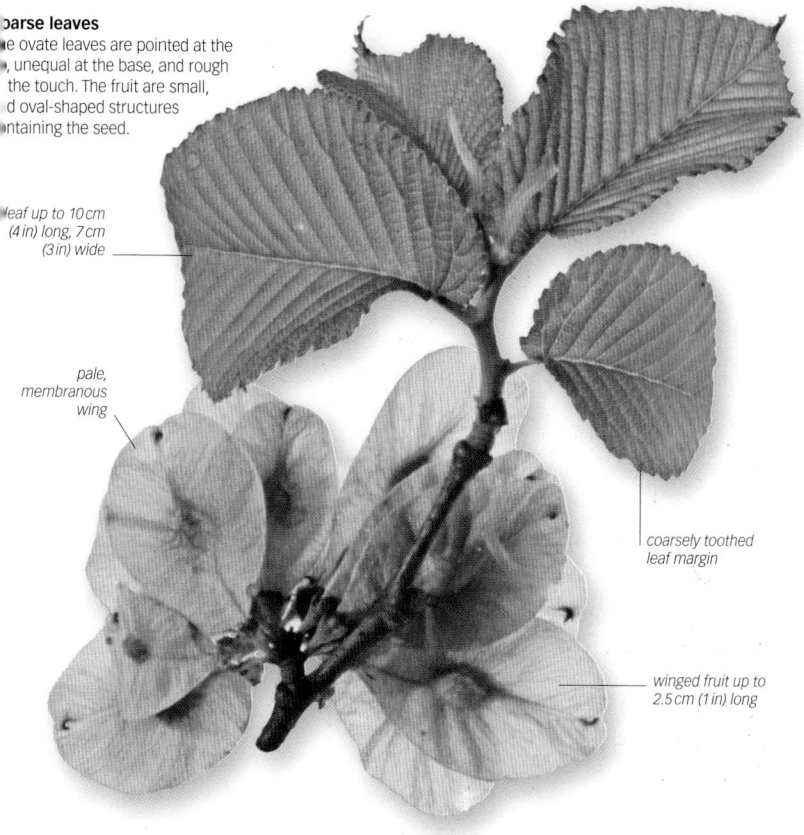


**PROFILE**

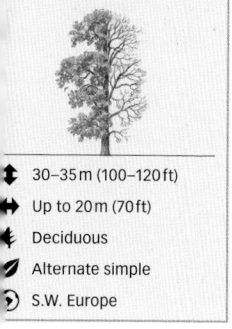


*Ulmus procera* (Ulmaceae)

# ENGLISH ELM

**Native to southwestern Europe**, this large, broadly columnar tree was once an important part of the landscape in England, and featured widely in the paintings of English landscape artists such as John Constable. Dutch elm disease led to its demise from the 1960s to 1980s. It is now believed that the English elm is not English at all, and was introduced into Britain from northwest Spain in the early Neolithic period.

The English elm has a grey-brown bark, which becomes regularly fissured into rough rectangular plates from an early age. The leaves are dark green on the upper surface and pale green on the underside, each with 10 to 12 pairs of veins. They turn golden yellow in autumn before falling. Small clusters of red flowers appear on bare shoots in early spring, followed by flattened, oval-shaped fruit (samara) containing paper-thin, winged seeds in summer.

**Japanese elm (*Ulmus japonica*)** With a more rounded, broadly spreading habit and larger leaves, this tree easily stands out from its cousin, the English elm.

## PROFILE

- Up to 30m (100ft)
- Up to 25m (80ft)
- Deciduous
- Alternate simple
- N. and W. Europe

**Papery fruit**
The wych elm fruit is a papery, hai disc known as a samara, borne in clusters, which carries seeds.

*seed carried in centre of disc*

*disc up to 5mm (¼in) wide*

*leaf up to 20cm (8in) long, 10cm (4in) wide*

## FEATURES

**Bark** Grey-brown, smooth; becomes lined with vertical fissures on maturity

*double-toothed leaf margin*

**Leaves** Dull green turning bright yellow in autumn

*Ulmus glabra* (Ulmaceae)

# WYCH ELM

**This medium to large**, broadly spreading, deciduous tree is found throughout western and northern Europe, from Russia to Portugal and north to Scandinavia. It survives well in exposed coastal areas and on low mountain slopes, especially in areas with high rainfall. It has strong and dense timber, which is resistant to deca by water. For centuries, hollowed out elm branches we used as water conduits, while sawn planks from the trunk were used to make coffin boards.

The wych elm has a short trunk that rapidly divides into large, ascending branches. Bright, red-purple flowe emerge in early spring before the leaves unfurl. The ova to obovate leaves are dull green and rough on the uppe surface and pale green on the underside, with grey hai They are coarsely and doubly toothed at the margins, and have unequal sides at the base.

**Chinese elm (*Ulmus parvifolia*)** With its small, leathery, and glossy green leaves, the Chinese elm is relatively easy to distinguish from the wych elm.

sharply toothed leaf margin

leaf up to 15 cm (6 in) long, 7 cm (3 in) wide

three-veined base

**Narrowly oval leaf**
The large, lanceolate to ovate leaves of the southern nettle tree taper to pointed tips and turn pale yellow in autumn before falling.

**PROFILE**

- Up to 25 m (80 ft)
- Up to 20 m (70 ft)
- Deciduous
- Alternate simple
- S. Europe, Middle East, N. Africa

**FEATURES**

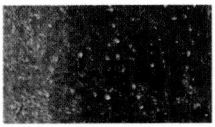

**Bark** Smooth and grey; develops corky warts and ridges with age

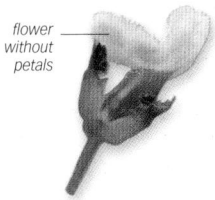


**Flowers** Small and green; borne either singly or in small clusters in spring

*Celtis australis* (Ulmaceae)

# SOUTHERN NETTLE TREE

**Also called European nettle** tree or Mediterranean hackberry, this broadly spreading tree has been cultivated in the British Isles since the 16th century. It is often planted for ornamental purposes and is resistant to air pollution. Its sweet and edible fruit can be eaten raw or cooked. Both leaves and fruit are believed to have some medicinal properties and are used to treat symptoms such as abdominal pain and colic.

The large leaves are rough and have a dark grey-green upper surface and a paler underside with a covering of bristly hairs. The flowers are hermaphroditic, with both male and female organs within each flower. Ovoid, purple-brown to blackish berry-like fruit are borne in short clusters and eaten by birds and other wildlife.

**Japanese hackberry (*Celtis sinensis*)** Reaching up to only 15 m (50 ft) in height, this tree is smaller than the southern nettle tree with smoother, smaller, glossy leaves.

**PROFILE**

- Up to 25 m (80 ft)
- Up to 20 m (70 ft)
- Deciduous
- Alternate simple
- North America

**Foliage and fruit**
Hackberry leaves are oval to ovate and pointed at the tip. The fruit is a small berry, turning from green to red, then ripening to purple-black.

**FEATURES**

**Flowers** Without petals; borne in leaf axils

*Celtis occidentalis* (Ulmaceae)

# HACKBERRY

**Also known as the nettle tree**, the leaves of the hackberry bear a distinct resemblance to the leaves of the common stinging nettle (*Urtica dioica*). This medium-sized, broadly columnar, deciduous tree is native to most of North America. It has been widely cultivated in Europe and elsewhere since the 17th century.

The bark is light grey, smooth when young, developing wart-like blemishes in maturity. The leaves are oval to ovate and roughly serrated around the margin, except for the lower third of the leaf. They are smooth, glossy, and rich green on the upper surface, and lighter green with slightly hairy veining on the underside. Male and female flowers are held separately on the same tree in spring. They are followed by fruit that are borne singly on thin, green stalks up to 2.5 cm (1 in) long.

**Mississippi hackberry (*Celtis laevigata*)** This tree is distinguished from the hackberry by its narrower, lanceolate leaves that are rarely serrated around the margins.

**PROFILE**

- Up to 30m (100ft)
- Up to 15m (50ft)
- Deciduous
- Alternate simple
- Caucasus region, N. Iran

**Vibrant green foliage**
Elliptic to ovate leaves are borne on hairy shoots. The leaves have distinct parallel veining, a bright green upper surface, and a pale green underside.

*coarsely toothed leaf margin*

*leaf has rough texture*

*leaf up to 10cm (4in) long*

**FEATURES**

**Bark** Smooth, silver-grey when young; flakes in old age

*Zelkova carpinifolia* (Ulmaceae)

# CAUCASIAN ELM

**Related to the genus *Ulmus***, this slow-growing, long-lived forest tree grows up to 30m (100ft) tall. The Caucasian elm is widely planted as an ornamental tree in parks, gardens, and arboreta in western Europe. It bears some resemblance to the common hornbeam (p.184), with a distinctive rounded shape, a short trunk, and a large mop-head of dense, ascending branches. The overall impression is that of a tree that was once pollarded (in which the top of the tree is cut off to encourage branching) but has long since been left unchecked.

The smooth bark is like that of the common beech (p.152) but flakes in maturity. The trunk has pronounced fluting with a buttressed base. Leaves are vibrant green and rough to the touch. Small green flowers are borne in the leaf axils in spring. The fruit is a small, rounded, pea-like capsule with pronounced ridging.

**Chinese zelkova (*Zelkova sinica*)** This is a small tree, up to 10m (30ft) tall, with slender branches and small, ovate to lanceolate leaves, 2.5–6cm (1–2½in) long.

**Keyaki leaves**
The leaves have 6 to 13 teeth on each side. They have a dark green upper surface and a paler underside with hairs.

*sharply toothed leaf margin*

*leaf up to 12 cm (5 in) long, 5 cm (2 in) wide*

*leaf ends slender t*

**PROFILE**

- Up to 40 m (130 ft)
- Up to 23 m (75 ft)
- Deciduous
- Alternate simple
- China, Japan, Korea

**FEATURES**

**Bark** Pale grey; peels or flakes in maturity to reveal light fawn-grey patches beneath

*Zelkova serrata* (Ulmaceae)

# KEYAKI

**Native to China, Japan, and Korea**, the broadly spreading keyaki grows in low-lying river valleys, where the soil is rich and deep. It was introduced into western cultivation in 1861, and since then it has become a popular tree for planting in large gardens and parks. In Japan, it grows as a forest tree at elevations of up to 1,200 m (4,000 ft) above sea level. Many old Japanese temples, especially in the Kyoto region are built of its strong and durable timber.

The smooth bark is rather like that of the common beech (p.152). The ovate leaves are slightly rough on the upper surface. They turn orange-red in autumn before falling. Small green male and female flowers appear in spring, followed by rounded fruit, up to 5 mm (¼ in) wide.

**Rounded crown**
An elm-like tree, the keyaki has light, ascendin lower branching and a rounded crown.

leaflet up to 13cm (5in) long

uit up to 5cm (2in) wide

mature leaflet, deep green with dull sheen

**ell-known nut**
e fruit that encases the familiar alnut is a round, green husk rried on a short, thick stalk.

**PROFILE**

- Up to 30m (100ft)
- Up to 15m (50ft)
- Deciduous
- Alternate compound
- S.E. Europe to Himalayas, China

**FEATURES**

**Bark** Light grey; develops narrow, vertical ridges with age

**Seeds** Brown walnut; containing edible kernels

*Juglans regia* (Juglandaceae)

# COMMON WALNUT

**This relatively slow-growing**, medium-sized to large deciduous tree is broadly spreading. It is indigenous to Greece through the Himalayan region to China. It has been widely cultivated elsewhere for its nuts and highly prized decorative timber since the Roman Empire. It was the Romans who introduced it to the British Isles. It was in cultivation in the USA by the 18th century.

The common walnut has a rounded canopy of long, spreading branches. Its aromatic leaves are pink-bronze when young. They consist of up to nine leaflets, growing from a main leaf stalk. Male and female flowers are borne on the same tree, both long, green catkins that appear in spring. Its fruit is a round, green husk, which may stain when handled.

**Butternut**
This tree (*Juglans cinerea*) has purple-grey bark and larger leaves than the common walnut.

## PROFILE

- Up to 30m (100ft)
- Up to 20m (70ft)
- Deciduous
- Alternate compound
- E. and C. USA

**Glossy leaflets**
The pinnate leaves consist of up to 17 leaflets, with toothed margins and pointed tips. The upper surface is glossy dark green, while the underside is hairy.

*leaflet up to 10cm (4in) long*

*yellow-green male catkin, up to 10cm (4in) long*

## FEATURES

**Fruit** Rounded, smooth husk; encasing edible nut

*Juglans nigra* (Juglandaceae)

# BLACK WALNUT

**Native to eastern and central USA**, this fast-growing tree has been widely cultivated in large gardens, parks, and arboreta in the temperate world. It has a pyramidal habit that spreads with age, and large leaves that turn bright yellow in autumn before falling. The tree is also prized for its timber, which is used for making cabinets.

The smooth, dark grey-brown bark develops fissures and ridges after about 30 years. Both male and female flowers are small and petal-less, appearing on the same tree in catkins in late spring and early summer. The grey-green female flowers are borne near the ends of shoots. The fruit is not as large as the common walnut (p.141), but has the same distinctive flavour.

**Late to leaf**
The broadly spreading black walnut's leaves appear late and the tree remains bare till early summer.

leaflet up to 15 cm (6 in) long

red stigma on female flower

ghtly toothed margin

sticky brown oot covered with hairs

**Leaflets and flowers**
The leaflets have a slightly hairy upper surface and a furry underside. Female catkins are similar to males, but can be told apart by their distinct red stigmas.

**PROFILE**

- Up to 25 m (80 ft)
- Up to 10 m (30 ft)
- Deciduous
- Pinnate
- Japan

**FEATURES**

**Bark** Grey-brown; becomes fissured and segmented into irregular plates

sticky, hairy husk

**Fruit** Green and rounded, sometimes oval; containing edible nut

*Juglans ailantifolia* (Juglandaceae)

# JAPANESE WALNUT

**As the name suggests**, this medium-sized, deciduous tree is native to Japan, but it has been planted elsewhere for ornamental purposes. It has the largest leaves among the walnuts and, when viewed from a distance, a denser appearance. It is a fast-growing species, with long spreading branches.

Each pinnate leaf may be up to 80 cm (32 in) long, and consists of up to 17 leaflets. Male and female flowers – both pendulous, green catkins – are borne separately on the same tree in late spring. Fruit are carried in clusters of up to 20, each a rounded, green husk containing the nut. The sticky husk is poisonous, and was used by the Japanese to catch fish. However, the walnut is edible, and has been eaten in Japan for many centuries.

**Ornamental tree**
The Japanese walnut tree is conical when young, but spreads with age. Its leaves are glossy, dark green.

**PROFILE**

- Up to 15 m (50 ft)
- Up to 8 m (25 ft)
- Deciduous
- Alternate simple
- N. China

**Fruit and leaves**
Borne in short clusters, the white mulberry's fruit look like elongated raspberries. The leaves are variable in shape, usually ovate to rounded.

*deeply toothed leaf margin*

*fruit up to 2.5 cm (1 in) long*

*leaf up to 20 cm (8 in) long, ending in long tip*

**FEATURES**

**Bark** Brown-orange, becomes gnarled from early age

**Fruit** Turn from green to red

*Morus alba* (Moraceae)

# WHITE MULBERRY

**A widely spreading**, medium-sized tree, the white mulberry is best known for being the food source of silkworms, which devour its leaves with gusto. Native to northern China, it is believed to have been introduced into Europe before 1596. Since then, it has become widespread across the temperate world.

The white mulberry's leaves are bright green and lustrous on the upper surface and paler on the underside. In autumn, they turn rich butter-yellow before falling. In some parts of the world, the leaves are used as fodder. The fruit can vary in colour, from white to pink to purple-red. It is edible, though usually less sweet and produced in less profusion than those of its more popular relative, the black mulberry (p.145).

**Paper mulberry**
This tree (*Broussonetia papyrifera*) is recognized by its spherical female flowers and orange-red fruit.

**PROFILE**

8–10m (25–30ft)
8–10m (25–30ft)
Deciduous
Alternate simple
W. Asia

**Edible berry**
Black mulberry fruit appear at the end of twigs, and ripen from green through red to dark purple. The leaves are rough and hairy.

*bright green, ovate leaf with coarsely serrated margin*

*leaf underside is lighter green and hairy*

*barely stalked fruit, borne in clusters*

**FEATURES**

**Male flowers** Small, green, cone-like structures

*Morus nigra* (Moraceae)

# BLACK MULBERRY

**Originally from western Asia**, the black mulberry quickly spread through human intervention and cultivation across temperate Asia and Europe. It reached the British Isles in the early 16th century, and North America thereafter. This tree has been popular for its edible fruit. A long-lived tree, several examples are known to be over 500 years old. Its orange-brown bark becomes fissured and cracked from an early age.

Its leaves are 12cm (5in) long and 10cm (4in) wide. Male and female flowers are normally borne on separate trees in early summer. These are followed by raspberry-like fruit on female trees. The fruit is edible when ripe and has an astringently sweet taste.

**Gnarled habit**
A broadly spreading tree, the black mulberry has an old appearance from a relatively early age.

**PROFILE**

- Up to 10m (30ft)
- Up to 10m (30ft)
- Deciduous
- Alternate simple
- S.W. Asia

**Distinctive leaves and fruit**
Fig leaves have three to five deep lobes – the middle lobe being the largest. The fruit are borne near the shoot tips.

*coarsely and bluntly toothed leaf margin*

*leaf up to 30cm (12in) long, 25cm (10in) wide*

*green, unripe fruit*

**FEATURES**

**Fruit** Pear-shaped, up to 5cm (2in) long; swell and ripen to purple-brown in second year

*Ficus carica* (Moraceae)

# COMMON FIG

**One of the earliest cultivated trees**, the small, shrubby, but broadly spreading common fig originates in southwest Asia. However, it is grown throughout warm regions across the world for its edible fruit. The fruit is also used in Graeco-Roman, Islamic, Ayurvedic and traditional Chinese medicine. In cooler regions, it is usually grown against a wall rather than as a free-standing tree.

The bark is mid-grey and smooth, with some patterning in old age. The trunk is short, sometimes twisted, while the branches are long and sinuous, starting from low down on the trunk and ending in stout and knobbly, upswept shoots. The easily recognizable leaves are large, leathery, and rough, with a shiny dark green upper surface and a paler, hairy underside. They have prominent veins and are heart-shaped at the base. Its uniquely shaped fruit are produced in summer near the tips of the shoots. Green in the first year, the fruit ripen over two years.

**PROFILE**

- Up to 15 m (50 ft)
- Up to 10 m (30 ft)
- Deciduous
- Alternate simple
- C. and S. USA

**Untoothed leaves**
The leaves are ovate, pointed at both ends, and untoothed. They are glossy, rich green on the upper surface and pale green on the underside.

*smooth leaf surface*

*leaf up to 10 cm (4 in) long, 5 cm (2 in) wide*

*eaf midrib*

**FEATURES**

**Bark** Orange-brown; with scaly ridges and uneven furrows

*fruit up to 10 cm (4 in) wide*

**Fruit** Green ripening to yellow; with an even, stippled surface and occasional brown hairs

*Maclura pomifera* (Moraceae)

# OSAGE ORANGE

**Native to central and southern USA**, this broadly spreading, ornamental tree was introduced into western cultivation in 1818. In the wild in the USA, it grows primarily in wet areas alongside rivers. Parts of the tree are used in food processing, pesticide production, and dye-making.

The tree has fleshy, yellow roots and a short trunk. Branches are often twisted and, when broken, ooze out a milky sap. They have sharp, green spines, normally at the base of leaf stalks. Small yellow-green male and female flowers, up to 1 cm (½ in) long, are borne in clusters on separate trees in early summer. The male flowers are borne in short racemes, while the females appear in clusters up to 1 cm (½ in) long. Female flowers ripen to become a large, spherical syncarp (multiple fruit), weighing up to 1 kg (2¼ lb). The tree is probably best known for this showy fruit, which looks similar to an orange. However, the fruit is inedible and, when fresh, full of sour milky juice.

## PROFILE

- Up to 30m (100ft)
- Up to 15m (50ft)
- Deciduous
- Alternate compound
- S.E. USA

**Pinnate leaves**
Leaves of the bitternut hickory consist of up to four pairs of opposite leaflets and one terminal leaflet.

*leaflet up to 15cm (6in) long, 7.5cm (3in) broad*

*leaflet has a serrated margin*

*green male catkin, up to 7.5cm (3in) long*

## FEATURES

**Bark** Grey and smooth; becomes thick, fissured, and ridged in maturity

**Fruit** Oval, thin, green shell; encasing bitter nut

*Carya cordiformis* (Juglandaceae)

# BITTERNUT HICKORY

**This large, broadly columnar, deciduous** tree is native to southeastern USA, from Minnesota to Texas. It is planted elsewhere in parks, gardens, and arboreta for its autumn leaf colour and ornamental ridged, grey bark. As the name suggests, its fruit are hard nuts and not palatable. They do, however, have a high oil content and were once crushed to produce lamp oil. The Native American word for hickory is "Pawcohiccora", which means nut oil.

A good way to distinguish this species from other hickories is its winter buds, which are long, slender, and bright yellow. Leaves are deep green on the upper surface and yellow-green on the underside. They turn golden yellow in autumn. Both male and female flowers are carried on separate catkins on the same tree in late spring. Male catkins ripen from green to gold.

**Pignut (*Carya glabra*)** Although its flowers and fruit are similar to the bitternut hickory, this tree is smaller, up to 22m (70ft) tall. Its orange-brown leaf bud is up to 0.8cm (½in) long.

**PROFILE**



- Up to 20 m (70 ft)
- Up to 12 m (40 ft)
- Deciduous
- Alternate compound
- E. USA

**ngnut hickory leaf**
e large compound leaf of this e normally consists of seven flets, three opposite pairs and e terminal leaflet.

**FEATURES**

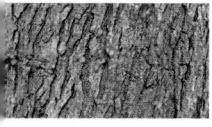

**Bark** Light grey, initially smooth; quickly develops shallow orange fissures

**Fruit** Yellow-green; borne in pairs or threes

*Carya laciniosa* (Juglandaceae)

# KINGNUT HICKORY

**Also known as big shellbark**, this tree was introduced into European cultivation in 1804. This slow-growing, medium-sized tree has a broadly columnar habit. It is now widely planted in ornamental collections for its large, attractive foliage and autumn leaf colour. The Latin name *laciniosa* means "with flaps", and refers to the way the shaggy bark curls away from the trunk.

The bark peels in thick vertical strips. Large, ovoid, bright leaf buds, up to 2.5 cm (1 in) long, open in spring to release the largest compound leaf of any hickory. The lanceolate to obovate-lanceolate leaves are up to 75 cm (30 in) long. The thick, tough leaflets are pale green with slightly hairy veins on the underside. They turn golden yellow in autumn. The big pear-shaped or rounded fruit are up to 5 cm (2 in) long, with a shell covering a sweet, edible, large nut.

**Pecan (*Carya illinoinensis*)** This tree is distinguished from the kingnut hickory by the number of leaflets on each pinnate leaf, usually 11 to 17, and its narrower, oval fruit.

terminal leaflet up to 20 cm (8 in) long, 10 cm (4 in) wide

toothed leaflet margin

leaflet tapers towards tip

**Pinnate leaves**
The leaves are more than 30 cm (12 in) long, with up to nine obova leaflets. They turn gold in autumn

**PROFILE**

- Up to 30 m (100 ft)
- Up to 15 m (50 ft)
- Deciduous
- Alternate compound
- E. USA

**FEATURES**

**Bark** Silver-grey; initially smooth, develops vertical orange fissures with age

fine hairs on leaf bud

**Leaf buds** Ovoid; fade from red-brown to pale fawn

**Fruit** Rounded to oval, yellow-green husk

*Carya tomentosa* (Juglandaceae)

# BIG-BUD HICKORY

**Also known as mockernut**, this broadly columnar, Nor American hickory is native east of a line from Minnesota t Texas. In the wild, it is the most abundant and widespread of the hickories. It is long lived, sometimes reaching 500 years old. The species name comes from the Latin word *tomentum*, meaning "covered with dense, short hairs". Th refers to the underside of the leaves and helps to identify the species. The tree is prized for its timber, which is stro and can withstand impact, making it the perfect wood for tool handles and sports equipment such as hockey sticks When burnt, the wood emits a fragrant smoke, which is used to smoke meat.

As the name implies, the big-bud hickory has a large leaf bud, which is up to 2 cm (¾ in) long. The leaves have slight sheen and are dark green on the upper surface, wit a paler underside. They emit a fragrance when crushed. Both the shoot and the leaf stalk are covered in fine, fawn-coloured hairs. The fruit has seams that resemble those of an old-fashioned rugby ball.

**PROFILE**

- 20–30 m (70–100 ft)
- Up to 15 m (50 ft)
- Deciduous
- Alternate compound
- E. North America

*obovate leaflet, up to 10 cm (4 in) long*

*atkins lustered n groups f three*

*two-thirds of leaflet serrated at margin*

**Long leaves**
The pinnate leaves are made up of five to seven leaflets, each with a long tip.

**FEATURES**

**Bark** Shaggy grey; curls in narrow, vertical strips

**Fruit** Oval to rounded, up to 3 cm (1¼ in) long; enclosing edible nut

*Carya ovata* (Juglandaceae)

# SHAGBARK HICKORY

**This is the most valuable** nut-producing tree in the USA, with a natural range extending from Quebec, Canada, to Texas, USA. It was one of the first North American trees to be introduced into Europe, arriving in 1629, and is widely planted for its autumn tints.

As the name suggests, it has shaggy, grey bark, which curls away from the tree in thin strips up to 30 cm (12 in) long, staying attached to the tree at the centre. This gives the trunk a rather dishevelled appearance. The pinnate leaves are deep yellow-green, turning brilliant golden yellow in autumn before falling. Small, yellowish green male and female flowers are borne on pendulous catkins in late spring. The thin, green husk of the fruit encases a sweet-tasting nut.

**Vigorous habit**
The shagbark hickory has a dense, broadly columnar habit and is widely planted for its autumn coloration.

## PROFILE

- Up to 40m (130ft)
- Up to 20m (70ft)
- Deciduous
- Alternate simple
- Europe, British Isles to Russia

**Beech nut and leaves**
A woody, brown husk covered with coarse bristles carries up to three triangular edible nuts.

*brown, woody husk*

*wavy-edged leaf, untoothed around margin*

*leaf up to 10cm (4in) long, 5cm (2in) wide*

## FEATURES

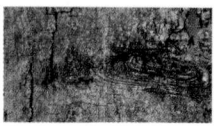

**Bark** Silver-grey; smooth throughout the tree's life

*Fagus sylvatica* (Fagaceae)

# COMMON BEECH

**Also known as European beech**, this majestic, broadly spreading tree takes its name "beech" from the Anglo-Saxon *boc* and the Germanic word *Buche*, both of which mean "book". In northern Europe, early manuscripts were written on thin tablets of beech wood and bound in beech boards. Nowadays, it is widely used for hedging because it retains its dead brown leaves throughout winter, thereby providing additional shelter.

Leaves are ovate to obovate, dark green on the upper surface and slightly paler beneath. New leaves are yellow-green, covered in fine hairs, and are edible, with a nutty flavour. Older leaves are tough and bitter. Yellow-green flowers appear in spring. Both male and female flowers are borne in separate clusters on the same tree.

**American beech**
This tree (*Fagus grandifolia*) is distinguished from common beech by its longer, narrower leaves and its suckering habit.

**PROFILE**

- Up to 40m (130ft)
- Up to 20m (70ft)
- Deciduous
- Alternate simple
- Switzerland, E. France

**oliage and fruit**
ne leaves range in colour from urple-green to deep purple, most black. The fruit is a small, val pod covered with bristles.

**FEATURES**

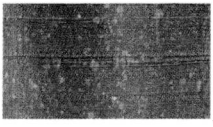

**Bark** Silver-grey, smooth throughout the life of the tree

*Fagus sylvatica* Purpurea Group (Fagaceae)

# PURPLE BEECH

**This large, broadly spreading tree** is neither a true species nor a garden creation, but rather a quirk of nature. Purple-leaved beeches were first spotted near Buchs, Switzerland, and in the Darney forest in eastern France around 1600. Shortly afterwards, they started being cultivated as an ornamental oddity, first in those regions and then further afield, soon becoming a favourite for planting in parks.

The purple beech is similar to common beech (p.152) in terms of its smooth, silver-grey bark and untoothed, wavy leaf margin. However, instead of being green, the leaves span various shades of purple – from vibrant pink-purple when young, to dark purple in maturity. They are also more oval and slightly smaller, with blunt tips.

**Weeping beech**
This tree (*Fagus sylvatica* 'Pendula') is distinguished from the purple beech by its rich green leaves.

## PROFILE

- Up to 30m (100ft)
- Up to 20m (70ft)
- Deciduous
- Alternate simple
- Forests of Caspian Sea, Caucasus, Turkey, Bulgaria, Iran

**Autumn leaves and fruit**
The leaves have up to 12 pairs of veins and become burnished gold in autumn. The fruit is a woody, bristly husk.

*leaf up to 12cm (5in) long*

*finely pointed leaf bud*

*husk up to 2.5cm (1in) long*

## FEATURES

**Bark** Smooth, light grey; sometimes with shallow fissures in maturity

**Leaves** Dark, rich green upper surface

*Fagus orientalis* (Fagaceae)

# ORIENTAL BEECH

**This large, broadly spreading tree** is in many ways similar to the common beech (p.152), with which it may hybridize on the boundary between their separate natural ranges. However, the oriental beech has larger leaves with more pairs of veins than the common beech, and can – given the right conditions – develop into an even larger tree.

The leaves are elliptic to obovate – at their widest above the middle. They have a wavy but untoothed margin and a pale green underside. Male and female flowers are small and yellow-green. However, while the male are drooping catkins, the female are erect inflorescences. They are borne in separate clusters on the same tree in spring. The flowers are followed by green, bristle-covered fruit husks, which become woody with age. Each husk contains up to three chestnut-brown, edible seeds.

**Chinese beech (*Fagus lucida*)** This is a smaller tree than the oriental beech, up to 15m (50ft) tall, with smaller and narrower, glossy green leaves, 5–8cm (2–3in) long.

**ebold's leaves and fruit**
e leaves are widest towards
e base. The fruit is a 1.5 cm-
in-) long, woody husk, held
a short, thick stalk.

**PROFILE**

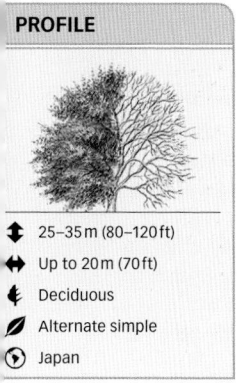

- 25–35 m (80–120 ft)
- Up to 20 m (70 ft)
- Deciduous
- Alternate simple
- Japan

*Fagus crenata* (Fagaceae)

# SIEBOLD'S BEECH

**Also known as the Japanese beech**, this large, broadly spreading tree is native to Japan, but has been widely planted in the West since its introduction in 1892. It is named after the 19th-century German physician and naturalist, Phillip Franz von Siebold. Siebold first identified the tree while working in Japan, where it is a dominant species in deciduous forests. The tree is one of the most popular species for bonsai (the art of growing miniature ornamental trees).

Siebold's beech is similar in outline to the common beech (p.152), with a large, rounded canopy. However, its leaves are more obovate in shape and the seed husks have flattened green whiskers at the base. Its bark is silver-grey and smooth, even in maturity. The leaves have 7 to 11 pairs of veins on the surface, and turn burnished gold in autumn. Male flowers are borne in catkins, while tiny female flowers are carried in leaf axils. The fruit is a husk, which splits into four lobes to reveal up to three edible seeds.

**PROFILE**



- 20m (70ft)
- Up to 15m (50ft)
- Deciduous
- Alternate simple
- Japan

**Tapering leaves**
The leaves of the Japanese beech are bright green on the upper surface and ovate to elliptic, tapering abruptly at both ends.

**FEATURES**

**Bark** Silver-grey; remains smooth even in maturity

*Fagus japonica* (Fagaceae)

# JAPANESE BEECH

**Although the name of this tree** may sometimes be confusingly given to Siebold's beech (p.155), the Japanese beech looks very different from *Fagus crenata*. This tree is much smaller in stature and often produces multiple stems, which gives it a shrublike appearance. It was introduced into western cultivation in 1907, but more than a hundred years later, it is still not a common tree and is rarely found outside botanical gardens and arboreta.

When they first unfurl from the leaf bud, the leaves are covered in dense white hairs, which may persist on the leaf underside. Each leaf has between 10 and 14 pairs of parallel leaf veins, all branching from a yellow-green midrib. In autumn, the leaves turn yellow-orange and persist on the tree until the start of winter. Both male and female flowers are borne on the same tree, and female flowers are pollinated by pollen carried on the wind. The seed is an angular nut, contained within a bristly, woody husk, which opens to release the seed in autumn.

**PROFILE**

- Up to 25 m (80 ft)
- Up to 15 m (50 ft)
- Deciduous
- Alternate simple
- C. Chile, W. Argentina

leaf up to 10 cm (4 in) long, 5 cm (2 in) wide

ripe husk, up to 1 cm (½ in) long

oblong to ovate, pendulous leaf

**ɔliage and fruit**
ıe leaves are distinguished from other ıembers of the *Nothofagus* genus by the ı to 18 pairs of parallel veins. The fruit ɔens from deep green to brown.

**FEATURES**

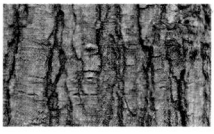

**Bark** Dark grey; becomes cracked and fissured in maturity

*Nothofagus alpina* (Fagaceae)

# RAULI SOUTHERN BEECH

**Earlier called *Nothofagus nervosa*** and *N. procera*, this broadly conical tree is native to central Chile and western Argentina, where it grows in the wild in the foothills of the Andes. It is a fast-growing species that produces excellent timber and is now planted in timber plantations in the northern hemisphere.

The tree has distinctive upswept branches. The leaves, at first glance, can be likened to those of the common hornbeam (p.184). They are deep green, sometimes bronze-green, on the upper surface and paler on the underside, with some hairs on the midrib and the veins. The shoots are green when young, becoming brown and rough with age. The fruit, borne at the base of each leaf, is a four-lobed husk containing three small nuts.

**Oval-leaved southern beech (*Nothofagus betuloides*)** This tree is distinguished by its smaller, more oval leaves, orange-brown shoots, and a tighter, denser crown.

**Leaves and fruit**
Antarctic beech leaves are oblong to ovate, crinkled, and slightly cupped along the margins. The fruit is borne at the base of leaves on side shoots.

**PROFILE**

- Up to 15m (50ft)
- Up to 10m (30ft)
- Deciduous
- Alternate simple
- South America

*Nothofagus antarctica* (Fagaceae)

# ANTARCTIC BEECH

**This fast-growing tree** is broadly columnar and inhabits mountainsides from Cape Horn to northern Chile, where it is known by the common name *ñirre*. It was introduced into western cultivation in 1830.

The bark is dark grey-brown, developing deep fissures and cracking into irregular plates from an early age. The crown can be quite open, with branches that are sporadically large and sometimes twisted. The shoots are olive-grey on the underside, with a slight covering of hairs. Leaf buds are ovoid, shiny red-brown, although they sometimes have a purple bloom. Antarctic beech leaves have a deep glossy green upper surface and a paler underside, with four pairs of parallel veins. When crushed, they may emit a honey-like fragrance. In autumn they turn orange, red, and yellow before falling. The fruit is a four-winged husk with up to three seeds.

**Myrtle beech (*Nothofagus cunninghamii*)** This evergreen beech has small, triangular leaves, which are up to 2cm (¾in) long. The leaves have tiny irregular teeth along the margins.

**Roble beech foliage**
The leaves are ovate to oval, sometimes almost oblong. They have 8 to 11 pairs of distinct veins.

**PROFILE**

- Up to 35 m (120 ft)
- Up to 20 m (70 ft)
- Deciduous
- Alternate simple
- Chile, Argentina

**FEATURES**

**Bark** Grey and smooth when young; becoming cracked and fissured with age

*Nothofagus obliqua* (Fagaceae)

# ROBLE BEECH

**Also known as the coyan beech**, the more common name for this tree is roble, which is the Spanish word for oak. In fact, in some respects, this large, broadly columnar tree does resemble the sessile oak (p.164). It produces tough, durable, oak-like timber, which in the past was used in shipbuilding and for making house beams and furniture. Today, it is widely planted as an ornamental tree, and grown alongside highways in some parts of southern Europe.

Its leaves are dark green on the upper surface and paler blue-green on the underside. Irregularly toothed along the margins, they have 8 to 11 pairs of distinct veins. In autumn, they turn golden yellow before falling. Small green flowers are produced at the base of leaves. Male flowers are borne singly; females, in threes. The fruit is a bristly husk containing up to three nuts.

**Menzies' red beech (*Nothofagus menziesii*)** This evergreen tree is told apart by its shiny, purple-brown bark and double-toothed, small, orbicular leaves, up to 1 cm (½ in) long and wide.

## PROFILE

- Up to 23 m (75 ft)
- Up to 20 m (70 ft)
- Evergreen
- Alternate simple
- Chile, Argentina

**Dense foliage**
Leaves are borne on shoots that are red-brown above and green below. The leaves overlap so densely that, from a distance, the whole tree appears black in colour.

## FEATURES

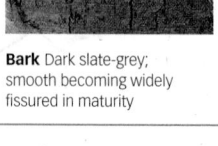

**Bark** Dark slate-grey; smooth becoming widely fissured in maturity

*Nothofagus dombeyi* (Fagaceae)

# COIGÜE SOUTHERN BEECH

**Also called Dombey's southern beech**, this broadly conical, evergreen tree is one of the most elegant of South American temperate trees. It was introduced into Europe in 1916. In this region, it may shed its leaves in winter, producing new ones in spring, with little evidence of a check in growth rate. In maturity, the tree resembles an old Atlas cedar (p.46), with an open arrangement of ascending branches, which bend outwards towards the tips.

The bark flakes to reveal orange-red new bark. Borne on slender shoots, the leaves are glossy black-green on the upper surface, and matt, pale green on the underside. Male flowers are small, but bright red and contrast with the evergreen foliage. The fruit is a small, bristly husk, enclosing three small nuts.

**New Zealand red beech (*Nothofagus fusca*)** Unlike the Coigüe southern beech, this tree's leaves are double-toothed with red veins on the underside, and turn dark red in autumn.

## PROFILE

- Up to 30m (100ft)
- Up to 20m (70ft)
- Deciduous
- Alternate simple
- Mediterranean, eastwards into S.W. Asia

**Spiky flowers**
Male and female flowers are clustered in small, creamy yellow, spike-like catkins.

*coarsely toothed leaf margin*

*sharply pointed leaf tip*

*rounded leaf base*

## FEATURES

**Fruit** Yellow-green husks

**Seed** Edible chestnut contained in a spiny husk

*Castanea sativa* (Fagaceae)

# SWEET CHESTNUT

**This fast-growing, broadly columnar**, ornamental tree is indigenous to warm, temperate regions. It is widely cultivated elsewhere for its fruit – an edible chestnut. The Romans in particular valued the tree as a source of food and introduced it to many parts of their empire, including the British Isles.

The bark is smooth and light grey at first, developing spiral fissures in maturity. In winter, this characteristic distinguishes this tree from the pedunculate oak (p.165). The oblong leaves are glossy, dark green on the upper surface and paler on the underside. They are up to 20cm (8in) long and 7.5cm (3in) wide, with coarsely toothed margins. Each tooth links to a vein running to the midrib. Small, creamy yellow flowers are borne on erect catkins that ripen in midsummer. The fruit appears in autumn, in a husk enclosing up to three chestnuts.

**Japanese chestnut (*Castanea crenata*)** This tree is smaller than the sweet chestnut with long, narrow, bristle-toothed leaves, which appear more crinkly than its European counterpart.

**Leaves and fruit**
The alternate leaves have a leathery texture. Up to three nuts are enveloped in a spiny husk, which takes two years to ripen.

**PROFILE**

- Up to 30 m (100 ft)
- Up to 12 m (40 ft)
- Evergreen
- Alternate simple
- USA (Oregon, California)

*Chrysolepis chrysophylla* (Fagaceae)

# GOLDEN CHESTNUT

This broadly conical, evergreen tree is often referred to as the golden chinkapin and, sometimes botanically, as *Castanopsis chrysophylla*. This is incorrect as the male and female flowers on *Castanopsis* are borne on separa catkins, whereas the male and female flowers on this tree are on the same catkin. The name "golden" refers to the underside of the leaf, which is covered with brigh golden hairs – an easy way of distinguishing it from oth members of the Fagaceae family.

The grey bark is smooth when young but develops fissures in maturity. The evergreen leaves are lanceolate to oblong, broad in the middle, and taper to a point at ea end. Fragrant male and female flowers are borne on erec catkins in summer. These are followed by dense clusters spiny husks, which contain three glossy brown nuts.

**American sweet chestnut (*Castanea dentata*)** The deciduous leaves are narrower and longer than those of the golde chestnut. They are hairless, with saw-toothed leaf margins.

**PROFILE**

- Up to 17 m (56 ft)
- Up to 15 m (50 ft)
- Evergreen
- Alternate simple
- W. USA

**Tanbark acorn**
The fruit of the tanbark oak is an ovoid acorn held within a short, stalked, bristly cup.

*acorn 2–3 cm (¾–1¼ in) long*

*hard, woody exocarp (shell)*

**FEATURES**

**Leaves** Oblong to elliptic, sharply toothed, leathery

*Lithocarpus densiflorus* (Fagaceae)

# TANBARK OAK

**As the name suggests**, this small to medium-sized, pyramidal evergreen is closely related to oak (*Quercus*), and displays some of the characteristics of this genus. It is native to California and Oregon on the North American west coast and was introduced into European cultivation in 1874. It has been regularly planted in parks, gardens, and arboreta since then.

The bark is a valuable source of tannin, a chemical used in the leather industry. It is grey-brown and smooth at first, becoming vertically fissured in maturity. Both the shoots and the leaves are covered with a soft, creamy white down when young.

The leaves are similar to those of the sweet chestnut (p.161) and are up to 10 cm (4 in) long and 5 cm (2 in) wide. They are dark, glossy green on the upper surface, with a paler green, sometimes almost white, underside. Fawn-coloured hairs surround the leaf veins. Clusters of small, creamy yellow flowers are borne on erect spikes in late spring and resemble the flowers of the sweet chestnut.

leaf up to 13 cm (5 in) long, 7.5 cm (3 in) wide

rounded, untoothed leaf lobe

glossy, dark green upper surface of lea

**Stalked foliage**
This tree has elliptic leaves, which taper towards the base. Each leaf is attached to the twig by a yellow stalk, up to 1.25 cm (½ in) long.

## PROFILE

- Up to 40 m (130 ft)
- Up to 25 m (80 ft)
- Deciduous
- Alternate simple
- Europe from Ireland and Iberia east to Turkey and Caucasus

## FEATURES

**Bark** Light grey, smooth for the first 30 years; developing deep vertical fissures afterwards

*Quercus petraea* (Fagaceae)

# SESSILE OAK

**Also known as the durmast oak**, this long-lived, broadly spreading tree produces strong, durable timber, which is attractively figured and has been used over the centuries for ship building, house construction, and for making furniture and wine barrels. In western Europe, the sessile oak often grows close to the pedunculate oak (p.165), and intermediate hybrids are regularly encountered.

The leaves have a dark green upper surface and a paler underside, with a slight covering of hairs. In late spring, the tree bears flowers in yellow-green, pendulous catkins. The seed is an acorn, one-third of which is enclosed in a scaly, unstalked cup, which is directly attached to the twig at its base.

**Hungarian oak**
This tree (*Quercus frainetto*) has obovate leaves, up to 20 cm (8 in) long, with large, deep, regular, oblong lobes

**Green acorn**
The pedunculate oak's young fruit is a small green acorn, one-third of which is held in a cup at the end of a stalk.

*small lobe at base of leaf*

*3–6 rounded lobes on either side of leaf margin*

*acorn up to 4 cm (1½ in) long*

## PROFILE

- 25–40 m (80–130 ft)
- Up to 30 m (100 ft)
- Deciduous
- Alternate simple
- Europe, W. Asia, N. Africa

## FEATURES

**Flowers** Long, pendulous, greenish yellow catkins

**Fruit** Acorn; green ripening to brown in first year

*Quercus robur* (Fagaceae)

# PEDUNCULATE OAK

**Also known as English or common oak,** this majestic, broadly spreading tree is found throughout Europe. It is usually found in lowlands, which allows its close relative sessile oak (p.164) to colonize upland regions of Europe. However, the two regularly hybridize where they meet, creating trees that may have characteristics of both species.

The pedunculate oak grows best on damp, rich, well-drained soils. It is long-lived, with many recorded veterans over 1,000 years old. The leaves are elliptic to obovate, tapering at the base. They are usually unstalked, or on shorter stalks than the sessile oak. The upper surface is deep green and the underside blue-green. The flowers are long, greenish yellow catkins. The fruit is borne on a stalk up to 10 cm (4 in) long.

**Pyrenean oak**
This tree (*Quercus pyrenaica*) has longer leaves, which are slightly hairy on the upper surface.

**Foliage and fruit**
Turkey oak leaves are elliptic to oblong and glossy dark green. The fruit are borne in cups covered in long, narrow scales.

## PROFILE



- Up to 40 m (130 ft)
- Up to 25 m (80 ft)
- Deciduous
- Alternate simple
- C. and S. Europe

## FEATURES

**Bark** Silver-grey, thick; deeply fissured in maturity

*Quercus cerris* (Fagaceae)

# TURKEY OAK

**This wide-spreading tree** is found across central and southern Europe, from France through to Turkey. It normally has a long, straight trunk with relatively little branching on the first third of the trunk's height. Unlike other oaks, it does not yield valuable timber because the timber cracks and splits when sawn. It has been widely cultivated across the rest of Europe since the 18th century and has become naturalized in many areas. It is often planted as an ornamental tree.

The leaves are variably lobed, but usually with shallower and more lobes than the sessile oak (p.164) and the pedunculate oak (p.165). Both male and female flowers are yellow-green pendulous catkins, borne separately on the same tree in early summer. The fruit is an acorn, held in a cup covered with bristle-like scales for half of its length.

**Chestnut-leaved oak (*Quercus castaneifolia*)** The leaves o this tree are oblong, tapering at both ends. They have coarse, triangular, sharply pointed teeth along the margins.

## PROFILE

- Up to 30m (100ft)
- Up to 30m (100ft)
- Evergreen
- Alternate simple
- S. Europe, Mediterranean region

**Leathery leaves**
Leaves are elliptic to ovate, leathery, and occasionally toothed with pale grey hairs on the underside.

*acorn up to 1.5cm (½in) long*

*dark green upper surface of leaf*

*sage green on leaf underside*

*leaf up to 7.5cm (3in) long, 5cm (2in) wide*

## FEATURES

**Bark** Grey-brown and smooth; develops shallow fissures and small plates with age

**Flowers** Male catkins are creamy grey

*Quercus ilex* (Fagaceae)

# HOLM OAK

**This evergreen oak** is also known as holly oak or evergreen oak. It has a rounded, domed shape, and dense branching. The profusion of leaves on the branches is such that, from a distance, the canopy looks solid and black. Little light or rainwater penetrates through the canopy to ground level, so the ground beneath this tree is normally bare, except for dry, brown, spent leaves. The holm oak is native to southern Europe and the Mediterranean but has been cultivated in northern Europe since the 16th century.

It is a valuable tree in coastal regions, providing shelter against wind and salt spray. During cold winters, up to 50 per cent of its leaves may be shed and replaced in spring. The male and female catkins appear separately on the same tree in summer. The fruit is a small, pointed acorn held in a fawn, scaly cup.

**Japanese chinquapin (*Castanopsis cuspidata*)** This small, bushy tree is distinguished by its larger, lighter green leaves, which have a long drawn-out tip, and a yellow-green midrib and petiole.

tapering lobe on leaf

leaf up to 20cm (8in) long

bristly lobe ends in fine point

**Deeply cut leaves**
The alternate leaves are cut into bristle-tipped lobes, and are often borne on stalks that are red at the base.

## PROFILE

- Up to 30m (100ft)
- Up to 20m (70ft)
- Deciduous
- Alternate simple
- E. North America

## FEATURES

**Fruit** Squat acorn; ripening in second year

**Leaves** Ruby-red mixed with gold, before falling in autumn

*Quercus rubra* (Fagaceae)

# RED OAK

**This fast-growing, broadly spreading** tree is native to eastern North America from Alabama, USA, to Nova Scotia and Quebec, Canada, where it grows further north than any other American oak. It is famed for its spectacular leaf colour displays in autumn. Introduced into Britain as early as 1724, the red oak has been wide planted as an ornamental species in the temperate world including western Europe.

It has a smooth, light grey bark, similar to beech whe young, which becomes deeply fissured in maturity. The leaves are large, oval or obovate-shaped, with distincti lobes, each ending in a fine point. They have a dull mat green upper surface, and pale blue-green underside, with tufts of fine, brown hairs in the vein axils (where the veins meet the midrib). The flowers are green-yellow, pendulous catkins, which appear in spring.

**Water oak (*Quercus nigra*)** This is a smaller, less vigorous tr than the red oak. It has smaller, wedge-shaped leaves with variab lobes, which are glossy, rich green on both sides.

**utumn leaves**
n autumn, the scarlet oak leaves radually change colour, sometimes ver four weeks, from green to ibrant scarlet before falling.

*eaf 15 cm (6 in) long, 10 cm (4 in) wide*

*large, angular lobe on side of leaf*

*petiole up to 4 cm (1½ in) long*

**PROFILE**

- Up to 30 m (100 ft)
- Up to 15 m (50 ft)
- Deciduous
- Alternate simple
- S.E. and C. USA

**FEATURES**

**Leaves** Dark, shiny green upper surface

*fruit 2 cm (¾ in) long*

**Fruit** Ovoid acorn, in shallow, scaled cup

*Quercus coccinea* (Fagaceae)

# SCARLET OAK

**Originating in the USA**, the scarlet oak is a large, attractive, pyramid-shaped tree. It was introduced into cultivation in 1691. Today it is widely planted throughout the northern hemisphere in parks and gardens for the autumn colours of its foliage.

The bark of the scarlet oak is silver-grey and smooth at first, but displaying warts and bumps. It matures to dark grey with shallow vertical fissures. The elliptic, occasionally oblong, leaves are shiny and pale green on the underside. They have three lobes on either side, each featuring spines towards the tip. Between the lobes, leaves may be cut almost to the midrib. The leaves are attached to red-brown shoots by thin, stalk-like petioles. The male flowers are borne in catkins at the tip of the previous year's shoots, while leaf axils bear the female flowers. The flowers of both sexes are pale green-brown.

**Pin oak (*Quercus palustris*)** The leaves of this tree are smaller than the scarlet oak, and are borne on longer petioles; and on the underside, carry tufts of brown hairs in the axils.

**PROFILE**

- Up to 20m (70ft)
- 20m (70ft)
- Evergreen
- Alternate simple
- W. Mediterranean, N. Africa, S.W. Europe

*leaf shiny dark green on upper surface*

**Cork oak leaves**
The leaves of this oak are variable, ranging from oval to oblong. Occasionally entire (smooth-edged), the leaves often have toothed margins.

*leaf up to 7.5cm (3in) long*

*broadly toothed leaf margin*

**FEATURES**

**Bark** Light brown, heavily fissured, corky

**Fruit** Slender, pointed acorn, up to 3cm (1¼in) long

*Quercus suber* (Fagaceae)

# CORK OAK

**The broadly spreading**, medium-sized cork oak is native to the western Mediterranean region, northern Africa, and the southern European Atlantic coast. It has been widely cultivated over many centuries for its thick, corky bark, which has been used to make cork products such as stoppers for wine bottles. Since the introduction of plastic corks and screw-top wine bottles, these trees have been neglected and felled right across the region but a move to return to cork stoppers may arrest the decline in this species.

Cork oak leaves are similar to those of the holm oak (p.167), with a pale green-grey, felt-covered underside. The male flowers are carried on weeping, yellow catkins in spring. The fruit is an acorn, green ripening to brown, and encased for half its length in a scaly cup.

**Lucombe oak (*Quercus* x *hispanica* 'Lucombeana')** This cultivated form of the hybrid between the Turkey oak (p.166) and the cork oak is much larger than the cork oak.

## PROFILE



- Up to 20 m (70 ft)
- 15 m (50 ft)
- Deciduous
- Alternate simple
- S. Europe from Spain to Caucasus

**bed foliage**
e leaves of the downy oak vary
om elliptic to obovate. The leaf
bes are normally irregular in size.

## FEATURES

**Bark** Dark grey; becomes fissured from an early age

**Fruit** Stalkless acorn, up to 4 cm (1 ½ in) long; green ripening to brown

*Quercus pubescens* (Fagaceae)

# DOWNY OAK

**This small to medium-sized**, broadly spreading tree has a large natural range, extending from Spain in the west to the Caucasus in the east. The downy oak is closely related to the sessile oak (p.164). Compared to its cousin, the smaller downy oak has a more shrublike appearance and ragged outline, and, as the name suggests, its leaves have more hairs.

The variable, lobed leaves are pale green on the underside with a dense covering of short, soft, grey-white hairs. The leaf petioles (stalks) are also covered with hairs. The leaf lobes may end in a small, sharp point, with a few indentations between the lobes extending more than halfway towards the leaf midrib. Clusters of male flowers are borne on pendulous yellow-green catkins in spring. The fruit is an acorn, contained in a hairy, scaly cup for up to half of its length.

**Lebanon oak (*Quercus libani*)** This tree has slender branches and glossy green, oblong-lanceolate leaves. The leaf margins have triangular, bristle-tipped teeth.

**Algerian oak leaves**
The leaves of this tree are large, oblong-ovate to obovate, sometimes oval. The largest lobe appear where the leaf is broades

## PROFILE

- Up to 30m (100ft)
- Up to 15m (50ft)
- Deciduous
- Alternate simple
- N. Africa, S.W. Europe

## FEATURES

**Bark** Dark grey, almost black; deeply fissured into small square plates

**Fruit** Acorn, up to 3cm (1¼in) long, carried in scaly cup

*Quercus canariensis* (Fagaceae)

# ALGERIAN OAK

**Also known as Mirbeck's oak**, this tree is native to northern Africa and southwestern Europe including the Canary Islands. It is reasonably hardy and survives much further north, where it is planted in parks, gardens and arboreta. In maturity, the Algerian oak has a dense rounded head of branches on top of a straight trunk. Although not strictly evergreen, many of its leaves remain green and stay on the tree through winter.

Each leaf has between 6 and 13 pairs of lobes, with a matt, slightly blue-green, hairy underside. The male flowers are bunched at leaf nodes in yellow pendulous catkins. The fruit is attached to the shoot by a 1cm- (½in-) long stalk.

**Young oak**
The Algerian oak is a larg narrowly columnar tree when young, broadening out in maturity.

**PROFILE**



- Up to 30m (100ft)
- Up to 6m (20ft)
- Deciduous
- Alternate simple
- Europe, N. Asia

**tkins and fruit**
ect female flowers develop into ndulous, cucumber-shaped fruit autumn. Leaves are dark green the upper surface and pale een on the underside.

**FEATURES**

**Bark** White or silver-grey; becomes corky with black fissures in old age

*Betula pendula* (Betulaceae)

# SILVER BIRCH

**The natural range of the silver birch** extends from Britain and Ireland, across Europe and northern Asia, to the Pacific Ocean. This narrowly weeping tree seldom reaches its full height potential, and is conical with upswept branches when young. It is hardy, being able to withstand intense cold and long periods of drought, and it seeds prolifically to establish itself on cleared ground. Also known as the warty birch, it has shoots covered in wart-like bumps, making them rough to the touch.

The leaves are borne on slender shoots and turn butter yellow in autumn. Both male and female flowers appear separately on the same tree in spring. The male flowers are borne in pendulous clusters. The green fruit ripen to brown and break up on the tree to release small, winged seeds.

**Grey birch (*Betula populifolia*)** This American counterpart of the silver birch is distinguished by its poplar-like leaves, which are borne on a long lax stalk and flutter in the slightest breeze.

**PROFILE**

- Up to 25 m (80 ft)
- Up to 6 m (20 ft)
- Deciduous
- Alternate simple
- N. Europe to N. Asia

*leaf up to 5 cm (2 in) long and wi*

*ovate to rounded leaf*

*upright fruiting female catkin*

**Leaves and fruiting catkins** The dark green leaves have tooth margins and taper to a point. The green, fruiting female catkin ripen and breaks off from the tree.

**FEATURES**

**Bark** Grey when young, matures to white during later years

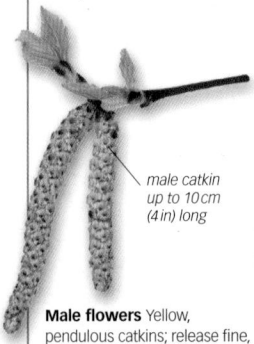


**Male flowers** Yellow, pendulous catkins; release fine, yellow pollen particles in spring

*Betula pubescens* (Betulaceae)

# DOWNY BIRCH

**Also known as white birch**, this hardy, broadly conical, deciduous tree has a natural range that extends across northern Europe into northern Asia. It thrives in poor soils and wet conditions, and grows right up into the Arctic region. It is called "downy" because of its soft, hairy shoots, a feature that distinguishes it from the silver birch (p.173), which has rough shoots. Other characteristics distinguishing these two birches include the less pendulous form an twisting branches of the downy birch.

While the bark on the tree's trunk is grey-white, its shoots and branches are a glossy, copper brown. The leaves are dark green on the upper surface and paler green on the underside, with hairy veins. Unlike the ma flowers, which are drooping catkins, the female flowers are upright, green catkins. They are borne separately from the male flowers on the same tree in spring. They turn brown when ripe and shed large amounts of small, papery, winged seeds.

**PROFILE**



- Up to 25m (80ft)
- Up to 6m (20ft)
- Deciduous
- Alternate simple
- W. China

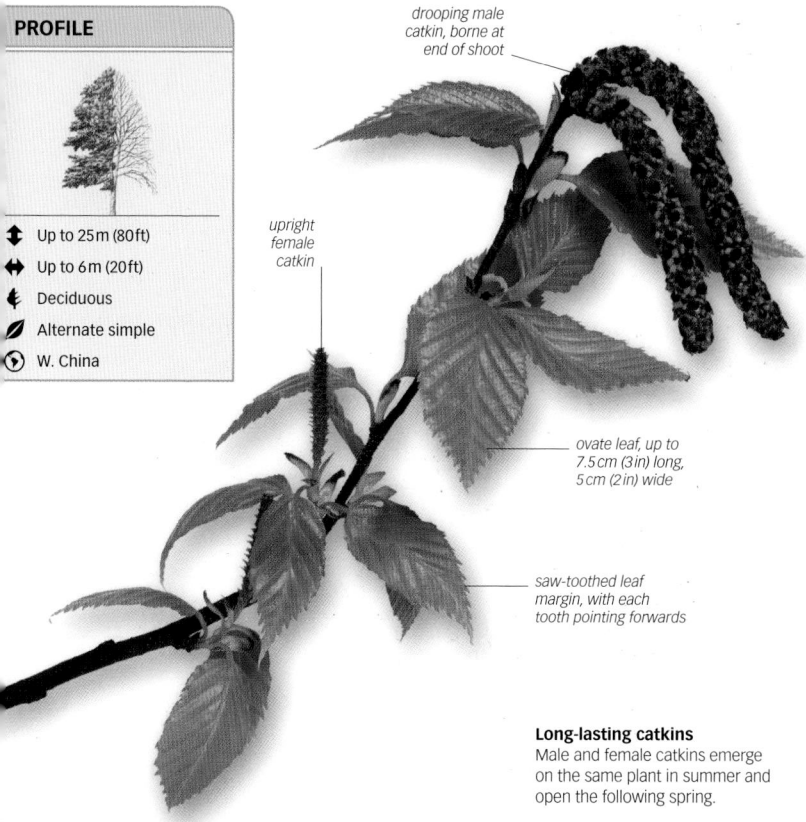


**Long-lasting catkins**
Male and female catkins emerge on the same plant in summer and open the following spring.

**FEATURES**

**Bark** Peels in thin strips, cream-pink when exposed

**Female flowers** Green catkins, borne upright

*Betula albosinensis* (Betulaceae)

# CHINESE RED-BARKED BIRCH

**This deciduous tree is best known** for its coppery to orange-red bark, which peels to reveal a fresh cream-pink surface beneath. This happens on the branches as well as the trunk. The tree is native to western China, where it grows high in mixed woodland in mountainous regions. It was introduced in Europe in 1901 by English plant collector Ernest H. Wilson, and has been planted around the temperate world ever since.

In spring, leaves emerge from small, sticky, red buds, and are covered in white down. This fades to reveal glossy mid-green leaves that turn golden yellow in autumn, before falling. Male and female flowers, carried in catkins, appear separately on the same tree. Female catkins break up to release hundreds of winged seeds.

**Chinese dwarf birch (*Betula chinensis*)** Apart from being a much smaller tree, with smaller sharply toothed leaves, this birch also lacks the striking bark of the Chinese red-barked birch.

**PROFILE**



- Up to 25 m (80 ft)
- Up to 6 m (20 ft)
- Deciduous
- Alternate simple
- Himalayan region, from S.W. China to Afghanistan

**Fruiting catkins**
The female catkins of the Himalayan birch ripen from green to brown in spring, and disintegrate on the tree to release small, winged seeds.

**FEATURES**

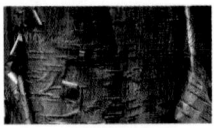

**Bark** Paper thin, peels off in horizontal strips

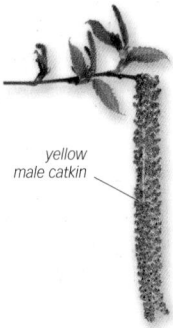


**Flowers** Male flowers borne on pendulous catkins

*Betula utilis* (Betulaceae)

# HIMALAYAN BIRCH

**This attractive birch** has a wide natural distribution throughout the Himalayan region, from Afghanistan in the west to southwestern China in the east. It is a broad conical, medium-sized deciduous tree. It occasionally reaches 25 m (80 ft) in height, but is usually smaller.

Within the wild population, the bark colour is extremely variable, ranging from pink-brown or orange-red, through to white. However, the orange-red form is most common in cultivation. The bark peels off in long, ribbon-like strips. The leaves are glossy dark green on the upper surface, and paler on the underside, with some hairs on the midrib. Each ovate leaf is distinctly veined, with up to 12 pairs of parallel veins. It is attached to hairy shoots by a short leaf stalk 1.25 cm (½ in) long. Pendulous male and upright female flowers are borne on the same tree in catkins.

**Monarch birch (*Betula maximowicziana*)** A bigger tree than the Himalayan birch, this related species can be easily distinguished by its much larger heart-shaped leaves.

**PROFILE**

- Up to 20 m (70 ft)
- Up to 6 m (20 ft)
- Deciduous
- Alternate simple
- E. to W. North America

*ovate leaves with shallow toothed margin and a tapered tip*

*pendulous male catkin, up to 10 cm (4 in) long*

*rough, dark brown shoot*

*young male catkin*

**rch male catkins**
ale catkins are initially green and come longer, yellow, and more ndulous as they mature. They oop from the shoot tips.

**FEATURES**

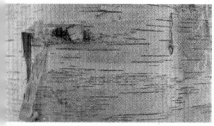

**Bark** Creamy white; peels in thin papery strips

**Leaves** Dark green to orange, before falling off in autumn

*Betula papyrifera* (Betulaceae)

# PAPER-BARK BIRCH

**This broadly conical, medium-sized** deciduous birch has a natural range that extends across North America, from the Atlantic to the Pacific coast. Native Americans used the tough, durable bark of this tree to cover their canoes and make them waterproof. As a result, the tree is often referred to as canoe birch. A hardy tree, it grows as far north as Alaska and Labrador, and was introduced into cultivation in Europe around 1750. It has been a popular addition to parks and gardens ever since.

The leaves are dark green and smooth on the upper surface, pale green on the underside, with veins lightly covered in fine hairs. In autumn, the leaves turn marmalade-orange before falling. The flowers are borne in catkins. Female catkins are up to 7.5 cm (3 in) long, ripen from green to brown, and disintegrate on the tree to release small, brown, winged seeds.

**Japanese cherry birch (*Betula grossa*)** This tree is distinguished by its dark bark, hornbeam-like leaves, and a unique fragrance, given off when its twigs are broken.

## PROFILE

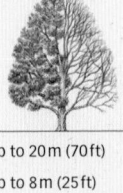

- Up to 20 m (70 ft)
- Up to 8 m (25 ft)
- Deciduous
- Alternate simple
- Russia, Japan, Korea

**Rough shoots**
The leaves and catkins of the Russian rock birch are carried on coarse, warty shoots.

*deeply serrated leaf margin*

*upright fruiting female catkin*

*leaf margin ends in a point*

*rough-textured shoot*

*leaf up to 9 cm (3½ in) long, 6 cm (2½ in) wide*

*drooping, yellow male catkin*

## FEATURES

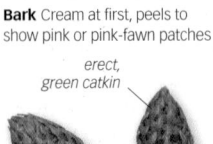

**Bark** Cream at first, peels to show pink or pink-fawn patches

*erect, green catkin*

**Female flowers** Upright, smaller than male catkins; ripening to brown

*Betula ermanii* (Betulaceae)

# RUSSIAN ROCK BIRCH

**This medium-sized, long-lived birch** is native to Japa and Korea, as well as parts of Russia. Sometimes called Erman's birch, it was introduced into cultivation in 1890. is a broadly conical tree, and one of relatively few birche to grow with multiple stems. A distinctive feature of this tree is the way its peeled bark shreds and hangs like a ragged fringe along the undersides of branches.

The bark is creamy, with a tint of pink, and stands ou particularly when the tree is bare in winter. The leaves a glossy dark green on the upper surface and paler on th underside. They are triangular to ovate, with 7 to 11 pai of impressed, parallel veins, and fawn-coloured hairs in the vein axils. Both male and female flowers are 4 cm- (1½ in-) long catkins. They are carried in separate clusters on the same tree in spring. Female catkins brea up on the tree to release small, winged seeds.

**Korean birch (*Betula costata*)** Though closely related to th Russian rock birch, this tree has leaves that are less heart-shape at the base and bark that has a greater pink tinge.

**PROFILE**



- 15–30 m (50–100 ft)
- Up to 15 m (50 ft)
- Deciduous
- Alternate simple
- C. and E. USA

**rooping male catkins**
ale flowers are borne in pendulous usters in spring before the leaves ıfurl. Female flowers appear on the me tree but in separate catkins.

*yellow male catkin, up to 7.5 cm (3 in) long*

**FEATURES**

**Bark** Peels in fine papery strips, making the tree appear shaggy

**Leaves** Ovate; up to 10 cm (4 in) long

*Betula nigra* (Betulaceae)

# RIVER BIRCH

**Also known as red birch**, this broadly spreading tree reaches 30 m (100 ft) in the wild but is smaller in cultivation. It occurs naturally from Maine in the east to Minnesota in central USA, and south to Texas, where, as the name suggests, it grows beside creeks and in low-lying marsh ground.

It has attractive pink-brown bark when young, turning purple-black with striking orange fissures with age. This feature has made it a popular ornamental species. The leaves have a deep green upper surface and a blue-green underside with silvery hairs on the veins. The flowers are borne in catkins. Female catkins are upright and green, males are pendulous.

**Yellow birch**
This tree (*Betula alleghaniensis*) has a shining yellow bark and more finely toothed leaf margins.

**PROFILE**

- Up to 25 m (80 ft)
- Up to 12 m (40 ft)
- Deciduous
- Alternate simple
- Europe, W. Asia, N. Africa

*up to 10 pairs of distinct, opposite leaf veins*

*green, unripe fruit*

*leaf up to 10 cm (4 in) long, 8 cm (3 in) wide*

**Circular leaves**
The common alder's leaves are obovate to circular, finely toothed, with a strongly indented midrib.

**FEATURES**

**Fruit** Brown woody cone, with scales opening to release numerous seeds

*Alnus glutinosa* (Betulaceae)

# COMMON ALDER

**This broadly conical tree** is native to Europe, western Asia, and North Africa. It is normally found growing in damp soil, often close to rivers and lakes. When its roots are submerged in water for long periods of time, it is able to create its own oxygen supply. Alder timber is water-durable and has been used to make boats, footwear, and the timber piles upon which Venice is built.

The tree has dark, grey-brown bark, which is lightly fissured from an early age. Its leaves are a shiny dark green on the upper surface and pale grey-green on the underside, with tufts of hairs in the leaf axils. Both male and female flowers are catkins. The male is greenish yellow, pendulous, and up to 10 cm (4 in) long. The female is upright, red, and oval-shaped, ripening into a small brown cone after fertilization.

**Oriental alder (*Alnus orientalis*)** This medium-sized alder is easily distinguished from the common alder by its sticky winter buds and its ovate, coarsely toothed, glossy leaves.

**PROFILE**

- Up to 20m (70ft)
- Up to 12m (40ft)
- Deciduous
- Alternate simple
- Europe

*leaf underside has grey hairs*

*leaf up to 10cm (4in) long, 5cm (2in) wide*

*fruit contains small, winged seeds*

**Leaves and cone-like fruit** The green fruit ripen to become brown, woody, cone-like structures. Leaves are matt dark green on the upper surface.

**FEATURES**

**Male flowers** Orange-yellow; borne on pendulous catkins

*Alnus incana* (Betulaceae)

# GREY ALDER

**Native to most of Europe** except for the British Isles, the grey alder is a fast-growing, medium-sized, broadly conical tree. It grows at elevations of up to around 1,000m (3,280ft) in the Caucasus mountains. This hardy species is regularly planted in cold, wet conditions where other trees may not thrive. It is also used to cover land being reclaimed after industrial activities such as mining and landfill. The tree gets its name from the dense covering of short grey hairs on the underside of the leaves.

The bark is dark grey and smooth, even in maturity. Leaves have an irregular, double-toothed margin, ending in a pointed tip. Flowers are borne clustered in catkins. Male and female flowers bloom separately on the same tree in early spring. The female catkin is erect and red. The fruit releases seeds after ripening, and remains on the tree for a long time.

**Sitka alder (*Alnus sinuata*)** Unlike the grey alder, this tree does not have a dense, hairy covering on the underside of the leaf. It is also much smaller and more shrublike in form.

**PROFILE**

- 30 m (100 ft)
- Up to 10 m (30 ft)
- Deciduous
- Alternate simple
- S. Italy, Albania, Corsica

*unripe fruit*

*immature male catkin*

*leaf underside pale green*

*glossy bright green upper surface of leaf*

*broadly heart-shaped leaf base*

**Bright green foliage**
Heart-shaped, occasionally almost round leaves are widely spaced on the shoots. Female catkins turn from pale brown to red.

**FEATURES**

*catkin 7.5 cm (3 in) long*

**Male flowers**
Long, drooping, yellow catkins

**Fruit** Ripen to brown, woody cone-like structures

*Alnus cordata* (Betulaceae)

# ITALIAN ALDER

**The broadly conical Italian alder** is the largest species of its genus. It is native to southern Italy, parts of Albania, and Corsica. It grows at elevations of up to 1,000 m (3,280 ft) above sea level on dry mountain slopes. This is unusual for a species of alder, as most require moist soil conditions to thrive. This tree takes its species name *cordata* from the fact that it produces cordate, or heart-shaped, leaves.

The bark is dull grey tinged with green, smooth at first, becoming fissured with age. Branches in the crown of the tree tend to have lighter bark. The leaves are up to 10 cm (4 in) long, with a sparse covering of hairs on the underside. They are sharply toothed around the margin except for the base of the leaf, which may be entire (smooth). Both male and female flowers appear separately on the same tree in early spring.

**Japanese alder (*Alnus japonica*)** This related tree has narrower, more pointed, elliptic leaves, and bears smaller male catkins in late winter or early spring.

**PROFILE**

- 15 m (50 ft)
- Up to 10 m (30 ft)
- Deciduous
- Alternate simple
- W. North America

**endulous male catkins**
e red alder flowers in
rly spring. Male flowers
e carried in pendulous
tkins, ripening to orange.

**FEATURES**

**Leaves** Up to 10 cm (4 in) long, 7.5 cm (3 in) wide, with slightly pointed tips

**Fruit**
Egg-shaped, woody brown; containing many winged seeds

*Alnus rubra* (Betulaceae)

# RED ALDER

**Also known as the Oregon alder**, this fast-growing tree is native to the west coast of the USA, from Alaska to California. It is prominent in the Cascade valleys and Coast Mountain areas, where it grows on areas of disturbed soil and along highways. It thrives in damp soil conditions, especially alongside creeks and rivers.

In the wild, the bark is normally silver-white and resembles white-barked birches; however, in cultivation the bark is usually relatively smooth and pewter-coloured with a pinkish tinge. The leaves have a dark green and smooth upper surface with reddish veining, and a pale grey-green underside with rusty red hairs along leaf veins. They are attached to thin red shoots by red petioles up to 3.5 cm (1 ½ in) long. Male and female flowers are borne separately on the same tree. The smaller, bright red female flowers ripen into cone-like fruit.

**Japanese green alder (*Alnus firma*)** Unlike the red alder, this smaller, shrublike tree has green petioles and no rust-coloured hairs on the underside of the leaf.

leaf up to 10cm (4in) long, 5cm (2in) wide

female catkin at tip of shoot

pendulous male catkin

**Hornbeam leaves and flowers**
The common hornbeam has ovate leaves that taper to a point. Male and female flowers are borne in separate catkins on the same tree in spring.

## PROFILE

- Up to 30m (100ft)
- Up to 20m (70ft)
- Deciduous
- Alternate simple
- Europe, W. Asia

## FEATURES

**Fruit** Ribbed nut at centre of three-lobed bracts, which ripen to buff in autumn

*Carpinus betulus* (Betulaceae)

# COMMON HORNBEAM

**This broadly spreading tree** is native to Europe, stretching from southern Britain and eastwards into Asia. It is sometimes confused with common beech (p.152) because of its silver-grey bark and similar-looking leaves.

However, the trunk and branches of hornbeam are distinctively angular, unlike those of beech. Distinctive serrations around the leaf margin also distinguish it from beech. Leaves have a dark green upper surface and pale green underside, with 10 to 13 pairs of parallel veins. In autumn, they turn a rich butter-yellow colour. Tiny, yellow male flowers are borne in catkins up to 5cm (2in) long. Female catkins are even smaller. Later, these develop into hanging clusters of fruit bracts. Green when young, the bracts stay on the tree throughout winter.

**Heartleaf hornbeam (*Carpinus cordata*)** This smaller, slow-growing tree can be easily distinguished by its large, heart-shaped leaves.

**emale flowers and foliage**
eaves have sharp serrations along
e margins. Female flowers develop
to papery clusters called bracts,
hich are bright green at first,
anging to pink-brown.

narrow, ovate leaf, up to 10 cm (4 in) long

coarsely toothed bract, up to 2 cm (3/4 in) long

## PROFILE

- 12–15 m (40–50 ft)
- Up to 8 m (25 ft)
- Deciduous
- Alternate simple
- Japan

## FEATURES

**Bark** Smooth, grey-purple; develops pink-grey, wavy, vertical stripes in maturity

**Male flowers** Bright yellow, pendulous; conspicuous in spring

*Carpinus japonica* (Betulaceae)

# JAPANESE HORNBEAM

**This is a wide-spreading**, relatively small tree, which is grown for its ornamental foliage. It is native to Japan and was introduced into western cultivation in 1895.

The shoot is thin but rough to the touch. Leaves are glossy deep green on the upper surface and paler on the underside. They have up to 24 pairs of prominent parallel veins, which give the leaves a corrugated appearance. The leaf margin is sharply toothed, with every third tooth pointing upwards. Male and female flowers are borne in drooping catkins on the same tree. The female flowers are green and relatively small. They develop into a hanging, bunched cluster of bracts, which resembles the fruit of *Ostrya*. Positioned beneath the bracts is the seed.

**Oriental hornbeam**
This small, bushy tree (*Carpinus orientalis*) has smaller leaves. Its seeds, attached to a single bract, are not borne in clusters.

**PROFILE**

- Up to 25 m (80 ft)
- 15 m (50 ft)
- Deciduous
- Alternate simple
- S.E. Europe, W. Asia

**Unripe fruit and leaf**
The leaves are broadly oval but heart-shaped at the base. The fruit when unripe is a green husk.

*irregular serrations around leaf margin*

*leaf up to 10 cm (4 in) wide*

*fruit covered in long bristles*

**FEATURES**

**Bark** Light grey-brown; turns distinctly corky in maturity

**Male flowers**
Up to 7.5 cm (3 in) long

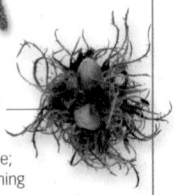

*edible, brown nut*

**Fruit** Edible; green ripening to brown

*Corylus colurna* (Betulaceae)

# TURKISH HAZEL

**This magnificent tree** is native to southeastern Europe and western Asia. It was introduced into cultivation in western Europe, including Britain, in the 16th century, and has been widely planted in parks and gardens since then. With its symmetrical, broadly conical form, it is ideally suited as an avenue or street tree.

The leaves have a dark green upper surface and are paler on the underside. Each leaf is irregularly serrated, and can grow up to 15 cm (6 in) long. In autumn, they turn a rich yellow before falling. Male and female flowers are carried in separate catkins on the same tree. Pendulous male flowers are yellow, while the smaller female catkins are red.

**Stately form**
In cultivation, the Turkish hazel normally has a short, straight trunk with a pyramid-shaped canopy.

## PROFILE

- Up to 20m (70ft)
- 15m (50ft)
- Deciduous
- Alternate simple
- S. Europe, W. Asia

**Pendulous fruit and leaves**
The fruit forms in hop-like clusters, with each husk containing a nut-like seed. The thick, stiff leaves have 12 to 15 pairs of veins.

*dark, glossy green upper surface of leaf*

*ovate leaf, 8–13cm (3–5in) long*

*double-toothed leaf margin*

*bladder-like, flat husk*

*fruit up to 5cm (2in) long*

## FEATURES

**Bark** Grey-brown; fissures into irregular loose flakes

*male flower up to 10cm (4in) long*

**Flowers** Male and female borne in catkins on the same tree

*Ostrya carpinifolia* (Betulaceae)

# HOP HORNBEAM

**This round-headed, broadly** spreading tree is native to southern Europe and western Asia. The name *Ostrya* is derived from the Greek word *ostrua*, which means "bone-like", referring to its hard, heavy timber. It was introduced into cultivation in 1724, and is admired for its autumn colours. Occasionally, the hop hornbeam produces long horizontal branches, which seem to defy gravity before they eventually need to be propped up.

Smooth at first, the bark cracks in flakes, which fall to reveal orange patches beneath. The leaves resemble those of the common hornbeam (p.184), and are pale green on the underside, with hairs in the vein axils (where the veins meet the midrib). They turn a clear bright yellow before falling in autumn.

**Ironwood**
This smaller tree (*Ostrya virginiana*) has hairy shoots and leaves with fewer veins.

**Leaves and flowers**
Fragrant flowers are borne in clusters of up to 10 in early to midsummer. The leaves vary from heart-shaped to almost rounded.

*pale green, leaf-like bract, up to 10 cm (4 in) long*

*leaf 5–7.5 cm (2–3 in) long*

*serrated leaf tapers abruptly to blunt tip*

*fragrant yellow flower, borne in drooping clusters*

**PROFILE**

- Up to 30 m (100 ft)
- Up to 20 m (70 ft)
- Deciduous
- Alternate simple
- Europe

*Tilia cordata* (Malvaceae)

# SMALL-LEAVED LIME

**Endemic to Europe, from Portugal** east to the Caucasus, this broadly columnar tree is known to have been regularly coppiced (trimmed back to stumps) in the past. When found growing wild in woodland, it is a good indicator that the woodland is old or even ancient. Some coppiced trees are believed to be over 2,000 years old.

The bark is silver-grey and smooth, becoming fissured from around 40 years of age. The inner bark, known as bast, is very fibrous and was often woven to make rope. Cordate, or heart-shaped, leaves are glossy green on the upper surface and blue-green on the underside, with some hairs in the vein axils. They turn yellow in autumn before falling. The flowers are accompanied by a narrow bract and develop into rounded fruits, up to 1 cm (½ in) wide. Each fruit has a green-grey felt-like surface and clusters are attached to the tree by a long stalk.

**Crimean lime (*Tilia* x *euchlora*)** This tree is easily distinguished from the small-leaved lime by its smaller size, pendulous lower branches, and glossy, deep green leaves.

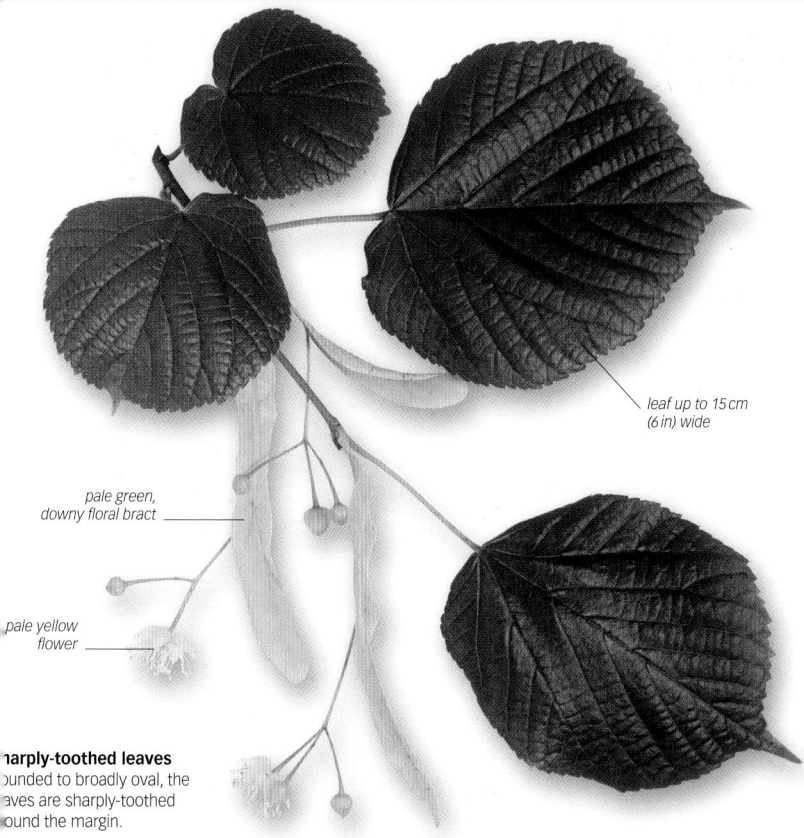


**harply-toothed leaves**
ounded to broadly oval, the
aves are sharply-toothed
ound the margin.

**PROFILE**

- Up to 30 m (100 ft)
- Up to 15 m (50 ft)
- Deciduous
- Alternate simple
- Europe, S.W. Asia

*Tilia platyphyllos* (Malvaceae)

# LARGE-LEAVED LIME

**Also known as the broad-leaved lime**, this large, broadly columnar ornamental tree has a round-domed canopy, a long, straight trunk, and graceful, arching branches. It is native to Europe and southwest Asia, and is commonly planted in parks and along avenues throughout this region.

The smooth, light grey bark develops some shallow fissures in maturity. Its leaves, large for this genus, are slightly hairy and deep green on the upper surface and light green on the underside, with dense hairs along the midrib and in the vein axils. The leaf stalks are covered in soft white hairs. Fragrant flowers are produced in pendulous clusters of up to six in early summer. A bract, up to 12.5 cm (5 in) long and 1.5 cm (½ in) wide, occurs alongside each flower cluster. The fruit is a pale green, downy nutlet borne on a long stalk in late summer.

**Japanese lime (*Tilia japonica*)** This tree has smaller leaves up to 8 cm (3 in) long. They are narrower, more heart-shaped at the base, and have a longer drawn-out tip.

**Foliage and flowers**
The leaves have sharply toothed margins and pointed tips. Fragrant flowers are borne in pendulous clusters of up to 10.

*broadly ovate leaf, heart-shaped at base*

*leaf up to 10cm (4 long and wide*

*yellow flower borne in small, drooping cluster*

*pale green, linear flower bract*

**PROFILE**

- 30–40m (100–130ft)
- Up to 15m (50ft)
- Deciduous
- Alternate simple
- Europe

**FEATURES**

**Fruit** Pea-like, light green; emerge in mid- to late summer

*Tilia* x *europaea* (Malvaceae)

# COMMON LIME

**Also known as the European lime**, this large, broadly columnar tree is a hybrid between the small-leaved lime (p.188) and the large-leaved lime (p.189). It is found naturally wherever the ranges of the two parents overlap – which is across most of Europe. The tree does not have the elegance of either parent and produces unsightly suckers around the base of its trun It is also prone to aphid attack, which results in a coatir of sticky aphid excrement known as honeydew.

The bark is grey to grey-brown, smooth when young, developing shallow, vertical fissures in maturity The leaves are dull dark green on the upper surface and pale green on the underside, with tufts of hairs in the main vein axils (where the veins meet the midrib). Th flowers, carried alongside a pale green bract in early summer, are followed by rounded fruit.

**Henry's lime (*Tilia henryana*)** This slow-growing Chinese lime has large leaves, which have prominent bristle-like teeth along the margins.

## PROFILE

- 20–30 m (70–100 ft)
- Up to 15 m (50 ft)
- Deciduous
- Alternate simple
- Switzerland

**Leaves and flowers**
This tree bears rounded to broadly ovate leaves. Small, strongly scented flowers are produced in pendant clusters in summer.

*lax stalk, up to 12 cm (5 in) long*

*white-felted underside of leaf*

*pale green flower bract*

*leaf up to 10 cm (4 in) long, 7.5 cm (3 in) wide*

*bud opens to creamy yellow flower*

## FEATURES

**Fruit** Rounded, light green, and pea-like

*Tilia tomentosa* 'Petiolaris' (Malvaceae)

# WEEPING SILVER LIME

**One of the most ornamental** of large trees, the weeping silver lime has a broadly columnar habit. Its long, arching branches are often likened to the vaulted ceiling of a cathedral. The weeping silver lime is a cultivar of silver lime (*Tilia tomentosa*), and is believed to have been first raised in Switzerland in the mid-1800s.

The bark is slate-grey, smooth when young, developing vertical fissures in maturity. Quite often, a graft union is evident as a slight swelling on the trunk between 2 m (6 ft) and 5 m (15 ft) from the ground. Weeping shoots hang from arching branches and carry leaves that have a dark green upper surface and a white-felted underside. The leaves flash a distinctive white and green as they flutter in the breeze.

**Oliver's lime**
This tree (*Tilia oliveri*) has a less weeping habit, hairless shoots, and a light silver-grey bark.

**Leaves and flowers**
The American basswood has large leaves, more than 25 cm (10 in) long and 20 cm (8 in) wide. Fragrant flowers bloom in early summer in pendulous clusters.

**PROFILE**

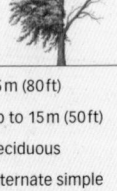

- 25 m (80 ft)
- Up to 15 m (50 ft)
- Deciduous
- Alternate simple
- E. North America

*Tilia americana* (Malvaceae)

# AMERICAN BASSWOOD

**Also known as American lime**, this tree is native to eastern North America, from New Brunswick, Canada, south to Tennessee and Arkansas, USA. "Bass" refers to the inner bark, which is extremely fibrous. Early European settlers would peel off strips of the bark and weave it into coarse rope. The tree is cultivated both within and outside North America, and was introduced into Europe in 1752.

The bark is grey-brown and smooth at first, becoming rough and corky, with long scaly ridges in maturity. The leaves, which feel slightly rough to the touch, are broadl ovate, sometimes almost rounded, with irregularly serrated leaf margins. Slightly shiny on the upper surfac the leaves are pale green underneath, with some tufts c hair in the vein axils. In winter, buds are a distinctive ligh green colour. The fruit is a woody, rounded drupe, covered in grey-brown hairs.

**Mongolian lime (*Tilia mongolica*)** Apart from its more compac rounded habit and smaller size, this tree also has smaller leaves, up to 7.5 cm (3 in) long, carried on red stalks.

immature male catkin emerges from leaf axil

bronze-coloured young leaf

male catkin up to 5 cm (2 in) long

**PROFILE**

- Up to 20 m (70 ft)
- Up to 15 m (50 ft)
- Deciduous
- Alternate simple
- Europe, N. Africa, N. Asia

**en flowers**
e and female flowers are borne ooping grey catkins on separate s, before the leaves emerge in winter or early spring.

**FEATURES**

**eaves** Broadly ovate to ounded, three-veined; borne n slender, flattened leaf stalks

*Populus tremula* (Salicaceae)

# ASPEN

**Also known as the European aspen**, this medium-sized deciduous tree is native to the whole of Europe and northern Asia, and is also indigenous to parts of North Africa. Its leaves tremble and quiver in the slightest breeze, hence its species name *tremula*.

Aspen is conical when young, becoming broadly spreading with age. It has light and dark grey, smooth bark, which becomes ridged at the base in maturity. Young leaves emerge in spring, fading to dull green with three prominent yellow-green veins at the base. They have a dark green upper surface and a pale grey-green underside. In late spring, tiny seeds covered in white, cottony hairs are released from green, capsule-like fruit. The hairs on the seeds help carry them in the air for some distance.

**Balsam poplar (*Populus balsamifera*)** An erect-branched habit and a shorter leaf petiole distinguish this tree from the aspen. In spring, the leaves emit a strong balsam-like fragrance.

ovate to triangular lea

slender, flattened petiole (leaf stalk)

leaf up to 8 cm (3 in) long and wide

**Glossy leaves**
Bronze-orange when new, leaves turn deep green on the upper surface. On the underside, they are pale sage-green with silver-grey down.

## PROFILE

- Up to 30 m (100 ft)
- Up to 25 m (80 ft)
- Deciduous
- Alternate simple
- W. Asia, Europe

## FEATURES

**Bark** Pale grey, dark, diamond-shaped pattern; develops large burrs with age

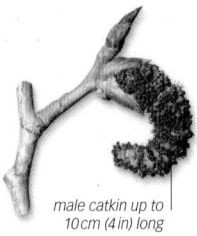


**Male flowers** Grey with red anthers; borne in drooping catkins in early spring

*Populus nigra* (Salicaceae)

# BLACK POPLAR

**This large, deciduous tree** is native to the whole of western Asia and Europe. It is a broadly spreading tree with long heavy branches. The black poplar inhabits riv valleys and damp areas throughout its natural range, bu in western Europe, including parts of the British Isles, it gives way to the Atlantic subspecies *P. nigra* subsp. *betulifolia,* which has downy shoots and young leaves.

The leaves emerge from large, conical, shiny buds, which smell of balsam when crushed. Male and female flowers are borne on separate trees. In late spring, tiny seeds, covered in white, cotton-wool-like hairs, are released from green fruit. They may be carried in the air for some distance.

**Hybrid poplar**
This tree (*P.* x *canadensi* bears lighter branches and grows faster than the black poplar.

**vate leaves**
ne Lombardy poplar bears triangular diamond-shaped leaves, carried on flattened, yellow-green petiole (leaf alk), up to 2.5 cm (1 in) long.

**PROFILE**

- Up to 30 m (100 ft)
- Up to 25 m (80 ft)
- Deciduous
- Alternate simple
- Europe, W. Asia

*Populus nigra* 'Italica' (Salicaceae)

# LOMBARDY POPLAR

**This narrowly columnar tree** is one of the most easily recognizable of all trees because of its slender, column-like outline and strongly ascending branching. It is not a true species but a distinctive male variety of the black poplar (p.194). This tree is believed to have naturally occurred in northern Italy in the early 1700s. Since then it has been widely propagated from cuttings, and is now one of the most common trees planted throughout the temperate world, especially in western Europe.

The bark is dark grey, with fluting and buttressing towards the trunk's base. The leaves are glossy bright green on the upper surface, with regular small, curved teeth along the leaf margins. Male catkins are up to 7.5 cm (3 in) long, deep red, turning red and yellow when shedding pollen in mid-spring. This tree does not produce female flowers.

**Chinese balsam poplar (*Populus szechuanica* var. *tibetica*)**
This poplar has a broadly columnar habit and large, broadly ovate leaves, which have a crimson midrib.

**PROFILE**

- Up to 20m (70ft)
- Up to 10m (30ft)
- Deciduous
- Alternate simple
- C. China

**Heart-shaped leaves**
The broadly ovate to heart-shaped leathery leaves have conspicuous red leaf stalks.

*leaf up to 35cm (14in) long, 20cm (8in) wide*

*bright green upper surface of leaf*

*shallow serration around leaf margin*

*stout, angled twig, covered in downy hairs*

**FEATURES**

**Bark** Grey-brown, smooth; becomes fissured in maturity

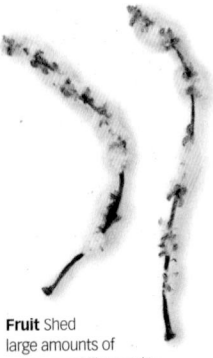

**Fruit** Shed large amounts of cotton-wool-like seeds

*Populus lasiocarpa* (Salicaceae)

# CHINESE NECKLACE POPLAR

**This broad-spreading tree** has among the largest leaves of any poplar. It tends to be open and gangly, with long-spreading, widely spaced branches, and can appear ungainly in winter, when bare.

In autumn, the leaves turn yellow, then crisp brown, making a clattering sound on windy days. In spring, stiff, yellow-green male and female flowers emerge in catkins borne on separate trees. The name "necklace" refers to the fruit, which appear as long, pendulous, green seed capsules in midsummer. These fruit ripen in late summer and release seeds to be dispersed by the wind.

**Black cottonwood**
This taller, fast-growing tree (*Populus trichocarpa*) has smaller leaves that smell of balsam.

## PROFILE

- Up to 26m (85ft)
- Up to 20m (70ft)
- Deciduous
- Alternate simple
- Europe (except British Isles), W. Asia, N. Africa

**Lobed leaves**
White poplar leaves vary in shape. Some are ovate and irregularly toothed, borne on short shoots.

*leaf up to 10cm (4in) long, 8cm (3in) wide*

*shiny, dark grey-green upper surface*

## FEATURES

**Bark** Light grey, pitted with small, black, diamond-shaped patches when young

*dense cover of white hairs on underside of leaf*

**Leaves** Variously shaped; can be maple-like, borne on vigorous shoots

*Populus alba* (Salicaceae)

# WHITE POPLAR

**This large, broadly conical tree** is often cultivated in coastal locations because of its ability to cope with onshore winds and salt spray. It is also planted alongside motorways and highways, where it withstands atmospheric pollution quite well.

The bark is coarsely cracked with vertical fissures in maturity. The leaves, borne alternately, are attached to the shoots by a 4cm- (1½in-) long hairy petiole (leaf stalk). Male and female flowers are borne on separate catkins before the leaves open. Male catkins are crimson and grey while the female are pale green, both up to 8cm (3in) long. The fruit is a green capsule, which opens to release seeds covered in fluffy, white hairs.

**Grey poplar**
This hybrid (*Populus* x *canescens*) has leaves with a greenish white, felt-like cover on the underside.

**PROFILE**

- Up to 25 m (80 ft)
- Up to 20 m (70 ft)
- Deciduous
- Alternate simple
- Europe, Asia

**Crack willow leaves**
Dark glossy green leaves are alternately arranged along stems. The leaves taper to a fine point.

*lanceolate leaf, up to 15 cm (6 in) long, 2.5 cm (1 in) wide*

*leaf tapers to fine point*

**FEATURES**

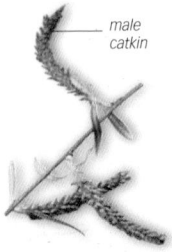


**Flowers** Lack petals; borne in catkins on separate trees; male are yellow, females green

*Salix fragilis* (Salicaceae)

# CRACK WILLOW

**This broadly spreading tree** is one of the largest willows. Often found growing alongside rivers and streams, it takes its name from the distinctive crack heard when a twig is snapped off the tree. The wood is brittle, and large branches are often broken off by high winds. The branches quite often take root where they touch the ground, and eventually another tree is formed, genetically the same as the parent.

The bark is dull grey, becoming heavily fissured and cracked from a relatively early age. Some stems may be as much as 2 m (6 ft) in diameter. The shoots are pale orange and conspicuous in late winter before new leaves appear. The leaves are lanceolate, tapering to a fine point. They are glossy dark green on the upper surface, with a raised central midrib, and blue-green on the underside. Small male and female flowers are borne in catkins.

**Grey sallow (*Salix cinerea*)** This is a much smaller tree than the crack willow. It can also be distinguished from the latter by its hairy, obovate leaves and stout, hairy twigs.

**PROFILE**



- Up to 25 m (80 ft)
- Up to 20 m (70 ft)
- Deciduous
- Alternate simple
- Europe, W. Asia

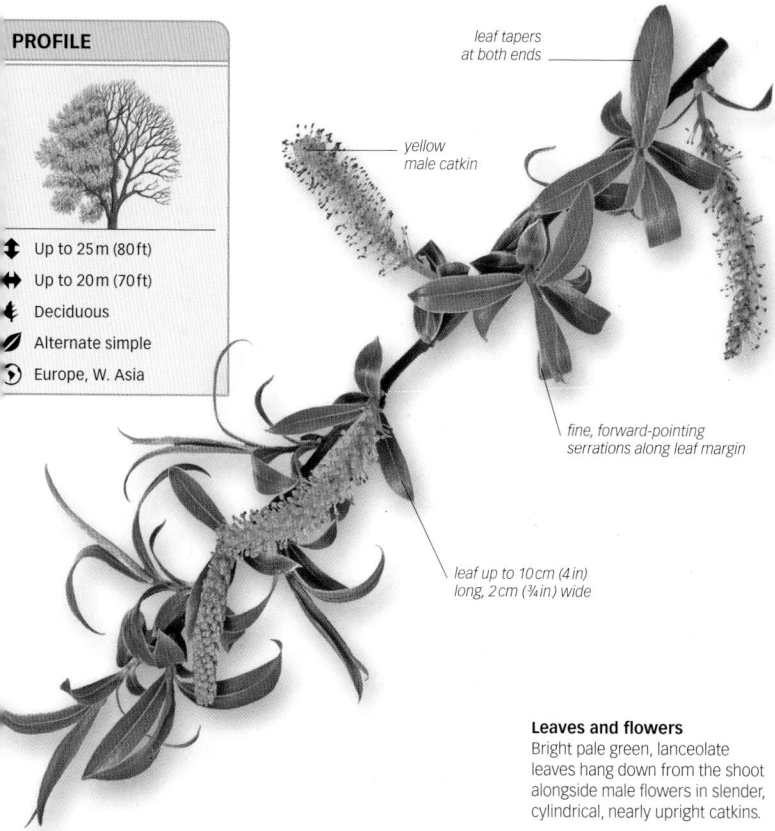


**Leaves and flowers**
Bright pale green, lanceolate leaves hang down from the shoot alongside male flowers in slender, cylindrical, nearly upright catkins.

**FEATURES**

**Bark** Brown-grey; develops coarse, vertical fissures with age

**Shoots** Slender, light grey-pink to olive-brown

*Salix alba* (Salicaceae)

# WHITE WILLOW

**A broadly columnar tree**, the white willow is native across Europe and western Asia. This medium-sized tree thrives in damp soils, and is normally found growing alongside rivers and near water meadows.

A dense coating of white hairs on the leaves gives this tree a silvery appearance, particularly when the leaves are stirred by the wind. Young leaves are coated with silver hairs on both sides; mature leaves retain hairs on the underside. Both male and female flowers are clustered in catkins on separate trees. They grow up to 6 cm (2½ in) long in spring. Green female flowers soon become fluffy with white-haired seeds.

**Bay willow**
This tree (*Salix pentrandra*) has olive-green shoots and glossy green leaves, which are aromatic when crushed.

## PROFILE



- Up to 25m (80ft)
- Up to 15m (50ft)
- Deciduous
- Alternate simple
- China

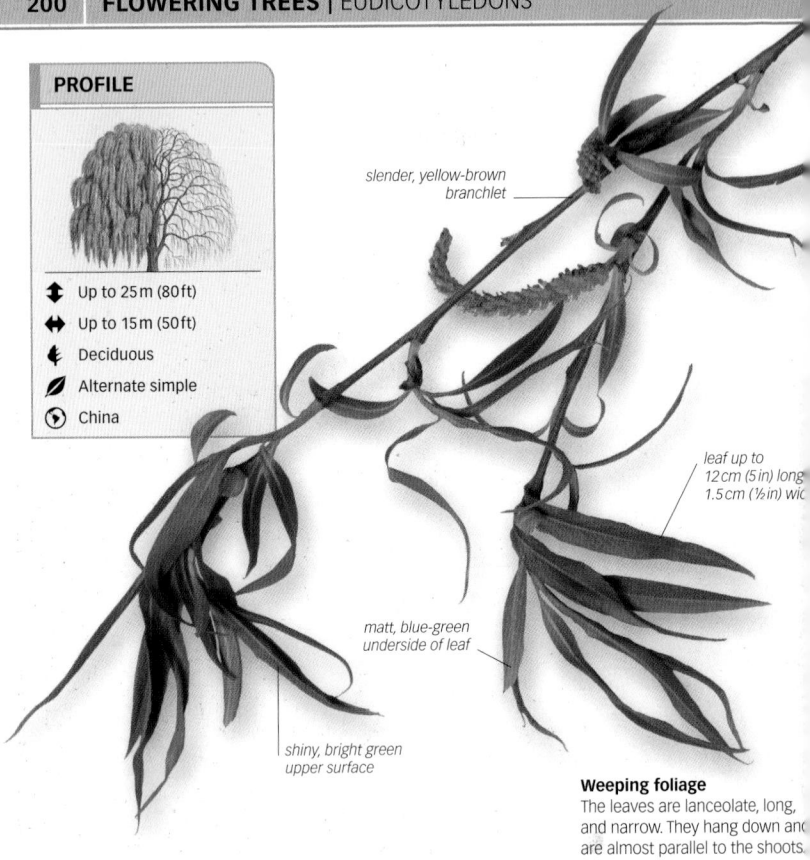


**Weeping foliage**
The leaves are lanceolate, long, and narrow. They hang down and are almost parallel to the shoots.

## FEATURES

**Bark** Cracked and vertically fissured, particularly in old age

**Male flowers**
Yellow-green, appear with young leaves in spring in slender catkins

*Salix babylonica* (Salicaceae)

# WEEPING WILLOW

**One of the best-known trees** of the temperate world, the weeping willow is commonly planted alongside rivers and lakes. It was introduced into the West towards the end of the 17th century and has long been cultivated elsewhere. It is a wide-spreading, medium-sized tree with a pendulous habit, featuring a wide head of relatively level branches from which long, pendulous branchlets descend almost vertically.

The leaves have shallow serrations along the margins. Male and female flowers are borne in separate trees. In recent years, this tree has been superseded by *Salix* x *sepulcralis* 'Chrysocoma' (p.203), which is a cultivar of a hybrid between the weeping willow (p.200) and the white willow (p.199). The hybrid has brighter yellow twigs and shoots, but is prone to attack from a canker disease, which produces an open wound.

**Dragon's claw willow (*Salix babylonica* var. *pekinensis* 'Tortuosa')** Unlike the weeping willow, this smaller columnar tree, up to 10m (30ft) tall, has twisted branches and twigs.

## PROFILE

- Up to 10m (30ft)
- Up to 10m (30ft)
- Deciduous
- Alternate simple
- Europe, W. Asia

**Goat willow catkins**
This tree bears male flowers in golden catkins. Soft, silvery, female catkins known as pussy willow are borne separately on female trees.

*tiny golden male flowers in catkins*

## FEATURES

**Bark** Dull grey; smooth, with minor fissures in maturity

**Leaves** Vary from oval to obovate or lanceolate, up to 10cm (4in) long

*Salix caprea* (Salicaceae)

# GOAT WILLOW

**Also known as pussy willow**, this small, broadly spreading tree sometimes resembles a large shrub of bushy habit. It seldom grows more than 10m (30ft) tall. The goat willow is native to the whole of Europe and western Asia and is found on all soil types in both upland and lowland regions. It produces a prolific amount of seed, which is dispersed by the wind and can easily colonize bare or cultivated land some distance from the tree.

The tree's young shoots are covered in fine grey down. The leaves have a dull green and wrinkled upper surface and a grey-green underside, with dense grey hairs. Male and female flowers are borne in catkins on separate trees in spring. The fruit is a grey-green capsule covered in soft down, which opens to release numerous tiny, airborne seeds.

**Common osier (*Salix viminalis*)** This tree is easily distinguished from the goat willow by its more shrubby habit with long, upright stems and longer, narrower leaves.

## PROFILE

- Up to 10m (30ft)
- Up to 8m (25ft)
- Deciduous
- Alternate simple
- W. and S. Europe, W. Asia, Himalayas

**Violet willow leaves**
The leaves are shiny dark green on the upper surface and glaucous blue-green on the underside, with a shallowly serrated margin.

## FEATURES

**Bark** Dark, almost purple-black; relatively smooth on older stems and trunks

**Male flowers** Borne in catkins, up to 5cm (2in) long

*Salix daphnoides* (Salicaceae)

# VIOLET WILLOW

**This broadly spreading tree** is native to western and southern Europe, and western Asia, including the Himalayan region. It has long been cultivated for its plum- or violet-coloured shoots which, when young, are covered with attractive white bloom. In cultivation, these trees are often coppiced every two to three years, so that multiple violet stems develop, growing up to 2–3m (6–10ft) tall. This is particularly effective in winter, when the stems are not masked by the foliage.

The lanceolate leaves remain green on the tree well into late autumn before falling. The leaf petiole is flushed crimson. White male catkins appear in early spring before the leaves emerge, becoming bright yellow as they mature. Grey-green female flowers are shorter and slender, ripening to release seed-bearing white "fluff" in late spring.

**Magnificent willow (*Salix magnifica*)** Unlike the violet willow this tree has oval or obovate magnolia-shaped leaves. It also bears attractive erect red and yellow catkins.

**Leaves and flowers**
The golden weeping willow bears leaves on long, pendulous, golden yellow secondary branches. The flowers, borne in catkins, appear along with leaves in mid-spring.

*leaf ends in tapered point*

*golden yellow shoot*

*bright yellow catkin*

**PROFILE**

- 20 m (70 ft)
- Up to 20 m (70 ft)
- Deciduous
- Alternate simple
- W. Asia

**FEATURES**

**Leaves** Lanceolate, slender; up to 13 cm (5 in) long, 2.5 cm (1 in) wide

*Salix* x *sepulcralis* 'Chrysocoma' (Salicaceae)

# GOLDEN WEEPING WILLOW

**A hybrid between** the white willow (p.199) and the weeping willow (p.200), this tree developed naturally where the ranges of the two species met in western Asia. Its cultivated form 'Chrysocoma' has been propagated for its vibrant golden shoots and graceful pendulous habit and is often seen growing alongside rivers and lakes. This broadly spreading tree has ascending primary branches, which support drooping secondary branches reaching the ground.

The bark is pale grey-brown with shallow corky fissures. Shoots and young twigs are golden yellow, and are best seen in winter when low sunlight hits the crown. Both male and female flowers are usually borne in the same catkin, although occasionally the catkins are made up of all male flowers.

***Salix fargesii*** This tree is distinguished by its small stature, red stems and leaf buds, and shiny mahogany-coloured bark.

## PROFILE

- 30–40m (100–130ft)
- Up to 30m (100ft)
- Deciduous
- Alternate simple
- Europe

**Lobed leaves**
The 3–5 lobed leaves of the London plane are glossy, dark green, and marked by conspicuous yellow veins.

*palmate leaf, up to 20cm (8in) lo 25cm (10in) wic*

*large, toothed lob*

*yellow veins usually meet near leaf base*

*green fruit, ripens to brown*

*stalk bears up to four fruit*

## FEATURES

**Bark** Light brown; flakes in large patches with age, exposing creamy patches

**Flowers** Red female and yellow male flowers borne on same tree

*Platanus* x *acerifolia* (Platanaceae)

# LONDON PLANE

**Among the most common trees** in towns and cities across the temperate world, the sprawling London plane is sometimes considered to be a form of the oriental plane (p.205). The general consensus is that it is an artificially created hybrid between the oriental plane and the American buttonwood (p.206) that emerged sometim before 1663. It can withstand both atmospheric pollution and pruning, and is thus commonly found in many cities.

Its bark is light brown, flaking in irregular scales. The leaves have a bright green upper surface but are paler on the underside, with conspicuous yellow veins and rusty hairs. The fruit are mace-like, bristly spheres that remain attached to the tree well after the leaves have fallen.

**Majestic tree**
The London plane is a larg broadly columnar, hybrid tree of garden origin, neve found growing in the wild.

**PROFILE**

- Over 30m (100ft)
- Up to 30m (100ft)
- Deciduous
- Alternate simple
- E. Mediterranean

*leaf up to 20cm (8in) long, 25cm (10in) wide*

*yellow-green stalk, up to 7.5cm (3in) long*

*globular, mace-like fruit, 2.5cm (1in) wide*

**eply lobed leaves**
e glossy, deep green leaves of
oriental plane are deeply cut
o five slender lobes. Globular fruit
borne on pendulous stalks.

**FEATURES**

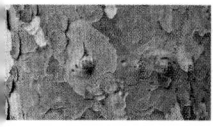

**Bark** Buff-grey; flakes to reveal cream-pink patches

*Platanus orientalis* (Platanaceae)

# ORIENTAL PLANE

**Native to the eastern Mediterranean**, the oriental plane is one of the largest temperate deciduous trees, with a trunk that can exceed 6m (20ft) in girth. It is also a long-lived tree – a tree on the Greek island of Kos is said to be of the time of Hippocrates, "the father of medicine".

The palmate leaves are shiny, rich green on the upper surface and pale green on the underside, with brown hairs along pronounced veins. In autumn, they turn bright yellow and then dull gold before falling. Once on the ground, they take a long time to decompose. In late spring, the oriental plane bears tiny flowers in pendulous, rounded clusters. They are followed by fruit attached in clusters of two to six on pendulous stalks. These remain on the tree well into winter.

**Large canopy**
The oriental plane has a wide-spreading canopy made up of long and large-limbed branches.

**PROFILE**

- Up to 35 m (120 ft)
- Up to 30 m (100 ft)
- Deciduous
- Alternate simple
- North America

**Palmately lobed leaves**
The leaves have three angular, pointed lobes. They have a sharply toothed margin with hair-covered veins on the underside.

**FEATURES**

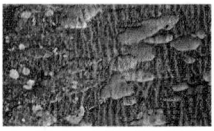

**Bark** Pale grey-brown trunk, smooth; flaking to reveal fresh, cream-coloured bark beneath

*Platanus occidentalis* (Platanaceae)

# BUTTONWOOD

**Also known as American sycamore**, this broadly spreading, large tree is native to North America where it grows into a magnificent specimen with a broad, open crown, and a trunk up to 5 m (15 ft) in diameter. It is favoured for planting in cities and parks, and provides shade in the summer months. When cultivated outside of North America, it seldom obtains the same noble stature, and often does not become well established. As with all members of the *Platanus* genus, it is tolerant of atmospheric pollution.

Unlike the bark on the trunk, the branches are blue-white, thin, and smooth. The leaves are bright, glossy green on the upper surface and pale green on the underside. New leaves are coated in soft, white down. Yellow male flowers and reddish female flowers appear in separate, rounded clusters on the same tree in late spring. The mace-like fruit are up to 2.5 cm (1 in) wide. They hang singly on thin stalks. Green when young, the fruit turn pink and then brown when ripe.

## PROFILE

- Up to 45 m (150 ft)
- Up to 15 m (50 ft)
- Deciduous
- Alternate simple
- E. USA, C. America

**Leaves and fruit**
Sweetgum leaves are palmately lobed and slightly toothed around the margin. The fruit is pendulous, long-stalked, and bristly.

*tapering leaf lobe*

*leaf up to 15 cm (6 in) long and wide*

## FEATURES

**Bark** Dark brown, smooth; becomes fissured into long vertical ridges with age

**Leaves** Change colour from orange, through bright red to purple in autumn

*Liquidambar styraciflua* (Hamamelidaceae)

# SWEETGUM

**Also known as satinwood**, this tree is native to the east coast of the USA and also parts of Central America. The sweetgum tree is one of the main constituents of the deciduous hardwood forests of North America. Its leaf shape can be confused with maple, a member of the *Acer* genus; however, maple leaves are borne in opposite pairs on a smooth shoot, whereas the leaves of the sweetgum are alternately positioned on corky shoots.

The leaves display five to seven tapering lobes, where the central lobe is normally the largest. Small, round, green-yellow male and female flowers appear in late spring. The fruit is up to 4 cm (1 ½ in) wide, borne in clusters, green ripening to brown.

**Changing habit**
The sweetgum has a broadly conical shape when young, but develops a rounded habit with age.

**Lobed leaves**
The palmate leaves are cut into five three-lobed sections. They are deep matt green on the upper surface, with a paler underside.

*deeply cut oblong lobe*

*leaf up to 8cm (3in) long and wide*

*slender petiole (leaf stalk)*

**PROFILE**

- Up to 25m (80ft)
- Up to 5m (15ft)
- Deciduous
- Alternate simple
- S.W. Turkey

**FEATURES**

**Bark** Orange-brown, thick; cracks with age into small, irregular-shaped plates

**Leaves** Turn from orange to red to gold in autumn

*Liquidambar orientalis* (Hamamelidaceae)

# ORIENTAL SWEETGUM

**This tree is commonly thought** of as the Asian version of the American sweetgum (p.207). However, oriental sweetgum is native to southwest Turkey and therefore not strictly Asian at all. In the wild, it is a medium-sized, broadly conical tree. In cultivation, it rarely attains half this size and is more bush-like in its habit. However, what it lacks in stature, it makes up for by providing some of the finest autumn leaf colours of any tree. The tree's resin has been used medicinally for over 700 years.

The leaves have five deeply cut lobes, the central lobe being the largest. Both male and female flowers are yellow-green and very small. They are borne separately on the same tree in spring. The rounded, pendulous fruit, up to 2.5cm (1in) long, are similar to those of the sweetgum (p.207). The fruit hang by a stalk up to 5cm (2in) long.

**Chinese sweetgum (*Liquidambar formosana*)** This species has duller, broader, green leaves with three to five lobes. They are more angular and hairier on the underside and the petiole (leaf stalk

## PROFILE



- Up to 25 m (80 ft)
- Up to 15 m (50 ft)
- Deciduous
- Alternate simple
- E. and S. North America

**Lustrous leaves**
The glossy leaves of the black tupelo are bright green on the upper surface and matt blue-green on the underside. Tiny flowers lie hidden amidst the leaves.

## FEATURES

**Bark** Smooth, dark grey; cracks and fissures into rough square plates in maturity

**Leaves** Turn yellow-orange to burgundy red in autumn

*Nyssa sylvatica* (Cornaceae)

# BLACK TUPELO

**Also known as black gum** or sour gum, black tupelo is native to eastern and southern North America from Ontario, Canada, in the north to New Mexico, USA, in the south. Since its discovery by Europeans in 1750, it has been extensively cultivated elsewhere and is often found in parks, gardens, and arboreta.

Both male and female flowers are small, green, and hard to see against the leaves. They are borne in long-stalked clusters on the same tree in summer. The edible fruit is a blueberry-coloured, egg-shaped, glossy berry, up to 1.5 cm (½ in) long. Although edible, the fruit is not particularly palatable, being rather sour, hence its alternative name – sour gum.

**Slender branches**
The black tupelo has slender, spreading branches and a broadly conical to columnar crown.

**PROFILE**



- 6–15 m (20–50 ft)
- Up to 11 m (35 ft)
- Deciduous
- Alternate simple
- C. China

**Summer foliage**
The leaves are shiny green on the upper surface and matt, pale green on the underside.

**FEATURES**

**Bark** Grey-brown, smooth; cracks and flakes with age

*Nyssa sinensis* (Cornaceae)

# CHINESE TUPELO

**This small, broadly conical tree** is related to both the black tupelo (p.209) and the water tupelo (*Nyssa aquatica*). It is indigenous to central China, where it grows in woodland in the shade of other trees, and was introduced into western cultivation in 1902.

The leaves emerge green-red from winter buds, but the red quickly fades to deep green. They turn red, orange, and yellow in autumn. The underside of the leaves have hairs on the margins and midrib. Male and female flowers are borne on the same tree in summer, in separate clusters, around leaf axils. They are five-petalled, small, and green, which makes them difficult to see among the foliage. The fruit is a purple-blue, egg-shaped berry up to 2.5 cm (1 in) long.

**Showy autumn foliage**
The Chinese tupelo is a beautiful sight in autumn, when the leaves turn a striking mix of colours.

## PROFILE

- 10–20m (30–70ft)
- Up to 15m (50ft)
- Deciduous
- Alternate simple
- Iran, E. Caucasus

**Bright green leaves**
The ovate, at times elliptic, leaves are glossy bright green on the upper surface, and dull green, with hairs, on the underside.

*shallowly toothed leaf margin*

*leaf 12cm (5in) long, 6cm (2½in) wide*

## FEATURES

*colourful autumn foliage*

**Leaves** Turn yellow, orange, red, and purple in autumn

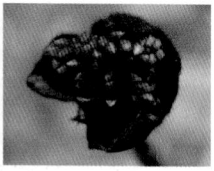

**Flowers** Small clusters of ruby-red anthers; appear on bare branches in winter

*Parrotia persica* (Hamamalidaceae)

# PERSIAN IRONWOOD

**Persian ironwood is a popular tree** in cultivation because of its beautiful autumn leaf colour. While in the wild it grows more upright, reaching 20m (70ft) tall, in cultivation, it is broadly spreading, occasionally reaching 15m (50ft) in height, and almost as much in width. It is named after German scientist and climber F. W. Parrot, who made the first European ascent of Mount Ararat in Turkey in 1829. In cultivation, the branches of this tree form an interlacing network reaching down to the ground, making it difficult to walk beneath the canopy.

The bark is dark brown and smooth. It flakes in patches to reveal light fawn-coloured new bark. Leaves often display bronze-red margins when young. They have wavy margins near the tips. Flowers are small and petalless with red anthers. The fruit is a small, nut-like, brown capsule, up to 1cm (½in) wide.

**X *Sycoparrotia semidecidua*** This hybrid between *Sycopsis* and *Parrotia* has leaves that are ovate, lighter green, and thinner than *Sycopsis*. Its flowers are orange-red, with yellow anthers.

## PROFILE

- 18–30m (60–100ft)
- Up to 20m (70ft)
- Deciduous
- Opposite simple or alternate simple
- Japan, W. China

**Cordate leaves**
The soft, thin leaves are heart-shaped, finely toothed around the margin, and as wide as they are long.

*shallowly toothed marg*

*seed pod*

*petiole up to 2.5cm (1in) long*

*leaf up to 7cm (3in) long and wide*

## FEATURES

**Bark** Grey-brown, smooth; becomes shallowly fissured with vertical cracks in maturity

**Leaves** Orange to apricot-flushed red or sulphur yellow in autumn

*Cercidiphyllum japonicum* (Cercidiphyllaceae)

# KATSURA TREE

**Katsura is one of the** most attractive deciduous trees in the northern hemisphere. It is one of the two species in the family Cercidiphyllaceae, the other being *Cercidiphyllum magnificum*. After katsura's introduction into western cultivation in 1881, it became a popular tree for planting in parks, gardens, and arboreta.

The bark is freckled with lighter coloured lenticels (pores). Held on lax, green-red petioles, the leaves are bright matt green on the upper surface and blue-green on the underside. However, by summer their upper surfac also turns blue-green. In autumn, they take on a variety o bright shades before eventually falling, giving off a sweet, caramel-like aroma as they begin to decompose. Bright red male flowers appear on side shoots before the leaves emerge in spring. Red female flowers develop on separat trees at the same time.

***Cercidiphyllum magnificum*** This is a smaller tree than the katsura tree, rarely reaching more than 10m (30ft) in height, with a smooth bark and larger, more coarsely toothed leaves.

## PROFILE

- Up to 10 m (30 ft)
- Up to 4 m (12 ft)
- Evergreen
- Alternate simple
- S. Ireland, W. France, Iberian Peninsula, countries bordering the Mediterranean

**'namental species**
th fruit ripening from flowers the previous year, the Killarney 'awberry tree bears fruit and wers at the same time.

## FEATURES

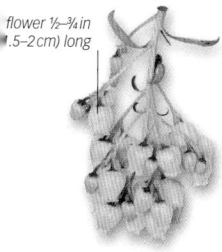


**Flowers** Creamy white, urn-shaped, borne in drooping clusters

**Fruit** Strawberry-like berry, green ripening to red

*Arbutus unedo* (Ericaceae)

# KILLARNEY STRAWBERRY TREE

**This broadly spreading tree** has become popular for garden planting. The name "Killarney" refers to a part of Ireland, where this tree is extremely common. It is often used for hedging around fields in this region.

Young bark is a rich, red-brown colour, which fades to a deep brown, and turns rough and fissured, giving the tree a gnarled appearance. The leaves are elliptic to obovate in shape. The flower clusters are up to 5 cm (2 in) long and are borne at the ends of shoots in autumn. The warty fruit ripens from green through yellow to red in autumn from flowers produced in the previous year. Though the fruit is edible, it tastes dry and is not particularly enjoyable.

**Garden tree**
The Killarney strawberry tree is small, with a broadly spreading habit and glossy green foliage.

## PROFILE

- Up to 10 m (30 ft)
- Up to 5 m (15 ft)
- Evergreen
- Alternate simple
- S.E. Europe

*elliptic to oval leaf with smooth margin*

*flower up to 6 mm (¼ in) long*

*leaf up to 10 cm (4 in) long, 5 cm (2 in) wide*

**Pitcher-like flowers**
Panicles of small flowers appear on short stalks in spring. Green-tinged at first, they open white at the ends of shoots, in upright clusters.

## FEATURES

**Bark** Red-brown to cinnamon; peels in ragged strips to reveal orange or cream new bark

*Arbutus andrachne* (Ericaceae)

# GRECIAN STRAWBERRY TREE

**Also known as Cyprus strawberry tree**, this small, broadly spreading tree is indigenous to southeast Europe, and has been in cultivation in warm, temperate regions of the world since 1724. Its canopy is dome-shaped, and it often develops low branching, and multiple stems – sometimes from just above ground level, giving it a shrublike appearance. When it is grown alongside Killarney strawberry tree (p.213), the two may cross-pollinate to produce the hybrid strawberry tree (*Arbutus* x *andrachnoides*).

The leaves are thick and leathery, glossy dark green on the upper surface, pale green on the underside, and with no serrations around the leaf margin. The fruit is a rounded red-orange berry, up to 1 cm (½ in) wide.

**Hybrid strawberry tree (*Arbutus* x *andrachnoides*)** Hardier than the Grecian strawberry tree, this tree has brighter, cinnamon-red bark and shoots, and it flowers in late autumn rather than spring.

## PROFILE



- Up to 40m (130ft)
- Up to 8m (25ft)
- Evergreen
- Alternate simple
- West coast of North America

**rge flower clusters**
ny, creamy white flowers are orne in erect panicles at the ds of shoots in spring.

## FEATURES

**Bark** Peels in papery flakes to reveal fresh green or cream colour beneath

**Fruit** Rounded, strawberry-like; changing from green to orange to red in early autumn

*Arbutus menziesii* (Ericaceae)

# MADRONE

**This broadly columnar tree** is called the Pacific or Californian madrone. It is the largest member of the Ericaceae family, growing up to 40m (130ft) in the wild, though it normally remains around half this height in cultivation. It is indigenous to the west coast of North America, from British Columbia, including Vancouver Island, Canada, south to California, USA. Madrone was introduced into Europe by Scottish plant collector David Douglas in 1827.

It has smooth and attractive red-pink bark, sometimes purple towards the base, which peels in papery flakes. The glossy leaves have pale blue-white undersides, and are borne on red petioles. The rough, strawberry-like fruits are covered in warts.

**Elegant evergreen**
The madrone is widely planted in parks, gardens, and arboreta across the northern temperate world.

**Flowers and leaves**
The fragrant flowers hang down in clusters, or singly, along the underside of the branches. Leaves are rich green, oval to elliptic.

*small, shallow teeth on leaf margin*

*golden anthers*

*bell-shaped, creamy white flower*

**PROFILE**

- Up to 10 m (30 ft)
- Up to 6 m (20 ft)
- Deciduous
- Alternate simple
- China, Japan, Korea

*Styrax japonicus* (Styracaceae)

# JAPANESE SNOWBELL

**As the name suggests**, this tree is native to Japan. However, Japanese snowbell is endemic to parts of China and Korea as well. It was introduced in the West in 1862, when botanical collector Richard Oldham brought a specimen from Japan. This was subsequently planted in the Royal Botanic Gardens at Kew, London.

The orange-brown bark develops fissures when the tree is around 30 years old. The leaves are 10 cm (4 in) long and 5 cm (2 in) wide, with a slight sheen on the upper surface. They are pale green and matt on the underside, and normally arranged in groups of three. In early summer, the canopy is covered in open flowers. Once pollinated, these develop into egg-shaped, grey-green fruit, each containing a single seed.

**Spreading form**
The Japanese snowbell often has a short trunk and widely spreading branches that emerge low on the trunk.

**preading raceme**
hinese snowbell tree bears white
owers, borne on terminal, upright,
ng racemes, which become lax
nd spreading over time.

**PROFILE**

- Up to 8m (25ft)
- Up to 3m (10ft)
- Deciduous
- Alternate simple
- C. and W. China

*Styrax hemsleyanus* (Styracaceae)

# CHINESE SNOWBELL TREE

**This slender, open-branched tree** is also known as Hemsley's storax, after William Hemsley, one-time keeper of the herbarium at the Royal Botanic Gardens, Kew, London. Native to central and western China, this tree grows on mountain slopes at an altitude of 2,700m (8,850ft) above sea level. It was introduced into western cultivation by English plant collector Ernest H. Wilson in 1900.

The Chinese snowbell tree has a dark brown and relatively smooth bark, even in maturity. The leaves are ovate to obovate, with pale green undersides, sometimes covered in hairs. The leaves have occasional blunt-edged serrations around the margins. A distinguishing feature of this species is its exposed, bright orange to chocolate-brown leaf bud. White flowers, occasionally with a slight pink blush, emerge from the ends of short shoots in late spring to early summer. Flowers are followed by down-covered, ovoid, grey-green fruit.

flower up to 3cm (1¼in) long

leaf up to 20cm (8in) long

yellow anthers on white flower

**Broadly ovate leaves**
On young trees, the large leaves can be irregularly shaped, but they are broadly ovate to orbicular on mature trees.

**PROFILE**

- Up to 14m (46ft)
- Up to 6m (20ft)
- Deciduous
- Alternate simple
- Japan

**FEATURES**

**Fruit** Grey-green, egg-shaped berry, carrying a single seed

*Styrax obassia* (Styracaceae)

# FRAGRANT SNOWBELL

**Also known as bigleaf storax**, this tree is indigenous to Japan. It was introduced into cultivation by British botanist Charles Maries in 1879. Today, despite its hardiness and beauty, it is not frequently cultivated.

The grey bark turns brown and fissured in maturity. In the second year, the bark on its shoots is chestnut-brown and flaky. Bright green on the upper surface, leaves have a paler underside with white down. Leaf petioles swell at the base to enclose the leaf bud. Fragrant, bell-shaped flowers are borne in lax, green, terminal racemes up to 20cm (8in) long, in early summer. These are followed by ovoid fruit, up to 1.5cm (½in) long and covered in pale brown hairs.

**Arching canopy**
The fragrant snowbell's open branches arch at the canopy to give it a round-headed appearance

## PROFILE

- Up to 20m (70ft)
- Up to 10m (30ft)
- Deciduous
- Alternate simple
- S.E. USA

**Bell-shaped flowers**
The white flowers hang in groups of three or four, along the underside of the branches in mid- to late spring.

*flower borne on long stalk*

*bright orange stamens*

*white, bell-shaped flower*

## FEATURES

*leaf up to 20cm (8in) long, 10cm (4in) wide*

**Leaves** Ovate to oblong; finely toothed along the margin

*slender beak tip*

**Fruit** Pendulous, angular capsule, attached to tree by 2cm- (¾in-) long stalk

*Halesia carolina* (Styracaceae)

# CAROLINA SNOWDROP TREE

**Also known as silverbell tree** or Carolina silverbell, this small, broadly conical tree is native to southeast USA, from Virginia south to Florida. It was discovered and introduced into cultivation in 1756. Since then, it has been widely planted elsewhere in the USA and in other parts of the western world. The botanical name *Halesia* commemorates the English clergyman and botanical author Dr Stephen Hales.

The bark of the tree is pale brown and smooth, becoming darker and scaly in maturity. The ovate to oblong leaves taper to a long point. They are bright green on the upper surface and pale green on the underside, with some hairs, especially around the leaf veins. In autumn, the leaves turn golden yellow before falling. Bell-shaped flowers are followed by pear-shaped, four-winged fruit capsules, which are green at first, ripening to brown.

**PROFILE**

- Up to 25 m (80 ft)
- Up to 15 m (50 ft)
- Deciduous
- Alternate simple
- S.E. USA

**Leaves and fruit**
The ovate to oblong leaves are borne alternately on the shoot. The pendulous, capsule-like fruit is up to 4 cm (1 ½ in) long and borne on a 2 cm- (¾ in-) long stalk. It ripens from green to brown.

**FEATURES**

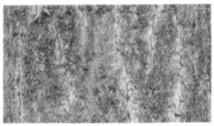

**Bark** Pale grey, with shallow, widely spaced, pink fissures; turns darker grey in maturity

**Flowers** Crocus-shaped; hang in clusters, normally of three

*Halesia monticola* (Styracaceae)

# MOUNTAIN SNOWDROP TREE

**This broadly spreading tree** is native to the mountains of southeast USA, from North Carolina to Georgia. It has been widely cultivated elsewhere, in the USA and around the world, since its introduction into European cultivation in about 1897. It is distinguished from the Carolina snowdrop tree (p.219) by its larger size, flowers, and fruit.

The shoot is grey-brown, and the leaf bud small and deep purple. The leaves are bright green on both sides, and turn yellow in autumn. White flowers, 3 cm (1 ¼ in) long, emerge from pale pink buds, borne on 2 cm- (¾ in-) long stalks. They hang beneath the branches in profusion, appearing in late spring and early summer.

**Cultivated habit**
The mountain snowdrop tree grows as a large shrub or a small-spreading tree in cultivation.

**PROFILE**

- 10–15 m (30–50 ft)
- Up to 8 m (25 ft)
- Deciduous
- Alternate simple
- Japan

**Camellia-like flowers**
These white, frilly petalled, open flowers appear singly in leaf axils in summer. When old, they fall in one piece from the tree.

*pale, shiny leaf underside*

*bright orange-yellow anthers*

*matt, dark green upper surface of leaf*

*roughly oval leaf, up to 10 cm (4 in) long, 4 cm (1½ in) wide*

**FEATURES**

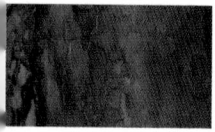

**Bark** Smooth, red-brown; flakes to reveal cream, pale orange, or light brown patches

*Stewartia pseudocamellia* (Theaceae)

# JAPANESE STEWARTIA

**A member of the same family** as the *Camellia*, this small to medium-sized tree produces very similar flowers. It is native to Japan and was introduced into western cultivation in the 1870s. It takes its generic name from John Stuart, the Earl of Bute and a patron of the Royal Botanic Gardens in Kew, London. For this reason, some books refer to it as Stuartia.

The tree becomes broadly columnar with age. The leaves are elliptic to ovate, finely toothed, and borne alternately on twigs. They sometimes have hairs in the vein axils on the underside. In autumn, the leaves range in colour from orange-red to purple before falling. The Japanese stewartia flowers in mid- to late summer, and the flowers are shed from the tree in one piece, rather than falling petal by petal. Its fruit is a woody, triangular, red-brown capsule, up to 2 cm (¾ in) long.

**Sawtooth pseudocamellia (*Stewartia serrata*)** This tree is distinguished by the neat, forward-pointing serrations on its leaf margins, and smaller flowers with a red blotch at the base.

**PROFILE**

- Up to 7 m (22 ft)
- Up to 7 m (22 ft)
- Deciduous
- Alternate simple
- C. China

*leaf up to 10 cm (4 in) long, 4 cm (1 ½ in) wide*

*pronounced vein on leaf*

*bright green leaf upper surface*

*bright orange anthers*

**Cup-shaped flowers** Creamy white flowers emerge in midsummer bearing frilly edged petals and clusters of bright orange anthers.

**FEATURES**

**Bark** Red-brown and smooth; flakes to reveal patches of fresh bark beneath

**Buds** Green, short-stalked, carried solitary in leaf axils

*Stewartia sinensis* (Theaceae)

# CHINESE STEWARTIA

**This small deciduous tree**, sometimes a large shrub, is native to Hubei province in central China. It was discovered and introduced into western cultivation by the English plant collector Ernest H. Wilson in 1901. Since then, it has been widely planted in gardens for its bark colouring, attractive summer flowers, and vibrant autumn leaf tints.

The thin bark flakes and peels to reveal patches of cream, fawn, or light grey fresh bark beneath. Densely borne leaves are bright green with a sheen on both surfaces. Elliptic to elliptic-oblong in shape, they display distinctly pronounced veins and a long, pointed, and curved tip. The leaves are alternately attached to crimson-purple shoots by a 1 cm- (½ in-) long, red, and slightly hairy petiole (stalk). In autumn, they turn bright crimson, orange, and yellow before falling. Upright flower buds open in midsummer to release beautiful camellia-like flowers up to 4–5 cm (1 ½–2 in) wide. The white flowers are slightly fragrant.

**oney flower**
nese ivory-white flowers, up-shaped at first, open up to cm (1 ½ in) wide, and contain ghly prized, rich nectar.

**PROFILE**

- 10–20 m (30–70 ft)
- Up to 8 m (25 ft)
- Evergreen
- Opposite simple
- Chile, Argentina

*Eucryphia cordifolia* (Eucryphiaceae)

# ULMO

**This elegant tree** grows in the foothills of the Andes mountain range, at an altitude of up to 700 m (2,300 ft) above sea level. It was first cultivated in Europe around 1851. In its native Chile and Argentina, it is currently threatened by logging and loss of habitat.

This densely branched tree is broadly conical. Its dark chocolate-brown, smooth bark is horizontally marked with fawn-coloured lenticels (raised pores). The leaves are oblong, wavy-edged with shallow, blunt serrations, occasionally heart-shaped at the base, and run to a broad, rounded tip. They are up to 8 cm (3 in) long and 3.5 cm (1 ½ in) wide. Four-petalled flowers, borne singly in leaf axils, appear in late summer. Purple-tipped stamens give the centre of the flowers a speckled appearance. The flowers' rich nectar is commercially harvested by beekeepers and sold as ulmo honey.

**Pinkwood (*Eucryphia moorei*)** With smaller flowers and pinnate leaves consisting of up to 13 slender leaflets, this Australasian tree is easily distinguished from the ulmo.

**Striking flowers**
Creamy or ivory-white flowers are produced in late summer. Sometimes these last well into early autumn.

**PROFILE**

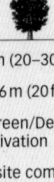

- 6–10 m (20–30 ft)
- Up to 6 m (20 ft)
- Evergreen/Deciduous in cultivation
- Opposite compound
- Chile

*Eucryphia glutinosa* (Eucryphiaceae)

# EUCRYPHIA

**This small, neat tree is evergreen** in its native Chile but usually deciduous in cultivation in Europe. It has a broadly columnar form, with a mass of strongly erect branches. Eucryphia, sometimes known as brush bush, was introduced into western cultivation in 1859, and is considered one of the most beautiful flowering trees.

Its bark is dark brown and relatively smooth even in old age. The leaves are pinnate, made up of three to five leaflets. Each leaflet has a prominent wavy margin, a shin dark green upper surface, and a pale green underside. In autumn, the leaves turn brilliant orange-red before falling. The four-petalled flowers emerge in the leaf axils in late summer and are normally borne in profusion on the tree. The fruit is an oval, woody capsule, up to 1.5 cm (½ in) long, and contains several seeds.

**Nyman's eucryphia (*Eucryphia* x *nymansensis*)** This garden cultivar has both simple and compound leaves on the same tree. It is more upright and freer flowering than eucryphia.

**Flowers and leaves**
Golden yellow, pendulous flowers are borne in profusion in spring. The trifoliate leaves are green.

**PROFILE**



- Up to 9 m (28 ft)
- Up to 5 m (15 ft)
- Deciduous
- Alternate compound
- C. and S. Europe

**FEATURES**

**Fruit** Green, hairy, bean-like seed pods, contain several small, round black seeds

*Laburnum anagyroides* (Fabaceae)

# COMMON LABURNUM

**Probably one of the most familiar** trees in cultivation, the common laburnum is small and broad-spreading. Native to southern and central Europe from France to Hungary and Bulgaria, it naturally occurs in mountainous regions at altitudes of up to 2,000 m (6,500 ft). It is also short-lived – between 50 and 60 years is considered a good age.

The bark is brown-grey and smooth, becoming shallowly fissured in maturity. Each leaf is composed of three leaflets, rich green on the upper surface, grey-green on the underside and covered with silver hairs when young. They are attached to the shoots by a short petiole (stalk). New shoots are olive-green, while winter buds are pale grey-brown and covered in silvery hairs. After flowering, seed pods develop and ripen to brown. They crack open on the tree to reveal poisonous seeds.

**Voss's laburnum (*Laburnum* x *watereri*)** This hybrid between *L. alpinum* and *L. anagyroides* produces larger flowers, borne in greater profusion. The leaves are slightly more hairy.

**PROFILE**

- Up to 12m (40ft)
- Up to 8m (25ft)
- Deciduous
- Alternate compound
- C. and S. Europe

**Drooping flowers**
Flowering in early summer, this tree has several small, pea-like flowers, widely spaced on slender racemes, which droop downwards from slender shoots.

*golden yellow flower, up to 2.5cm (1in) long*

**FEATURES**

**Leaves** Trifoliate, deep shiny green on both surfaces

*Laburnum alpinum* (Fabaceae)

# ALPINE LABURNUM

**Also known as the Scotch laburnum**, this small, wide spreading tree is native to the mountains of central and southern Europe and has been cultivated elsewhere since the end of the 14th century. It copes better with harsh winter conditions than the common laburnum (p.225), hence it is frequently planted along roads and tracks in Scotland – from where it gets its alternative name.

The bark is brown-grey and smooth, becoming only shallowly fissured in maturity. New shoots are olive-green bearing pale grey-brown winter buds covered in silver-grey hairs. Trifoliate leaves are attached to shoots by a short green petiole (stalk). Each leaflet is up to 10cm (4in) long and 5cm (2in) wide. Flowers are borne in hanging panicles up to 40cm (16in) long. The fruit are flat, green seed pods which ripen to brown. They contain hard-coated, round, black, poisonous seeds.

**Mount Etna broom (*Genista aetnensis*)** Slender, green, almost leafless shoots and yellow, pea-like flowers, borne in erect clusters along shoots, distinguish this tree from the Alpine laburnum.

## PROFILE

- Up to 10m (30ft)
- Up to 5m (15ft)
- Deciduous
- Alternate simple
- Middle East

*leaf up to 12cm (5in) long and wide*

*leaf upper surface yellow-green to blue-green*

*pale blue-green leaf underside*

*bright, rosy pink flowers, borne in clusters of 3–6*

**Flowers on old wood**
As rounded to heart-shaped leaves unfurl in spring, clusters of bright pea-flowers are borne along old shoots.

## FEATURES

**Bark** Grey-brown, creased; fine brown fissures in maturity

**Fruit** Long, thin, purple-tinted seed pod

*Cercis siliquastrum* (Fabaceae)

# JUDAS TREE

**This small, broadly spreading** deciduous tree is said to be the tree on which Judas Iscariot hanged himself after betraying Christ. However, its name is more likely to have been derived from "Judea's tree", referring to the region of its origin, now Israel and Palestine, where the tree occurs commonly. It has long been cultivated across Europe for its bright pink flowers, and it grows particularly well in hot, dry, sunny conditions. Older trees may develop a pronounced leaning habit.

The broad leaves are held on pink-red shoots by a pink petiole, from which light green-yellow leaf veins radiate. In summer, the flowers grow into conspicuous seed pods, up to 12cm (5in) long and 2cm (¾in) wide, which stay on the tree until winter.

**Eastern redbud**
This small, round-headed tree (*Cercis canadensis*) has paler flowers and thinner, bright green leaves.

**Leaves and flowers**
Bipinnate leaves are up to 50 cm (20 in) long. Borne on soft, green shoots they give the tree a "feathery" appearance. Fragrant flowers appear in summer.

**PROFILE**

- Up to 12 m (40 ft)
- Up to 10 m (30 ft)
- Deciduous
- Alternate compound
- Iran, China, Taiwan, Korea

*Albizia julibrissin* (Fabaceae)

# PINK SIRIS

**Sometimes mistaken for** the silver wattle (p.229), this broadly spreading, flat-topped tree is native to Iran, China, Taiwan, and Korea. Also known as the silk tree, it was introduced into western cultivation by the English botanist Ernest H. Wilson in 1918. The pink siris is a beautiful sight when in flower, making it a popular street plant in the USA. However, the tree is not completely hardy and struggles in northern USA and in parts of northern Europe.

The bark of the pink siris is dark brown and smooth. Foliage is similar to the silver wattle, with leaves made up of numerous small, tapering, bright green leaflets, each up to 1 cm (½ in) long. The flowers are borne on erect stalks in late summer to early autumn. They have fluffy clusters of salmon-pink stamens that fade to lemon at the base, making them look like pink powder puffs from a distance. The fragrance of the flowers is like that of freshly cut hay. Seeds are borne in flat, light brown pea-like pods, up to 15 cm (6 in) long.

**PROFILE**

- 20–25 m (70–80 ft)
- Up to 10 m (30 ft)
- Evergreen
- Alternate compound
- S.E. Australia, Tasmania

**Vibrant flower cluster**
The tiny flowers have sulphur-yellow stamens, and are borne on a panicle up to 10 cm (4 in) long.

*flower up to 1 cm (½ in) wide*

*small, linear leaflet*

*bipinnate leaf*

*blue-green shoot*

**FEATURES**

**Fruit** Glaucous green seed pod, ripening from green to brown

*Acacia dealbata* (Fabaceae)

# SILVER WATTLE

**Also known as mimosa**, this tender, temperate, medium-sized tree is prized by florists the world over for its delicate, feathery foliage and fragrant, yellow flowers. Native to southeast Australia and Tasmania, this broadly conical tree is a popular ornamental street tree in Mediterranean countries, but does not grow as well in cooler climates further north.

The bark is smooth, ranging between grey-green to almost glaucous blue when young, and turning darker and more brown in maturity. The leaves have a matt, mid-green upper surface and a sage-green underside. In the southern hemisphere, the tree blooms in summer, while in the north, this usually translates into early spring. The flowers are rounded with numerous yellow stamens, which are slightly fragrant. Its fruit is a seed pod containing several round, brown seeds.

**Cootamundra wattle (*Acacia baileyana*)** Although similar to the silver wattle, this tree tends to be smaller and with many branches. Its smaller, bipinnate leaves are slightly more glaucous.

## PROFILE



- Up to 40m (130ft)
- Up to 20m (70ft)
- Evergreen
- Transitions from compound to simple
- E. Australia, Tasmania

**Adult foliage**
In maturity, blackwood acacia leaves are alternate and undivided. The flowers have rounded heads and contain numerous pale yellow stamens.

## FEATURES

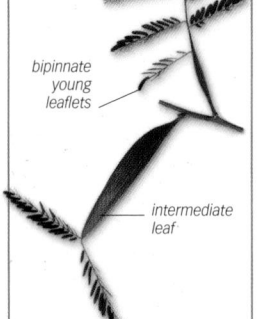


**Leaves** Transition from bipinnate to simple with age

*Acacia melanoxylon* (Fabaceae)

# BLACKWOOD ACACIA

**Also known as the sally wattle** or the Australian blackwood, this pyramid-shaped tree reaches up to 40m (130ft) in height, though it normally remains much shorte It has a range that extends from southern Queensland to central Tasmania. It grows at 1,000m (3,280ft) above sea level in the Tasmanian rainforest.

The straight trunk has dark brown bark, smooth when young, vertically cracking into flaking plates with age. The tree is sometimes coppiced (cut back) and stumps may produce dull green phyllodes (flattened leaf stalks). Bluish white shoots bear leaves that are mid-green on the uppe surface and blue-green on the underside. Bipinnate youn leaves give the tree a feathery appearance. The mildly fragrant flowers are borne on panicles (branched flower stalks) up to 10cm (4in) long and are followed by reddish brown fruit pods that contain flat, rounded seeds.

**Oven's wattle (*Acacia pravissima*)** Unlike blackwood acacia this large shrub or small tree has arching branches and triangular phyllodes that are more prominent than the leaves.

## PROFILE

- Up to 6 m (20 ft)
- Up to 6 m (20 ft)
- Deciduous
- Opposite or alternate or borne in whorls of three
- China, Korea, N.E. India

**Crinkly flowers**
Deep lilac-pink flowers with crinkly petals are borne in branched flower clusters.

*flowers held in panicle, up to 15 cm (6 in) long*

## FEATURES

**Leaves** Obovate; up to 5 cm (2 in) long, 2.5 cm (1 in) wide

*Lagerstroemia indica* (Lythraceae)

# CRAPE MYRTLE

**This wide-spreading, flat-topped tree** is native to China, Korea, and parts of northeast India. It is widely planted on streets and in parks and gardens throughout the southern states of the USA, India, and much of the Mediterranean. Further north, it is rather tender and requires shelter and a sunny area.

The bark is thin, smooth, and light fawn. It flakes to reveal patches of mottled grey, pink, and cinnamon beneath. The trunk can have multiple stems, and both the trunk and the main branches are sometimes angular or ribbed, rather like the common hornbeam (p.184). The leaves are deep green, thick, tough, and privet-like. In autumn, they turn orange or red before falling.

**Summer flowers**
The broad canopy of crape myrtle bears flowers in profusion from midsummer to early autumn.

## PROFILE

- Up to 25 m (80 ft)
- Up to 15 m (50 ft)
- Deciduous
- Alternate simple
- Europe, W. Asia

**Wild cherry blossoms**
Borne in clusters, the fragrant flowers open in spring, just befo or as the leaves emerge.

*elliptic leaf, up to 15 cm (6 in) long*

*large, white, five-petalled flower*

*flower up to 3 cm (1 ¼ in) wide*

## FEATURES

**Bark** Grey-red, smooth, turning red-brown when mature

**Fruit** Round, shiny cherries, up to 1.5 cm (½ in) wide

*Prunus avium* (Rosaceae)

# GEAN

**Also known as wild cherry** or mazzard, this hardy, broadly columnar tree has a natural range spanning Europe and western Asia. It commonly grows on the edge of woodland or in small clearings, but is also likely to be found in city parks, motorway embankments, and farmlar copses. Gean is the parent of many domestic sweet cherries grown for their edible fruit.

In maturity, the bark turns glossy, sometimes peeling with light brown horizontal bands of lenticels (pores). The leaves, up to 5 cm (2 in) wide, have a sharply serrated margin and end in a short point. They are deep green on the upper surface and pale green on the underside. They turn orange, red, or yellow in autumn. A bitter fruit is borne in summer.

**St Lucie cherry**
This tree (*Prunus mahaleb* can be told apart from gea by its darker bark, smaller stature, and rounded habi

**Serrated leaves**
The bird cherry tree's dark matt green leaves are finely serrated around the margin and run to a short point at the tip.

*leaf ends in abrupt point*

*leaf up to 10 cm (4 in) long*

**PROFILE**

- Up to 15 m (50 ft)
- Up to 15 m (50 ft)
- Deciduous
- Alternate simple
- N. Europe, Asia, China, Japan

**FEATURES**

**Bark** Smooth, dark grey; emits an acrid scent when scratched

**Flowers** White, slightly fragrant; borne in upright racemes in mid- to late spring

*Prunus padus* (Rosaceae)

# BIRD CHERRY

**This deciduous, hardy**, small to medium-sized tree is extremely beautiful when in bloom, and has given rise to a number of ornamental cultivars, which are now popularly grown in gardens across the northern hemisphere. As the name suggests, this tree produces a cherry-like fruit, which is relished by birds but is bitter to the human palate.

The leaves turn orange-red in autumn before falling. Small flowers are borne in upright racemes, 10–15 cm (4–6 in) long. These become lax, spreading, and pendulous as the flowers open. The flowers are followed by small, round to egg-shaped berries, up to 1 cm (½ in) wide. Initially green, the berries ripen to red, then black.

**Spreading habit**
With a conical habit in youth, the bird cherry becomes rounded, with drooping branches, in maturity.

**PROFILE**

- Up to 10m (30ft)
- Up to 10m (30ft)
- Evergreen
- Alternate simple
- Portugal, Spain, S.W. France

*flowers borne in long, narrow raceme, up to 25cm (10in) long*

*creamy white flower, with five petals*

*ovate, elliptic leaf, tapers to short point*

*shallow, rounded serrations along leaf margin*

**Flowers and leaves**
Creamy white flowers are reminiscent of the lily of the valley. Leaves are dark green on the upper surface and paler on the underside.

**FEATURES**

**Fruit** Egg-shaped; green, ripening through red to black

*Prunus lusitanica* (Rosaceae)

# PORTUGUESE LAUREL

**A small to medium-sized tree**, the Portuguese laurel is perhaps taller in its natural habitat. It is grown around the Mediterranean region as a single specimen, like bull bay (see p.96), and is quite often clipped into architectural forms. Elsewhere, it is grown as a dense, luxuriant hedge or screen. It has been cultivated in this way since the 17th century, or perhaps even earlier.

The bark is dark slate-grey to grey-brown and relatively smooth even in maturity. Dark glossy green leaves are up to 10cm (4in) long and 5cm (2in) wide. Small flowers borne in early summer are scented, although not necessarily pleasantly. Long clusters of fruit follow the flowers. Individual fruits are widely spaced along the stalk.

**Broadly spread habit**
The evergreen Portuguese laurel is shrubby and multi-stemmed, and serves well as a hedge or screen.

**PROFILE**

- Up to 15 m (50 ft)
- Up to 10 m (30 ft)
- Deciduous
- Alternate simple
- W. China

willow-like leaf, up to 10 cm (4 in) long

egg-shaped, crimson berry, borne singly or in pairs on long stalks

finely toothed leaf running to long, pointed tip

**rimson cherry**
e fruit of the Tibetan cherry
nerges as a yellow berry in
tumn, ripening to crimson-red.

**FEATURES**

**Bark** Deep-red, smooth; peels occasionally

flower up to 2 cm (¾ in) wide

orange-tipped stamen

**Flowers** White; produced in spring after leaves appear

*Prunus serrula* (Rosaceae)

# TIBETAN CHERRY

**Native to Tibet and other parts** of western China, this compact but broadly spreading, small, deciduous tree was first introduced into western cultivation by British plant collector Ernest H. Wilson in 1908. It reaches up to 15 m (50 ft) in the wild, but is usually shorter in cultivation.

The Tibetan cherry is generally considered to be among the most attractive of all trees due to its bark, which looks like highly polished mahogany furniture. It is divided into horizontal sections by bands of light brown stomata (microscopic pores) and is particularly striking under the winter sun, when the tree is bare. Small, white, and relatively inconspicuous flowers appear in spring, while tiny, berry-like, purely ornamental fruit emerge in autumn.

**Himalayan cherry (*Prunus rufa*)** Its peeling, reddish brown, ornamental bark is similar to that of Tibetan cherry. It has rusty haired young shoots and small clusters of pale pink flowers.

## PROFILE



- 4–10 m (12–30 ft)
- 6 m (20 ft)
- Deciduous
- Alternate simple
- W. Asia, N. Africa

**Leaves and fruit**
A fleshy, yellow fruit covered with velvety hairs encloses the edible almond seed.

## FEATURES

**Flowers** Borne singly or in pairs in early spring

**Seeds** White, edible; carried in woody shells

*Prunus dulcis* (Rosaceae)

# ALMOND

**Known widely for its fruit**, this small tree has a natural distribution extending across northern Africa and western Asia. However, since the Roman period it has been cultivated elsewhere and is now naturalized throughout the Mediterranean region and southern Europe.

The grey-black bark is smooth at first, cracking into small squares on maturity. Green, young twigs turn purple and then grey. Dark green to yellow-green leave may appear curled and wrinkled due to a fungal diseas known as peach leaf curl. Five-petalled flowers are whi sometimes faintly blushed pink, and produced singly or in pairs in early spring before the leaves emerge. The fr is covered in a grey-green, thick, leathery coat called a hull. Inside the hull is a hard shell, or stone, which contains the edible seed.

**Apricot (*Prunus armeniaca*)** This tree mainly differs from almond in its edible, fleshy, yellow fruit, which ripens to orange-r and its ovate-shaped smaller leaves.

## PROFILE

- Up to 10m (30ft)
- Up to 6m (20ft)
- Deciduous
- Alternate simple
- Europe

**Succulent fruit**
The fruit is an ovoid drupe with a thin skin, green at first turning red-purple. The succulent flesh inside ripens to a golden hue.

*leaf margin bluntly serrated*

*leaf up to 7.5cm (3in) long*

*fruit up to 7.5cm (3in) long*

*fruit coated in a blue-white bloom*

## FEATURES

**Bark** Brown-grey, developing fissures with age

**Flowers** Fragrant, borne in spring, before leaves appear

*Prunus domestica* (Rosaceae)

# PLUM

**Also known as garden plum**, the original natural distribution of this small, broadly spreading tree is unknown. It may have developed as a hybrid between *Prunus spinosa* and *Prunus cerasifera*, both of which are native to the Caucasus region between Europe and Asia. Today, the plum is naturalized across much of Europe and is widely cultivated for its fruit throughout temperate regions of the world.

The tree has a broad and spreading crown. When young, its bark is smooth and has a slight sheen. The leaves are elliptic to obovate, up to 2.5cm (1in) wide, with a dull grass-green upper surface and slightly blue-green underside. Cherry-like white flowers, 2.5cm (1in) wide, are borne on bare branches. The sharp- to sweet-tasting, fleshy fruit grows up to 5cm (2in) wide. It contains a single flattened seed, known as a stone.

**Sour cherry (*Prunus cerasus*)** Sour cherry has small, red, circular fruit, up to 2.5cm (1in) wide, which ripens to black. As indicated by its name, the fruit has a very sharp, acidic taste.

**PROFILE**

- Up to 7 m (22 ft)
- Up to 6 m (20 ft)
- Deciduous
- Alternate simple
- Japan

*flower consists of five notched petals*

**Notched petals**
White or pale pink flowers emerge from pink buds. The flowers are up t 2 cm (¾ in) wide and appear singly c in small clusters of two or three.

**FEATURES**

**Leaves** Bronze-red in spring, fade to mid-green before turning bright red and gold

*Prunus incisa* (Rosaceae)

# FUJI CHERRY

**This hardy, slow-growing**, deciduous Japanese cherr was first cultivated in 1910 from wild trees growing near Mount Fuji on Honshu, the main island of Japan. When introduced into the western world shortly afterwards, it became hugely popular, and was widely planted in gardens and parks. Many trees at that time were graftec onto faster-growing root-stock, which resulted in incompatible and oversized growth at the trunk's base.

Young trees have an upright habit with ascending branches, while older trees are more wide-spreading. The grey-brown, smooth bark cracks in maturity. The flowers open before the leaves in early spring and are borne towards the ends of side twigs, off the main branch. The purple-black, egg-shaped fruit is up to 8 mm (⅜ in) long.

**Japanese apricot**
This tree (*Prunus mume*) is much smaller than the Fuji cherry and its deeper pink flowers appear earlie in the year.

**Double-petalled flowers**
The flowers are white, or white flushed pink, double-petalled, and without fragrance. They are borne in short-stalked clusters of two to five in spring.

**PROFILE**

- Up to 5 m (15 ft)
- Up to 5 m (15 ft)
- Deciduous
- Alternate simple
- China, Japan

*Prunus serrulata* (Rosaceae)

# HILL CHERRY

**A small, flat-topped tree** with spreading branches, the hill cherry is grown as an ornamental tree in botanic gardens and arboreta. It is believed to be the first cultivated Japanese cherry to be introduced into the West, arriving in Britain via Canton, China, in 1822. The species is known to have been cultivated in Japan for at least 1,000 years; however, some botanists believe it may not be a true species, but arose as a variant from an unknown species of Chinese cherry.

The bark is grey-brown, with a slight sheen and horizontal banding. The leaves are oval to lanceolate, up to 13 cm (5 in) long and 5 cm (2 in) wide, with a long tapered point and a finely serrated margin. Their upper surface is bright green, while the underside is blue-green. The fruit (seldom produced) is an inedible, small, circular, red cherry.

**Great white cherry (*Prunus* 'Taihaku')** This beautiful Japanese cherry of garden origin is distinguished by its large, dazzling white, single flowers, up to 8 cm (3 in) wide.

**Spike-like racemes**
Creamy white flowers are carried at the end of shoots in spreading to drooping, spike-like racemes in late spring or early summer.

*leaf up to 12 cm (5 in) long, 5 cm (2 in) wide*

*smooth, glossy, dark green, leaf upper surface*

*pale green leaf underside*

*flower up to 1 cm (½ in) wide*

**PROFILE**

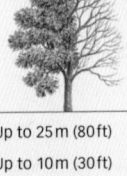

- Up to 25 m (80 ft)
- Up to 10 m (30 ft)
- Deciduous
- Alternate simple
- E. and C. North America

**FEATURES**

*black ripe cherry*

**Fruit** Round, edible cherry; red ripening to black

*Prunus serotina* (Rosaceae)

# RUM CHERRY

**Also known as black cherry**, this medium-sized, broadly columnar tree is native to eastern and central North America, from Nova Scotia, Canada, to Mexico and Guatemala. It is called rum cherry because its fruit were once used by early North American settlers to flavour rum. Commonly found in woodland, it does not thrive as a single specimen in exposed regions.

The bark is dark grey and smooth, becoming horizontally fissured in maturity. It emits a distinctive, peppery odour when scratched. The leaves are elliptic to lanceolate, tapering to a point. They are finely toothed around the margin and have some hairs along the midrib. Rum cherry is a member of the bird cherry (p.233) group and carries its flowers in racemes (pendulous clusters) up to 15 cm (6 in) long. Its fruit is a round cherry up to 1 cm (½ in) in diameter.

**Kanzan flowering cherry (*Prunus serrulata* 'Kanzan')** This tree is distinguished from the rum cherry by its profusion of large pink flowers, smaller size, and spreading habit.

## PROFILE



- Up to 10m (30ft)
- 10m (30ft)
- Deciduous
- Alternate simple
- China

**Peach blossom**
The flowers of the peach tree are pale to deep pink or red, and are produced before the leaves appear in early spring.

## FEATURES

**Leaves** Shape varies from lanceolate to oblong-elliptic

**Fruit** Edible, rounded drupe, containing stone-like seed

*Prunus persica* (Rosaceae)

# PEACH

**This small, spreading tree** has been cultivated for its fruit since time immemorial. The species name *persica* derives from an early European belief that this tree came from Persia (Iran). However, botanists now believe that the peach is probably native to China, and was introduced into Persia and much of the Mediterranean region, along the Silk Road, long before Christianity.

The bark is dark grey, smooth at first, becoming cracked into irregular plates in maturity. The leaves are up to 16cm (6in) long and 3cm (1¼in) wide. They have a slight sheen on the upper surface, with a pale green, matt underside. The flowers are produced either singly or, occasionally, in pairs. The edible, orange-yellow fruit grows up to 7cm (3in) wide, and has a velvety soft skin. It encloses yellow or whitish flesh, which becomes sweet and juicy when ripe. The flesh surrounds a large, deeply pitted seed, or stone. The stone has a pale brown woody husk, is oval in shape, and is up to 2.5cm (1in) long.

**PROFILE**

- 10–20 m (30–70 ft)
- Up to 15 m (50 ft)
- Deciduous
- Alternate simple
- Japan

*leaf sharply toothed at margin*

**Flowering cherry**
Delicate pink flowers emerge in mid-spring against a backdrop of bronze-tinted foliage.

*bronze-red young leaf*

*rose-pink flower, 3–4 cm (1 1/4–1 1/2 in) wide*

*flowers have notched petals*

**FEATURES**

**Bark** Chestnut-brown with slight sheen; regularly marked with fawn-coloured, linear lenticels ("breathing" pores)

*long, slender leaf tip*

**Leaves** Dramatic shades of orange in early to mid-autumn

*Prunus sargentii* (Rosaceae)

# SARGENT'S CHERRY

**Named after Charles Sargent**, first director of the Arnold Arboretum in Jamaica Plain, Massachusetts, USA this tree was introduced into Europe in 1890 by British plant collector Ernest H. Wilson. It is one of the larger Japanese flowering cherries, forming an open-rounded outline when mature.

At the base of the trunk on older trees, surface roots splay outwards, sometimes for several metres, before disappearing underground. The shoots and buds are dark red-brown. Elliptic to obovate leaves end in a long, slender tip. They are bronze-coloured when unfurling, fading to yellow and then dark green. Flowers are single, rose-pink, and borne profusely in clusters of four to five pairs in mid-spring, among emerging foliage.

**Mount Fuji cherry**
This tree (*Prunus* 'Shirotae') has a short-trunked, wide-spreading habit and snow-white flowers.

## PROFILE

- Up to 12m (40ft)
- 6m (20ft)
- Deciduous
- Alternate simple
- Europe

**Hawthorn flowers**
Strongly scented, creamy white flowers are produced in dense clusters on shoots around mid-spring.

*dark green upper surface of leaf*

*pink anther*

*leaf cut deep, until near midrib*

## FEATURES

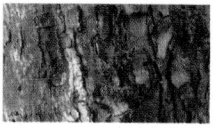

**Bark** Dull brown, smooth; becomes fissured with shallow, vertical cracks in maturity

**Fruit** Berry-like, initially green, ripening to red

*Crataegus monogyna* (Rosaceae)

# COMMON HAWTHORN

**This slow-growing tree** is often found growing in hedgerows and on open land, although it will grow on the edge of woodland too. Extremely hardy, it can withstand exposure, strong winds, and cold temperatures. It has been used in farming for centuries to shelter and enclose animal stock, particularly in upland areas. A regularly clipped hawthorn hedge makes an effective windbreak, with its strong mesh of small, thorny branches.

The bark is smooth at first, becoming fissured, with shallow, vertical, orange-coloured cracks in maturity. Variously shaped leaves have paler undersides with some hairs in the vein axils. Creamy white flowers are followed by small berry-like fruit, known as haws. Initially green, haws ripen to red in autumn and remain on the tree well into winter, when they become a valuable food source for migrating birds.

**Oriental thorn (*Crataegus laciniata*)** This small ornamental tree has deeply cut, hairy leaves, which are darker green on the upper surface, and its fruit are more yellowish red.

**Glossy red fruit**
This tree bears oval, red fruit, or haws, which remain on the tree till late autumn, sometimes winter, before being eaten by birds.

*shallow-lobed leaf with toothed margin*

*leaf up to 5 cm (2 in) long and wide*

*fruit up to 2.5 cm (1 in) long*

**PROFILE**

- Up to 10 m (30 ft)
- Up to 8 m (25 ft)
- Deciduous
- Alternate simple
- N.W. and C. Europe

**FEATURES**

**Flowers** Creamy white, pungently scented, with five petals and pink-orange anthers

**Variant** Young leaves of *Crataegus laevigata* 'Gireoudii' are mottled cream and pink

*Crataegus laevigata* (Rosaceae)

# MIDLAND HAWTHORN

**This hardy, broadly spreading tree** takes its name from an area in central England, where it grows in profusion, and is an accepted indicator species for evidence of ancient woodland. It is native to northwest and central Europe, where it is commonly found in hedgerows and on woodland edges. It differs from common hawthorn (p.243) in its leaves, which are less deeply lobed, and its flowers, which have two styles (female part of flower) as opposed to one in the common hawthorn.

The bark is grey-brown, smooth at first, cracking into small plates in maturity. Leaves are ovate to obovate, glossy dark green on the upper surface, paler on the underside. Thorns, up to 2 cm (¾ in) long, are sporadically borne on tips of twigs. Flowers appear in small but dense clusters in late spring. These are followed by small, oval fruit, each containing two hard seeds.

***Crataegus dsungarica*** This small hawthorn is distinguished from the midland hawthorn by its profusion of thorns, larger flowers, and fruit, which turn purple-black rather than red.

**PROFILE**

- Up to 12 m (40 ft)
- Up to 6 m (20 ft)
- Deciduous
- Alternate simple
- C. China

**Tapering leaves**
The leaves are elliptic to ovate, and taper to a fine point with some hairs along the midrib and main veins.

*bright grass-green leaf upper surface*

*finely toothed leaf margin*

*pale green leaf underside*

*small, rounded fruit, up to 1 cm (½ in) wide*

*fruit borne on ng, slender stalk*

**FEATURES**

**Flowers** Fragrant, white with pink flush; with five broad, overlapping petals

*Malus hupehensis* (Rosaceae)

# HUPEH CRAB

**This broadly spreading tree** is one of the most beautiful of all small deciduous trees. It reaches up to 12 m (40 ft) in its native land among the mountains of Hupeh Province in central China. In cultivation, however, it is normally smaller with stiff, ascending branches. In China, its leaves are used to make a drink called red tea. It was introduced into western cultivation in 1900 by the English plant collector Ernest H. Wilson.

Its bark is purple-brown with irregular plates that flake to reveal fresh, orange-brown bark beneath. Its flowers are pink as buds, but open white with a rose flush in spring. In a good year, they are borne in such profusion that the whole tree canopy seems to be covered in blossoms. Its fruit is greenish yellow, ripening to a small, slightly flattened, red "apple", pendulously borne in clusters of three or four.

**Allegheny serviceberry (*Amelanchier laevis*)** This tree has soft, lanceolate leaves, which emerge a bronze-pink colour amidst a profusion of star-like flowers in early spring.

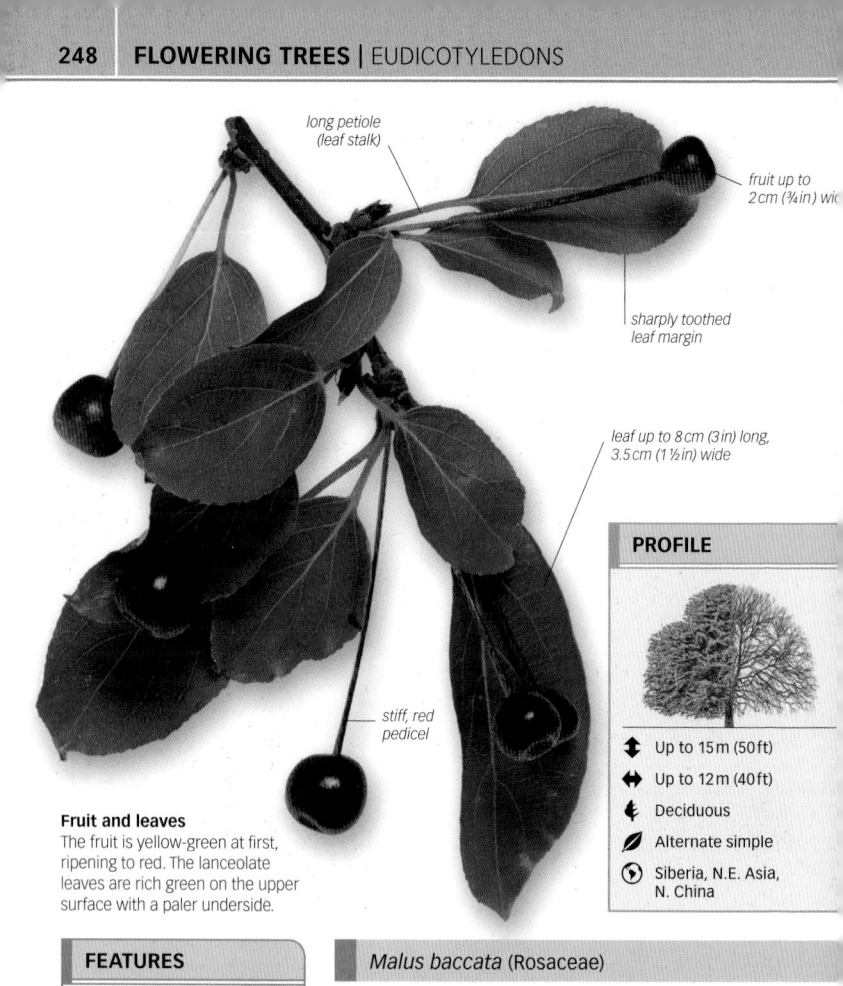


**Fruit and leaves**
The fruit is yellow-green at first, ripening to red. The lanceolate leaves are rich green on the upper surface with a paler underside.

**PROFILE**

- Up to 15 m (50 ft)
- Up to 12 m (40 ft)
- Deciduous
- Alternate simple
- Siberia, N.E. Asia, N. China

**FEATURES**

**Flowers** White; up to 3.5 cm (1½ in) wide

*Malus baccata* (Rosaceae)

# SIBERIAN CRAB

**Native to Siberia**, as well as other parts of northeast Asia and northern China, this small to medium-sized tree is hardy, round-crowned, and slightly pendulous. It was first cultivated as an ornamental specimen outside this region in 1784. Today it is found in parks, gardens, and arboreta throughout western Europe and North America.

The bark is smooth at first, flaking into irregular patches with age to reveal a lighter, grey-brown bark beneath. The leaves are somewhat similar to those of the common pear (p.250). They are attached to the shoots by a 5 cm-(2 in-) long, slender petiole (leaf stalk). Fragrant flowers have widely parted petals surrounding a central cluster of yellow anthers. They are borne in mid-spring in groups of five, each on a stiff pedicel up to 6 cm (2½ in) long. The globular fruit remains on the tree well into winter.

**Pillar crab (*Malus tschonoskii*)** Unlike the Siberian crab, this tree is erect with long, upright branches. Additionally, the leaves are coated with grey-white hairs on the underside.

## PROFILE

- Up to 10m (30ft)
- Up to 6m (20ft)
- Deciduous
- Alternate simple
- Originated in W. Asia; exists today in cultivation worldwide

**Variable fruit**
The fruit is variable in colour and taste, with creamy white flesh surrounding five chambers (carpels), each bearing one to three seeds.

*leaf up to 12cm (5in) long, 6cm (2½in) wide*

*fruit up to 9cm (3½in) wide*

## FEATURES

**Bark** Grey-brown, smooth; fissures into irregular-shaped plates with age

**Flowers** Five-petalled, fragrant; white with pink tinge that fades over time

*Malus domestica* (Rosaceae)

# CULTIVATED APPLE

**Also known as orchard apple**, this is a small, broadly spreading tree grown throughout the world for its edible fruit. It was originally cultivated in western Asia and probably arose as a hybrid of several *Malus* species including *M. sylvestris* and *M. sieversii*. Today there are more than 7,500 known cultivars, each one producing a slightly different fruit, flower, form, or size.

Its bark peels in thin flakes to lift and reveal lighter brown, new bark beneath. The leaves are deep green on the upper surface and paler on the underside. They have a pointed tip, serrated margin, and a slightly downy underside. They are borne on a 5cm- (2in-) long petiole. The fragrant flowers are up to 3.5cm (1½in) wide. The juicy, edible fruit matures in late summer.

**Spreading tree**
The cultivated apple tree is broadly spreading, with a rounded head and hairy, young shoots.

## PROFILE

- Up to 15 m (50 ft)
- Up to 12 m (40 ft)
- Deciduous
- Alternate simple
- Originated in W. Asia; exists today in cultivation worldwide

**Variable fruit**
Pears vary in shape and colour depending on the cultivar: from rounded to pear-shaped; green, speckled brown, russet, or red.

## FEATURES

**Flowers** White, five-petalled, with purple-red anthers; borne in clusters in spring

*Pyrus communis* (Rosaceae)

# COMMON PEAR

**This tree is believed to be a hybrid** that originated in western Asia over 2,000 years ago, like the orchard apple (p.249). It has been cultivated throughout the western world for centuries, with several popular cultivars having been raised at Versailles, France, in the 17th century. Today, there are over 1,000 different cultivars available commercially, each one with slightly different form, size, fruit, or flowers.

The common pear is a broadly columnar, upright, small to medium-sized tree. It has distinctive spur shoots, which occasionally develop into spines and give the crown a slightly angular appearance. The bark is dark grey, fissuring into small irregular plates in maturity. Its leaves are glossy dark green on the upper surface, paler on the underside. The edible fruit is sweet and juicy, with creamy white flesh, which surrounds small, hard, brown seeds.

**Wild Himalayan pear (*Pyrus pashia*)** This can be distinguished from the common pear by its tangled mass of spiny branches, and its smaller brown fruit, which are speckled with cream dots.

leaf twists along its length

urple nther

leaf up to 10 cm (4 in) long, less than 4 cm (1 ½ in) wide

flower up to 2.5 cm (1 in) wide

**owers in clusters**
eamy white flowers with rple anthers are borne in dely spaced clusters along e branches in spring.

**PROFILE**

- Up to 10 m (30 ft)
- Up to 7 m (22 ft)
- Deciduous
- Alternate simple
- Russia, Caucasus region, W. Asia

**FEATURES**

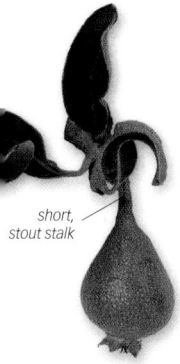


**Fruit** Green when young, ripening to russet brown; borne in late summer

*Pyrus salicifolia* (Rosaceae)

# WILLOW-LEAVED PEAR

**This small, broadly weeping tree** is also known as the weeping silver-leaved pear. The most ornamental of pears, it is native to Russia, Turkey, and northern Iraq. It was introduced in the West by the German botanist and explorer P. S. Pallas, who discovered it in 1780. Today it is commonly planted in gardens and parks. It is not a long-lived tree.

Its bark is pale grey, becoming vertically fissured in maturity. The leaves are narrowly lanceolate, usually untoothed, and tapering at both ends. They also display a twist along their length. Young leaves are covered with a silvery white down, which extends to the pendulous shoots. Mature leaves are sage green and smooth. The five-petalled flowers appear on short shoots in spring. The fruit is a small, hard pear, up to 3 cm (1 ¼ in) long. Hairy when young, it turns smooth with age.

**Sand pear (*Pyrus pyrifolia*)** Also called the Chinese pear or Asian pear, this tree has ovate, toothed, glossy green leaves, up to 12 cm (5 in) long, which turn deep red in autumn.

## PROFILE

- Up to 20 m (70 ft)
- Up to 7 m (22 ft)
- Deciduous
- Alternate compound
- Asia, Europe

**Sharply toothed leaflets**
The pinnate leaves, up to 20 cm (8 in) long, carry up to 15 leaflets that are sharply toothed along the margin and taper to a point.

*leaflet up to 5 cm (2 in) long*

*fruit borne in pendulous clusters*

*round, red berry up to 1 cm (½ in) wide*

## FEATURES

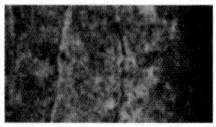

**Bark** Silver-grey, smooth, shiny even in maturity

*creamy white flower, up to 1 cm (½ in) wide*

**Flowers** Fragrant, borne in dense clusters, up to 15 cm (6 in) wide, in late spring

*Sorbus aucuparia* (Rosaceae)

# ROWAN

**This broadly conical, deciduous tree** is native to the whole of Asia and Europe. In mountainous regions of northern Europe, it can grow up to 1,000 m (3,280 ft) above sea level – hence its other name mountain ash. It is a particularly hardy tree and can withstand exposure better than most members of the *Sorbus* genus. Its berries are an important food source for birds. In some regions of Europe, a rowan tree planted outside the house is considered protection against evil spirits.

The leaves have a fresh green upper surface and a blue-green underside. In autumn, they turn yellow or red before falling. The fruit is borne towards the end of summer on stalks up to 2 cm (¾ in) long and remains on the tree until eaten by birds.

**Japanese rowan**
This tree (*Sorbus commixta*) has larger leaflets than the mountain ash, and red, long-pointed winter buds.

red, oval to rounded berry

**eaves and berries**
e leaves are ovate
elliptic with irregular,
allow serrations around
e margins. Clusters of red
erries are borne in summer.

**PROFILE**

15 m (50 ft)
Up to 20 m (70 ft)
Deciduous
Alternate simple
N., W., and C. Europe

**FEATURES**

**Flowers** Creamy white, fragrant; up to 1 cm (½ in) wide

*Sorbus aria* (Rosaceae)

# WHITEBEAM

**Native to north**, west, and central Europe, the whitebeam is a small to medium-sized tree of calcareous uplands. It thrives on thin chalk and limestone soils. It is sometimes referred to as the weather tree, due to the fact that in windy conditions – often the precursor to low pressure – the wind flips the leaves over, revealing their white underside. This is taken by some as a sign that rains are imminent.

The leaves are up to 9 cm (3½ in) long and 5 cm (2 in) wide. Initially pale green, they turn matt green on the upper surface and white on the underside. A dense covering of silver-white hairs extends down the leaf stalks. The flowers are clustered in flattened heads, each up to 8 cm (3 in) wide. The fruit is a rough, red berry with fawn speckles.

**Rounded habit**
Conical when young, the whitebeam matures into a broadly columnar tree with a rounded habit.

**PROFILE**

- Up to 15 m (50 ft)
- Up to 12 m (40 ft)
- Deciduous
- Alternate simple
- N.W. Europe

**Swedish whitebeam flowers**
The dull white flowers of this tree are individually small, but they are borne in large, flattened clusters up to 12.5 cm (5 in) wide.

*yellowish white stamens*

*flower 2 cm (¾ in) wide, with five petals*

**FEATURES**

**Fruit** Deep red, oval berry, up to 1 cm (½ in) long

*Sorbus intermedia* (Rosaceae)

# SWEDISH WHITEBEAM

**A medium-sized tree**, the Swedish whitebeam is native to northwest Europe including much of southern Scandinavia. It is an extremely hardy tree that thrives in exposed conditions, and can tolerate localized pollution – hence its popularity as an urban street tree. It is also used to restore land previously affected by industrial pollution as it can grow on impoverished soils.

The bark is grey and shiny at first, cracking into uneven flakes on maturity. The irregularly lobed leaves are dark green with a slight sheen on the upper surface and pale green on the underside, with a dense covering of short, white hairs. The dull white flowers are followed by fruit at the end of summer.

**Arching branches**
The Swedish whitebeam has a broad crown. Its arching branches become pendulous towards the tip.

## PROFILE



- Up to 20m (70ft)
- Up to 15m (50ft)
- Deciduous
- Alternate simple
- N. Europe, N. Africa

**Flowers and leaves**
Small flowers appear in late spring to early summer. Leaves are dark green on the upper surface, and pale green on the underside.

## FEATURES

**Bark** Grey-brown; develops irregular plates with age

**Fruit** Oval-shaped, warty berry, up to 1.5cm (½in) long

*Sorbus torminalis* (Rosaceae)

# WILD SERVICE TREE

**Also known as the chequer tree**, the wild service tree is easily distinguished from the members of the genus *Sorbus* by its stiff, maple- or plane-shaped leaves. Before the introduction of hops, its fruit were used to flavour beer – hence the frequently found English pub name: "The Chequers".

Smooth at first, the grey-brown bark cracks into irregular plates, flaking off to reveal fresh, rust-brown bark beneath. Winter leaf buds are distinctly olive-green. The leaves are deeply cut into sharply toothed lobes, and fixed alternately on olive-brown shoots by yellow-green stalks up to 5cm (2in) long. In autumn, the leaves turn yellow-brown before falling. Erect clusters of russet brown fruit follow in early autumn.

**Broadly columnar tree**
The medium-sized wild service tree has a broadly columnar habit and distinctive leaves.

**PROFILE**

- Up to 30 m (100 ft)
- Up to 12 m (40 ft)
- Deciduous
- Alternate compound
- W., C. and S. Europe; N.W. Africa; S.W. Asia

**Leaves and fruit**
The pinnate leaves are up to 25 cm (10 in) long and consist of 13 to 21 oblong leaflets. The greenish-brown fruit is sometimes flushed red.

*fruit up to 4 cm (1½ in) in diameter*

*yellow-green leaflet, up to 6 cm (2½ in) long, 1 cm (½ in) wide*

*serrated margin on top half of leaflet*

**FEATURES**

**Flowers** Creamy white, with five petals

*Sorbus domestica* (Rosaceae)

# SERVICE TREE

**Although it is larger in size**, at first glance the service tree resembles the rowan (p.252). This broadly columnar medium- to large-sized tree may occasionally be up to 30 m (100 ft) tall. It is native to western, central, and southern Europe; northwest Africa; and southwest Asia. However, it is rare in some of these regions; for example it is found growing wild in only a few locations in the British Isles. It is sometimes referred to as the true service tree to distinguish it from the similar-named wild service tree (p.255).

The brown bark is smooth on young trees, but becomes fissured and flaky in maturity. Winter buds are green and sticky. In late spring, flowers are densely borne in flattened clusters known as corymbs, which are up to 14 cm (5½ in) wide. The fruit is either apple-shaped (var. *pomifera*) or pear-shaped (var. *pyrifera*).

**Apple-fruited service tree (*Sorbus domestica* var. *pomifera*)** This tree can be distinguished from the service tree by its redder, more rounded, apple-shaped fruit.

**PROFILE**

- 5–10 m (15–30 ft)
- Up to 5 m (15 ft)
- Deciduous
- Alternate compound
- C. and W. China

*leaflet with pointed tip*

*sharply toothed margin on top half of leaflet*

*flower up to 7 mm (¼ in) wide*

**Spring blooms**
The white, five-petalled flowers of the Hupeh rowan bloom in late spring, in dense clusters up to 10 cm (4 in) wide.

**FEATURES**

**Fruit** Rounded, white to pink in colour, up to 1 cm (½ in) wide

*Sorbus hupehensis* (Rosaceae)

# HUPEH ROWAN

**Also known as the Chinese** mountain ash, this small, broadly columnar, deciduous tree is native to central and western China. Introduced into western cultivation in 1910, it is now widely grown in parks, gardens, and arboreta throughout the temperate world. It is a popular ornamental tree in Europe and North America, where it produces a compact crown of slender, ascending, purple-brown branches.

The bark is grey-brown to purplish brown. It is smooth when young, with a slight sheen, becoming flaky in maturity. The leaves are ash-like, pinnate, and, unlike most other rowans, blue-green in colour. Each pinnate leaf is made up of 11 to 17 oval-shaped leaflets that turn brilliant red in autumn. The flowers are slightly fragrant. The fruit is borne in loose, drooping bunches in autumn, and persists into winter.

**Vilmorin's rowan (*Sorbus vilmorinii*)** This tree has smaller pinnate leaves, each with 19 to 25 oblong to elliptic, round-tipped leaflets. The fruit is smaller and deep pink.

**PROFILE**

- 6–8 m (20–25 ft)
- Up to 5 m (15 ft)
- Deciduous
- Alternate compound
- W. Himalayas

narrowly elliptic leaflet, up to 5 cm (2 in) long

leaflet tapers to a point

rounded fruit, up to 1 cm (½ in) wide

fruit borne on pendulous, red-stalked panicle

**Foliage and fruit**
The leaves are pinnate and made up of 15 to 19 leaflets. Fruit ripen from pink to white, and look like waxy marbles.

**FEATURES**

**Flowers** Five-petalled, soft pink, carried in dense clusters in late spring

*Sorbus cashmiriana* (Rosaceae)

# KASHMIR ROWAN

**This small, broadly conical tree** was first described from specimens collected in Kashmir, northern India, in 1901. However, it was not cultivated outside its natural range of the western Himalayas until the 1930s. Since then it has been widely planted throughout the temperate world and is a prized addition to gardens and arboreta.

It has grey, sometimes red-grey, bark that remains relatively smooth even in maturity. The winter leaf buds are conical and distinctly pink-red. Leaves are pinnate, up to 15 cm (6 in) long. Each leaflet is deep green on the upper surface and pale green on the underside, with a fine covering of silver-grey hairs. Leaflets are sharply serrated along the margins. Slightly fragrant, light pink flowers up to 1.5 cm (½ in) wide are carried in lax corymbs up to 10 cm (4 in) in width in late spring. These are followed by berry-like, pink-coloured fruit, which turn to white when ripe. They persist on the tree long after the leaves have fallen in early winter.

slender-pointed leaflet

scarlet fruit, each up to 1 cm (½ in) wide

leaflet up to 10 cm (4 in) long, 5 cm (2 in) wide

**Fruit and leaves**
Large, lax, rounded heads of fruit up to 15 cm (6 in) wide grow alongside grass-green leaves with grey-green undersides.

**PROFILE**

- Up to 10 m (30 ft)
- Up to 10 m (30 ft)
- Deciduous
- Alternate compound
- S.W. China

**FEATURES**

**Leaves** Rich red in autumn before falling

red, conical bud

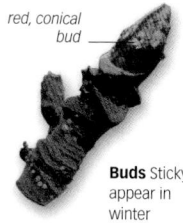

**Buds** Sticky; appear in winter

*Sorbus sargentiana* (Rosaceae)

# SARGENT'S ROWAN

**This medium-sized rowan** is native to the mountains of Sichuan in southwest China. It was collected by British plant collector Ernest H. Wilson in 1908 for the Arnold Arboretum in Jamaica Plain, Massachusetts, USA, and was named after the arboretum's director, Charles Sprague Sargent. Known for its attractive fruit and autumn colour, this tree has rigid, widely spreading branches.

The bark is plum-brown and smooth, even in maturity. The leaves are pinnate and up to 35 cm (14 in) long. They consist of 7 to 11 leaflets that have fine hairs and serrations around the upper half of the margin. The leaf stalks are bright crimson-red. The large winter buds are similar to those of the horse chestnut (p.281), but more conical and red. In early summer, small, creamy white flowers are borne in large, dense corymbs (flat-topped clusters of flowers) up to 20 cm (8 in) wide.

**Chinese mountain ash (*Sorbus scalaris*)** Unlike Sargent's rowan, this tree has leaves with more than 30 small leaflets. They have a glossy green upper surface and grey hairs on the underside.

**PROFILE**

- 15–20m (50–70ft)
- Up to 15m (50ft)
- Deciduous
- Alternate simple
- E. Himalayas, Burma

*creamy white flower, up to 1cm (½in) wide*

*serrated margin around top half of leaf*

*deep green leaf, 15cm (6in) long*

**Corymbs and leaves**
The flowers are borne in dense clusters (corymbs) on thick, woolly stalks. Leaves are large and oval to almost round in shape.

**FEATURES**

*small white hairs on underside*

**Leaves** Green-white on underside; up to 15cm (6in) long and wide

*Sorbus thibetica* (Rosaceae)

# TIBETAN WHITEBEAM

**This silvery, white-leaved whitebeam** was originally collected from the Himalayas in the 1920s. It is rarely seen in cultivation in its true form, and is mainly represented by the cultivar 'John Mitchell'. This cultivar is named after the one-time curator of Westonbirt Arboretum in Gloucestershire, England, who selected this form and planted it at Westonbirt in 1938.

A large-sized rowan, it has wide-spreading branches and a broad, rounded head of dense foliage. Its silver-grey bark is smooth and shiny at first but becomes darker and lightly fissured in maturity. The pungently scented flowers have purple-orange anthers and are similar to those of the common hawthorn (p.243). They are carried densely on corymbs (flat-topped flower clusters) up to 10cm (4in) wide. The fruit is apple-shaped, up to 1cm (½in) wide, green ripening to russet-brown.

***Sorbus megalocarpa*** This tree is distinguished by its broadly obovate, coarsely toothed leaves with little hairs on the underside and its large, marble-sized, brown, speckled fruit.

## PROFILE

- Up to 6 m (20 ft)
- Up to 6 m (20 ft)
- Deciduous
- Alternate simple
- S.E. Europe, S.W. Asia

**Roselike flowers**
The white flowers have five well-spaced petals around a central cluster of purple anthers and golden stamens.

*bright green leaf, up to 15 cm (6 in) long*

*flower up to 5 cm (2 in) wide*

*minutely toothed leaf margin*

## FEATURES

**Fruit** Russet brown; shaped like a flattened pear

*Mespilus germanica* (Rosaceae)

# MEDLAR

**This small, broadly spreading**, deciduous tree is native to southwest Asia and southeast Europe. It has long been cultivated for its fruit, which is edible and tasty, though considered an acquired taste by some. This is probably due to the need to "blet" the fruit before eating. This means allowing the fruit to overripen until it becomes like a soft pear. Once bletted, the fruit tastes like cinnamon-flavoured stewed apple.

The bark is smooth and dull brown, becoming fissured and flaking with age. The elliptic to lanceolate, stalkless leaves are faintly hairy on both sides. The flowers are borne singly at the ends of shoots in early summer. The fruit is up to 5 cm (2 in) long and 3 cm (1 ¼ in) wide and has an open top surrounded by a calyx, similar to a rose hip – the fruit of the rose.

**Quince *(Cydonia oblonga)*** This tree is distinguished by its broadly elliptic to rounded leaves, green shoots, pale pink flowers and large, green-yellow, pear-shaped fruit.

**PROFILE**

- Up to 25 m (80 ft)
- 15 m (50 ft)
- Deciduous
- Alternate compound
- USA

flowers in pendulous raceme up to 20 cm (8 in) long

reddish brown calyx

smooth leaflet margin

leaflet up to 5 cm (2 in) long

ovate to elliptic leaflet, grass green on upper surface

**Leaves and flowers**
Pinnate leaves, up to 30 cm (12 in) long, have 11 to 21 lax leaflets. Pea-like, fragran white flowers are borne in early summer.

**FEATURES**

**Fruit** Reddish to dark brown, hanging pod bears black seeds

*Robinia pseudoacacia* (Fabaceae)

# BLACK LOCUST

**Native to the Appalachian Mountains**, from Pennsylvania to Georgia, this large, broadly columnar tree is now naturalized throughout the USA. The black locust was one of the first American trees to be introduced into Europe in 1601.

The smooth, grey-brown bark becomes fissured and vertically ridged with age. The branch wood often breaks to form scars on old trees. On mature trees, suckers from the roots can rise up to 10 m (30 ft) away from the trunk. The sharply pointed leaves are blue-green on the underside, and may have two spines at the base. The fruit is an oblong pod up to 10 cm (4 in) long. It splits open in late summer to reveal black seeds.

**Golden-leaved robini**
Unlike the black locust, this cultivated variety (*Robinia pseudoacacia* 'Frisia') has bright golden yellow leaves and a smaller stature.

## PROFILE



- Up to 30m (100ft)
- Up to 20m (70ft)
- Deciduous
- Alternate compound
- N. China

**Ovate leaflets**
The pinnate leaves are alternately arranged on blue-green shoots. Up to 25cm (10in) long, each leaf has 9 to 17 opposite leaflets.

## FEATURES

**Bark** Light grey, smooth; develops regular vertical fissures in maturity

**Flowers** White, pea-like; borne on pendulous panicles

*Sophora japonica* (Fabaceae)

# JAPANESE PAGODA TREE

**Despite its name**, this broadly columnar tree is native to northern China and not Japan. However, it has been widely cultivated in Japan for centuries, particularly in temple gardens in and around Kyoto. It was introduced into western cultivation in 1753. When grown from seed, it may take up to 30 years to produce flowers.

The bark is reminiscent of that of the common ash (p.300). The leaves are blue-green and slightly hairy on the underside, and emerge from buds only in early summer. Fragrant white flowers are carried on terminal, pendulous, widespread panicles, up to 25cm (10in) long, in late summer. The flowers are more abundant after hot summers. The fruit is a pod, green ripening to brown, up to 7.5cm (3in) long. It contains up to six seeds.

**Kowhai (*Sophora tetraptera*)** This small, evergreen tree has pinnate leaves, with 20 to 40 ovate to elliptic leaflets, each up to 3cm (1¼in) long, and yellow, tubular flowers.

## PROFILE



- Up to 30 m (100 ft)
- Up to 15 m (50 ft)
- Deciduous
- Alternate compound
- N. China

**Pinnate leaves**
The pinnate leaves are up to 75 cm (30 in) long. They consist of 11 to 19 leaflets held on a bright red petiole (stalk), up to 1.5 cm (½ in) long.

## FEATURES

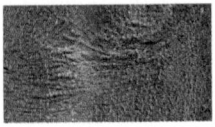

**Bark** Slate-grey, relatively smooth; develops vertical, light patterning in maturity

**Fruit** Winged seed; yellow-brown, tinged with red when ripe

*Ailanthus altissima* (Simaroubaceae)

# TREE OF HEAVEN

**One of the fastest growing** of all temperate Asian trees, the tree of heaven was introduced into western cultivation in 1751. This large, broadly columnar tree produces extensive suckers from its roots, and has bee known to lift paving slabs and crack pavements up to 15 m (50 ft) from the trunk.

Leaves consist of 11 to 19 leaflets, which have some serration near the base. Borne in late spring, they are bright red at first, developing a deep green upper surface and a pale blue-green underside later. Yellow-green male and female flowers are borne in large panicles on separate trees in summer. Female trees bear winged seeds in ash-like, orange-red bunches, up to 30 cm (12 in) long.

**Pollution-resistant tree**
The tree of heaven is wide planted in towns and citie for its ability to withstand atmospheric pollution.

**Bipinnate foliage**
In summer, this tree bears large, bipinnate leaves, 1 m (3 ft) long, consisting of up to 14 leaflets.

*leaflet up to 7.5 cm (3 in) long*

*ovate, untoothed leaflet*

**PROFILE**

- Up to 20 m (70 ft)
- 8–10 m (25–30 ft)
- Deciduous
- Alternate compound
- C. and E. USA

**FEATURES**

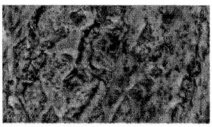

**Bark** Dark grey, red-tinged, with deep fissures

**Fruit** Seed capsule, glaucous-green when unripe

*Gymnocladus dioicus* (Fabaceae)

# KENTUCKY COFFEE TREE

**This large, broadly columnar**, sometimes spreading tree is native to central and eastern USA. Early European settlers would roast and use its seeds to make a substitute coffee-like drink – hence the reference to coffee in its name.

The Kentucky coffee tree is rather sparse looking, with branches that remain bare until towards their tips. The leaves are produced late in the season, and for a while in spring the tree shows no signs of life because the leaf buds are small and so easily missed. The leaflets are bronze when young, developing a dark green upper surface and a blue-green underside in summer. They turn golden yellow in autumn. Greenish white, fragrant flowers, up to 2.5 cm (1 in) wide, are borne in conical panicles, up to 10 cm (4 in) long. The flowers are followed by broad-bean-like seed pods, up to 25 cm (10 in) long and 5 cm (2 in) wide. Glaucous-green at first, they ripen to red-brown. The seed pods contain up to nine seeds set within a sweet-tasting pulp.

**PROFILE**

- 20–30 m (70–100 ft)
- Up to 20 m (70 ft)
- Deciduous
- Alternate compound
- C. and E. USA

**Honey locust leaves**
The leaves are pinnate, sometimes bipinnate (where the leaflets themselves are pinnate). Each leaf has up to 36 oblong-lanceolate leaflets.

*leaflet tapers to a broad tip*

*glossy bright green upper surface of leaflet*

*leaflet up to 4 cm (1½ in) long*

**FEATURES**

**Flowers** Small, yellow-green, up to 1 cm (½ in) wide; borne in racemes up to 7.5 cm (3 in) long in early to midsummer

*Gleditsia triacanthos* (Fabaceae)

# HONEY LOCUST

**This broadly spreading tree** is best identified by its ferocious thorns, which cover its trunk and main branches. Its native habitat extends from New England to Texas in the USA, and it has been cultivated in Europe since its introduction in 1700. It is widely planted in city streets because of its tolerance to heat, dust, drought, and airborne pollutants. Unlike other members of the pea family, the honey locust does not produce the typical "wing and keel" pea flower.

The bark is grey-brown, smooth when young, developing clusters of sharp spines, up to 7.5 cm (3 in) long, in maturity. Leaves are frond-like in appearance and lack a terminal leaflet. The leaflets have slight serrations along the margins. The shoots are green and may carry smaller spines next to each leaf bud. The seed-bearing fruit is a large, twisted, pendulous pod up to 45 cm (18 in) long. Green at first, it ripens to olive-brown.

**ellow-wood leaves**
e pinnate leaves are 20–30 cm
-12 in) long, with 5 to 11 broadly
ate to oval leaflets.

*leaflet up to 13 cm (5 in) long, 7 cm (3 in) wide*

*dark green upper surface of leaflet*

## PROFILE

- Up to 15 m (50 ft)
- Up to 20 m (70 ft)
- Deciduous
- Alternate compound
- S.E. USA

## FEATURES

**Bark** Smooth grey to light brown in colour

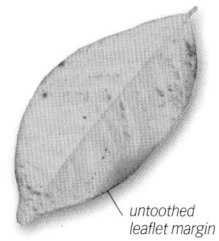


**Leaves** Bright clear yellow in autumn

*Cladrastis kentukea* (Fabaceae)

# YELLOW-WOOD

**Also known as virgilia**, this broadly columnar tree was introduced into Europe in 1812. It is a small to medium-sized tree with a broad and rounded crown. It takes its name from its yellow heartwood, which is used to make furniture, gunstocks, and decorative items.

The shoots are green and downy when young, turning yellow-green, and then red-brown, with age. The leaflets are dark green on the upper surface, while the underside is pale green and covered with fine hairs. White, mildly fragrant flowers are produced in early summer. They are borne in wisteria-like, pendulous racemes. These are followed by fruit, which are smooth pods, green ripening to brown. They contain two to six dark brown seeds.

**Low-branched tree** Yellow-wood normally has low branching and a wide crown of upright, spreading branches.

**PROFILE**

- Up to 30 m (100 ft)
- Up to 15 m (50 ft)
- Evergreen
- Alternate simple
- South Australia, Tasmania

*oval, woody seed capsule, up to 5 mm (¼ in) long*

*lanceolate, blue-green mature leaf*

*mature leaf, 12 cm (5 in) long, 4 cm (1½ in) wide*

**White flowers**
In summer, flowers with numerous creamy yellow stamens are borne in clusters of three in the leaf axil

**FEATURES**

**Bark** Mottled grey-green and copper; flakes in long strips to reveal cream surface below

**Leaves**
Glaucous silver-blue, stalkless; carried in opposite pairs when young

*Eucalyptus gunnii* (Myrtaceae)

# CIDER GUM

**This large, broadly columnar**, fast-growing evergreen is native to Tasmania, where it grows in moist mountain forests up to 1,300 m (4,265 ft) above sea level. One of the hardiest of all *Eucalyptus* species, it is widely planted in temperate regions as an ornamental tree and for timber. The attractive juvenile foliage is highly valued by flower arrangers and florists. In order to maintain this foliage, trees are regularly coppiced (trimmed down to stumps), to stimulate the growth of new shoots.

The juvenile leaves are rounded and up to 4 cm (1½ in) long. They are virtually stalkless, and are carried in opposite pairs on pink, bloomy shoots. Mature leaves are alternate and hang down from limp branchlets. The flowers are slightly fragrant, and after pollination, develop into dry, grey seed capsules that are open at one end.

**Urn gum (*Eucalyptus urnigera*)** This tree is easily distinguished by its smaller stature, dark, glossy green, waxy leaves, and urn-shaped seed capsules.

**PROFILE**

- Up to 25 m (80 ft)
- Up to 8 m (25 ft)
- Evergreen
- Alternate simple
- Tasmania

**laucous leaves**
oth young and mature leaves e thick, fleshy, and blue-green th a waxy coating. They are orne on blue-green shoots.

**FEATURES**

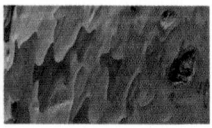

**Bark** Smooth, mottled grey-white; peels in vertical strips to reveal creamy white layer

*Eucalyptus coccifera* (Myrtaceae)

# MOUNT WELLINGTON PEPPERMINT

**Also known as** the Tasmanian snow gum, this large tree is one of the hardiest and most attractive of the eucalyptus trees. In Tasmania it grows in the central mountain ranges up to 1,400 m (4,590 ft) above sea level. A broadly spreading, fast-growing species, it was first introduced into Britain around 1840, and has been widely planted across Europe since then.

Juvenile leaves are rounded to oval-shaped, while mature leaves are lanceolate. The foliage emits a peppermint fragrance when crushed. Flowers, with numerous yellow stamens, are borne in clusters in the leaf axils in early summer. The fruit is a small, woody, funnel-shaped capsule that contains several seeds. Blue-green and bloomy at first, it ripens to grey-brown.

**Tasmanian blue gum (*Eucalyptus globulus*)** Unlike its cousin, this tree has leathery, lanceolate leaves, up to 30 cm (12 in) long and 5 cm (2 in) wide. They emit a eucalyptus scent.

**PROFILE**

- Up to 45 m (150 ft)
- Up to 20 m (70 ft)
- Evergreen
- Transitions from opposite to alternate simple
- S.E. Australia, Tasmania

*light greenish blue young leaf with copper tint*

*lanceolate, mature leaf*

**Mountain gum leaves** Young leaves are rounded, stalkless,and borne opposite on blue-green shoots; they become lanceolate with age.

**FEATURES**

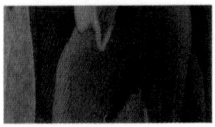

**Bark** Patchwork of grey-brown, salmon-pink, or red-brown

*adult leaf up to 18 cm (7 in) long*

**Leaves** Lanceolate, glaucous-blue in maturity

*Eucalyptus dalrympleana* (Myrtaceae)

# MOUNTAIN GUM

**This broadly columnar tree**, also known as white mountain gum or broad-leaved kindling bark, grows up to 45 m (150 ft) in its native habitat. But high in the mountains of New South Wales, 1,300 m (4,265 ft) above sea level, it seldom reaches more than half this size, and may even be shrubby.

The tree has a straight trunk with beautiful patchwork bark, which peels in long, ragged strips to reveal patches of white or fawn beneath. Juvenile and mature leaves, which vary in shape and arrangement, are often borne together on the tree. The flowers are fragrant and white, with yellow stamens. They are borne in groups of three, in umbrella-shaped flower clusters in the leaf axils in summer. The flowers are a good source of honey. Seeds are contained in a green hemispherical capsule, ripening to woody brown.

**Silver gum (*Eucalyptus cordata*)** This small tree is up to 15 m (50 ft) tall. It has angular, almost square, shoots; heart-shaped juvenile leaves; and white bark mottled green and purple.

**Yellow gum leaves**
Mature leaves are lanceolate, bronze when young, turning glossy apple-green with age. The fruit is a stalkless capsule, ripening from blue-green to woody brown.

## PROFILE



- 40–60 m (130–200 ft)
- Up to 20 m (70 ft)
- Evergreen
- Transitions from opposite to alternate
- Tasmania

## FEATURES

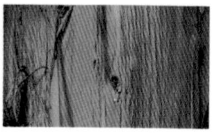

**Bark** Brown or pink-red in maturity; flakes in long, linear strips to reveal paler bark

*Eucalyptus johnstonii* (Myrtaceae)

# YELLOW GUM

**This narrowly columnar tree**, also known as the Tasmanian yellow gum, is one of the largest *Eucalyptus* species. It reaches up to 60 m (200 ft) in height in its native habitat. It is fast-growing, with some specimens having been known to put on more than 2 m (6 ft) of growth in a year. The tree was introduced into Europe in 1886.

The bark is blue-grey when young, and, when shed, accumulates in piles around the base of the tree's straight trunk. Juvenile leaves are rounded, thick and fleshy, and stalkless. They are borne in opposite pairs on distinctive deep red, young shoots. Mature leaves are lanceolate, bright green, and borne alternately on the stem. The flowers are fragrant, creamy white with yellow stamens, borne in umbels (clusters) of three in the leaf axils in summer. The fruit is a capsule, borne in threes. Each capsule contains several seeds.

**Snow gum (*Eucalyptus pauciflora*)** This tree is distinguished from the yellow gum by its sickle-shaped leaves, up to 20 cm (8 in) long, and light grey, almost white bark.

sharply toothed leaf margin

drawn-out, pointed leaf tip

heart-shaped leaf base

leaf paler green with hairs on underside

lax, white bract, up to 20 cm (8 in) long

**Conspicuous flower bracts**
Two unequal bracts enclose small flowers with lilac anthers, which are clustered in round heads. The leaves are broadly ovate.

**PROFILE**

- Up to 25 m (80 ft)
- Up to 15 m (50 ft)
- Deciduous
- Alternate simple
- China

**FEATURES**

**Bark** Brown, smooth at first; becomes fissured in maturity

**Fruit** Green, ripening to purple-brown

*Davidia involucrata* (Cornaceae)

# POCKET HANDKERCHIEF TREE

**This Chinese tree was introduced** in the West by English plant collector Ernest H. Wilson in 1901. It is also known as the dove tree or ghost tree. All three common names refer to the hanging white bracts, which surround the flower in spring.

The brown bark, initially smooth, develops orange-brown cracks, and fissures into irregular plates. Shiny, bright green leaves grow up to 15 cm (6 in) long and curl in hot or dry weather to reduce water loss. The flower heads are up to 1 cm (½ in) wide. The fruit is a green, circular husk, borne singly on a 4 cm- (1 ½ in-) long stalk. It contains a hard nut with several seeds inside.

**Showy blossom**
In spring, the flower bracts are conspicuous on this large, broadly conical, sometimes spreading tree

**PROFILE**

- Up to 12 m (40 ft)
- 12 m (40 ft)
- Deciduous
- Alternate compound
- China, Korea

*flower up to 1 cm (½ in) long*

*oblong to ovate leaflet, up to 10 cm (4 in) long*

*heavily lobed leaflet has toothed margin*

**Foliage and flowers**
Up to 45 cm (18 in) long, the pinnate, and sometimes bipinnate, leaf carries 11 to 13 leaflets. The flowers appears in summer.

**FEATURES**

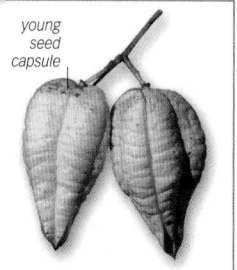


**Fruit** Bladder-like seed capsule, green ripening to yellow-brown

*Koelreuteria paniculata* (Sapindaceae)

# PRIDE OF INDIA

**Also known as the golden-rain tree** or China tree, this medium-sized, broadly spreading tree is native to China and Korea. It has, however, been widely planted in parks, gardens, and arboreta throughout India and the temperate world since its introduction into wider cultivation in 1763.

The young bark is pale brown and smooth, becoming fissured in maturity. Pinnate leaves are matt and dark green on the upper surface, paler with a pink midrib on the underside. They are borne in spring on long and arching shoots, which gradually fade from red through pink to light green by high summer. Clusters of bright golden yellow flowers are carried in open panicles, up to 45 cm (18 in) long.

**Ornamental foliage**
Planted for its flowers and unusual fruit, the pride of India tree has a graceful, broadly spreading form.

## PROFILE

- Up to 20 m (70 ft)
- Up to 15 m (50 ft)
- Deciduous
- Alternate simple
- China, Japan, Taiwan

**Flower cluster**
In early summer, tiny, four-petalled flowers are borne in clusters (corymbs) above the foliage, at regular intervals along horizontal branches.

*oval leaf, up to 15 cm (6 in) long, with dark green, shiny upper surface*

*small, creamy white flower*

*erect flower stalk*

*hairy, pale blue-green leaf underside*

## FEATURES

**Flower buds** Green, in broad, flattened corymbs, up to 15 cm (6 in) wide

**Fruit** Rounded, blue-black berries, on pink-red stalks

*Cornus controversa* (Cornaceae)

# WEDDING-CAKE TREE

**Also known as the table dogwood**, this broadly spreading, medium-sized tree came into western cultivation before 1880. Its common names refer to its symmetrical, horizontal branches, which gradually grow shorter towards the top of the tree in tiers, like the layers of a wedding cake.

It is one of the only two dogwoods to have alternate leaves, while the rest have opposite leaves. The bark is smooth, grey to light brown, and becomes lightly fissured in maturity. The distinctly veined leaves turn rich plum-red in autumn before falling. The flowers are followed by clusters of small berries in autumn.

**Variegated table dogwood**
This cultivar (*Cornus controversa* 'Variegata') has narrower, variegated leaves with a striking silver-cream margin.

## PROFILE

- 3–10 m (10–30 ft)
- Up to 8 m (25 ft)
- Deciduous
- Opposite simple
- Japan, China, Korea

*tiny, green flower bobble*

*bract, up to 5 cm (2 in) long, tapers to a point*

*untoothed leaf margin*

*roughly oval leaf, up to 7.5 cm (3 in) long*

**Bract-enclosed flowers**
Flower clusters are surrounded by four creamy white or pink-white bracts, positioned on upright stalks above the dark green foliage.

## FEATURES

**Leaves** Pink, red, and purple in autumn before falling

**Fruit** Red, globular; borne in clusters on long stalks

*Cornus kousa* (Cornaceae)

# JAPANESE DOGWOOD

**Also known as the** Japanese strawberry tree, this tree is commonly planted in gardens throughout the temperate regions of the world. Indigenous to Japan, it was introduced into western cultivation in 1875. A Chinese variety of this tree was discovered by Ernest H. Wilson in 1907, and is also cultivated in Europe.

The Japanese dogwood has a rich red-brown bark, which flakes to reveal cream- or fawn-coloured new bark beneath. The leaves have a shiny upper surface and a paler underside, with tufts of brown hairs in the leaf vein axils. The tiny, green flowers appear in early summer, and develop into strawberry-like, edible fruit in late summer.

**Chinese dogwood**
This large tree (*Cornus kousa* var. *chinensis*) has larger leaves, which are smooth around the margin; and creamy white flower bracts, which turn pink.

## PROFILE

- 25 m (80 ft)
- Up to 15 m (50 ft)
- Deciduous
- Opposite simple
- W. North America

**Erect flowers**
Flowers are borne at shoot ends on erect stalks, enclosed by four to seven bracts. The variable leaves are obovate to oval in shape.

*creamy white, often blushed pink, petal-like bract, up to 7.5 cm (3 in) long*

*dark green leaf, up to 15 cm (6 in) long, 7.5 cm (3 in) wide*

*cluster of small, green-purple flowers with yellow stamens*

*elliptic, pointed leaf with untoothed margin*

## FEATURES

**Leaves** Turn yellow or red in autumn before falling

**Fruit** Rounded, strawberry-like, carried on long stalks

*Cornus nuttallii* (Cornaceae)

# PACIFIC DOGWOOD

**With a natural habitat** ranging from British Columbia to California, the Pacific dogwood has been cultivated in parks and gardens outside this region since its discovery in 1835. In cultivation, this tree rarely attains its full height, often growing as a large, multi-stemmed shrub, or small tree up to 10 m (30 ft) tall. This medium-sized, broadly conical tree produces the largest bracts of any dogwood species.

The smooth purple-grey bark cracks into irregular plates in maturity. The leaves are pale green, with a fine coating of hairs on the underside. In late spring, flowers appear in dense hemispherical clusters, up to 2.5 cm (1 in) wide, followed by small, red fruit.

**American flowering dogwood**
This smaller related tree (*Cornus florida*) has four bracts that enclose flower heads in winter.

## PROFILE

- Up to 15 m (50 ft)
- Up to 15 m (50 ft)
- Deciduous
- Opposite compound
- N. and N.E. China, Korea, Japan

**eaf and leaflets**
ne pinnate leaves of the Amur ork tree grow up to 40 cm 6 in) long. Each leaf consists f up to 13 ovate leaflets.

## FEATURES

**Bark** Grey, thick, deeply fissured, and corky

**Fruit** Stalked clusters of smooth, rounded, green berries, ripen to shiny black

*Phellodendron amurense* (Rutaceae)

# AMUR CORK TREE

**As implied by its name,** the bark of this tree has been used in China in much the same way as that of the cork oak (p.170). It is native to Amur, a region straddling the border between China and Russia, as well as parts of Korea and Japan. The Amur cork tree has been in western cultivation since 1885. However, in recent years it has become an invasive species, and is now listed as a noxious weed in some states in the USA, such as Massachusetts.

Its pinnate leaves may look like those of the common ash (p.300) with leaflets up to 5 cm (2 in) wide. The underside of each leaflet is pale green, with tufts of hair at the base of the midrib. The flowers are small and white, with yellow anthers, borne on terminal panicles up to 15 cm (6 in) long.

**Spreading form**
Until recently, the broadly spreading, medium-sized Amur cork tree was often planted in the USA.

**Flowers in corymbs**
Pungently scented flowers are carried in domed corymbs (flat-topped flower clusters) up to 15 cm (6 in) wide.

*dark green upper surface of leaflet*

*leaflet up to 12 cm (5 in) long*

*creamy white flowers, with yellow anthers*

*pale green underside of leaflet*

*leaf stalk fades from deep pink to yellow-green*

**PROFILE**

- Up to 15 m (50 ft)
- Up to 15 m (50 ft)
- Deciduous
- Opposite simple
- China, Korea

*Tetradium daniellii* (Rutaceae)

# EUODIA

**This tree is also called** the bee-bee tree because its flowers attract honey bees and appear at a time when few other trees are in bloom. Its botanical name commemorates William Daniell, a British army surgeon and botanist who, in the 1860s, collected specimens of the tree in China. However, it was not introduced into western cultivation until 1905.

The bark is grey and smooth, even in maturity. Pinnate leaves, up to 40 cm (16 in) long, carry 7 to 11 elliptic, oval to lanceolate leaflets. The leaves turn pale yellow in autumn before falling. In summer, small flowers are followed by clusters of spherical fruit, which ripen from red-brown to black. Each fruit contains tiny, black seeds.

**Fast-growing tree**
The euodia is a broadly spreading, medium-sized, deciduous tree. It grows rapidly to become as wide as it is tall.

**PROFILE**

- Up to 20m (70ft)
- Up to 15m (50ft)
- Evergreen
- Alternate simple
- Europe, W. Asia, N. Africa

**Densely clustered berries** Fruit of the common holly tree is a spherical, smooth berry, borne in dense groups clustered along the shoots in winter.

**FEATURES**

**Flowers** Purple-tinged or white; male and female appear on separate trees

*Ilex aquifolium* (Aquifoliaceae)

# COMMON HOLLY

**This easily recognizable**, broadly columnar, medium-sized tree is extremely hardy. Its dense foliage provides welcome shelter in exposed mountainous and coastal locations. Holly has long been cultivated in gardens and has given rise to numerous, common garden cultivars. In the western world, holly is closely linked to Christmas celebrations.

The bark is silver-grey and smooth even in maturity. Elliptic to ovate leaves are thick and stiff. They are glossy, dark green, and waxy on the upper surface; light green on the underside; and variable around the margin. Some leaves bear sharp, strong spines, others may have no spines at all. Male and female flowers are borne on separate trees. They are small, clustered into the leaf axils, and appear in early summer. The fruit ripen from green to bright red and are eaten by birds in winter.

**Horned holly (*Ilex cornuta*)** It is easy to distinguish this Chinese holly from the common holly by its distinct, rectangular leaves displaying up to five angular spines.

**PROFILE**

- Up to 10m (30ft)
- Up to 6m (20ft)
- Evergreen
- Alternate simple
- C. and W. China

*leaf up to 4cm (1½in) long*

*sharply pointed, central lobe of leaf*

**Angular lobes**
The leaves have three to seven angular lobes, all ferociously spined, with the central lobe elongated and pointed.

**FEATURES**

**Bark** Slate-grey, smooth

**Fruit** Bright red, spherical berries; carried in clusters in autumn

*Ilex pernyi* (Aquifoliaceae)

# PERNY'S HOLLY

**This narrowly conical tree**, sometimes large shrub, is native to central and western China. It was discovered in 1858 by Abbé Paul Perny, a French Jesuit missionary. However, it was another 40 years before it was introduced into western cultivation. Today, it is commonly planted in botanical gardens and arboreta.

The leaves, which are borne on thick, leathery stalks, are deep glossy green on the upper surface and paler on the underside. They are oblong, sometimes almost triangular, and occasionally trident-shaped. The branches of Perny's holly are erect, ascending, and then arching. The flowers are cream to pale yellow and slightly fragrant. Male and female flowers are borne on separate trees, in tight clusters, on the leaf axils. The fruit is a rounded, red berry, carried on erect shoots. Borne in autumn, it persists on the tree well into winter.

***Ilex corallina*** This tree is easily distinguished from Perny's holly by its wavy-edged, lanceolate leaves, up to 8cm (3in) long. These are normally spineless, though toothed.

## PROFILE

- Up to 30 m (100 ft)
- Up to 15 m (50 ft)
- Deciduous
- Opposite compound
- Native to Greece and Albania, is naturalized across temperate regions

*creamy white flower with five petals*

*flowers in branched cluster*

*yellow blotch on flower, turns pink*

**Conical panicles**
The creamy white flowers are borne in large clusters in spring. These are conical and upright, up to 25 cm (10 in) tall.

## FEATURES

**Leaves**
Compound palmate, bright green, strongly veined

**Fruit** Rounded green husk with spines; up to 6 cm (2½ in) wide

*Aesculus hippocastanum* (Sapindaceae)

# COMMON HORSE CHESTNUT

**Perhaps one of the most common** large trees in cultivation, the common horse chestnut is indigenous only to Greece and Albania. This broadly columnar tree has been widely planted in the temperate world since its introduction in 1650. In recent years, it has come under attack from a leaf-mining moth and a bleeding canker bacterium, both of which are causing widespread damage to trees across Europe.

The bark is grey to brown-orange and smooth, turning shallowly fissured and scaly in maturity. Leaves consisting of up to seven obovate leaflets, each up to 25 cm (10 in) long, turn golden brown before falling in mid-autumn. Winter buds are large, rich red-brown, and sticky. The rounded fruit contains one to three seeds.

**California buckeye (*Aesculus californica*)** This American species has much smaller leaves and flowers than the common horse chestnut, and its flowers are borne in summer.

**Compound palmate leaves**
The leaves have five to seven leaflets, all meeting the leaf stalk at a common point.

*rough, slightly pear-shaped, green fruit*

*pink petiole (leaf stalk)*

*obovate to broadly lanceolate leaflet, up to 25 cm (10 in) long*

**PROFILE**

- 25–30 m (80–100 ft)
- Up to 12 m (40 ft)
- Deciduous
- Opposite compound
- N. India, N.W. Himalayas

**FEATURES**

**Flowers** White to pale pink; borne on erect panicles up to 25 cm (10 in) long

**Seed** Dark brown, enclosed in green husk

*Aesculus indica* (Sapindaceae)

# INDIAN HORSE CHESTNUT

**This large, broadly columnar tree** is native to north India and the northwest Himalayas, where it grows in the foothills up to 3,000 m (9,840 ft) above sea level. Introduced into western cultivation in 1851, it is planted in parks, gardens, and arboreta across the temperate world, especially Europe and North America.

The bark is grey-brown and smooth, even in maturity. Bronze-coloured leaflets emerge in spring, turning glossy grass green in summer and yellow in autumn. Borne in summer, the flowers have a red or yellow blotch at the base. They are more slender than the flowers of the common horse chestnut (p.281). The fruit is a green husk, ripening to brown. It opens to reveal up to three seeds, smaller than those of the common horse chestnut.

**Chinese horse chestnut (*Aesculus chinensis*)** This tree is smaller than the Indian horse chestnut, with smaller leaves and white flowers that are borne on thinner panicles.

**PROFILE**

- 20–30 m (70–100 ft)
- Up to 15 m (50 ft)
- Deciduous
- Opposite compound
- Japan

*red blotch on flower base*

**Flowers and leaves** Creamy white flowers, amidst shiny dark grey-green leaves, are borne in spring.

*flowers borne in erect panicle, up to 25 cm (10 in) long*

**FEATURES**

**Fruit** Almost spineless, up to 1.5 cm (½ in) long

*Aesculus turbinata* (Sapindaceae)

# JAPANESE HORSE CHESTNUT

**This broadly columnar tree** is similar in appearance to the common horse chestnut (p.281). It is widely planted in its native Japan as an ornamental species in parks and gardens. Elsewhere, it is not as common although regularly found in botanic gardens and arboreta across temperate regions of the world. It is slower-growing than the common horse chestnut, with smaller flowers, which are not carried in such profusion. However, it has larger leaves, which turn bright orange in autumn.

The bark is brown and smooth when young, flaking in maturity. Winter buds are red-brown, glossy, and sticky. The ovate leaves are compound palmate, consisting of a maximum of seven deeply veined leaflets up to 40 cm (16 in) long. They have fine, uneven toothed margins and rusty hairs along the midrib on the pale green underside. The egg-shaped fruit ripens to brown and cracks to reveal up to three shiny dark brown seeds.

**Conical panicles**
Flowers ranging in colour from pink to deep crimson are borne on branched, conical flower clusters.

*flower with five petals*

*flowers borne on panicle up to 20cm (8in) long*

**PROFILE**

- Up to 20m (70ft)
- Up to 10m (30ft)
- Deciduous
- Opposite compound
- Germany

**FEATURES**

**Leaves** Compound palmate, made of five to seven leaflets

*fruit up to 5cm (2in) wide*

**Fruit** Rounded, green husk; ripening to dull brown

*Aesculus* x *carnea* (Sapindaceae)

# RED HORSE CHESTNUT

**With its bright pink-red flowers**, this popular hybrid tree is easily told apart from the common horse chestnut (p.281), which is one of its parents, the other being the American red buckeye (p.286). Little is known about the origins of this broadly columnar species, but it possibly occurred naturally in Germany in the early 1800s.

The bark is dull brown and smooth when young, developing shallow fissures and breaking into flaking plates with age. The mid- to dark green leaves consist of obovate leaflets up to 25cm (10in) long. They have pronounced parallel veins and are joined at the base to a long, pink-green stalk. The fruit, sometimes covered in spines, splits in segments to reveal up to three shiny brown seeds.

**Blooming in spring**
The canopy of the large red horse chestnut starts blooming from mid- to late spring.

**ellow flower clusters**
early summer, pale yellow flowers
e borne on stalks in erect, elongated,
anicles (branched clusters) that are
to 15 cm (6 in) long.

*pink blotch on flower*

**PROFILE**

- Up to 30 m (100 ft)
- Up to 12 m (40 ft)
- Deciduous
- Opposite compound
- S.E. USA

**FEATURES**

**Leaves** Orange-red in fall before being shed

**Fruit** Green ripening to brown; carry up to three seeds

*Aesculus flava* (Sapindaceae)

# SWEET BUCKEYE

**This large, round-headed** but broadly conical tree is native to the southeastern United States, from where it was introduced into Europe in 1764. It is the only buckeye (or horse chestnut) to produce yellow flowers and is sometimes referred to as the yellow buckeye.

The bark is brown-gray, flaking in maturity into large, irregular-shaped scales. Branches tend to be horizontal, sometimes drooping, with a characteristic upward sweep at the tip. The leaves are compound palmate, each consisting of five bright to deep green leaflets, which are narrowly elliptic and up to 6 in (15 cm) long. They are joined to a pea-green, sometimes pink, leaf stalk at a common point. The fruit is a smooth, rounded to oblong husk, up to 2 in (5 cm) long. It ripens to split in segments to reveal two to three shiny brown seeds.

**Ohio buckeye (*Aesculus glabra*)** This tree can be distinguished from the sweet buckeye by its tall, thin, pale green-yellow flowers and its elliptic leaflets, which are up to 8 in (20 cm) long.

**PROFILE**

- Up to 7 m (22 ft)
- Up to 3 m (10 ft)
- Deciduous
- Opposite compound
- S.E. USA

**Erect flowers**
The red buckeye has four-petalled flowers, which bloom in early summer. The leaves are compound palmate with elliptic leaflets.

*flowers borne in erect, open panicle, up to 20 cm (8 in) long*

*slender, bright crimson-red flower*

*leaflet up to 15 cm (6 in) long*

**FEATURES**

**Leaves** Five glossy, dark green leaflets, each on a short stalk

**Fruit** Pear-shaped, russet-green ripening to light brown; appears after flowers

*Aesculus pavia* (Sapindaceae)

# RED BUCKEYE

**Native to the coastal plains** of southeastern USA, from North Carolina to Florida, and west to the Mississipp River basin, this tree grows in moist woods and thickets. Sometimes no more than a shrub, it is a small, broadly spreading tree. The red buckeye tree is one of the parent of the hybrid red horse chestnut (p.284) and gives the red colouring to the latter's flowers. It was introduced into the western world in 1711 and has been cultivated in parks, gardens, and arboreta since then.

The red buckeye has dark grey bark, smooth at first, which cracks into irregular plates in maturity. The leaves are made up of sharply toothed, elliptic leaflets. Each leaflet is borne on a yellow-pink petiole (leaf stalk) up to 18 cm (7 in) long. In autumn, the leaves turn orange and red. This tree produces small fruit, which open to reveal one or two glossy, mahogany-coloured seeds.

**Sunrise horse chestnut (*Aesculus* x *neglecta* 'Erythroblastos')** This tree is distinguished by its salmon-pink leaves in spring and panicles of creamy yellow flowers.

## PROFILE

- Up to 20m (70ft)
- Up to 10m (30ft)
- Deciduous
- Opposite simple
- Europe, N. Africa, S.W. Asia

**Leaves and fruit**
The palmate, lobed leaves of the field maple have yellow-green veins on the upper surface. The fruit is borne in pendulous clusters.

*leaf dark green on upper surface*

*two winged seedcases (keys) arranged in pairs*

*leaf borne on green or pink-green petiole*

*leaf up to 7.5cm (3in) long and wide*

## FEATURES

**Bark** Pale grey-brown, smooth; becomes corky in maturity

**Flowers** Small, greenish yellow; borne in erect terminal clusters in spring

*Acer campestre* (Sapindaceae)

# FIELD MAPLE

**This medium-sized**, broadly columnar tree is normally shorter than its maximum height of 20m (70ft). Also known as hedge maple, this tree, along with common hawthorn (p.243), serves as a field boundary hedge across its natural range. Some European specimens of this long-lived tree are known to be over 500 years old.

The bark becomes corky with age and this extends to relatively small branches, giving them a "winged" appearance. The palmate leaves have five rounded lobes and are pale green on the underside. The leaf stalk, or petiole, exudes a milky liquid when crushed or broken. In autumn, the leaves may turn bright golden yellow or orange before falling. The tree produces a typical green, two-winged seedcase, which ripens to light brown, sometimes remaining on the tree into early winter.

**Rough-barked maple (*Acer triflorum*)** This related species is distinguished from the field maple by its trifoliate leaves and heavily fissured bark.

**PROFILE**

- 30m (100ft)
- Up to 20m (70ft)
- Deciduous
- Opposite simple
- Iberian peninsula to Ukraine

*coarsely toothed leaf margin*

*flower cluster up to 7.5cm (3in) long*

**Leaves and flowers**
Sycamore leaves are borne on pink-green petioles. The flowers hang in dense, pendulous clusters, appearing at the same time as leaves in spring.

**FEATURES**

*leaf up to 20cm (8in) wide*

**Leaves** Palmate with five lobes; deep green upper surface, pale green underside

*wing 2.5cm (1in) long*

**Fruit** Two-winged seed, borne in clusters in early summer

*Acer pseudoplatanus* (Sapindaceae)

# SYCAMORE

**In some parts of the world** this large, broadly columnar tree is known as the plane tree, although it is not part of the *Platanus* genus. The sycamore is native to a region extending from the Iberian Peninsula to the Ukraine. Although not native to Britain, it is now extremely common there, having become naturalized many centuries ago. A hardy tree, it is resistant to strong winds and exposure to salt-laden air in coastal regions.

Its grey bark is smooth at first, becoming greyish-pink in maturity with irregular flaking plates. The leaves turn yellow in autumn. Lime-green leaf buds are very conspicuous in winter. The fruit, a two-winged seed, is pink-green when unripe and matures to light brown in autumn.

***Acer pseudoplatanus* 'Brilliantissimum'**
Unlike the sycamore, this small, slow-growing cultivar produces dramatic shrimp-pink leaves in spri

**PROFILE**

- Up to 30m (100ft)
- Up to 20m (70ft)
- Deciduous
- Opposite simple
- Europe, S.W. Asia

*bright green leaf upper surface*

*leaf ends in slender, sharp tip*

*sharply toothed leaf margin*

*two-winged fruit*

**Foliage and seeds**
The palmate leaves with five angular lobes are borne on long, slender, pink-yellow petioles. The seeds develop in early autumn.

**FEATURES**

**Bark** Light fawn-grey and smooth when young; develops ridges and fissures in maturity

**Flowers** Small, bright yellow, sometimes red; borne in spring as leaves emerge

*Acer platanoides* (Sapindaceae)

# NORWAY MAPLE

**This fast-growing tree** is native to southwestern Asia and Europe, including southern Scandinavia. It has been widely cultivated within its native region and elsewhere in the temperate world for centuries. Broadly conical, it is planted as an ornamental tree in parks, gardens, urban areas, and alongside roads.

The Norway maple is prone to damage from grey squirrels, which strip the bark, sometimes killing large branches across the crown. The leaves, glaucous on the underside, are up to 15cm (6in) long and wide. In autumn they turn striking shades of gold, orange, and red before falling. Small flowers are borne in conspicuous drooping clusters in spring. The green-yellow, often pink-blushed, fruit is a typical *Acer* two-winged seed. It is borne in pendulous clusters, up to 5cm (2in) long, ripening to a fawn colour in autumn.

***Acer platanoides* 'Schwedleri'** This cultivar is distinguished from the Norway maple by its rich crimson-purple-coloured leaves, which are especially vibrant in spring.

## PROFILE

- 20 m (70 ft)
- Up to 15 m (50 ft)
- Deciduous
- Opposite simple
- Turkey, Iran, Caucasus, W. China

**Palmate leaves**
The leaves have five to seven broad lobes, each running to a fine point. The fruit – a two-winged seed – is borne in clusters.

*lobe ends in fine point*

*leaf up to 10 cm (4 in) long*

*two-winged seed*

## FEATURES

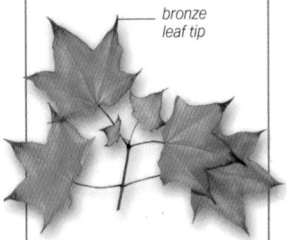


**Leaves** Butter-yellow in autumn before falling

**Flowers** Small, greenish yellow, appear in spring

*Acer cappadocicum* (Sapindaceae)

# CAUCASIAN MAPLE

**An attractive large maple**, this tree is native to Turkey, Iran, the Caucasus between Europe and Asia, and western China. The large, stately, broadly spreading Caucasian maple was introduced into western Europe in 1838. Since then, it has become a popular choice for planting in parks, gardens, and arboreta.

The bark is similar to the common ash (p.300), light grey and smooth at first, developing shallow, vertical fissures in maturity. The leaves are palmate, growing up to 15 cm (6 in) wide. Grass-green on the upper surface, they are paler on the underside, with tufts of hairs in the vein axils. The fruit is green when young, growing up to 4 cm (1 ½ in) long. It turns light brown on ripening and is shed from the tree in late autumn.

**Top-heavy tree**
The Caucasian maple has rounded crown borne on a little-branched trunk, abou 4 m (12 ft) from ground leve

## PROFILE

- Up to 15m (50ft)
- Up to 10m (30ft)
- Deciduous
- Opposite simple
- China

**Variable leaves**
The faintly lobed leaves are variable in shape, but are often rounded at the base. The fruit is a two-winged seed.

*leaf up to 15cm (6in) long, 8cm (3in) wide*

*wing of seedcase angled downwards*

*irregularly serrated leaf margin*

*leaf ends in short, curved point*

## FEATURES

**Bark** Smooth, with vertical white and green stripes

**Leaves** Turn orange-red, before falling in autumn

**Flowers** Yellow-green, borne in clusters

*Acer davidii* (Sapindaceae)

# PÈRE DAVID'S MAPLE

**Native to China,** this tree is often referred to as Snake-bark maple – a generic term for a whole group of the *Acer* genus. From China, it was introduced into the West in 1879 by English botanist Charles Maries. A small, broadly columnar tree, it was named after French Jesuit missionary and plant collector, Père (Father) David. Many clones and cultivars, such as 'George Forrest' and 'Ernest Wilson', are now grown in parks and gardens.

The variable leaves range from ovate to oblong-lanceolate. Small flowers emerge in spring just after the leaves. Green-yellow, often blushed pink fruit ripen to light-brown. They are borne in pendulous clusters up to 7.5cm (3in) long in autumn.

**Père David's maple 'George Forrest'**
Spreading branches and dark green leaves attached to shoots by red petioles distinguish this cultivar (*A. Davidii* 'George Forrest').

**PROFILE**

- 15 m (50 ft)
- Up to 6 m (20 ft)
- Deciduous
- Opposite compound
- C. China

**Fruit and leaves**
This tree produces pairs of pale green, winged seeds, covered with soft down. Its leaves have three elliptic leaflets.

*blunt teeth on each side of leaf*

*blue-green leaf underside*

*leaf dark green on upper surface*

*leaf up to 10 cm (4 in) long*

*wing approximately 3 cm (1¼ in) long, ripens to light brown*

**FEATURES**

**Bark** Cinnamon-red; smooth at first, peels in papery flakes

**Flowers** Borne on hairy stalks, in drooping clusters in spring

*Acer griseum* (Sapindaceae)

# PAPERBARK MAPLE

**Probably one of the finest** trees for bark colour, the small, broadly columnar paperbark maple is native to central China. It was discovered by Ernest H. Wilson in 1901, and almost immediately became a garden favourite throughout the temperate world.

Its bark is distinctive in winter, when low sunlight shines through the translucent bark peelings, which appear in thin flakes and curl back on themselves. The leaves are glaucous blue-green on the underside, with a light covering of hairs, reminiscent of oaks in shape. In autumn, they turn from orange, through red, to burgundy before falling. The fruit ripens from green to light brown, remaining on the tree well into winter.

**Golden Japanese maple**
*Acer shirasawanum* 'Aureum' has a plain, light brown bark and golden, palmate leaves.

## PROFILE

- Up to 30m (100ft)
- Up to 15m (50ft)
- Deciduous
- Alternate simple
- S.E. Canada, N.E. USA

**Autumn colours**
In autumn, dark matt green, palmate leaves of the red maple turn a vibrant, bright scarlet red before falling.

*leaf up to 10cm (4in) long and wide*

*shallow-lobed leaf*

*lobe reaches halfway to base of leaf*

*coarsely serrated leaf margin*

## FEATURES

**Flowers** Small, bright red; borne in clusters on short stalks in early spring

*Acer rubrum* (Sapindaceae)

# RED MAPLE

**The large, broadly columnar** red maple has a natural range from eastern Newfoundland and Ontario in Canada to Florida and Texas in the USA. This tree is normally found growing in deep, damp soils.

The bark remains dark grey and smooth in maturity. The leaves have three or five lobes with glaucous blue-green, almost white, undersides, and yellow hairs around the leaf veins. The showy flowers are borne on bare branches before the leaves appear. These are followed by pairs of pale green, downy, winged seeds, each wing being around 2.5cm (1in) long. These turn red and green, ripening to light brown, and stay on the tree into winter.

**Vibrant autumn hue**
The striking red maple is one of the main constituents of the "American fall" leaf colour displays.

**PROFILE**

- 8–15m (25–50ft)
- Up to 10m (30ft)
- Deciduous
- Opposite simple
- Japan, China, Taiwan, Korea

*pair of winged seeds, up to 1cm (½in) long*

*red-tinged fruit wing*

*leaf margin has forward-facing serration*

*palmate leaf, up to 10cm (4in) wide, with pointed lobes*

**Japanese maple foliage**
Slender shoots end in paired, lobed leaves varying in shape. Clusters of rich green, winged fruit ripen to red in summer.

**FEATURES**

**Leaves** Five or seven pointed lobes; bright red, orange, or yellow in autumn

*Acer palmatum* (Sapindaceae)

# JAPANESE MAPLE

**The smooth Japanese maple** was first known to Europeans in 1783. However, a trade embargo with Japan delayed its introduction into western cultivation until 1820. This tree is widely planted throughout the world and has given rise to hundreds of garden cultivars.

It has a smooth, grey-brown bark, even in maturity. Some variants have leaves that are cut inbetween the lobes almost to the midrib. In spring, as new leaves emerge, small burgundy-red flowers with yellow stamens are borne in upright, stalked clusters, becoming drooping later. The winged fruit are borne in clusters of up to 20 seeds. Some remain on the tree even after the leaves have fallen.

**Japanese maple cultivar**
This cultivar (*A. palmatum* 'Osakazuki') has bright red autumn foliage and regular, seven-lobed leaves.

**Autumn leaves**
Palmate, almost rounded, leaves have 5 to 11 pointed lobes. Green at first, leaves turn to red, orange, yellow, or wine-purple in autumn.

*toothed lobe tapers to a point*

**PROFILE**

- Up to 10m (30ft)
- Up to 10m (30ft)
- Deciduous
- Opposite simple
- Japan

**FEATURES**

**Flowers** Purple-red, with lemon-yellow stamens; borne in pendulous, stalked clusters

**Seeds** Winged; borne in pairs on long stalks

*Acer japonicum* (Sapindaceae)

# FULLMOON MAPLE

**Native to the Japanese islands** of Hokkaido and Honshu, this tree was introduced into western cultivation in 1864. Today it is rarely seen in cultivation, having been replaced by many of its own cultivars such as 'Aconitifolium' and 'Vitifolium'. It has a sprawling form, with low branches to ground level.

The bark is silver grey-brown and smooth, even in maturity. The slightly crinkly leaves have a pale green, hairy underside. Its toothed leaves are up to 12.5 cm (5 in) long and wide. Small flowers are borne in hairy clusters just as the leaves emerge in spring. Green winged seeds, up to 2.5 cm (1 in) long, ripen to red and finally brown in late summer.

**Vine-leaved Japanese maple**
This tree (*Acer japonicum* 'Vitifolium') has larger vine-shaped leaves with up to nine shallowly cut lobes.

**PROFILE**

- Up to 35 m (120 ft)
- Up to 15 m (50 ft)
- Deciduous
- Opposite simple
- E. North America

palmate leaf, up to 15 cm (6 in) long and wide

leaf lobe tapers to a point

**Five-lobed leaves**
Sugar maple leaves have five prominent, tapered lobes that run to long points. The leaves have a mid- to dark green upper surface.

**FEATURES**

**Bark** Smooth, brown-grey; becomes shallowly fissured, flaking in maturity

**Leaves** Bright scarlet, gold, or yellow in autumn, before falling

*Acer saccharum* (Sapindaceae)

# SUGAR MAPLE

**This large, broadly columnar tree** is native to eastern North America, from Quebec south to Missouri. Besides being known for maple syrup, the sugar maple is also known for its timber, which is hard and resistant to wear, and has been used to make dance floors. It is a common tree in cultivation outside its natural range, both in North America and throughout the northern hemisphere, in parks, gardens, and arboreta.

Sugar maple leaves have a pale green underside, with hairs in the leaf axils. Small, yellowish green flowers are borne in drooping, open clusters in early spring, just as the new leaves appear. The fruit is a pair of winged seeds, up to 2.5 cm (1 in) long, bright green ripening to brown and persisting on the tree well into autumn.

**Sugary sap**
Maple syrup is made from sap tapped from the bark c the sugar maple. The sap is boiled to produce syrup.

## PROFILE

- Up to 30 m (100 ft)
- Up to 15 m (50 ft)
- Deciduous
- Opposite simple
- E. North America

**Silver maple foliage**
The leaves have five large lobes ending in a sharp point. They are held on lax petioles, or leaf stalks, up to 15 cm (6 in) long.

*sharply toothed leaf lobe*

*palmate leaf*

*lobed leaf, up to 15 cm (6 in) long and wide*

## FEATURES

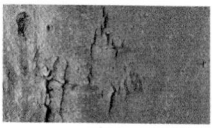

**Bark** Smooth, grey; becomes flaky; shoots may emerge from beneath it

**Leaves** Palmate; turning bright yellow in autumn

*Acer saccharinum* (Sapindaceae)

# SILVER MAPLE

**One of the fastest growing maples** in North America, the silver maple is a broadly columnar, large tree with a natural range that extends across eastern North America. Since its introduction into Europe in 1725, it has been widely planted in parks and arboreta. This tree is sometimes referred to as the American version of a sycamore (p.288), but it has a more refined habit and foliage.

The broad leaves have a light green upper surface and a blue-green to silver underside with some hairs. Small, greenish yellow flowers, without petals, are clustered on young shoots as leaves emerge in spring. The fruit are winged seeds, up to 2.5 cm (1 in) long, bright green ripening to brown.

**Elegant habit**
The silver maple has a light, open crown and bicoloured leaves, which catch the light as they flutter in the breeze.

## PROFILE

- 15–20m (50–70ft)
- Up to 10m (30ft)
- Deciduous
- Opposite compound
- C. North America

**Box elder leaves**
The leaves of the box elder, unlike many related maple trees, are pinnate. Each leaf consists of up to seven variably shaped leaflets.

*bright green leaf upper surface*

*hairy, light green leaf underside*

*leaf up to 10cm (4in) long*

## FEATURES

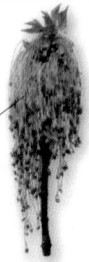

*flowers borne in tassel-like clusters*

**Flowers** Small, yellow-green, with drooping stamens

**Fruit** Downwards-pointing seed with two wings; up to 2cm (¾in) long

*Acer negundo* (Sapindaceae)

# BOX ELDER

**Also called the ash-leaved maple**, the box elder is a broadly columnar, light, and open-branched tree. It grows wild across central North America, particularly alongside rivers and where soil is moist. The species was introduced into Europe as early as 1688.

Box elder bark is brown to silver-grey, thin and smooth when young, remaining relatively so into maturity. The leaves are similar to those of the unrelated common elder (*Sambucus nigra*). The leaflets are sometimes lobed and arranged along leaf stalks in pairs, with one larger, final leaflet at the end. Their autumn colour tends to be yellow and muted. Small male and female petal-less flowers are borne on separate trees in spring as the leaves emerge. They are carried in drooping clusters from the outermost twigs. The fruit is typical of the *Acer* genus – a seed with two incurved wings, arranged in pairs.

**Henry's maple (*Acer henryi*)** Unlike box elder, its pinnate leaves consist of three narrower leaflets. Borne on pink petioles (stalks), they develop a bright red and orange tint in autumn.

**PROFILE**



- Up to 25 m (80 ft)
- Up to 12 m (40 ft)
- Deciduous
- Opposite simple
- W. North America

**Leaves and fruit**
Each palmate leaf of the Oregon maple has either five or seven large lobes. The fruit has paired wings set at right angles.

**FEATURES**

**Flowers** Yellow-green, borne in conspicuous, pendulous clusters in spring

*Acer macrophyllum* (Sapindaceae)

# OREGON MAPLE

**Characterized by its large leaves**, the Oregon maple is indigenous to a region stretching from British Columbia, Canada, to California, USA. This majestic, large, broadly columnar tree was introduced into cultivation in 1812.

The bark is smooth and grey-brown, becoming heavily and vertically fissured in maturity. On older specimens, the trunk may grow up to 1.5 m (5 ft) wide at chest height. The leaves are up to 25 cm (10 in) long and 30 cm (12 in) wide. They are shiny dark green on the upper surface and paler on the underside. Each leaf is carried on a long, buff-coloured, sometimes red, petiole (leaf stalk). The leaves turn deep yellow and orange to brown in autumn. Slightly fragrant flowers emerge around the same time as the leaves begin to grow in spring. The young, green fruit has an initial covering of fawn-coloured hairs. It has large, smooth wings up to 5 cm (2 in) long. It ripens to brown, and persists on the tree well into autumn.

**PROFILE**

- Up to 40 m (130 ft)
- Up to 20 m (70 ft)
- Deciduous
- Opposite compound
- Europe

*white, faintly hairy midrib on underside of leaflet*

*shallow-toothed leaflet margin*

*distinctive black leaf bud*

*winged seed up 4 cm (1½ in) long*

*leaflet up to 12 cm (5 in) long*

**Ash keys**
The fruit is a pendulous cluster of flattened, winged seeds known as keys. Initially green, it turns light brown to grey when mature.

**FEATURES**

**Flowers** Appear in late winter clustered along previous year's shoots

*Fraxinus excelsior* (Oleaceae)

# COMMON ASH

**Native to most of Europe**, from the Pyrenees to the Caucasus, this broadly columnar tree is one of the largest European deciduous trees. It is a common species in woodland, field boundaries, and open moorland, particularly on calcareous limestone soil. It has become invasive in some urban areas, seeding itself with ease into gardens and parks. It has a light, airy crown with relatively few, large, heavy branches and a trunk that tends to be straight and clean.

The bark is pale fawn-grey when young, becoming fissured with age. The leaves are pinnate and up to 30 cm (12 in) long. They consist of up to 12 pairs of ovate-oblong or lanceolate leaflets, which are rich green on the upper surface, with a slightly paler underside. Distinctive black leaf buds appear in winter. The fruit sometimes persist on the tree through winter.

**Golden ash (*Fraxinus excelsior* 'Jaspidea')** Unlike the common ash, this tree has golden yellow young shoots and yellowish branches, which are especially obvious in winter.

leaflet up to 10 cm (4 in) long, 5 cm (2 in) wide

creamy white flowers

roundly toothed leaflet margin

**Fluffy clusters**
Borne in large, fluffy, open clusters (panicles), the flowers are upright at first, drooping in late spring.

**PROFILE**

- Up to 20 m (70 ft)
- Up to 15 m (50 ft)
- Deciduous
- Opposite compound
- S. Europe, S.W. Asia

**FEATURES**

**Fruit** Single, flat, winged seed, up to 4 cm (1½ in) long; ripening to pale brown

*Fraxinus ornus* (Oleaceae)

# MANNA ASH

**This broadly spreading**, medium-sized tree is native to southern Europe and southwestern Asia. It has been widely cultivated in parks, gardens, and arboreta throughout Europe since before 1700. Unlike most ash trees, manna ash produces large panicles of creamy white, fragrant flowers in spring. Manna sugar, a form of sweetener tolerated by diabetics, is derived from the sap of this tree.

The bark is fawn-grey and smooth, even in maturity. Winter buds are brown and shaped like a bishop's mitre. The leaves are pinnate, up to 20 cm (8 in) long, and consist of five to nine oblong-ovate leaflets. Matt green on the upper surface, the leaflets have a pale green underside. In autumn, they turn bright yellow before falling. Fruit are borne in long, pendulous clusters and remain on the tree late into autumn.

**Himalayan manna ash (*Fraxinus floribunda*)** This species has larger flower panicles than the manna ash and larger leaflets that are up to 12 cm (5 in) long, with a shiny upper surface.

**Sparsely toothed leaflets**
The leaves are pinnate, up to 35 cm (14 in) long. They consist of up to nine short-stalked (except for the termina leaflet), sparsely toothed leaflets.

## PROFILE



- Up to 28 m (92 ft)
- Up to 15 m (50 ft)
- Deciduous
- Opposite compound
- E. North America

## FEATURES

**Bark** Grey, with prominent, narrow fissures, which become deep in maturity

*Fraxinus americana* (Oleaceae)

# WHITE ASH

**Also known as American ash**, this large, broadly columnar tree is native to eastern North America, from Nova Scotia to Texas and Florida. It was introduced into cultivation in 1724 and is now planted in parks and cities throughout North America and in parts of Europe. The tree is highly prized for its strong, white timber, which is used to make mallets, baseball bats, hockey sticks, and rowing oars.

The winter leaf buds are rusty brown and borne on olive-green shoots. Leaves are dark green on the upper surface and distinctively pale green to almost white beneath. Small, purple male and female flowers appear in clusters on separate trees in spring, before the leaves emerge. The fruit is a 5 cm- (2 in-) long winged seed, ripening from green to brown. It is carried in dense, pendulous clusters throughout autumn and early winter.

**Green ash (*Fraxinus pennsylvanica*)** This tree has pinnate leaves with up to 11 leaflets, each up to 15 cm (6 in) long. The leaflets are green, rather than white, on the underside.

**Sharp, uneven serrations**
The pinnate leaves, up to 25cm (10in) long, consist of up to 13 lanceolate, jagged-toothed, and widely spaced leaflets.

**PROFILE**

- 18–25m (60–80ft)
- Up to 12m (40ft)
- Deciduous
- Opposite compound
- S. Europe, N. Africa, W. Asia

**FEATURES**

**Bark** Grey-brown, displaying vertical fissures

*Fraxinus angustifolia* (Oleaceae)

# NARROW-LEAVED ASH

**This broadly columnar tree** has the narrowest leaves among the members of the *Fraxinus* genus. It was introduced into cultivation around 1800. There are several distinctive cultivars related to this species, including 'Raywood', which has leaves that turn an attractive plum-purple in autumn.

The shoots are olive-green; winter buds are dark brown and covered in a dense down. The leaves are similar to those of the common ash (p.300), but are narrower and hang downwards from the shoots. They are slightly paler and without hairs on the underside. Small, relatively inconspicuous, green to purple-green flowers are borne in clusters in early spring before the leaves unfurl. The fruit are flattened, winged seeds, each up to 4cm (1½in) long. They are borne in hanging, fawn-coloured clusters, which persist well into winter.

**Pallis's ash (*Fraxinus pallisiae*)** This tree's pinnate leaves have only seven leaflets. These are more triangular and less shiny than those of the narrow-leaved ash.

## PROFILE

- Up to 7 m (22 ft)
- Up to 5 m (15 ft)
- Deciduous
- Opposite compound
- C. China

**Pinnate leaves**
The leaf is composed of five, occasionally seven, leaflets borne on purple-green leaf stalks.

*dark green upper surface of leaflet*

*leaflet up to 10 cm (4 in) long, 5 cm (2 in) wide*

## FEATURES

**Bark** Light grey; smooth, even in maturity

**Buds** Light grey; covered with fine down in winter

**Flowers** Creamy white; borne in loose clusters

*Fraxinus sieboldiana* (Oleaceae)

# CHINESE FLOWERING ASH

**This slow-growing tree** from central China was previously named *Fraxinus mariesii*. It was introduced into western cultivation in 1878, when English plant collector Charles Maries sent it from China to nurserymen Veitch & Sons. Although beautiful when in flower, this broadly spreading tree is uncommon in cultivation and rarely seen in parks and gardens.

It has a round-headed, bushy form in maturity. The leaves are up to 18 cm (7 in) long, and have leaflets that are dark green on the upper surface and silver-green on the underside. They turn yellow and gold before being shed in fall. The flowers emerge in late spring. The fruit are deep purple, single-winged samaras, borne in late summer. They ripen to a light brown colour.

**Chinese ash (*Fraxinus chinensis*)** A larger, more vigorous tree than the Chinese flowering ash, this tree, up to 15 m (50 ft) tall, bears plump, brownish black winter buds covered in light grey hairs.

**PROFILE**

- Up to 20m (70ft)
- Up to 12m (40ft)
- Deciduous
- Opposite simple
- S.E. USA

*flowers borne in upright panicle*

*leaf up to 25cm (10in) long, 15cm (6in) wide*

*broadly ovate leaf*

**rumpet-shaped flowers** wo-lipped, white flowers with ellow and purple spots are orne in large, open panicles n mid- to late summer.

**FEATURES**

**Bark** Light grey-brown; loose, flaking in patches in maturity

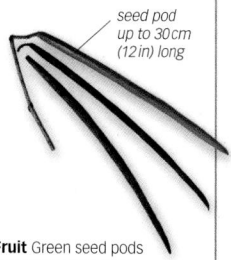


**Fruit** Green seed pods ripening to brown; stay on tree for one year

*Catalpa bignonioides* (Bignoniaceae)

# INDIAN BEAN TREE

**This medium-sized tree's name** refers to Native Americans, rather than the Indian subcontinent. Native Americans used to dry, paint, and then wear the seeds of this species as decoration. A broadly spreading and highly ornamental tree, it is one of the last to bloom, waiting until mid- to late summer to produce its orchid-like flowers. The Indian bean tree is common in towns and cities throughout the northern hemisphere, mainly due to the fact that it tolerates localized atmospheric pollution very well.

The lax, soft leaves are heart-shaped at the base, and run to a tapered point. They are rarely lobed. Bronze-coloured in spring, they quickly fade to grass green on the upper surface, paler on the underside with an occasional covering of hairs. The flowers are white with yellow and purple markings.

**Golden-leaved Indian bean tree (*Catalpa bignoniodes* 'Aurea')** This tree has golden yellow leaves, relatively sparse panicles of flowers, and a smaller stature than the Indian bean tree.

**PROFILE**

- Up to 20m (70ft)
- Up to 12m (40ft)
- Deciduous
- Opposite simple
- W. China

*leaf up to 15cm (6in) long, 12cm (5in) wide*

*flowers borne in dense clusters*

*long, slender point at leaf tip*

*lax petiole*

**Pink flowers**
Delicate, bell-shaped, pink flowers are borne in dense clusters in midsummer.

**FEATURES**

**Bark** Dark grey, becomes scaly; peels to reveal grey-pink, fresh bark beneath

**Variant** Seed pod variant from subspecies 'Duclouxii'

*Catalpa fargesii* (Bignoniaceae)

# FARGES' CATALPA

**This broadly columnar**, medium-sized, deciduous tree was named after the French Jesuit missionary Père Paul Guillaume Farges, who discovered it in western China in 1896. It is now widely grown in both North America and Europe for its delicate pink flowers, which appear in early to midsummer, several weeks earlier than those on the tree's American cousin, the Indian bean tree (p.305).

The leaves are lax and soft, broadly ovate, with a small side lobe that may or may not be present. Borne singly on a long petiole (stalk), the leaves are bronze-coloured when they first emerge from the bud. By late spring, they become deep green, with a slight sheen on the upper surface, and paler on the underside. The light pink flowers have maroon spots and yellow blotches at the entrance to the flower throat. Around 15 flowers are borne in large, open panicles, which are up to 15cm (6in) long. These are followed by pendulous seed pods up to 45cm (18in) long. Slender, green, ripening to dark brown, they appear in summer, persisting on the tree till autumn.

## PROFILE

- Up to 20m (70ft)
- Up to 12m (40ft)
- Deciduous
- Opposite simple
- C. and E. China

**Upright panicles**
Open, erect panicles up to 30cm (12in) tall, bear trumpet-shaped flowers in late spring.

*brown, felted flower bud*

*blotchy yellow on inner surface*

*flower up to 5cm (2in) long*

*lilac to pale-purple on outer surface*

## FEATURES

**Leaves** Large, heart-shaped at base; with a large, shallow lobe on either side

**Fruit** Green, pointed, egg-shaped capsule ripening to woody brown

**Seeds** Winged, borne in green fruit, dispersed by wind

*Paulownia tomentosa* (Scrophulariaceae)

# FOXGLOVE TREE

**Also known as the princess tree**, or the empress tree, this fast-growing, medium-sized, deciduous tree was introduced into western cultivation in 1834. Since then, the foxglove tree has become popular for planting in parks, gardens, and arboreta. It takes its genus name from Anna Pavlovna, the daughter of Tsar Paul I of Russia.

The bark is grey and smooth, even in maturity, similar to that of the common beech (p.152). The leaves are ovate, up to 45cm (18in) long and wide – even larger on coppiced regrowth. They are lax and soft, dark green on the upper surface, lighter on the underside, and covered in fine, sticky hairs. Fragrant, tubular flowers are borne in upright open panicles.

**Columnar habit**
The foxglove tree is rounded to broadly columnar with very stout shoots that are hairy when young.

**PROFILE**

Up to 22 m (72 ft)

Up to 10 m (30 ft)

Deciduous

Alternate compound

China, Japan, E. Himalayas

*pea-sized fruit*

*leaflet tapers to a point*

**Ovate leaflets**
The large, pinnate leaves of this tree consist of broadly ovate leaflets running to a slender point

**FEATURES**

**Bark** Light grey-brown, smooth; becomes vertically fissured in maturity

*Rhus verniciflua* (Anacardiaceae)

# VARNISH TREE

**Also known as Chinese lacquer tree**, this fast-growing, medium-sized, deciduous tree has been cultivated in Europe since before 1862. Broadly conical when young, it develops a rounded habit in maturity. Its name refers to the fact that its sap is the source of the varnish used to give a high-gloss finish to Chinese and Japanese lacquerware. In China, oil is also extracted from the fruit to make candles. However, all parts of the tree are poisonous and contact with skin can cause irritation and blistering.

The varnish tree's branches are long and gangly, and sparsely covered with large, pinnate leaves up to 60 cm (24 in) long. These consist of 9 to 19 leaflets, each up to 15 cm (6 in) long. They are rich, glossy green on the upper surface, and paler with a fine covering of hairs on the underside. In summer, small, yellowish white flowers are produced in large, pendulous panicles. These are followed by clusters of berry-like, yellowish green fruit.

**lowers in long panicles**
hinese sumach bears small, reamy yellow flowers, carried in onical panicles, in summer.

**PROFILE**

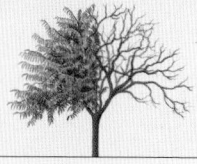

- Up to 20m (70ft)
- Up to 8m (25ft)
- Deciduous
- Alternate compound
- China

*Rhus potaninii* (Anacardiaceae)

# CHINESE SUMACH

**Also known as Potanin's sumach**, this tree is named after the Russian explorer and botanist Grigori Potanin, who discovered and recorded the species in northern China. The broadly spreading, medium-sized tree has been cultivated in the west for at least 100 years and is found in parks, gardens, and arboreta throughout Europe. In the wild in China, it has a neat, round-topped shape. However, in cultivation, it is likely to be multi-stemmed and spreading.

The bark is grey-pink and smooth. The long and spreading branches are bare except for the ends, which carry large, pinnate leaves. The leaves, up to 35cm (14in) long, are borne on hairy shoots and carry 7 to 11 leaflets, which run to a fine point. The leaflets are dark green on the upper surface, paler on the underside, and usually turn bright red or pink-purple in autumn. The tree bears flowers in summer, and these are followed by rounded, green, berry-like fruit, which are covered in fine hairs. The fruit turn red when ripe.

**PROFILE**

- Up to 25 m (80 ft)
- Up to 20 m (70 ft)
- Evergreen
- Alternate simple
- Malaysia, Indonesia, Pacific Ocean islands

**Leaves and fruit**
Breadfruit leaves are large, with six to nine pointed lobes. The greer fruit, borne singly or in clusters of two or three at ends of branches, is rounded to rugby-ball shaped.

*leaf up to 90 cm (36 in) long*

**FEATURES**

**Bark** Grey, smooth; releases sticky white latex

**Fruit** Green, rounded to oval; up to 20 cm (8 in) long with warty skin

*Artocarpus altilis* (Moraceae)

# BREADFRUIT

**This fast-growing tree** is native to Malaysia, Indonesia, and the Pacific Ocean islands. However, it has been cultivated in other parts of the tropics for centuries. Broadly columnar, it has ascending, arching branches and a dense crown of foliage. When cooked, its fruit tastes like freshly baked bread. The most famous transportation of this plant was by Captain Bligh aboard HMS *Bounty* in 1789. He was tasked with transporting breadfruit plants from Tahiti in the Pacific to the West Indies. The lavish attention paid to the plants rather than the sailors caused a mutiny along the way.

The rough, ovate leaves are deep glossy green on the upper surface, paler on the underside. Tiny male and female flowers are borne in profusion on the same tree. They appear on a capitulum, which is a flower-head like a false fruit. The actual fruit weighs up to 5 kg (11 lb). Its greer outer skin has hexagon-shaped discs. Inside, the milky flesh looks a little like that of a melon. It is starchy when unripe and usually fragrant when ripe.

**ackfruit foliage**
he leaves are dark green with a light sheen on the upper surface nd pale green with some down n the underside.

## PROFILE



- Up to 20m (70ft)
- Up to 20m (70ft)
- Evergreen
- Alternate simple
- S.E. Asia; known only in cultivation

## FEATURES

**Bark** Relatively smooth, reddish brown to grey

**Fruit** Very large, up to 90cm (36in) long, 50cm (20in) wide

*Artocarpus heterophyllus* (Moraceae)

# JACKFRUIT

**The jackfruit is believed** to have originated from southern India, but has been so widely cultivated throughout Asia that it is now difficult to pinpoint its natural range. Rather like breadfruit (p.310), the fruit of the jackfruit tree are cultivated for their edible flesh. The tree is fast-growing, broadly columnar, and medium-sized, with a single trunk that branches into a dense crown of foliage.

The mature, dark green leaves are leathery. Both male and female flowers are borne on the same tree. Small and green, the flowers emerge directly from the trunk and main branches. They are followed by rounded to oval fruit, weighing up to 20kg (44lb), which are borne on woody stalks directly attached to the trunk and main branches. The fruit has waxy flesh inside, which may be pink or golden yellow with a strong, unpleasant odour, but a sweet taste rather like sour banana. The jackfruit flesh is a nutritious carbohydrate used in many dishes, from custards to curries.

**PROFILE**

- 15–30m (50–100ft)
- Up to 30m (100ft)
- Semi-evergreen
- Alternate simple
- Southeast Asia

**Cordate leaves**
Bo leaves are heart-shaped, with an elongated, slightly curved tip.

*leaf up to 20cm (8in) long, 12cm (5in) wide*

*pale yellow leaf midrib*

*flexible leaf stalk, up to 10cm (4in) long*

**FEATURES**

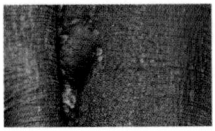

**Bark** Smooth, grey; develops vertical fluting and buttressing in maturity

*Ficus religiosa* (Moraceae)

# BO TREE

**According to Buddhist beliefs**, the Buddha attained enlightenment under the bo tree, also known as the sacred fig. This long-lived species (some specimens are believed to be 2,000 years old) is sacred to both Buddhists and Hindus, and is usually grown close to temples. Its native habitat extends from India and Pakistan to Indonesia, but it is widely planted outside these countries, including subtropical areas of the USA.

A wide-spreading tree, its trunk may extend up to 3m (10ft) in diameter in maturity. With age, some surface roots start radiating from the trunk's wide base. Aerial roots may also hang down from the branches. The leaves range in colour from bright green to blue-green, with a pale yellow midrib and veining. The flowers are red but very small. Both male and female flowers are borne on the same tree. The fruit is a small fig, up to 1.5cm (½in) long, green ripening to purple. It is borne in rounded and stalkless clusters along the twigs.

glossy leaf, up to 25 cm (10 in) long

pale yellow leaf midrib

**Distinctive leaves**
The leaves are leathery, elliptical, and blunt-tipped. They have prominent pale yellow veining.

**PROFILE**

- 20–25 m (70–80 ft)
- Up to 20 m (70 ft)
- Evergreen
- Alternate simple
- India

**FEATURES**

**Aerial roots** Grow down to the ground; thicken once they reach the soil

*Ficus benghalensis* (Moraceae)

# BANYAN TREE

**The banyan is one of the oldest** and largest trees on Earth, with specimens more than 5,000 years old still in existence. One banyan in the botanic garden near Kolkata (Calcutta), India, has a crown circumference approaching 1 km (0.6 miles). As with other fig trees, banyans are stranglers, starting life as a seed deposited by a bird among the branches of another tree. This seed develops aerial roots that eventually strangle the host tree. The tree's low-spreading branches grow more aerial roots, some of which develop into secondary trunks – old trees can have hundreds of such trunks. The canopy of the banyan tree casts a dense shade.

The bark is pale grey and relatively smooth. The leaf buds are covered by two scales, which fall as the leaves grow. The leaves are bronze-pink when young, turning dark green in maturity. The banyan produces numerous small flowers. The fruit is a spherical fig, up to 2 cm (¾ in) wide, borne in pairs in the leaf axils. It is green and ripens to scarlet.

*leaf up to 10cm (4in) long, 5cm (2in) wide*

**Smooth, leathery leaves**
Ovate to elliptic leaves are glossy green on the upper surface, paler on the underside, and thinner in texture than most fig leaves.

**PROFILE**

- Up to 30m (100ft)
- Up to 20m (70ft)
- Evergreen
- Alternate simple
- S. Asia to N. Australia

*Ficus benjamina* (Moraceae)

# WEEPING FIG

**In cool regions of the world**, this tree is commonly grown as a houseplant. However, in the tropics it is a broadly spreading, eventually weeping, large evergreen tree. It is native to south and southeast Asia, north Australia, and southwest Pacific but has been widely cultivated throughout the tropics. The weeping fig is a graceful tree with strongly ascending branches that weep at the tips. Like most figs, it is a strangler, developing aerial roots that descend to form a dense latticework around the main trunk.

The bark is pale grey, sometimes almost white, and exudes white latex. The alternate leaves shimmer in the slightest breeze. Green-cream flowers are small and not very visible. The fruit are small rounded figs, which are borne in pairs in the leaf axils nearest the ends of the twigs. They ripen from green to pink, then turn scarlet before ripening to purple, and eventually black.

leaf 15–30cm (6–12in) long

**Large, elliptic leaves**
This fig tree bears alternate leaves, dark green on the upper surface, golden brown on the underside, which bleed a milky sap when cut.

**PROFILE**

- Up to 60m (200ft)
- Up to 60m (200ft)
- Evergreen
- Alternate simple
- E. Australia

*Ficus macrophylla* (Moraceae)

# MORETON BAY FIG

**This broadly spreading tree** is indigenous to eastern Australia, from Queensland in the north to New South Wales and Lord Howe Island in the south. It is widely cultivated as an ornamental tree across warmer parts of the world, including the Mediterranean and California, USA. It is known as a strangler because its seedling germinates in the canopy of a host tree and lives as an epiphyte – growing on another tree non-parasitically – until its aerial roots touch the ground.

The bark is light brown to grey, smooth, developing heavy buttressing and surface, snake-like roots in maturity. The small flowers require pollination by a specific wasp, known simply as the fig wasp. The fruit is a fig, up to 2.5cm (1in) wide, green ripening to purple with lighter spots.

**Buttressed trunk**
The Moreton Bay fig's massive base and equally large spread make it suitable for wide open spaces.

**PROFILE**



- Up to 60m (200ft)
- Up to 60m (200ft)
- Evergreen
- Alternate simple
- S. and S.E. Asia

**Glossy green leaves**
The thick leaves of the Indian rubber tree mature from pink to dark green, turning glossy and smooth, with a leathery texture.

**FEATURES**

**Bark** Light brown, smooth; releases sticky, milky-white latex when cut

*Ficus elastica* (Moraceae)

# INDIAN RUBBER TREE

**Native to the eastern Himalayas**, northeast India, Burma, and Malaysia, this large, broadly spreading fig is as wide as it is tall. It was the original source of rubber until the Brazilian *Hevea brasiliensis* rubber tree was discovered. As with most tropical figs, this tree is a strangler. It develops secondary trunks from aerial roots, and has long, sinuous, surface roots, which splay out for several metres from the main trunk.

The oblong to elliptic leaves have a single, distinct midrib and a pointed tip. They are arranged spirally on the shoots, which are at the ends of long, bare branches. The fruit is an oval, stalkless fig, up to 2cm (¾in) long, borne in pairs in the leaf axils towards the ends of the twigs. The greenish yellow figs are produced all year round. The tree begins to bear fruit from around 20 years of age.

**Signature foliage**
The leaves are tough, waxy, bright green with a slight sheen on the upper surface. The fruit are green, rounded, and pendulous.

**PROFILE**

- Up to 15 m (50 ft)
- Up to 15 m (50 ft)
- Evergreen
- Opposite simple
- Caribbean, Florida Keys, S.E. Mexico

*Clusia rosea* (Clusiaceae)

# AUTOGRAPH TREE

**This tree thrives in coastal regions**, being tolerant of salt spray, high winds, and saline soil. Its common name refers to its leaves, which are so thick that words can be carved on to them – they have even been used to make playing cards. A strangler, the medium-sized, spreading autograph tree begins its life as an epiphyte. Once attached to the ground, it quickly develops a sprawling habit, with horizontal branches and a dense crown.

The bark is light grey and smooth. The leaves have a bright green upper surface that contrasts with their pale green underside. Flowers are 10 cm (4 in) wide, consisting of seven fleshy, white petals surrounding a cluster of green-yellow stamens. They are short-lived, opening in the late afternoon and beginning to turn brown and die by the following morning. The flower buds are globular, mostly white with a pink blush. The fruit are glossy green, globular capsules up to 5 cm (2 in) wide. When mature, they split to release small, orange-white seeds.

**Cacao leaves**
The leaves are oblong to elliptic, with a short pointed tip. Leathery and smooth, they have a pale underside.

## PROFILE



- Up to 10 m (30 ft)
- Up to 8 m (25 ft)
- Evergreen
- Alternate simple
- C. America

## FEATURES

**Bark** Rich brown, relatively smooth throughout life

**Fruit** Ovoid; ripening from green to orange and maroon, then brown

*Theobroma cacao* (Malvaceae)

# CACAO

**This small, spreading tree** provides cocoa – the key ingredient of chocolate. Cacao is indigenous to Central America, but has been widely cultivated in the West Indies, Africa, Java, and Sri Lanka for its seeds – cocoa beans – which are roasted and ground to produce cocoa butter.

It has alternately arranged, large pendulous leaves. The creamy yellow to pink flowers, up to 1 cm (½ in) wide each have five petals. They emerge directly from the trunk and larger branches in spring, and sporadically at other times of the year too. These are followed by the fruit – a pod, shaped like a rugby ball and marked by longitudinal ribbing. These are attached to the trunk and main branches by short, woody stalks. They contain up to 100 purple cocoa beans, up to 2 cm (¾ in) long, each set in a pleasantly flavoured, yoghurt-like pulp.

**Cupuacu (*Theobroma grandiflorum*)** This tree is easily distinguished by its larger, oval fruit, which are covered in a brown, "fuzzy" suede coat, and larger leaves, up to 35 cm (14 in) long.

**PROFILE**

- 10–25 m (30–80 ft)
- Up to 30 m (100 ft)
- Deciduous
- Alternate simple
- C. Tropical Africa, Arabian Peninsula

white flower, up to 15 cm (6 in) wide

yellow-tipped stamen

**Showy white flower**
Baobab flowers have crinkled petals and numerous yellow or purple stamens. The flowers hang singly from branches on long cords.

**FEATURES**

**Bark** Mid-grey, smooth

**Fruit** Brown, pitcher-shaped; up to 30 cm (12 in) long, 10 cm (4 in) wide

*Adansonia digitata* (Malvaceae)

# AFRICAN BAOBAB

**This is the most widespread** of the eight species of *Adansonia* (baobabs), and the only species native to central tropical Africa and parts of the Arabian Peninsula. The majority of the other species are native to Madagascar. Several of African baobab's largest specimens are believed to be more than 1,000 years old.

The African baobab is a large tree, with a massive trunk that may attain a circumference of 30 m (100 ft). The leaves are glossy dark green and rounded. They are divided into five to nine leaflets, each up to 15 cm (6 in) long, with a pale green midrib. The tree may remain bare for more than half the year. Its flowers open at night to release a pungent scent like that of over-ripe melon, which is attractive to fruit bats – the tree's primary pollinator. The fruit hang on long stalks; they contain up to 30 seeds, surrounded in an acidic, edible pulp.

**Madagascan baobab (*Andansonia madagascarionsis*)**
Unlike the African baobab, this tree is native to Madagascar. It is also smaller in stature and bears dark red flowers.

**PROFILE**

- Up to 60m (200ft)
- Up to 20m (70ft)
- Semi-evergreen
- Alternate compound
- Central and South America; Africa; S. Asia

*leaflet broadest below its centre*

*leaflet up to 15cm (6in) long*

*leaflet tapers to a narrow tip*

**Long-stalked leaves**
Kapok leaves are up to 30cm (12in) wide, and divided into five to nine lanceolate leaflets. The leaves are held on long, slender stalks.

**FEATURES**

**Bark** Silver-grey, often covered with thick spines

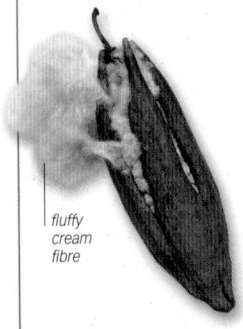


**Fruit** Banana-shaped brown pod, up to 15cm (6in) long

*Ceiba pentandra* (Malvaceae)

# KAPOK

**This tree occurs naturally** in Central and South America, Africa, and southern Asia. This shows that it existed 250 million years ago when all three continents were interconnected and made up part of the supercontinent known as Pangea. By far the highest population of kapok is in Central America, where the ancient Mayan civilization considered the tree to be sacred. It is a large, broadly conical, semi-evergreen tree, reaching up to 60m (200ft) in height.

The kapok's trunk base is heavily buttressed in mature specimens. In spring, this tree bears small, fragrant flowers in clusters. These flowers, up to 2cm (¾in) wide, have five pale yellow, waxy petals, which curve back on themselves to reveal five extended stamens. The flowers are followed by long, leathery fruit pods, which split open vertically to release seeds surrounded by masses of fibre. The fibre, also known as kapok, was once used as a filling for, among other things, pillows and life jackets.

**PROFILE**

- Up to 20m (70ft)
- Up to 20m (70ft)
- Deciduous
- Alternate compound
- South America

**Silk floss flowers**
The flowers are bright rose-pink with five petals. The inner side of each petal usually becomes white towards the base.

*purple markings on inside of petal*

*long, curved, pink pistil, initially enclosed by petals*

**FEATURES**

**Bark** Grey-green; pockmarked with thick, blunt thorns

*Chorisia speciosa* (Malvaceae)

# SILK FLOSS TREE

**Native to South America**, the silk floss tree, also called *Cebia speciosa*, is cultivated elsewhere as an ornamental tree in parks and gardens. This fast-growing, broadly spreading, medium-sized tree is attractive while in flower.

The bark is marked with blunt thorns. The density of the thorns varies from tree to tree, and thorns may appear on larger branches as well. The base of the trunk may become distended in maturity. The green, compound leaves are up to 25cm (10in) wide, and consist of five to seven narrowly elliptic leaflets, each up to 12cm (5in) long. The leaf margins are irregularly toothed, and leaflets are borne on a long leaf stalk. Hibiscus-like flowers emerge from bulging green buds in the leaf axils from spring into summer, and grow up to 15cm (6in) wide. These are followed by ovoid to pear-shaped woody pods, 20cm (8in) long. The pods contain black seeds surrounded in fluffy material, which resembles sheep's wool – rather like the kapok (p.320).

## PROFILE

- Up to 40 m (130 ft)
- Up to 30 m (100 ft)
- Semi-evergreen
- Alternate simple
- Tropical South America

**Flower cluster**
Pale yellow flowers are borne above the leaves, in panicles up to 10 cm (4 in) long. Each flower has six unequal-sized petals.

*flower 2.5 cm (1 in) wide*

*bud opens to six-petalled flower*

## FEATURES

**Bark** Light grey; smooth when young, fissures vertically in maturity

**Leaves** Narrowly oblong, dark green, leathery

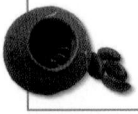

**Fruit** Brown, hard-shelled, woody, 10–12 cm (4–5 in) wide

*Bertholletia excelsa* (Lecythidaceae)

# BRAZIL NUT TREE

**As the name suggests**, this large, semi-evergreen tree is native to Brazil, but it also inhabits other countries bordering the Amazon basin. It is a typical emergent rainforest tree – standing above the canopy with a long, straight trunk devoid of branches for two thirds of its length and topped by a crown made up of long branches with dark foliage. The tree's trunk exceeds 2 m (6 ft) in width.

The bark, on maturity, resembles that of a mature common ash (p.300). The leaves are up to 35 cm (14 in) long and 15 cm (6 in) wide, each with pronounced veining and a pale green central midrib. In the dry season, they turn bronze-red before falling. The fruit is shaped like a cannonball with a flattened top. Each fruit may weigh up to 2 kg (4 ½ lb). Inside are the hard-shelled seeds known as Brazil nuts.

**PROFILE**



- Up to 7 m (22 ft)
- Up to 8 m (25 ft)
- Evergreen
- Alternate simple
- C. America, South America, West Indies

**Fruit and leaves**
The annatto fruit is an egg-shaped husk. Leaves are bright green and broadly ovate.

**FEATURES**

**Flowers** Cup-shaped, pale pink; borne in clusters

**Seeds** Small; exude bright red colour when crushed

*Bixa orellana* (Bixaceae)

# ANNATTO

**This small, broadly spreading tree** has a multi-stemmed, shrublike habit, and is native to Central and South America as well as the West Indies. It is a popular plant for cultivation in tropical gardens because of its attractive flowers and useful seeds. The annatto is best known as the source of a bright red dye, which comes from the seeds. The dye obtained is used to colour cosmetics, such as lipstick, and food, such as smoked fish and red-veined cheese.

The bark is light grey-brown and smooth. Leaves are faintly glossy, growing up to 15 cm (6 in) wide. The flowers are clustered at the ends of twigs on smaller branches. They are up to 5 cm (2 in) wide, with five petals surrounding a central cluster of pink stamens. The fruit is a husk that ripens from yellow to red, borne in clusters of four to five at the ends of twigs and can grow up to 7 cm (3 in) long. Each husk contains up to 50 red seeds.

**PROFILE**

- 20–25 m (70–80 ft)
- Up to 20 m (70 ft)
- Evergreen
- Alternate simple
- S. India, Sri Lanka

**Vibrant green foliage**
Ebony leaves are borne alternately on stems. The leaves are paler with dark markings on the underside.

**FEATURES**

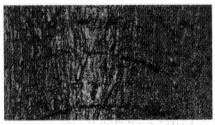

**Bark** Dark grey; peels off in rectangular flakes in maturity

*Diospyros ebenum* (Ebenaceae)

# EBONY

**There are several trees** with the commercial name ebony, but this species – with its dense black, extremely hard heartwood – is the best known. It is native to southern India and Sri Lanka. Ebony is most valued for its timber, which has a wide variety of uses, from woodturning and carving to furniture making. In the wild, it is a slow-growing, medium-sized, evergreen tree, reaching about 20–25 m (70–80 ft) tall.

The tree has oblong-elliptic leaves, with blunt tips. Although male and female flowers are borne on separate trees, they are similar in appearance. They are small, up to 2 cm (¾ in) wide, with four dull white, thick petals. The female flowers are borne singly, while the male flowers bloom in clusters of up to 15. The female flowers are followed by the fruit, which is an edible rounded berry – similar in appearance to a small persimmon. It is 2 cm (¾ in) wide, green when young, ripening to black, and held in a green woody cup that was the old flower sepal.

**Papaya leaves**
Large leaves are borne on lax leaf stems. They are palmately divided into deeply cut lobes.

**PROFILE**

- Up to 7m (22ft)
- Up to 4m (12ft)
- Evergreen
- Alternate simple
- Central and South America

**FEATURES**

**Flowers** Male and female borne on separate trees

**Fruit** Fleshy; green ripening to orange-yellow

*Carica papaya* (Caricaceae)

# PAPAYA

**Also known as the pawpaw**, this fast-growing, short-lived, small, columnar, evergreen is native to Central and South America but is also grown elsewhere for its juicy, edible fruit. Although it takes on tree-like proportions, the papaya is not strictly a tree but a long-lived, herbaceous plant. It displays a single stem with spirally arranged leaves that grow only from the top. The trunk does not lay down wood, as in a normal tree, and always remains soft.

Papaya bark is light brown and regularly patterned with scars where old leaf stems were attached. Towards the crown and growing tip, the stem colour is bright green. Dark glossy green leaves have five to seven lobes, each with further incisions. The small, waxy flowers are similar to frangipani (*Plumeria*). Cream to greenish white in colour, they appear in the leaf axils, and develop into a pear-shaped fruit. Around 15–45cm (6–18in) long, the fruit hangs close to the stem and consists of yellowish orange pulp and black seeds.

*deep cleft divides leaf apex into two rounded lobes*

*deep olive-green leaf, up to 12 cm (5 in) long, 15 cm (6 in) wide*

**Orchid-like flower**
Camel's hoof tree has lilac-pink, five-petalled flowers, resembling an orchid. The flowers bloom in clusters on short stalks.

**PROFILE**

- Up to 10 m (30 ft)
- Up to 10 m (30 ft)
- Evergreen
- Alternate simple
- Hong Kong

*Bauhinia* x *blakeana* (Fabaceae)

# CAMEL'S HOOF TREE

**Shaped like a camel's hoof**, the distinctive leaves of this tree aid in its identification. This tree is also known as the Hong Kong orchid tree, and is widely cultivated across the tropics and subtropics. It is a hybrid between the orchid tree (*B. variegata*) and the purple camel's hoof tree (*B. purpurea*), and was discovered near the ruins of a Hong Kong house around 1880. It is believed that all the trees of this species in cultivation today are derived from one plant, which was propagated from the 1880 specimen and then grown in the Hong Kong botanic garden.

This fast-growing, medium-sized tree has a broadly spreading habit, often with multiple stems. It has a smooth, grey-green bark. The leaves are orbicular (disc-shaped), thick, and leathery. The tree bears highly fragrant flowers, up to 15 cm (6 in) wide, borne in clusters of two to three at the tips of branchlets. Flowers have deep burgundy or purple streaks on just one of their five petals.

**PROFILE**

- Up to 20m (70ft)
- Up to 20m (70ft)
- Semi-evergreen
- Alternate compound
- Madagascar

*widely spread, vermillion petal*

**Showy flowers**
When the flamboyant tree is in bloom, the profusion of its bright vermillion flowers almost obscures the delicate, bipinnate foliage.

**FEATURES**

**Fruit** Hang down en masse from branches; green at first, ripening to brown

*Delonix regia* (Fabaceae)

# FLAMBOYANT TREE

**This broadly-spreading tree** originates from Madagascar, where it is now endangered in the wild. However, the flamboyant tree is widely cultivated across tropical and subtropical regions of the world as an ornamental tree. It is also known as the flame tree or royal poinciana, and in India, gulmohar, which translates from Hindi as "peacock flowers", a reference to its showy, bright orange-red flowers.

The flamboyant tree has smooth, light brown bark and a short trunk, which quickly breaks into long, horizontal branches. The leaves, up to 60cm (24in) long, are frond-like, similar to that of the jacaranda (p.333). They have a bright green upper surface and a paler underside. Flowers are borne in spring or early summer. They have five petals, four of which are an intense vermillion, while the fifth, normally the central petal, is streaked with cream, red, and yellow. The flowers are followed by long, flattened, and pendulous seed pods, which grow up to 60cm (24in) long and 5cm (2in) wide.

**PROFILE**

- 10–25 m (30–80 ft)
- Up to 15 m (50 ft)
- Evergreen
- Opposite simple
- Coastal regions of E. Africa, India, S.E. Asia, W. Pacific islands, N. Australia

*seedling up to 75 cm (30 in) long*

**Pendulous fruit** The fruit is a dark brown, leathery, pear-shaped pod. Seeds germinate within the pods while still on the tree.

**FEATURES**

**Leaves** Shiny, bright green upper surface, paler underside, with warty spots

**Aerial roots** Prop roots arch down from lower trunk to anchor tree to seabed

*Rhizophora mucronata* (Rhizophoraceae)

# ASIATIC MANGROVE

**This broadly spreading**, multi-stemmed evergreen tree is native to coastal regions of East Africa, India, southeast Asia, western Pacific islands, and northern Australia. It grows with its roots in salt water and has its own inbuilt desalination mechanism and defences against waterlogging.

The tree's bark is light grey. Its aerial roots anchor it to the seabed giving the tree a stilted appearance. Its obovate leaves are up to 19 cm (7 in) long and 10 cm (4 in) wide. They have a sharply pointed tip and turn from green to red-brown. Creamy white, four-petalled flowers, up to 2 cm (3/4 in) wide, are borne in clusters of three to five in the leaf axils. The fruit are pods, up to 5 cm (2 in) long, also borne in the leaf axils. They contain seeds that germinate into seedlings on the parent tree, growing straight and long before dropping from the tree.

**Red mangrove (*Rhizophora mangle*)** This tree is recognized by its more pronounced arching roots, smaller leaves up to 12.5 cm (5 in) long and 5 cm (2 in) wide, and pale yellow flowers.

fruit up to 3cm (1¼in) long

elliptic leaflet, up to 20cm (8in) long

**Leaves and fruit**
The trifoliate, leathery leaves are spirally arranged on the shoot. The green, capsule-like fruit ripens to woody brown.

**PROFILE**

- Up to 40m (130ft)
- Up to 20m (70ft)
- Semi-evergreen
- Alternate compound
- Brazil, Venezuela

**FEATURES**

**Bark** Pale grey-brown; smooth throughout life

*Hevea brasiliensis* (Euphorbiaceae)

# RUBBER TREE

**This fast-growing, large**, semi-evergreen, broadly columnar tree is indigenous to both the Amazon river basin in Brazil and the Orinoco river basin in Venezuela. It has been widely planted elsewhere in tropical regions, such as in Malaysia, because it is the main source of natural rubber for commercial use.

Rubber can be tapped from the trees when they are six years old. This is done by cutting a slanting groove in the outer bark and allowing the milky white latex to ooze out into a collecting cup. Trees that are no longer tapped retain V-shaped scars on their otherwise smooth bark for many years and are a good identification feature.

The leaves are dark green on the upper surface, paler on the underside. They may turn orange-red and fall in the dry season. Small, greenish white, fragrant flowers appear in the leaf axils in short, erect panicles. The fruit is a smooth, three-lobed capsule. When fully ripe, it bursts open with a loud crack to release the seeds inside.

**Narrow, lax leaves**
Lanceolate leaves of the mango tree are pale green on the underside and hang down on long leaf stalks.

*glossy, deep green upper surface of leaf*

*pale yellow midrib*

*pronounced veining on leaf surface*

**PROFILE**

- 30 m (100 ft)
- 15 m (50 ft)
- Evergreen
- Alternate simple
- India, E. Asia

**FEATURES**

**Bark** Smooth grey-brown; turns dark, furrowed with age

**Fruit** Green ripening to yellow, orange, or red

*Mangifera indica* (Anacardiaceae)

# MANGO

**Native to India, mango** has been widely cultivated throughout the tropics for millennia. It was grown in East Asia as early as 500 BCE. Today, it is probably the best known and most popular of all tropical fruit and is regularly eaten worldwide.

The trunk of this tree may become buttressed in maturity. New leaves emerge copper-red and are very lax. The leaves are up to 30 cm (12 in) long and 7.5 cm (3 in) wide, and hang from 10 cm- (4 in-) long leaf petioles (stalks). Flowers are tiny, pale yellow, cream, or pale pink, and clustered in hundreds along terminal flower stalks. Flowers are followed by fruit borne in hanging, stalked bunches. The size of the fruit is variable, but normally similar to that of the avocado (p.111).

**Large, dense habit**
The largest cultivated fruit tree, the mango has a trunk that carries a dense crown of dark, luxuriant foliage.

**PROFILE**

- Up to 20 m (70 ft)
- Up to 20 m (70 ft)
- Semi-evergreen
- Alternate compound
- C. America, West Indies

*leaflet up to 7 cm (3 in) long, 3 cm (1 1/4 in) wide*

*dark green leaflet*

**Sickle-shaped leaflets**
The mahogany leaves consist of four to eight pairs of ovate to sickle-shaped leaflets. There is no terminal leaflet.

**FEATURES**

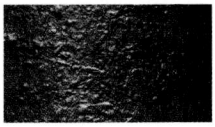

**Bark** Dark red-brown, scaly

*pod up to 4 in (10 cm) long, 2 1/2 in (6 cm) wide*

**Fruit** Oval, woody capsules; contain up to 50 winged seeds

*Swietenia mahagoni* (Meliaceae)

# MAHOGANY

**This slow-growing tree** is probably best known as the source of one of the world's most valued timbers. Mahogany is a medium-sized, broadly columnar, semi-evergreen tree with upward-sweeping branches. It has dense, durable wood, which has a rich, red colour and can be polished to a high shine. It has been favoured by furniture makers ever since it was discovered in Central America and the West Indies in the 17th century. Unfortunately, due to overcutting, it is now endangered in the wild, and its timber should only be obtained from trees grown in managed plantations.

The mahogany's trunk may become buttressed with age. The pinnate leaves are up to 25 cm (10 in) long with four to eight pairs of leaflets. Flowers are small, greenish yellow to white, and fragrant, emerging in early summer and persisting on the tree until early autumn. They are borne in branched clusters in the leaf axils. The fruit is a woody capsule, stalked and upright with winged seeds.

**Teak leaves**
The tree bears rough, leathery, and rich green leaves. Each leaf has a wavy margin.

**PROFILE**

- Up to 35m (120ft)
- Up to 20m (70ft)
- Deciduous
- Opposite simple
- India, Indonesia, Malaysia, Burma

**FEATURES**

**Bark** Pale grey; flakes in maturity to reveal yellow patches beneath

*Tectona grandis* (Lamiaceae)

# TEAK

**Teak is not only the common name** of this broadly columnar, fast-growing tree, but also of its timber and wood products. The tree is grown across the world for its timber and has been naturalized in many tropical countries, including parts of Africa and the Caribbean.

The trunk develops vertical fluting with age. New leaves emerge in the wet season and are followed by small, fragrant, white flowers. The leaves are borne on thick petioles, up to 4cm (1½in) long, and are laden with soft, white hairs on the underside. Flowers are carried in panicles up to 40cm (16in) long and 30cm (12in) wide. The fruit are round, fleshy, and purplish red, ripening to brown.

**Teak timber**
Since its introduction into Europe in the early 1800s, teak has been widely used to make furniture.

**Trumpet-shaped flowers**
Vibrant lilac-blue, trumpet-shaped flowers are carried in erect flower clusters.

*flower up to 5 cm (2 in) long*

*panicle up to 30 cm (12 in) long*

*bipinnate leaf, up to 45 cm (18 in) long*

**PROFILE**

- Up to 15 m (50 ft)
- Up to 15 m (50 ft)
- Deciduous
- Opposite compound
- Paraguay, S. Brazil, N. Argentina

*Jacaranda mimosifolia* (Bignoniaceae)

# JACARANDA

**One of the best known** subtropical trees, the jacaranda is native to South America but has been cultivated in almost every part of the world where there is no risk of frost. It is broadly spreading and medium-sized with an open, branched crown.

The bark is dark grey and smooth when young, becoming scaly in maturity. The leaves are fern-like, with a maximum of 20 pairs of pinnae, each carrying up to 28 pairs of bright green, ovate to elliptic 1 cm- (½ in-) long leaflets. The overall effect is reminiscent of mimosa – hence the species name. Flowers appear in spring and summer. The fruit is a 5 cm- (2 in-) wide, flat brown pod, which contains many winged seeds.

**Jacaranda in bloom**
The mature tree produces a striking mass of lilac-blue flowers, which last for around two months.

## PROFILE

- 10–35 m (30–120 ft)
- Up to 20 m (70 ft)
- Semi-evergreen
- Opposite compound
- Tropical Africa

**Tulip-like flowers**
This tree bears fragrant blooms that are bright reddish orange on the outside and golden yellow inside. They have frilly, gold-rimmed borders.

*curved, pitcher-shaped flower, up to 15 cm (6 in) long*

## FEATURES

**Bark** Pale grey, smooth

**Leaves** Pinnate, up to 60 cm (24 in) long; with 9 to 21 leaflets

*Spathodea campanulata* (Bignoniaceae)

# AFRICAN TULIP TREE

**Also known as flame of the forest**, this tree is widely grown throughout the tropical and subtropical world in parks and gardens. It is especially popular in subtropical regions of the USA, and in India, where it is planted as a street tree. Although considered an evergreen, it sheds its leaves in dry summers.

The African tulip tree carries a few low branches, but develops a thick, dense crown of foliage. The leaves consist of ovate, dark green leaflets, each with a slight sheen. The flower buds are like bunches of small, yellow-brown bananas. Hundreds of winged seeds are contained within smooth, woody seed pods that are up to 20 cm (8 in) long and 5 cm (2 in) wide.

**Best in bloom**
One of the finest flowering trees of the tropics, the African tulip tree is primar native to Uganda.

**PROFILE**

- 15 m (50 ft)
- Up to 10 m (30 ft)
- Evergreen
- Opposite simple
- N.W. South America

*leaf deep green on upper surface*

**Smooth leaves**
The leaves are ovate to lanceolate, with a slight sheen on the upper surface.

*pale green underside of leaf*

*leaf up to 15 cm (6 in) long*

**FEATURES**

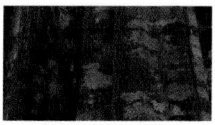

**Bark** Grey, smooth at first; becomes fluted in maturity

**Flowers** Fragrant, white to pink, occasionally red; up to 5 mm (¼ in) wide

*Cinchona officinalis* (Rubiaceae)

# QUININE TREE

**The discovery of this** broadly spreading tree led to one of the most important medical advancements in human history. The bark of the quinine tree and related *Cinchona* species is the only known natural source of quinine, a chemical compound that is an effective treatment for malaria.

This tree is native to the western region of the Amazon rainforest, in Ecuador and Peru, and it was the Quechua Indians of Peru that discovered its medicinal properties. By the early 17th century, the Jesuits had introduced it into Europe.

As the tree matures, the trunk develops deep, long fluting. The leaves, up to 6 cm (2 ½ in) wide, have smooth margins. The small, fragrant flowers are tubular-shaped and borne in open-stalked terminal panicles. Both the flowers and the panicles are covered in fine, silvery-white hairs. The fruit is a green ovoid-shaped capsule, up to 1.5 cm (½ in) long, which ripens to brown and splits open to reveal numerous winged seeds.

# GLOSSARY

**ACHENE**
A small, dry and hard, one-seeded fruit that does not split open for seed distribution.

**AGGREGATE FRUIT**
A cluster of many ripened ovaries (fruits) produced from a single flower. Examples are strawberry, raspberry and blackberry.

**ALTERNATE**
Describes leaves that are borne singly at each node, in two vertical rows, on either side of an axis.

**ANGIOSPERM**
A seed-producing plant that encloses its seeds in a fruit and produces flowers. All flowering trees are angiosperms.

**ANTHER**
In flowering plants, the structure on the stamen that contains pollen.

**ARIL**
Coat that covers some seeds; often fleshy and brightly coloured.

**AXIL**
The angle formed by a leaf or lateral branch with the stem.

**AXILLARY**
Borne in an axil, usually referring to flowers.

**BARK**
The outer layers of the stem of a woody plant, which protect the plant from water loss, cold, infection and mechanical damage.

**BASAL ANGIOSPERM**
*See* primitive angiosperm.

**BIPINNATE**
A compound leaf arrangement in which the leaflets are themselves pinnate.

**BRACT**
Modified leaf at the base of a flower or flowerhead. A bract may be small and scale-like, or large and petal-like, or it may resemble normal foliage.

**BRACTEOLE**
Secondary bract sheathing a flower in an inflorescence.

**BURR**
1. Prickly, spiny, or hooked fruit, seed head, or flowerhead.
2. Woody outgrowth on the trunk of some trees.

**BUTTRESS**
Trunk base that is fluted or swollen, giving stability to a tree in shallow soil conditions.

**CALCAREOUS**
Describing soil that contains calcium carbonate and so is alkaline in nature.

**CALYX (PL. CALYCES)**
Collective name for sepals, joined or separate, which form the outer whorl of the perianth.

**CAPSULE**
A type of dry fruit that splits open to disperse ripe seed – sometimes called a pod.

**CARPEL**
Female flower part consisting of a style, a stigma, and an ovary.

**CATKIN**
A type of inflorescence, usually pendulous, in which scale-like bracts and tiny, often petalless flowers are arranged in a spike.

**CLADE**
A group of species that includes all the evolutionary descendants from a single common ancestor.

**CLONE**
A genetically identical group of plants derived from one individual by vegetative reproduction.

**COLUMNAR**
A tree shape that is significantly taller than it is broad, with parallel sides.

**COMPOUND**
Describes a leaf divided into leaflets.

**CONE**
The seed-bearing or pollen-bearing structure of conifer trees.

**CONICAL**
Widest at the bottom, tapering towards the top.

**COPPICE**
An area of woodland where trees are periodically cut back to ground level in order to encourage the growth of new shoots from the stumps.

**CORDATE**
A leaf that is heart shaped.

**COROLLA**
1. Collective name for petals.
2. Inner whorl of perianth segments in some monocotyledons.

**CORYMB**
Broad, flat-topped or domed inflorescence of stalked flowers or flowerheads arising at different levels on alternate sides of an axis.

**COTYLEDON**
The first food-containing leaf of a plant embryo that is formed inside the seed. Monocotyledon seeds generally have a single cotyledon, dicots (such as eudicotyledons and primitive angiosperms) two, and those of conifers have a variable number.

**CULTIVAR**
Contraction of "cultivated variety". A cultivated plant that retains distinct characteristics when propagated.

**CYME**
Branched inflorescence with each axis ending in a flower.

**DECIDUOUS**
A tree that loses its leaves and remains leafless for some months of the year, usually in winter (temperate zones) or the dry season (tropical zones).

**DIGITATE**
A palmate compound leaf divided into five leaflets arising from a single basal point.

**DIOECIOUS**
A plant that has male and female flowers on different plants.

**DRUPE**
A type of fruit consisting of a soft outer wall and one or more inner hard "stones" each containing a seed. Fruits of cherries, plums and date palms are drupes.

**LLIPTIC**
flat leaf shape that is broadest t the centre, tapering towards ach end.

**MBRYO**
young plant at a rudimentary tage of development. In seed lants, including seed trees, the mbryo is encased in a seed until grows into a seedling during ermination.

**NDOCARP**
he inner layer of a fruit nmediately around the seed; e endocarp forms the hard stone" of drupes.

**NDOSPERM**
erm given to the specialized food tore within the fertilized seed of ngiosperms (flowering plants) that ourishes the embryo during ermination.

**NTIRE**
leaf margin that is without teeth.

**PIPHYTE**
plant that has no roots in the soil nd lives above the ground surface, upported by another plant.

**VERGREEN**
tree that bears leaves hroughout the year.

**XOCARP**
he outermost "skin" of a fruit

**ASCICLE**
tight cluster of leaves or stalked owers that diverge very little. or instance, the needle-like eaves of many pine trees arise n fascicles.

**OLLICLE**
ry fruit, formed from a single arpel, that splits along one side to elease one or more seeds.

**ORM**
ny variant of a species.

**RUIT**
structure of a plant that evelops from the ovary of a lower and contains one or more eeds. Fruit can be simple, like erries, or compound, where he fruits of separate flowers re merged.

**AMETE**
ell or nucleus that participates in exual fusion.

**GENUS**
A category in classification consisting of a group of closely related species, and denoted by the first part of the scientific name, e.g. *Pinus* in *Pinus pinea*.

**GERMINATION**
The changes undergone by a reproductive body, such as a seed, immediately prior to and including the first indications of growth.

**GLABROUS**
Hairless.

**GLAUCOUS**
Covered with a bloom, or blueish white or bluish grey.

**GLOBOSE**
Spherical.

**GYMNOSPERM**
A seed-producing plant that doesn't enclose its seeds in a fruit. Many gymnosperms carry their seeds on cones.

**HABIT**
The growth form of a tree, including its size, shape, and orientation.

**HERBACEOUS**
A non-woody plant that normally lives for more than one season, usually dying back at the end of the growing season and overwintering by means of underground rootstocks.

**HERITAGE TREE**
A tree that has some important cultural or historical significance.

**HERMAPHRODITE**
Any organism that has both male and female sex organs; in a tree, where the male and female reproductive organs are borne on the same tree.

**HYBRID**
Naturally or artificially produced offspring of genetically distinct parents of different species. Hybrids show new characteristics. Hybrid names include the names of both parent species separated by an "x", such as *Tilia* x *euchlora*.

**INDICATOR SPECIES**
A species that by its presence (or absence) shows the type of environmental conditions that prevail.

**INFLORESCENCE**
Arrangement of flowers around a single axis (stem).

**LANCEOLATE**
Leaf that is broadest below the centre, tapering to a narrow tip.

**LATERAL**
1. Located on or to the side of an axis.
2. Side shoot arising from the stem of a plant.

**LAX**
Describes an arrangement of structures, such as a cluster of flowers, that is loose instead of compact and crowded.

**LEADING SHOOT**
The terminal shoot of a main branch.

**LEAFLET**
Single division of a compound leaf. Also known as a pinna.

**LEAF AXIL**
The angle between the upper surface of a leaf and the branch from which it is growing. A bud often grows in the leaf axil. Also, where a vein comes off the midrib of a leaf.

**LENTICEL**
Raised pore on the surface of bark or some fruits that provides access for air to the inner tissues.

**LOBE**
A protruding part of a leaf or a flower.

**MARGIN**
The edge of a leaf blade. Leaf margins may be smooth (entire), lobed, or serrated

**MESOCARP**
The soft, fleshy, middle portion of the wall of a succulent fruit between the skin and the hard layer.

**MIDRIB**
Primary (usually central) vein running from the stalk to the tip of a leaf or leaflet. Also called midvein.

**MONOECIOUS**
A plant that has separate male and female parts on the same individual.

**MONOTYPIC**
A taxonomic group with a single species, such a family that contains only one genus or a genus with only one species.

**MUTATION**
A random change in the genetic makeup of an organism, in its genes or chromosomes; mutations may be passed on through generations.

**NATIVE**
A species that occurs naturally in a particular region, as opposed to one that has been introduced.

**NATURALIZED**
A non-native species that has become established in the wild in a region where it was introduced.

**NODE**
Point on a stem, sometimes swollen, at which leaves, leaf buds, and shoots arise.

**OBLANCEOLATE**
Leaf shape that is broadest above the centre, tapering to a narrow basal point. Also called inversely lance-shaped (lanceolate).

**OBLONG**
Describes a leaf shape with two sides of roughly equal length.

**OBLONG-ELLIPTIC**
Describes a leaf shape that is oblong with ends that are round.

**OBOVATE**
A leaf shape that is egg-shaped in outline and broadest above the middle.

**OPPOSITE**
A leaf arrangement in which the leaves are borne in pairs at each node, in the same place but on opposite sides of an axis.

**OVARY**
The lower, wide vessel-like section of the female part of a flower that contains one or more ovules. After fertilization – and the ovules become seeds – the ovary develops into a fruit.

**OVATE**
Describes a leaf shape that is broadest below the middle.

**OVOID**
Describes a solid form that is broadest below the middle; usually refers to a fruit.

**OVULE**
Structure that contains the egg of a seed plant. Ovules are encased in an ovary in flowering plants, but naked in gymnosperms (conifers, ginkgo, and cycads). After fertilization, the ovule becomes the seed.

**PALMATE**
A compound leaf that is lobed or divided in a hand-like fashion into leaflets arising from a single basal point.

**PANICLE**
An elongated, branched flower cluster, with stalked flowers.

**PEA-LIKE**
A flower with an erect standard petal, two lateral wing petals, and two lower, keeled petals enclosing the stamens and pistil.

**PEDICEL**
The stalk supporting a flower, flowerhead, or fruit.

**PETAL**
One of the parts of the corolla of a flower. It is often brightly coloured to attract pollinating animals.

**PETIOLE**
The stalk of a leaf.

**PERENNIAL**
A plant that normally lives for more than one season.

**PERIANTH**
Collective term for the corolla and calyx.

**PERICARP**
The tissues that makes up fruit derived from an ovary: divided into exocarp, mesocarp, and endocarp.

**PHLOEM**
Plant tissue consisting of microscopic vessels that transport water and dissolvedfood (such as sugars) throughthe plant.

**PHOTOSYNTHESIS**
A process whereby a plant uses light energy to make food and oxygen.

**PINNA (PL. PINNAE)**
One of the main divisions of a feather-like compound leaf, such as a fern frond.

**PINNATE**
A compound leaf arrangement in which the leaflets (pinnae) are arranged either alternately or in opposite pairs on a central axis.

**PIONEER SPECIES**
A species that is usually the first to colonize inhospitable sites and cleared ground, leading the way for other vegetation. Pioneer species improve soil quality and protect land from erosion.

**PISTIL**
Female reproductive organ of a flower, composed of one or several fused or separate carpels.

**POLLARD**
To prune the tops of trees in such a way as to encourage new growth in the form of a dense head of foliage.

**POLLEN**
Tiny grains produced by seed plants that contain male gametes (sex cells) for fertilizing the female egg.

**PRIMITIVE ANGIOSPERM**
A group of flowering plants with certain primitive features that diverged away from the main evolutionary line of flowering plants before others. Also called basal angiosperms.

**RACEME**
Inflorescence of stalked flowers radiating from a single, unbranche axis, with the youngest flowers near the tip.

**SAMARA**
A type of dry fruit with papery "wings" that can be carried by wind, thus dispersing seed farther from the parent tree. Samaras are either single-winged (as in most maples) or multi-winged.

**SEMI-DECIDUOUS OR SEMI-EVERGREEN**
A tree that loses its leaves for only a short period during the yea or that sheds a proportion of its leaves periodically but is never entirely leafless.

**SEED**
Developmental stage of a seed plant, consisting of an encapsulated embryo.

**SEPAL**
One of the parts of the calyx of a flower, usually small and leaf-like, and enveloping the unopened flower bud.

**SERRATED**
Describes the margin of a leaf which has sharp "teeth" pointing forwards, like the edge of a saw.

**SIMPLE**
Undivided, as in a leaf

**SPECIES (ABBREV. SP.)**
A classification category defining a group of similar plants that and usually interbreed, e.g. Scots pine (*Pinus sylvestris*) is one species.

**SPERM**
A male reproductive cell capable of fertilization.

**SPIKE**
An inflorescence in which stalkless flowers are arranged on an unbranched axis.

**SPORE**
A single cell containing half the quantity of genetic material of typical body cells. Unlike gametes, spores can divide and grow without being fertilized. Tree ferns are the only trees that reproduce by spores.

**STAMEN**
Male part of a flower, usually composed of an anther borne on a filament.

**STAMINAL TUBE**
A structure formed from joined stamens.

**STIGMA**
Female part of a flower at the tip of the pistil that receives pollen.

**STIPULE**
Leaf-like or bract-like structure borne at the point where a leaf-stalk arises from a stem.

**STOMA (PL. STOMATA)**
Tiny adjustable pore on the surface of a plant that allows for the exchange of gases for photosynthesis and respiration.

**STRANGLER**
A plant that initially uses another plant (known as the host) for support, before out-competing the host for light and water. Several members if the *Ficus* genus are stranglers.

**STROBILUS**
A cone-like reproductive structure, such as the seed-bearing structure of conifer trees.

**STYLE**
Female part of flower connecting the ovary and the stigma.

**SUBULATE**
Awl-shaped.

**SUBSPECIES (ABBREV. SUBSP.)**
A category of classification, below species, defining a group within a species, often isolated geographically but able to interbreed with others of the same species.

**SUCKER**
1. Shoot that arises below the soil level, usually from the roots rather than from the stem or crown of the plant.
2. Shoot that arises from the stock of a grafted or budded plant.

**SYNCARP**
An aggregate or multiple fruit that is produced from fused pistils; the individual fruits join together in a mass and grow together to form a single fruit.

**TEPAL**
The term that is given to the sepals and petals when they are indistinguishable from one another as in the case of primitive angiosperms.

**TERMINAL**
The position at the end of a stem or shoot.

**TRIFOLIATE**
Three leaves, or a leaf made up of three separate leaflets.

**UMBEL**
Flat or round-topped inflorescence in which numerous stalked flowers are borne in a terminal position from a single point.

**VARIEGATED**
Having more than one colour; usually used to describe leaves.

**VARIETY (ABBREV. VAR.)**
A naturally occurring variant of a species.

**VEIN**
A vascular bundle (bundle of transport vessels) running through a leaf.

**WHORL**
An arrangement of several identical structural parts in a circle around the same point. For instance, petals make up the whorl of the corolla.

**WOODY PLANT**
A plant that has wood: a type of strengthening tissue made from thick-walled vessels of xylem tissue. For example; trees, shrub, and woody climbers such as ivy.

**XYLEM**
Plant tissue consisting of microscopic thick-walled vessels that transport water and dissolved minerals through the plant.

# LIST OF TREE FAMILIES

The following is a list of all tree families covered in this book along with the genera included within each family and the relevant pages numbers. These family names are the most up to date at the time of going to print. However, readers should be aware they may find alternative family names still being used elsewhere.

**Anacardiaceae** *Mangifera* (p.330), *Rhus* (pp.308–309)

**Aquifoliaceae** *Ilex* (pp.279–280)

**Araucariaceae** *Araucaria* (pp.28–p.29), *Wollemia* (p.30)

**Arecaceae** *Butia* (p.117), *Chamaerops* (p.115), *Cocos* (p.119), *Phoenix* (p.116), *Trachycarpus* (p.114)

**Asparagaceae** *Cordyline* (p.118), *Dracaena* (p.120)

**Betulaceae** *Alnus* (pp.180-183), *Betula* (pp.173–179), *Carpinus* (pp.184–185), *Corylus* (p.186), *Ostrya* (p.187)

**Bignoniaceae** *Catalpa* (pp.305–306), *Jacaranda* (p.333), *Spathodea* (p.334)

**Bixaceae** *Bixa* (p.323)

**Caricaceae** *Carica* (p.325)

**Cephalotaxaceae** *Cephalotaxus* (pp.31–32)

**Cercidiphyllaceae** *Cercidiphyllum* (p.212)

**Clusiaceae** *Clusia* (p.317)

**Cornaceae** *Cornus* (pp.274–276), *Davidia* (p.272), *Nyssa* (pp.209–210)

**Cupressaceae** *Athrotaxus* (p.60–61), *Calocedrus* (p.39), *Chamaecyparis* (p.40, pp.43–44), *Cryptomeria* (p.42), *Cunninghamia* (p.68), *Cupressus* (pp.51–52), *Fitzroya* (p.45), *Glyptostrobus* (p.70), *Juniperus* (pp.53–55), *Metasequoia* (p.67), *Platycladus* (p.58), *Sequoia* (p.62), *Sequoiadendron* (p.63), *Taxodium* (p.66), *Thuja* (pp.56–57), *Thujopsis* (p.59), x *Cuppressocyparis* (p.41)

**Dicksoniaceae** *Dicksonia* (p.23)

**Ebenaceae** *Diospyros* (p.324)

**Ericaceae** *Arbutus* (pp.213–215)

**Eucommiaceae** *Eucommia* (p.124)

**Eucryphiaceae** *Eucryphia* (pp.223–224)

**Euphorbiaceae** *Hevea* (p.329)

**Fabaceae** *Acacia* (p.229–230), *Albizia* (p.228), *Bauhinia* (p.326), *Cercis* (p.227), *Cladrastris* (p.267), *Delonix* (p.327), *Gleditsia* (p.266), *Gymnocladus* (p.265), *Laburnum* (pp.225–226), *Robinia* (p.262), *Sophora* (p.263)

**Fagaceae** *Castanea* (p.161), *Chrysolepis* (p.162), *Fagus* (pp.152–156), *Lithocarpus* (p.163), *Nothofagus* (pp.157–160), *Quercus* (pp.164–172)

**Ginkgoaceae** *Ginkgo* (p.26)

**Hamamelidaceae** *Liquidambar* (pp.207–208), *Parrotia* (p.211)

**Juglandaceae** *Carya* (pp.148–151), *Juglans* (pp.141–143)

**Lamiaceae** *Tectona* (p.332)

**Lauraceae** *Cinnamomum* (p.112), *Laurus* (pp.107–108), *Persea* (p.111), *Sassafras* (p.127), *Umbellularia* (p.128)

**Lecythidaceae** *Bertholletia* (p.322)

**Lythraceae** *Lagerstroemia* (p.231)

**Magnoliaceae** *Liriodendron* (p.105–106), *Magnolia* (pp.96–103), *Michelia* (p.104)

**Malvaceae** *Adansonia* (p.319), *Ceiba* (p.320), *Chorisia* (p.321), *Theobroma* (p.318), *Tilia* (pp.188–192)

**Meliaceae** *Swietenia* (p.331)

**Monimiaceae** *Laurelia* (p.109)

**Moraceae** *Artocarpus* (pp.310–311), *Ficus* (p.146, pp.312–316), *Maclura* (p.147), *Morus* (pp.144–145)

**Myrtaceae** *Eucalyptus* (pp.268–271), *Luma* (p.126), *Metrosideros* (pp.122–123)

**Oleaceae** *Fraxinus* (pp.300–304), *Ligustrum* (p.130), *Olea* (p.129), *Phillyrea* (p.131)

**Pinaceae** *Abies* (pp.71–75), *Cedrus* (pp.46–48), *Larix* (pp.76–78), *Picea* (pp.80–93), *Pseudolarix* (p.79), *Pseudotsuga* (pp.49–50), *Tsuga* (pp.64–65)

**Pittosporaceae** *Pittosporum* (p.132)

**Platanaceae** *Platanus* (pp.204–206)

**Podocarpaceae** *Podocarpus* (p.34), *Prumnopitys* (p.33) *Saxegothaea* (p.35)

**Proteaceae** *Embothrium* (p.125)

**Rhizophoraceae** *Rhizophora* (p.328)

**Rosaceae** *Crataegus* (pp.243–245), *Malus* (pp.246–249), *Mespilus* (p.261), *Prunus* (pp.232–242), *Pyrus* (pp.250–251), *Sorbus* (pp.252–260)

**Rubiaceae** *Cinchona* (p.335)

**Rutaceae** *Phellodendron* (p.277), *Tetradium* (p.278)

**Salicaceae** *Populus* (pp.193–197), *Salix* (pp.198–203)

**Sapindaceae** *Acer* (pp.287–299), *Aesculus* (pp.281–286), *Koelreuteria* (p.273)

**Sciadopityaceae** *Sciadopitys* (p.69)

**Scrophulariaceae** *Paulownia* (p.307)

**Simaroubaceae** *Ailanthus* (p.264)

**Styracaceae** *Halesia* (pp.219–220), *Styrax* (pp.216–218)

**Taxaceae** *Torreya* (p.36), *Taxus* (pp.37–38)

**Theaceae** *Stewartia* (pp.221–222)

**Ulmaceae** *Celtis* (pp.137–138), *Ulmus* (pp.133–136), *Zelkova* (pp.139–140)

**Winteraceae** *Drimys* (p.110)

# INDEX

Page numbers in **bold** are for main page entries.

## A


*Abies alba* **71**
*Abies cephalonica* 71
*Abies concolor* 74
*Abies delavayi* 73
*Abies grandis* 75
*Abies koreana* **73**
*Abies lasiocarpa* 75
*Abies nordmanniana* **72**
*Abies numidica* 72
*Abies procera* **74**
acacia, blackwood **230**
*Acacia baileyana* 229
*Acacia dealbata* **229**
*Acacia melanoxylon* **230**
*Acacia pravissima* 230
*Acer* 19
*Acer campestre* 287
*Acer cappadocicum* **290**
*Acer davidii* **291**
*Acer griseum* **292**
*Acer henryi* 298
*Acer japonicum* 295
*Acer macrophyllum* 299
*Acer negundo* 298
*Acer palmatum* 7, 294
*Acer platanoides* **289**
*Acer pseudoplatanus* **288**
*Acer rubrum* **293**
*Acer saccharinum* **297**
*Acer saccharum* **296**
*Acer shirasawanum* 292
*Acer triflorum* 287
acorn 19
*Adansonia digitata* 3**19**
adaptations to habitats 10–15
adelgid, hemlock woolly 65
*Adiantum* 26
aerial roots 22
*Aesculus californica* 281
*Aesculus carnea* **284**
*Aesculus chinensis* 282
*Aesculus flava* **285**
*Aesculus glabra* 285
*Aesculus hippocastanum* 7, **281**
*Aesculus indica* **282**
*Aesculus* x *neglecta* 'Erythroblastos' 286
*Aesculus pavia* **286**
*Aesculus turbinata* **283**
African baobab **319**
African tulip tree **334**
*Agathis australis* 29
*Ailanthus altissima* **264**
*Albizia julibrissin* **228**
alder,
  common **180**
  grey **181**
  Italian **182**
  Japanese 182
  Japanese green 183
  Oregon **183**
  Oriental 180
  red **183**
  Sitka 181
Algerian fir 72
Algerian oak **172**
Allegheny serviceberry 247
alligator juniper 53
almond **236**
*Alnus cordata* **182**
*Alnus firma* 183
*Alnus glutinosa* 1**80**
*Alnus incana* **181**
*Alnus japonica* 182
*Alnus orientalis* 180
*Alnus rubra* **183**
*Alnus sinuata* 181
alpine fir 75
Alpine laburnum **226**
alternate leaves 16
Amazon rainforest 6, 11
*Amelanchier laevis* 247
*Amelanchier lamarckii* 246
American arbor-vitae **57**
American ash **302**
American basswood **192**
American beech 152
American flowering dogwood 276
American lime **192**
American sweet chestnut 162
American sycamore **206**
Amur cork tree **277**
Anacardiaceae 308–309, 330
*Andansonia madagascarionsis* 319
Angiospermae 7, 24, **94**
angiosperms **94**
  basal **95**
annatto **323**
Antarctic beech **158**
anther 18, 94
apple **249**
  common crab **246**
  cultivated 246, **249**
  orchard 246, **249**
  sour **246**
apple-fruited service tree 256
apricot 236
  Japanese 238
Aquifoliaceae 279–280
*Araucaria araucana* **28**
*Araucaria heterophylla* **29**
Araucariaceae 28–30
arbor-vitae,
  American **57**
  Chinese **58**
*Arbutus andrachne* **214**
*Arbutus* x *andrachnoides* 214
*Arbutus menziesii* **215**
*Arbutus unedo* **213**
*Archaeopteris* 6
Arecaceaea 114, 117, 119
Arizona cypress 52
Armand's pine 88
Arolla pine 87
*Artocarpus altilis* **310**
*Artocarpus heterophyllus* **311**
ash,
  American **302**
  Chinese 304
  Chinese flowering **304**
  Chinese mountain **257**, 259
  common **300**
  golden 300
  green 302
  Himalayan manna 301
  manna **301**
  mountain **252**
  narrow-leaved **303**
  Pallis's 303
  white **302**
ash-leaved maple **298**
Asian pear 251
Asiatic mangrove **328**
Asparagaceae 118, 120
aspen **193**
  European **193**
*Athrotaxus laxifolia* **61**
*Athrotaxus selaginoides* **60**
Atlas cedar **46**
Australian blackwood **230**
Austrian pine 87
*Austrocedrus chilensis* 57
autograph tree **317**
avocado 95, **111**
azarole 245


## B


bald cypress **66**
balsam poplar 193
  Chinese 195
bananas 113
banyan tree **313**
baobab 13
  African **319**
  Madagascan 319
bark 8, 16
  broad-leaved kindling **270**
  Winter's **110**
basal angiosperms **95**
basswood, American **192**
*Bauhinia* x *blakeana* **326**
*Bauhinia purpurea* 326
*Bauhinia variegata* 326
bay,
  bull **96**
  California **128**
bay laurel **107**
bay willow 199
bean tree,
  golden-leaved Indian 305
  Indian **305**
bee-bee tree **278**
beech,
  American 152
  Antarctic **158**
  Chinese 154
  Coigüe southern **160**
  common **152**
  coyan **159**

Dombey's southern **160**
European **152**
hedgerows 15
Japanese 155, **156**
Menzies' red 159
myrtle 158
New Zealand red 160
Oriental **154**
oval-leaved southern 157
purple **153**
rauli southern **157**
roble **159**
Siebold's **155**, 156
weeping 153
berries 8, 9, 19
*Bertholletia excelsa* **322**
*Betula albosinensis* **175**
*Betula alleghaniensis* 179
*Betula chinensis* 175
*Betula costata* 178
*Betula ermanii* **178**
*Betula grossa* 177
*Betula maximowicziana* 176
*Betula nigra* **179**
*Betula papyrifera* **177**
*Betula pendula* **173**
*Betula populifolia* 173
*Betula pubescens* **174**
*Betula utilis* **176**
Betulaceae 173–187
Bhutan pine **92**
big-bud hickory **150**
big-cone pine 90
big shellbark **149**
bigcone fir **49**
bigleaf magnolia, Japanese 102
bigleaf storax **218**
Bignoniaceae 305–306, 333–334
birch,
canoe **177**
Chinese dwarf 175
Chinese red-barked **175**
downy **174**
Erman's **178**
grey 173
Himalayan **176**
Japanese cherry 177
Korean 178
monarch 176
paper-bark **177**
red **179**
river **179**
Russian rock **178**
silver **173**
warty **173**
white **174**
yellow 179
birches 12
bird cherry **233**
bitternut hickory **148**
*Bixa orellana* **323**
Bixaceae 323
black cherry **240**
black cottonwood 196
black gum **209**
black locust **262**
black mulberry **145**
black pine, Japanese 85
black poplar **194**, 195
black tupelo **209**, 210
black walnut **142**
blackwood, Australian **230**
blackwood acacia **230**
bleeding canker 281
blue gum, Tasmanian 269
bo tree **312**
bonsai 54
box, jasmine **131**
box elder **298**
Brazil nut tree 11, **322**
breadfruit **310**
Brewer's weeping spruce **84**
broad-leaved kindling bark **270**
broad-leaved lime **189**
broom, Mount Etna 226
*Broussonetia papyifera* 144
brush bush **224**
buckeye *see also* horse chestnut
California 281
Ohio 285
red 284, 286
sweet 285
yellow 285
bull bay **96**
*Butia capitata* **117**
butternut 141
buttonwood 204, **206**


# C


cabbage palm **118**
cacao **318**
California bay **128**
California buckeye 281
California laurel **128**
California nutmeg **36**
California olive **128**
Californian madrone **215**
*Calocedrus decurrens* **39**
cambium 9
camel's hoof tree, purple 326
camel's hoof tree **326**
camellia 221
Campbell's magnolia **101**
camphor tree **112**
Canadian hemlock **65**
Canary Island date palm **116**
Canary Island laurel **108**
Canary Island pine **91**
canoe birch **177**
canopy 8
capsules, spore 22
carbon dioxide 6, 9, 14
*Carica papaya* **325**
Caricaceae 325
Carolina snowdrop tree **219**, 220
carpel 95
*Carpinus betulus* **184**
*Carpinus cordata* 184
*Carpinus japonica* **185**
*Carpinus orientalis* 185
*Carya cordiformis* **148**
*Carya glabra* 148
*Carya illinoinensis* 149
*Carya laciniosa* **149**
*Carya ovata* **151**
*Carya tomentosa* **150**
*Castanea crenata* 161
*Castanea dentata* 162
*Castanea sativa* 7, **161**
*Castanopsis cuspidata* 167
catalpa, Farges' **306**
*Catalpa bignonioides* 'Aurea' 305
*Catalpa bignonioides* **305**
*Catalpa fargesii* **306**
Caucasian elm **139**
Caucasian fir **72**
Caucasian maple **290**
Caucasian spruce **81**
*Cebia speciosa* see *Chorisia speciosa*
cedar,
Atlas **46**
Chilean 57
Cyprian 48
deodar **47**
incense **39**
Indian **47**
Japanese **42**, 60
summit **61**
Tasmanian **60**
western red **56**
white 51, **57**
cedar of Lebanon 46, **48**, 51
*Cedrus atlantica* **46**
*Cedrus brevifolia* 48
*Cedrus deodara* **47**
*Cedrus libani* **48**
*Ceiba pentandra* **320**
cellulose 9
*Celtis australis* **137**
*Celtis laevigata* 138
*Celtis occidentalis* **138**
*Celtis sinensis* 137
Central Africa tropical forests 11
Cephalotaxaceae 31–32
*Cephalotaxus* 36
*Cephalotaxus fortunei* **31**
*Cephalotaxus harringtonia* **32**
Cercidiphyllaceae 212
*Cercidiphyllum japonicum* 17, **212**
*Cercidiphyllum magnificum* 212
*Cercis canadensis* 227
*Cercis siliquastrum* **227**
*Chamaecyparis formosensis* 40
*Chamaecyparis lawsoniana* **40**
*Chamaecyparis nootkatensis* **44**
*Chamaecyparis obtusa* **43**
*Chamaecyparis pisifera* 43
*Chamaecyparis thyoides* 44
*Chamaerops humilis* **115**
chequer tree **255**
cherry,
bird 233
black 240
Chinese 239
Fuji 238 *see also* cherry, Mount Fuji
great white 239
hill **239**
Himalayan 235
Mount Fuji 242 *see also* Fuji cherry
pink-blossomed 240

rum 240
Sargent's 242
sour 237
St Lucie 232
sweet 232
wild 121, 232
cherry birch, Japanese 177
chestnut,
American sweet 162
Chinese horse 282
common horse 7, **281**
golden **162**
Indian horse **282**
Japanese 161
Japanese horse **283**
red horse **284**
sunrise horse 286
sweet 7, **161**
chestnut-leaved oak 166
Chile pine **28**
Chilean cedar 57
Chilean fire bush **125**
Chilean laurel **109**
Chilean myrtle **126**
white 126
Chilean sassafras **109**
Chilean yew **33**
China tree **273**
Chinese arbor-vitae **58**
Chinese ash 304
Chinese balsam poplar 195
Chinese beech 154
Chinese dwarf birch 175
Chinese cherry 239
Chinese dogwood 275
Chinese elm 136
Chinese evergreen magnolia 104
Chinese fir **68**
Chinese flowering ash **304**
Chinese fringe tree 129
Chinese horse chestnut 282
Chinese juniper **54**
Chinese mountain ash 259
Chinese necklace poplar **196**
Chinese plum yew **31**
Chinese privet **130**
Chinese red-barked birch **175**
Chinese mountain ash **257**
Chinese snowbell tree **217**
Chinese stewartia **222**
Chinese sumach **309**
Chinese swamp cypress **70**
Chinese sweetgum 208
Chinese tulip tree **106**
Chinese tupelo **210**
Chinese weeping willow **200**
Chinese yew 38
Chinese zelkova 139
chinquapin, Japanese 167
*Chionanthus retusus* 129
chlorophyll 9
chocolate 318
*Chorisia speciosa* **321**
Christmas tree 71, 72, 80, 85
New Zealand **123**
*Chrysolepis chrysophylla* **162**
Chusan palm **114**
cider gum **268**
*Cinchona officinalis* **335**
*Cinnamomum camphora* **112**
*Cladrastis kentukea* **267**
classification 7
climate 6
*Clusia rosea* **317**
Clusiaceae 317
coastal habitats 14
coastal redwood **62**
cockspur thorn (hawthorn) 94, **245**
cocoa 318
coconut 113, **119**
*Cocos nucifera* **119**
coffee tree, Kentucky **265**
Coigüe southern beech 35, **160**
Colorado white fir 74
common alder **180**
common ash **300**
common beech **152**
common crab apple **246**
common elder 298
common fig **146**
common hawthorn **243**
common holly **279**
common hornbeam **184**
common horse chestnut **281**
common juniper **53**
common laburnum **225**
common lime **190**
common oak 17, **165**
common osier 201
common pear **250**
common walnut **141**
common yew **37**
compound leaves 16, 113
cones 8, 9, 19
conifer trees 6, 7, **27**, 95
coniferous forests 10
Cootamundra wattle 229
*Cordyline australis* **118**
cordylines 113
cork oak **170**
cork tree, Amur **277**
Cornaceae 209–210, 272, 274–276
*Cornus controversa* **274**
*Cornus controversa* 'Variegata' 274
*Cornus florida* 276
*Cornus kousa* **275**
*Cornus kousa* var. *chinensis* 275
*Cornus nuttallii* **276**
Corsican pine **87**
*Corylus colurna* **186**
cottonwood, black 196
cotyledons 113, 121
cow's tail pine **32**
coyan beech **159**
crab,
Hupeh **247**
pillar 248
Siberian **248**
crab apple, common **246**
crack willow **198**
crape myrtle **231**
*Crataegus azarolus* 245
*Crataegus crus-galli* **245**
*Crataegus dsungarica* 244
*Crataegus laciniata* 243
*Crataegus laevigata* **244**
*Crataegus monogyna* **243**
Crimean lime 188
*Cryptomeria japonica* **42**
cucumber magnolia 96
cultivars 7
cultivated apple **249**
*Cunninghamia konishii* 68
*Cunninghamia lanceolata* **68**
Cupressaceae 39–45, 51–63, 66–68, 70
*Cupressocyparis leylandii*, X **41**
*Cupressus arizonica* 52
*Cupressus lusitanica* 51
*Cupressus macrocarpa* 14, **51**
*Cupressus sempervirens* 19, **52**
cupuacu 318
cyanides 95
*Cyathea australis* 23
Cyatheaceae 22
Cyatheales 22
Cycadophyta 24
cycads, evolution 6
*Cydonia oblonga* 261
cypress,
Arizona 52
bald **66**
Chinese swamp **70**
hinkoi **43**
Italian 19, **52**
Lawson **40**
Leyland **41**
Mediterranean **52**
Monterey 14, **51**
Nootka **44**
Patagonian **45**
pond 66
sawara 43
swamp 15, **66**
Taiwan 40
white 44
Cyprian cedar 48
Cyprus strawberry tree **214**


# D


date palm 113
Canary Island **116**
*Davidia involucrata* **272**
dawn redwood **67**
Dawson's magnolia **97**
Delavay's fir 73
*Delonix regia* **327**
deodar cedar **47**
desert habitats 13
*Dicksonia antarctica* **23**
Dicksoniaceae 22, 23
dicotyledons 95
dioecious 18
*Diospyros ebenum* **324**
divisions (classification) 7
dogwood,
American flowering 276
Chinese 275
Japanese **275**
Pacific **276**
table **274**
variegated table 274
Dombey's southern beech **160**

double fertilization 94
Douglas fir 49, **50**
  Japanese 50
  large-coned **49**
dove tree **272**
downy birch **174**
downy oak **171**
*Dracaena draco* **120**
dragon spruce 80
dragon tree 13, **120**
dragon's blood tree **120**
dragon's claw willow 200
*Drimys lanceolata* 110
*Drimys winteri* **110**
drip tip leaves 11
drooping juniper 54
drupes 113
Dunkeld larch **77**
durmast oak **164**
Dutch elm **133**
dwarf birch, Chinese 175
dwarf fan palm **115**

# E

eastern hemlock **65**
eastern redbud 227
Ebenaceae 324
ebony **324**
egg cells 22, 24, 94
elder,
  box **298**
  common 298
elm,
  Caucasian **139**
  Chinese 136
  Dutch **133**
  English 17, **135**
  European hybrid **133**
  European white **134**
  fluttering **134**
  Japanese 135
  Siberian 134
  smooth-leaved 133
  wych 133, **136**
*Embothrium coccineum* **125**
embryo 22, 24, 94
empress tree **307**
endangered tree species 6
Engliah oak 7, **165**
English elm 17, **135**
Ericaceae 213–215
Erman's birch **178**
erosion, soil 6
*Eucalyptus* 60, 121
*Eucalyptus coccifera* **269**
*Eucalyptus cordata* 270
*Eucalyptus dalrympleana* **270**
*Eucalyptus globulus* 269
*Eucalyptus gunnii* **268**
*Eucalyptus johnstonii* **271**
*Eucalyptus pauciflora* 271
*Eucalyptus urnigera* 268
eucommia **124**
*Eucommia ulmoides* **124**
Eucommiaceae 124
*Eucryphia* **224**
*Eucryphia cordifolia* **223**
*Eucryphia glutinosa* **224**
*Eucryphia moorei* 223
*Eucryphia* x *nymansensis* 224
eucryphia, Nyman's 224
Eucryphiaceae 223–224
Eudicotyledoneae 7
eudicotyledons 7, 94, **121**
euodia **278**
Euphorbiaceae 329
European aspen **193**
European beech **152**
European fan palm 113, **115**
European hybrid elm **133**
European larch **76**
European lime **190**
European nettle tree **137**
European silver fir **71**
European white elm **134**
evergreen magnolia, Chinese 104
evergreen oak 7, **167**
evolution of trees 6

# F

Fabaceae 225–230, 262–263, 265–267, 326–327
Fagaceae 152–172
*Fagus crenata* **155**, 156
*Fagus grandifolia* 152
*Fagus japonica* 156
*Fagus lucida* 154
*Fagus orientalis* **154**
*Fagus sylvatica* **152**
*Fagus sylvatica* 'Pendula' 153
*Fagus sylvatica* Purpurea Group **153**
families (classification) 7
fan palm,
  dwarf **115**
  European 113, **115**
Farges' catalpa **306**
fern, maidenhair 26
fertilization 9, 24,
  double 94
*Ficus* 121
*Ficus benghalensis* **313**
*Ficus benjamina* 11, **314**
*Ficus carica* **146**
*Ficus elastica* **316**
*Ficus macrophylla* **315**
*Ficus religiosa* **312**
field maple **287**
fig,
  common **146**
  Moreton Bay **315**
  sacred **312**
  weeping 11, **314**
figs 121
filament 18
fir,
  Algerian 72
  alpine 75
  bigcone **49**
  Caucasian **72**
  Chinese **68**
  Colorado white 74
  Delavay's 73
  Douglas 49, **50**
  European silver **71**
  grand **75**
  Greek 71
  Japanese Douglas 50
  Korean **73**
  large-coned Douglas **49**
  luanta 68
  noble **74**
  Nordman 72
fire bush, Chilean **125**
*Fitzroya cupressoides* **45**
flaky juniper **55**
flamboyant tree **327**
flame of the forest **334**
flame tree **327**
flooding 14, 15
Florida Everglades 15
floss tree, silk **321**
flowering ash, Chinese **304**
flowering dogwood, American 276
flowering trees 7, **94**, 113
flowers 8, 94
  identifying 18
fluttering elm **134**
forest, flame of the **334**
forest zones 10
'fossil tree' 67
foxglove tree **307**
fragrant snowbell **218**
frangipani 325
*Fraxinus americana* **302**
*Fraxinus angustifolia* **303**
*Fraxinus chinensis* 304
*Fraxinus excelsior* **300**
*Fraxinus excelsior* 'Jaspidea' 300
*Fraxinus floribunda* 301
*Fraxinus mariesii* 304
*Fraxinus ornus* **301**
*Fraxinus pallisiae* 303
*Fraxinus pennsylvanica* 302
*Fraxinus sieboldiana* **304**
fringe tree, Chinese 129
fruits 8, 9, 19, 24, 94
Fuji cherry **238**
fullmoon maple **295**

# G

garden plum **237**
gean **232**
genera (classification) 7
'General Sherman' 63
generic name (classification) 7
*Genista aetnensis* 226
genus (classification) 7
ghost tree **272**
giant Himalayan pink tulip tree **101**
giant redwood **63**
gin 53
*Ginkgo biloba* 14, **26**
Ginkgophyta 24, 25
ginkgos 7, **25**
*Gleditsia triacanthos* **266**
*Glyptostrobus pensilis* **70**
Gnetophyta 24
goat willow **201**
golden ash 300
golden chestnut **162**

golden Japanese maple 292
golden larch **79**
golden-leaved Indian bean tree 305
golden-leaved robinia 262
golden-rain tree **273**
golden weeping willow **203**
grand fir **75**
grasses 95, 113
grasslands, evolution of 6
great white cherry 239
Grecian strawberry tree **214**
Greek fir 71
green alder, Japanese 183
green ash 302
grey alder **181**
grey birch 173
grey poplar 197
grey sallow 198
groups (classification) 7
gulmohar **327**
gum,
  black **209**
  cider **268**
  mountain **270**
  silver 270
  snow 271
  sour **209**
  Tasmanian blue 269
  Tasmanian snow **269**
  Tasmanian yellow **271**
  urn 268
  white mountain **270**
  yellow **271**
gums 121
*Gymnocladus dioica* **265**
gymnosperms, evolution 6

# H

habitats 10–15, 19
hackberry **138**
  Japanese 137
  Mediterranean **137**
  Mississippi 138
*Halesia carolina* **219**
*Halesia monticola* **220**
Hamamelidaceae 207–208, 211
handkerchief tree, pocket **272**
hawthorn,
  common 15, **243**
  Midland **244**
hawthorn (thorn), cockspur 94
hazel, Turkish **186**
heartleaf hornbeam 184
heat island effect 14
heaven, tree of **264**
hedge maple **287**
hedgerow habitats 15
hemlock,
  Canadian **65**
  eastern **65**
  Japanese 65
  mountain 64
  western **64**
hemlock woolly adelgid 65
Hemsley's styrax **217**
Henry's lime 190
Henry's maple 298
*Hevea brasiliensis* 316, **329**
hiba **59**
hickory,
  big-bud **150**
  bitternut **148**
  kingnut **149**
  shagbark **151**
hill cherry **239**
Himalayan birch **176**
Himalayan cherry 235
Himalayan juniper **55**
Himalayan larch 78
Himalayan manna ash 301
Himalayan pear, wild 250
Himalayan pink tulip tree, giant **101**
Himalayan white pine **92**
hinoki cypress **43**
Hippocastanaceae 282–284
Holford's pine 93
holly 15
  common **279**
  horned 279
  Perny's **280**
holly oak **167**
holm oak 7, **167**
Hondo spruce 83
honey locust **266**
Hong Kong orchid tree **326**
hoof tree, camel's **326**
hop hornbeam **187**
hornbeam 12
  common **184**
  heartleaf 184
  hop **187**
  Japanese **185**
  Oriental 185
horned holly 279
horse chestnut 7 *see also* buckeye
  Chinese 282
  common 281
  Indian 282
  Japanese 283
  red 284
  sunrise 286
Hungarian oak 164
Hupeh crab **247**
Hupeh rowan **257**
husk 9
hybrid elm, European **133**
hybrid larch **77**
hybrid magnolia **98**
  Veitch's 101
hybrid poplar 194
hybrid strawberry tree 214
hybrids 7

# I

identifying trees 16–19
*Ilex aquifolium* **279**
*Ilex corallina* 280
*Ilex cornuta* 279
*Ilex pernyi* **280**
incense cedar **39**
India, pride of **273**
Indian bean tree **305**, 306
  golden-leaved 305
Indian cedar **47**
Indian horse chestnut **282**
Indian rubber tree **316**
inflorescence 113
ironwood 187
  Persian **211**
Italian alder **182**
Italian cypress 19, **52**

# J

jacaranda **333**
*Jacaranda mimosifolia* **333**
jackfruit **311**
Japanese alder 182
Japanese apricot 238
Japanese beech 155, **156**
Japanese bigleaf magnolia 102
Japanese black pine 85
Japanese cedar **42**, 60
Japanese cherry birch 177
Japanese chestnut 161
Japanese chinquapin 167
Japanese dogwood **275**
Japanese Douglas fir 50
Japanese elm 135
Japanese green alder 183
Japanese hackberry 137
Japanese hemlock 65
Japanese hornbeam **185**
Japanese horse chestnut **283**
Japanese larch **78**
Japanese lime 189
Japanese magnolia, Northern 100
Japanese maple 7, **294**
  golden 292
  vine-leaved 295
Japanese pagoda tree **263**
Japanese plum yew **32**
Japanese rowan 252
Japanese snowbell **216**
Japanese spice tree 108
Japanese stewartia **221**
Japanese strawberry tree **275**
Japanese umbrella pine **69**
Japanese walnut **143**
Japanese yew 37
jasmine box **131**
jelly palm **117**
Joshua tree 13
Judas tree **227**
Juglandaceae 141–142, 148–151
*Juglans ailantifolia* **143**
*Juglans cinerea* 141
*Juglans nigra* **142**
*Juglans regia* **141**
juniper,
  alligator 53
  Chinese **54**
  common **53**
  drooping 54
  flaky **55**
  Himalayan **55**
  prickly 55
  scaly-leaved Nepal **55**
*Juniperus chinensis* **54**
*Juniperus communis* **53**
*Juniperus deppeana* 53

*Juniperus oxycedrus* 55
*Juniperus recurva* 54
*Juniperus squamata* **55**

# K

kapok **320**
karo 132
Kashmir rowan **258**
katsura tree 17, **212**
kauri pine 29
keaki **140**
Kentucky coffee tree **265**
Killarney strawberry tree **213**
kindling bark, broad-leaved **270**
King Billy pine **60**
King William pine **60**, 61
kingnut hickory **149**
'knees' 15, 66, 70
*Koelreuteria paniculata* **273**
kohuhu **132**
Korean birch 178
Korean fir **73**
Korean pine 92
kowhai 263

# L

laburnum,
  Alpine **226**
  common **225**
  Scotch **226**
  Voss's 225
*Laburnum alpinum* 225, **226**
*Laburnum anagyroides* **225**
*Laburnum* x *watereri* 225
lacebark pine **88**
*Lagerstroemia indica* **231**
Lamiaceae 332
larch,
  Dunkeld **77**
  European **76**
  golden **79**
  Himalayan 78
  hybrid **77**
  Japanese **78**
  Siberian 76
large-coned Douglas fir **49**
large-leaved lime **189**, 190
*Larix decidua* **76**
*Larix griffithii* 78
*Larix kaempferi* **78**
*Larix laricina* 77
*Larix* x *marschlinsii* **77**
*Larix sibirica* 76
Lauraceae 107–109, 111–112, 127–128
laurel 95
  bay **107**
  California **128**
  Canary Island **108**
  Chilean **109**
  Portuguese **234**
*Laurelia sempervirens* **109**
*Laurus azorica* **108**
*Laurus nobilis* **107**
Lawson cypress **40**
leaf fall, seasonal 12
leaves 8, 9, 16–17
Lebanon, cedar of **48**, 51
Lebanon oak 171
Lecythidaceae 322
lenticels 8, 15, 16
*Lepidodendron* 6
Leyland cypress **41**
*Libocedrus bidwillii* 56
*Ligustrum lucidum* **130**
Likiang spruce 81
lilies 113
lily tree 97
lime,
  American **192**
  broad-leaved **189**
  common **190**
  Crimean 188
  European **190**
  Henry's 190
  Japanese 189
  large-leaved **189**, 190
  Mongolian 192
  Oliver's 191
  small-leaved **188**, 190
  weeping silver **191**
*Lindera benzoin* 107
*Lindera obtusiloba* 108
Linnean system 7
*Liquidambar formosana* 208
*Liquidambar orientalis* **208**
*Liquidambar styraciflua* **207**
*Liriodendron chinensis* **106**
*Liriodendron tulipifera* **105**
*Lithocarpus densiflorus* **163**
liverworts 22
loblolly magnolia **96**
locust,
  black **262**
  honey **266**
lodgepole pine 27, **89**
*Lodoicea maldivica* 113
Loebner's magnolia 98
Lombardy poplar **195**
London plane 14, **204**
luanta fir 68
Lucombe oak 170
*Luma apiculata* **126**
*Luma chequen* 126
Lythraceae 231

# M

Macedonian pine 86
*Maclura pomifera* **147**
Madagascan baobab 319
Madagascar rainforest 6
madrone, Californian/Pacific **215**
magnificent willow 202
magnilian, Sprenger's **102**
*Magnolia acuminata* 96
*Magnolia campbellii* **101**
*Magnolia dawsoniana* **97**
*Magnolia delavayi* 104
*Magnolia denudata* 97, 98
*Magnolia grandiflora* **96**
*Magnolia kobus* 98, 100
*Magnolia liliiflora* 98, 103
*Magnolia* x *loebneri* 95, 98
*Magnolia obovata* 102
*Magnolia sargentiana* **99**
*Magnolia* x *soulangeana* **98**
*Magnolia sprengeri* **102**
*Magnolia stellata* 98, **100**
*Magnolia tomentosa* 100
*Magnolia tripetala* 99
*Magnolia* x *veitchii* 101
*Magnolia wilsonii* **103**
magnolia,
  Campbell's **101**
  Chinese evergreen 104
  cucumber 96
  Dawson's **97**
  hybrid **98**
  Japanese bigleaf 102
  loblolly **96**
  Loebner's 95, 98
  Mulan 103
  Northern Japanese 100
  Sargent's **99**
  saucer **98**
  star **100**
  Veitch's hybrid 101
  Wilson's **103**
Magnoliaceae 96–106
magnolias 95
magnoliids 95
mahogany **331**
maidenhair fern 26
maidenhair tree 6, 25, **26**
male cells 24, 25
*Malus baccata* **248**
*Malus domestica* **249**
*Malus hupehensis* **247**
*Malus sieversii* 249
*Malus sylvestris* **246**, 249
*Malus tschonoskii* 248
Malvaceae 188–192, 318–321
*Mangifera indica* **330**
mango **330**
mangrove 10
  Asiatic **328**
  habitat 14
  red 328
  tall-stilted **328**
manna ash **301**
  Himalayan 301
maple,
  ash-leaved **298**
  Caucasian **290**
  field **287**
  fullmoon **295**
  golden Japanese 292
  hedge **287**
  Henry's 298
  Japanese 7, **294**
  Norway **289**
  Oregon **299**
  paperbark **292**
  Père David's **291**
  red **293**
  rough-barked 287
  silver **297**
  snake-bark 291
  sugar **296**
  vine-leaved Japanese 295
mayten 131

*Maytenus boaria* 131
mazzard **232**
Mediterranean cypress **52**
Mediterranean hackberry **137**
medlar **261**
Meliaceae 331
Menzie's red beech 159
mespil, snowy 246
*Mespilus germanica* **261**
*Metasequoia glyptostroboides* **67**
*Metrosideros excelsa* **123**
*Metrosideros robusta* **122**
Mexican white pine **93**
michelia, sweet **104**
*Michelia doltsopa* **104**
Midland hawthorn **244**
mimosa **229**
minerals 8, 9
Mirbeck's oak **172**
Mississippi hackberry 138
mockernut **150**
monarch birch 176
Mongolian lime 192
monkey puzzle tree **28**
monocotyledons 7, 94, 95, **113**
monoecious 18
Monterey cypress 14, **51**
Monterey pine **90**
Moraceae 144–147, 310–316
Moreton Bay fig **315**
*Morus alba* **144**
*Morus nigra* **145**
mosses 22
Mount Etna broom 226
Mount Fuji cherry 242
Mount Wellington peppermint **269**
mountain ash **252**
  Chinese **257**, 259
mountain gum **270**
  white **270**
mountain habitats 13
mountain hemlock 64
mountain pepper 110
mountain pine 91
mountain snowdrop tree **220**
Mulan magnolia 103
mulberry,
  black **145**
  paper 144
  white **144**
*Myrisitica fragrans* 36
Myrtaceae 122–123, 126, 268–271
myrtle,
  Chilean **126**
  crape **231**
  Oregon **128**
  white Chilean 126
myrtle beech 158
*Myrtus luma* see *Luma apiculata*

# N

narrow-leaved ash **303**
necklace poplar, Chinese **196**
Nepal juniper, scaly-leaved **55**
nettle, stinging 138
nettle tree **138**
  European **137**
  southern **137**
New Zealand Christmas tree **123**
New Zealand red beech 160
*ñirre* **158**
noble fir **74**
Nootka cypress **44**
Nordman fir 72
Norfolk Island pine **29**
Northern Japanese magnolia 100
Norway maple **289**
Norway spruce **80**
*Nothofagus alpina* **157**
*Nothofagus antarctica* **158**
*Nothofagus betuloides* 157
*Nothofagus cunninghamii* 158
*Nothofagus dombeyi* **160**
*Nothofagus fusca* 160
*Nothofagus menziesii* 159
*Nothofagus nervosa* see *N. alpina*
*Nothofagus obliqua* **159**
nut tree, Brazil **322**
nutmeg,
  California **36**
  true 36, 95
nuts 8, 19
Nyman's eucryphia 224
*Nyssa aquatica* 210
*Nyssa sinensis* **210**
*Nyssa sylvatica* **209**

# O

oak 12, 121
  Algerian **172**
  chestnut-leaved 166
  common 17, 19, **165**
  cork **170**
  downy **171**
  durmast **164**
  English 7, **165**
  evergreen 7, **167**
  holly **167**
  holm 7, **167**
  Hungarian 164
  Lebanon 171
  Lucombe 170
  Mirbeck's **172**
  pendunculate **165**
  pin 169
  Pyrenean 165
  red 7, **168**
  scarlet **169**
  sessile **164**
  Turkey **166**
  water 168
Ohio buckeye 285
*Olea europaea* **129**
Oleaceae 129–131, 300–304
olive **129**
  California **128**
Oliver's lime 191
orange, Osage **147**
orchard apple **249**
orchid tree 326
  Hong Kong **326**
orchids 95
orders (classification) 7
Oregon alder **183**
Oregon maple **299**
Oregon myrtle **128**
Oriental alder 180
Oriental beech **154**
Oriental hornbeam 185
Oriental pear 251
Oriental plane **205**
Oriental spruce **81**
Oriental sweetgum **208**
Oriental thorn 243
Osage orange **147**
osier, common 201
*Ostrya* 185
*Ostrya carpinifolia* **187**
*Ostrya virginiana* 187
oval-leaved southern beech 157
ovary 18, 94
Oven's wattle 230
ovule 9, 24, 25, 27, 94
oxygen 6, 8, 9, 14, 15

# P

Pacific dogwood **276**
Pacific madrone **215**
Pacific yew **38**
pagoda tree, Japanese **263**
pahautea 56
Pallis's ash 303
palm 6, 95, 113
  cabbage **118**
  Canary Island date **116**
  Chusan **114**
  date 113
  dwarf fan **115**
  European fan 113, **115**
  jelly **117**
  pindo **117**
  Seychelles 113
  windmill **114**
Palmae 116
palmate leaves 16
papaya **325**
paper-bark birch **177**
paper mulberry 144
paperbark maple **292**
*Parrotia persica* **211**
Patagonian cypress **45**
*Paulownia tomentosa* **307**
'pawcohiccora' 148
pawpaw **325**
peach **241**
peach leaf curl fungal disease 236
pear 19
  Asian 251
  common **250**
  Oriental 251
  sand 251
  weeping silver-leaved **251**
  wild Himalayan 250
  willow-leaved **251**
pecan 149
pedunculate oak **165**
pepper, mountain 110
peppermint, Mount Wellington **269**
Père David's maple **291**

Perny's holly **280**
*Persea americana* **111**
Persian ironwood **211**
petals 18, 94, 95
*Phellodendron amurense* **277**
*Phillyrea latifolia* **131**
phloem 9
*Phoenix canariensis* **116**
photosynthesis 8, 9, 95
*Picea abies* **80**
*Picea asperata* 80
*Picea breweriana* **84**
*Picea glauca* 82
*Picea jezoensis* 83
*Picea likiangensis* 81
*Picea omorika* **83**
*Picea orientalis* **81**
*Picea sitchensis* **82**
pignut 148
pillar crab 248
pin oak 169
Pinaceae 46–50, 64–65, 71–93
pindo palm **117**
pine,
  Armand's 88
  Arolla 87
  Austrian 87
  Bhutan **92**
  big-cone 90
  Canary Island **91**
  Chile **28**
  Corsican **87**
  cow's tail **32**
  Himalayan white **92**
  Holford's 93
  Japanese black 85
  Japanese umbrella **69**
  kauri 29
  King Billy **60**
  King William **60**
  Korean 92
  lacebark **88**
  lodgepole 27, **89**
  Macedonian 86
  Mexican white **93**
  Monterey **90**
  mountain 91
  Norfolk Island **29**
  Scots **85**
  stone **86**
  umbrella **86**
  water **70**
  Weymouth 89
  Wollemi **30**
pink-blossomed cherry 240
pink siris **228**
pink tulip tree **101**
pinkwood 223
pinnate leaves 16
Pinophyta 24
*Pinus armandii* 88
*Pinus ayacahuite* **93**
*Pinus bungeana* **88**
*Pinus canariensis* **91**
*Pinus cembra* 87
*Pinus coulteri* 90
*Pinus contorta* var. *latifolia* **89**
*Pinus* x *holfordiana* 93
*Pinus koraiensis* 92
*Pinus mugo* 91
*Pinus nigra* 87
*Pinus nigra* subsp. *laricio* **87**
*Pinus peuce* 86
*Pinus pinea* **86**
*Pinus radiata* **90**
*Pinus strobus* 89
*Pinus sylvestris* **85**
*Pinus thunbergii* 85
*Pinus wallichiana* **92**
Pittosporaceae 132
*Pittosporum crassifolium* 132
*Pittosporum tenuifolium* **132**
plane, London 14, **204**
  oriental **205**
plane tree (sycamore) 288
Platanaceae 204–206
*Platanus* x *acerifolia* 14, **204**
*Platanus occidentalis* **206**
*Platanus orientalis* **205**
*Platycladus orientalis* **58**
plum **237**
  garden **237**
plum-fruited yew **33**
plum yew,
  Chinese **31**
  Japanese **32**
*Plumeria* 325
pneumatophores 15, 66
pocket handkerchief tree **272**
pod seeds 19
podocarp, willow-leaf **34**
Podocarpaceae 33–35
*Podocarpus andinus* see *Prumnopitys andina*
*Podocarpus nubigenus* 35
*Podocarpus salignus* **34**
poinciana, royal **327**
pollen grains 24, 27, 94, 121
pollen tube 24, 25, 121
pollination 9, 18, 27, 94, 113
pollution 6, 14
pond cypress 66
poplar,
  balsam 193
  black **194**
  Chinese balsam 195
  Chinese necklace **196**
  grey 197
  hybrid 194
  Lombary **195**
  white **197**
*Populus alba* **197**
*Populus balsamifera* 193
*Populus* x *canadensis* 194
*Populus* x *canascens* 197
*Populus lasiocarpa* **196**
*Populus nigra* **194**
*Populus nigra* 'Italica' **195**
*Populus nigra* subsp. *betulifolia* **194**
*Populus szechuanica* var. *tibetica* 195
*Populus tremula* **193**
*Populus trichocarpa* 196
Portuguese laurel **234**
Potanin's sumach **309**
prickly juniper 55
pride of India **273**
primitive angiosperms 7, 94, **95**
Prince Albert's yew **35**
princess tree **307**
privet,
  Chinese **130**
  shining **130**
prop roots 14
Proteaceae 125
prothallus 22
*Prumnopitys andina* **33**
*Prunus* 121
*Prunus armeniaca* 236
*Prunus avium* 121, **232**
*Prunus cerasifera* 237
*Prunus cerasus* 237
*Prunus domestica* **237**
*Prunus dulcis* **236**
*Prunus incisa* **238**
*Prunus lusitanica* **234**
*Prunus mahaleb* 232
*Prunus mume* 238
*Prunus padus* **233**
*Prunus persica* **241**
*Prunus rufa* 235
*Prunus sargentii* **242**
*Prunus serotina* **240**
*Prunus serrula* **235**
*Prunus serrulata* **239**, 240
*Prunus serrulata* 'Kanzan' 240
*Prunus 'shirotae'* 242
*Prunus spinosa* 237
*Prunus* 'Taihaku' 239
pseudocamellia, sawtooth 221
*Pseudolarix amabilis* **79**
*Pseudotsuga japonica* 50
*Pseudotsuga macrocarpa* **49**
*Pseudotsuga menziesii* **50**
Pteridophyta 22
purple beech **153**
purple camel's hoof tree 326
pussy willow **201**
Pyrenean oak 165
*Pyrus communis* **250**
*Pyrus pashia* 250
*Pyrus pyrifolia* 251
*Pyrus salicifolia* **251**


# Q


*Quercus* 121
*Quercus canariensis* **172**
*Quercus castaneifolia* 166
*Quercus cerris* **166**
*Quercus coccinea* **169**
*Quercus frainetto* 164
*Quercus* x *hispanica* 'Lucombeana' 170
*Quercus ilex* 7, **167**
*Quercus libani* 171
*Quercus nigra* 168
*Quercus palustris* 169
*Quercus petraea* **164**
*Quercus pubescens* **171**
*Quercus pyrenaica* 165
*Quercus robur* 7, 17, 19, **165**
*Quercus rubra* **168**

)uercus suber 170
uince 261
uinine tree **335**

# R

ainfall 6
ainforests 6
ata **122**
auli southern beech **157**
Ravenala madagascariensis 113
ed alder **183**
ed-barked birch, Chinese **175**
ed beech,
Menzie's 159
New Zealand 160
ed birch **179**
ed buckeye 284, **286**
ed cedar, western **56**
ed horse chestnut **284**
ed mangrove 328
ed maple **293**
ed oak 7, **168**
edbud, eastern 227
edwood,
coastal **62**
dawn **67**
giant **63**
esin 27
Rhizophora 14
Rhizophora mangle 328
Rhizophora mucronata **328**
Rhizophoraceae 328–329
Rhus potaninii **309**
Rhus verniciflua **308**
iver birch **179**
obinia, golden-leaved 262
Robinia pseudoacacia **262**
Robinia pseudoacacia 'Frisia' 262
oble beech **159**
ock birch, Russian **178**
oots 8
Rosaceae 232–261
ough-barked maple 287
ough tree fern 23
owan **252**
Hupeh **257**
Japanese 252
Kashmir **258**
Sargent's **259**
Vilmorin's 257
oyal poinciana **327**
ubber tree 11, **329**
Indian **316**
Rubiaceae 335
um cherry **240**
Russian rock birch **178**
Rutaceae 277–278

# S

sacred fig **312**
Salicaceae 193–203
Salix alba **199**
Salix babylonica **200**, 203
Salix babylonica var. pekinensis 'Tortuosa' 200
Salix caprea **201**
Salix cinera 198
Salix daphnoides **202**
Salix fargesii 203
Salix fragilis **198**
Salix magnifica 202
Salix pentrandra 199
Salix x sepulcralis 'Chrysocoma' 200, **203**
Salix viminalis 201
sallow, grey 198
sally wattle **230**
salt 14
Sambucus nigra 298
sand pear 251
Sapindaceae 7, 273, 281–299
Sapindales 7
Sargent's cherry **242**
Sargent's magnolia **99**
Sargent's rowan **259**
sassafras **127**
Chilean **109**
Sassafras albidum **127**
satinwood **207**
saucer magnolia **98**
sawara cypress 43
sawtooth pseudocamellia 221
Saxegothaea conspicua **35**
scaly-leaved Nepal juniper **55**
scarlet oak **169**
Sciadopityaceae 69
Sciadopitys verticillata **69**
Scotch laburnum **226**
Scots pine **85**
Scrophulariaceae 307
seed dispersal 9
seed trees 7, **24**
seeds 8, 19, 24, 27, 94
sepals 18, 94, 95
Sequoia sempervirens **62**
Sequoiadendron giganteum **63**
Serbian spruce 13, **83**
serviceberry, Alleghenny 247
service tree **256**
apple-fruited 256
true **256**
wild **255**, 256
sessile oak **164**
Seychelles palm 113
shagbark hickory **151**
shellbark, big **149**
shining privet **130**
Siberian crab **248**
Siberian elm 134
Siberian larch 76
Siebold's beech **155**, 156
silk floss tree **321**
silk tree **228**
silver birch **173**
silver fir, European **71**
silver gum 270
silver-leaved pear, weeping **251**
silver lime, weeping **191**
silver maple **297**
silver wattle **229**
silverbell tree **219**
Simaroubaceae 264
siris, pink **228**
Sitka alder 181
Sitka spruce **82**
small-leaved lime **188**, 190
smooth Japanese maple **294**
smooth-leaved elm 133
snake-bark maple 291
snow gum 271
Tasmanian **269**
snowbell,
fragrant **218**
Japanese **216**
snowbell tree, Chinese **217**
snowdrop tree,
Carolina **219**
mountain **220**
snowy mespil 246
soft tree fern **23**
soil erosion 6
Sophora japonica **263**
Sophora tetraptera 263
Sorbus aria **253**
Sorbus aucuparia **252**
Sorbus cashmiriana **258**
Sorbus commixta 252
Sorbus domestica **256**
Sorbus domestica var. pomifera 256
Sorbus hupehensis **257**
Sorbus intermedia **254**
Sorbus megalocarpa 260
Sorbus sargentiana **259**
Sorbus scalaris 259
Sorbus tibetica **260**
Sorbus torminalis **255**
Sorbus vilmorinii 257
sorrel tree **128**
sour apple **246**
sour cherry 237
sour gum **209**
Southeast Asia tropical forests 11
southern beech,
Coigüe **160**
Dombey's **160**
oval-leaved 157
rauli **157**
southern nettle tree **137**
Spathodea campanulata **334**
species name (classification) 7
sperm cells 22, 25
Spermatophyta 24
spice bush 107
spice tree, Japanese 108
spore trees 7, **22**
spores 22
Sprenger's magnolia **102**
spruce,
Brewer's weeping **84**
caucasian **81**
dragon 80
Hendo 83
Likiang 81
Norway **80**
Oriental **81**
Serbian 13, **83**
Sitka **82**
white 82
Yezo 83
St Lucie cherry 232
stamen 18, 95

star magnolia **100**
starch 8, 9
stewartia,
  Chinese **222**
  Japanese **221**
*Stewartia pseudocamellia* **221**
*Stewartia serrata* 221
*Stewartia sinensis* **222**
stigma 18, 121
stilt roots 14
stinging nettle 138
stone pine **86**
storax, bigleaf **218**
storax, Hemsley's **217**
strawberry tree,
  Cyprus **214**
  Grecian **214**
  hybrid 214
  Japanese **275**
  Killarney **213**
strobili (cones) 27
Stuartia 221
style 18
Styracaceae 216–220
*Styrax hemsleyanus* **217**
*Styrax japonicus* **216**
*Styrax obassia* **218**
subdivision (classification) 7
sucrose 9
sugar maple **296**
sugars 9
sumach,
  Chinese **309**
  Potanin's **309**
summit cedar **61**
sunrise horse chestnut 286
swamp cypress 15, **66**
  Chinese **70**
Swedish whitebeam **254**
sweet buckeye **285**
sweet cherry 232
sweet chestnut 7, **161**
  American 162
sweet michelia **104**
sweetgum **207**
  Chinese 208
  oriental **208**
*Swietenia mahagoni* **331**
sycamore **288**
  American **206**
*Sycopsis* **211**


# T


table dogwood **274**
  variegated 274
Taiwan cypress 40
*Taiwania cryptomeriodes* 42
tall-stilted mangrove **328**
tamarack 77
tanbark oak **163**
tannins 95
Tasmanian blue gum 269
Tasmanian cedar **60**
Tasmanian snow gum **269**
Tasmanian yellow gum **271**
Taxaceae 36–38
*Taxodium distichum* 15, 66
*Taxodium distichum* var. *imbricarium* 66
*Taxus baccata* **37**
*Taxus brevifolia* **38**
*Taxus chinensis* 38
*Taxus cuspidata* 37
teak **332**
*Tectona grandis* **332**
temperate broadleaf forests 10
temperate habitats 12
tepals 18, 95
*Tetradium daniellii* **278**
Theaceae 221–222
*Theobroma cacao* **318**
*Theobroma grandiflorum* 318
thorn, Oriental 243
thorn (hawthorn), cockspur 94, **245**
*Thuja occidentalis* **57**
*Thuja orientalis* see *Platycladus orientalis*
*Thuja plicata* **56**
*Thujopsis dolabrata* **59**
Tibetan cherry **235**
Tibetan whitebeam **260**
*Tilia americana* **192**
*Tilia cordata* **188**
*Tilia* x *euchlora* 188
*Tilia* x *europaea* **190**
*Tilia henryana* 190
*Tilia japonica* 189
*Tilia mongolica* 192
*Tilia oliveri* 191
*Tilia platyphyllos* **189**
*Tilia tomentosa* 'Petiolaris' **191**
*Torreya californica* **36**
*Trachycarpus fortunei* **114**
traveller's tree 113
tree fern 6, 22
  rough 23
  soft **23**
tree line 13
tree of heaven **264**
'tree of life' 119
tree rings 9
tropical broadleaf forests 10
tropical habitats 11
tropical rainforests 10
true service tree **256**
trunk 8
*Tsuga canadensis* **65**
*Tsuga heterophylla* **64**
*Tsuga mertensiana* 64
*Tsuga sieboldii* 65
tulip tree **105**
  African **334**
  Chinese **106**
  pink **101**
tupelo,
  black **209**
  Chinese **210**
Turkey oak **166**
Turkish hazel **186**


# U


Ulmaceae 133–140
ulmo **223**
*Ulmus glabra* **136**
*Ulmus* x *hollandica* **133**
*Ulmus japonica* 135
*Ulmus laevis* **134**
*Ulmus minor* 133
*Ulmus parvifolia* 136
*Ulmus procera* 17, **135**
*Ulmus pumila* 134
*Umbellularia californica* **128**
umbrella pine **86**
  Japanese **69**
umbrella tree 99
urban habitats 14
urn gum 268
*Urtica dioica* 138


# V


variegated table dogwood 274
varnish tree **308**
Veitch's hybrid magnolia 101
Vilmorin's rowan 257
vine-leaved Japanese maple 295
violet willow **202**
virgilia **267**
von Linné, Carl 7
Voss's laburnum 225


# W


walnut,
  black **142**
  common **141**
  Japanese **143**
warty birch **173**
water flow 6
water oak 168
water pine **70**
wattle,
  Cootamundra 229
  Oven's 230
  Sally **230**
  silver **229**
weather patterns 6
weather tree **253**
wedding-cake tree **274**
weeping beech 153
weeping fig 11, **314**
weeping silver-leaved pear **251**
weeping silver lime **191**
weeping spruce, Brewer's **84**
weeping willow **200**
  golden **203**
Wellingtonia 63
western hemlock **64**
western red cedar **56**
wetland habitats 15
Weymouth pine 89
white ash **302**
white birch **174**
white cedar 51, **57**
white cherry, great 239
white Chilean myrtle 126
white cypress 44
white elm, European **134**
white fir, Colorado 74
white mountain gum **270**
white mulberry **144**
white pine,

Himalayan **92**
Mexican **93**
white poplar **197**
white spruce 82
white willow **199**, 200, 203
whitebeam **253**
Swedish **254**
Tibetan **260**
wild cherry 121, **232**
wild Himalayan pear 250
wild service tree **255**
willow,
bay 199
crack **198**
dragon's claw 200
goat **201**
golden weeping **203**
magnificent 202
pussy **201**
violet **202**
weeping **200**
white **199**
willow-leaf podocarp **34**
willow-leaved pear **251**
Wilson's magnolia **103**
wind pollination 27
windmill palm **114**
winged seeds 19
Winter's bark 35, **110**
Winteraceae 110
Wollemi pine **30**
*Wollemia nobilis* **30**
wood 8, 24, 113, 121
wych elm 133, **136**

X

X *Cupressocyparis leylandii* **41**
X *Sycoparrotia semidecidua* 211
xylem 9, 24

Y

yellow birch 179
yellow buckeye **285**
yellow gum **271**
Tasmanian **271**
yellow-wood **267**
yew,
Chilean **33**
Chinese 38
Chinese plum **31**
common **37**
Japanese 37
Japanese plum **32**
Pacific **38**
plum-fruited **33**
Prince Albert's **35**
Yezo spruce 83
yuccas 113

Z

zelkova, Chinese 139
*Zelkova carpinifolia* **139**
*Zelkova serrata* **140**
*Zelkova sinica* 139

# ACKNOWLEDGMENTS

Produced in collaboration with the **Smithsonian Institution** in Washington D.C., USA, the world's largest museum and research complex. This renowned research centre is dedicated to public education, national service, and scholarship in the arts, sciences, and history.
**Smithsonian Enterprises:** Kealy Wilson, Product Development Coordinator; Ellen Nanney, Licensing Manager; Brigid Ferraro, Director of Licensing; Carol LeBlanc, Vice President

The publisher would like to thank the following: Derek Harvey for additional text and advice; Jane Parker for the index; Monica Byles for proofreading; Lili Bryant for editorial assistance; Sophia Tampakopoulos, Jacket Design Development Manager; Jonny Burrows for icon design; Jacqui Swann and Fiona Macdonald for design assistance; Sam Priddy, Fiona Macdonald, and Jonny Burrows for their help on the photoshoots; and Jenny Faithfull and Julia Harris-Voss for additional picture research.

Thanks to the following for assistance with photoshoots: Katrina Podlewska at The Forestry Commission National Arboretum Westonbirt, Gloucestershire and the Westonbirt volunteers Mike Westgate, Rosemary Westgate, Val Taylor, Peter Higginbotham, Brian Marsh, Sue Bradley Jones; Matthew Hall at Batsford Arboretum, Gloucestershire; and Andrew Conner at The Royal Botanic Gardens, Kew, London

The publisher would like to thank the following for their kind permission to reproduce their photographs:

(Key: a-above; b-below/bottom; c-centre; f-far; l-left; r-right; t-top)

**1 Corbis:** Fumio Tomita/amanaimages. **3 Getty Images:** Laszlo Podor Photography. **5 Tony Russell:** (bl, br). **6 Dorling Kindersley:** Thomas Marent (tr). **7 Alamy Images:** Martin Hughes-Jones (br). **9 Dorling Kindersley:** Alan Buckingham (cr). **11 Dinesh Valke:** (br). **13 Dorling Kindersley:** Paul Whitfield (tr). **14 Corbis:** Bob Krist (tr). **20-21 Corbis:** Mark Karrass. **23 Dorling Kindersley:** The Royal Botanic Gardens, Kew (cl, bl). **26 Tony Russell:** (cl). **27 Getty Images:** National Geographic/Ralph Lee Hopkins (b). **28 Tony Russell:** (t). **29 Ardea:** John Mason (JLMO) (cl). **30 Tony Russell:** (cl, b, t). **34 Dorling Kindersley:** The Forestry Commission at Westonbirt, The National Arboretum (cl, br); The Royal Botanic Gardens, Kew (t). **Tony Russell:** (bl). **36 Tony Russell:** (bl). **37 Tony Russell:** (cl). **38 Tony Russell:** (t, b). **39 Tony Russell:** (bl). **40 Tony Russell:** (cla). **41 Dorling Kindersley:** Batsford Arboretum (t, cl). **44 Dorling Kindersley:** Batsford Arboretum (t, cl). **45 Tony Russell:** (bl). **46 Tony Russell:** (cl). **47 Tony Russell:** (cl). **48 Tony Russell:** (b). **49 Tony Russell:** (bl, cl, tr). **50 Tony Russell:** (cl). **51 Tony Russell:** (cl). **52 Dorling Kindersley:** (t); Batsford Arboretum (cl). **53 Tony Russell:** (cl). **54 Tony Russell:** (tl). **55 Dorling Kindersley:** The Forestry Commission at Westonbirt, The National Arboretum (t). **56 Dorling Kindersley:** Batsford Arboretum (t, cl). **59 Tony Russell:** (bl). **60 Tony Russell:** (bl, tr). **61 Tony Russell:** (cl). **62 Tony Russell:** (cl). **63 Dorling Kindersley:** Paul Whitfield © Rough Guides (cl). **64 Tony Russell:** (cl). **65 Tony Russell:** (cl, bl). **66 Tony Russell:** (bl). **68 Tony Russell:** (tl, cl). **69 Dorling Kindersley:** Batsford Arboretum (t, cl). **70 Dorling Kindersley:** The Forestry Commission at Westonbirt, The National Arboretum (cl). **72 Corbis:** Harpur Garden Library (t). **73 Dorling Kindersley:** The Royal Botanic Gardens, Kew (cl). **74 Tony Russell:** (cl). **78 Tony Russell:** (cla). **79 Dorling Kindersley:** The Forestry Commission at Westonbirt, The National Arboretum (b). **80 Tony Russell:** (cl). **81 Tony Russell:** (cl). **83 Tony Russell:** (b). **84 Tony Russell:** (cl, bl). **85 Tony Russell:** (cl). **86 Tony Russell:** (cl). **88 Getty Images:** Steve Taylor (cl). **89 Tony Russell:** (cl). **91 Alamy Images:** Krystyna Szulecka Photography (t). **Tony Russell:** (bl, cl). **93 Tony Russell:** (bl). **96 FLPA:** Francois Merlet (bl). **99 Tony Russell:** (t, b). **100 Tony Russell:** (t). **102 Dorling Kindersley:** The Forestry Commission at Westonbirt, The National Arboretum (cl); The Royal Botanic Gardens, Kew (t). **103 Alamy Images:** Roger Phillips (t). **Tony Russell:** (b). **104 Tony Russell:** (t). **105 Alamy Images:** Science Photo Library (br).

**Tony Russell:** (cl). **106 Alamy Images:** FLPA (bl). **Dorling Kindersley:** (t); The Royal Botanic Gardens, Kew (cl). **108 Tony Russell:** (t). **109 Dorling Kindersley:** The Forestry Commission at Westonbirt, The National Arboretum (t, b). **111 Dorling Kindersley:** The Royal Botanic Gardens, Kew (cl). **114 Tony Russell:** (br). **115 Dorling Kindersley:** The Royal Botanic Gardens, Kew (cl). **116 © Plantdatabase.co.uk:** (t). **Tony Russell:** (cl). **117 Getty Images:** Garden Picture Library/Mark Bolton (t). **118 Dorling Kindersley:** The Royal Botanic Gardens, Kew (t, cl, bl). **120 Alamy Images:** Blickwinkel (cl). **122 Tony Russell:** (t). **123 Dorling Kindersley:** The Royal Botanic Gardens, Kew (t, cl). **124 Tony Russell:** (cl). **126 Getty Images:** Matt Anker (bl). **131 Dorling Kindersley:** The Forestry Commission at Westonbirt, The National Arboretum (cl). **133 Alamy Images:** Cath Evans (bl); tbkmedia.de (tr). **134 Dorling Kindersley:** The Royal Botanic Gardens, Kew (t, cl). **135 Alamy Images:** Frank Blackburn (t). **136 Alamy Images:** Steve Taylor ARPS (t). **Dorling Kindersley:** The Forestry Commission at Westonbirt, The National Arboretum (cl, bl). **137 Dorling Kindersley:** The Forestry Commission at Westonbirt, The National Arboretum (t, cl). **Peter Greenwood:** (b). **138 Dan Mullen:** (bl). **139 Dorling Kindersley:** The Royal Botanic Gardens, Kew (t, cl). **140 Dorling Kindersley:** Batsford Arboretum (t, cl). **141 Tony Russell:** (cl). **144 Alamy Images:** Blickwinkel (bl); mauritius images GmbH (cl). **148 Alamy Images:** Blickwinkel (bl). **149 Dorling Kindersley:** The Forestry Commission at Westonbirt, The National Arboretum (cl, t); The Royal Botanic Gardens, Kew (bl). **150 Dorling Kindersley:** The Forestry Commission at Westonbirt, The National Arboretum (cl, bl); The Royal Botanic Gardens, Kew (t, clb). **151 Alamy Images:** Blickwinkel (bl). **153 Dorling Kindersley:** The Forestry Commission at Westonbirt, The National Arboretum (t, cl). **154 Dorling Kindersley:** Batsford Arboretum (cl); The Forestry Commission at Westonbirt, The National Arboretum (bl). **155 naturepl.com:** Nature Production (t). **156 Dorling Kindersley:** The Forestry Commission at Westonbirt, The National Arboretum (t). **Tony Russell:** (bl). **157 Dorling Kindersley:** The Forestry Commission at Westonbirt, The National Arboretum (t, cl). **159 Dorling Kindersley:** The Royal Botanic Gardens, Kew (t). **160 Dorling Kindersley:** The Forestry Commission at Westonbirt, The National Arboretum (t, cl). **163 Steven J. Baskauf:** (t). **Tony Russell:** (bl). **164 Dorling Kindersley:** Batsford Arboretum (t, cl). **165 Tony Russell:** (cl). **166 Dorling Kindersley:** Batsford Arboretum (t, bl). **167 Tony Russell:** (cl). **170 Dorling Kindersley:** Batsford Arboretum (t); The Royal Botanic Gardens, Kew (cl). **171 Alamy Images:** Cuboimages srl (bl). **Dorling Kindersley:** The Forestry Commission at Westonbirt, The National Arboretum (t, cl). **172 Alamy Images:** Shapencolour (bl). **Dorling Kindersley:** The Forestry Commission at Westonbirt, The National Arboretum (t, cl). **183 Alamy Images:** Florapix (t). **Corbis:** Martin B. Withers/Frank Lane Picture Agency (cl). **185 Dorling Kindersley:** The Forestry Commission at Westonbirt, The National Arboretum (cl). **186 Dorling Kindersley:** The Forestry Commission at Westonbirt, The National Arboretum (t, cl, bl). **187 Dorling Kindersley:** The Forestry Commission at Westonbirt, The National Arboretum (t, cl). **194 Dorling Kindersley:** The Forestry Commission at Westonbirt, The National Arboretum (cl). **Fotolia:** alessandrozocc (bl). **195 Photolibrary:** (t). **196 Dorling Kindersley:** The Forestry Commission at Westonbirt, The National Arboretum (cl, bl, t). **197 Dorling Kindersley:** The Forestry Commission at Westonbirt, The National Arboretum (cl, t). **199 Tony Russell:** (bl). **200 Dorling Kindersley:** The Forestry Commission at Westonbirt, The National Arboretum (cl). **201 Dorling Kindersley:** The Forestry Commission at Westonbirt, The National Arboretum (bl, cl). **202 Dorling Kindersley:** The Forestry Commission at Westonbirt, The National Arboretum (cl). **Tony Russell:** (bl). **203 Tony Russell:** (bl). **204 Tony Russell:** (bl). **205 Tony Russell:** (cl). **207 Dorling Kindersley:** Batsford Arboretum (cl). **208 Dorling Kindersley:** The Forestry Commission at Westonbirt, The National Arboretum (t, cl, bl). **209 Dorling Kindersley:** The Forestry Commission at Westonbirt, The National Arboretum (cl). **210 Dorling Kindersley:** The Forestry Commission at Westonbirt, The National Arboretum (t, cl). **211 Dorling Kindersley:** Batsford Arboretum (t). **Tony Russell:** (b). **212 Dorling Kindersley:** (t); Batsford Arboretum (cl). **215 Fotolia:** Chungking (bl). **218 Tony Russell:** (bl). **220 Dorling Kindersley:** Batsford Arboretum (t, cl). **Tony Russell:** (bl). **222 Dorling Kindersley:** The Forestry Commission at Westonbirt, The National Arboretum (t, cl); The Royal Botanic Gardens, Kew (bl). **225 Tony Russell:** (bl). **232 Tony Russell:** (cl, tr). **233 Dorling Kindersley:** The Forestry Commission at Westonbirt, The National Arboretum (t, cl). **234 Tony Russell:** (bl). **239 Alamy Images:** imagebroker (t). **240 Alamy Images:** WILDLIFE GmbH (bl). **242 Tony Russell:** (cl). **243 Tony Russell:** (cl). **245 Dorling Kindersley:** The Forestry Commission at Westonbirt, The National Arboretum (cl); The Royal Botanic Gardens, Kew (t). **246 Dorling Kindersley:** The Royal Botanic Gardens, Kew (cl). **Tony Russell:** (t). **249 Tony Russell:** (cl). **250 Getty Images:** Thomas Marent (bl). **253 Getty Images:** Bob Gibbons/Oxford Scientific (t). **254 Alamy Images:** Blickwinkel (c). **258 Photolibrary:** Anne Green - Armytage (bl). **259 Tony Russell:** (bl). **262 Tony Russell:** (bl). **263 Dorling Kindersley:** Batsford Arboretum (t, cl). **Tony Russell:** (bl). **264 Dorling Kindersley:** Batsford Arboretum (t, cl). **265 Wikipedia:** hardyplants (bl). **266 Tony Russell:** (cl). **267 Dorling Kindersley:** The Forestry Commission at Westonbirt, The National Arboretum (cl, t). **269 © Plantdatabase.co.uk:** (cl). **271 James Wood:** (t). **272 Dorling Kindersley:** Batsford Arboretum (cl, bl). **274 Tony Russell:** (bl). **276 Tony Russell:** (bl). **280 Dorling Kindersley:** The Forestry Commission at Westonbirt, The National Arboretum (cl, t). **Tony Russell:** (bl). **283 Alamy Images:** Blickwinkel (bl). **Tony Russell:** (t). **285 Alamy Images:** Blickwinkel (bl). **287 Tony Russell:** (cl). **289 Tony Russell:** (cl). **295 Tony Russell:** (bl, t). **296 Dorling Kindersley:** Batsford Arboretum (t, cl). **297 Dorling Kindersley:** Batsford Arboretum (cl, t). **298 Dorling Kindersley:** The Forestry Commission at Westonbirt, The National Arboretum (t). **302 Dorling Kindersley:** The Forestry Commission at Westonbirt, The National Arboretum (t, cl). **304 Dorling Kindersley:** The Forestry Commission at Westonbirt, The National Arboretum (t, cl, clb). **305 Dorling Kindersley:** Batsford Arboretum (cl). **306 Dorling Kindersley:** Batsford Arboretum (cl); The Forestry Commission at Westonbirt, The National Arboretum (bl). **308 Dorling Kindersley:** The Forestry Commission at Westonbirt, The National Arboretum (t, cl). **309 Tony Russell:** (t). **310 Dorling Kindersley:** The Royal Botanic Gardens, Kew (cl). **311 Dorling Kindersley:** The Royal Botanic Gardens, Kew (t, cl). **312 Dorling Kindersley:** The Royal Botanic Gardens, Kew (cl). **313 Dorling Kindersley:** The Royal Botanic Gardens, Kew (t, cl). **314 Dinesh Valke:** (t). **315 Tony Russell:** (t, b). **316 Dorling Kindersley:** The Royal Botanic Gardens, Kew (t, cl). **317 Eric Hunt:** (t). **318 Dorling Kindersley:** The Royal Botanic Gardens, Kew (t, cl, bl). **319 Alamy Images:** Blickwinkel (bl). **R McRobbie:** (t). **320 Tony Russell:** (cl). **321 Tony Russell:** (bl). **322 FLPA:** Silvestre Silva (t). **Tony Russell:** (clb). **323 Tony Russell:** (cl). **326 Tony Russell:** (t). **327 Alamy Images:** Arco Images GmbH (bl). **Fotolia:** Christian Musat (t). **328 Alamy Images:** Leonid Serebrennikov (cl). **FLPA:** Konrad Wothe/Minden Pictures (t). **Photolibrary:** (bl). **329 Tony Russell:** (t). **331 Alamy Images:** Inga Spence (t). **332 Alamy Images:** Sajith Sivasankaran (t). **Photolibrary:** Ron Giling (cl). **333 Tony Russell:** (t). **334 Dorling Kindersley:** The Royal Botanic Gardens, Kew (cl, bl). **Tony Russell:** (t). **335 Alamy Images:** Wildlife GmbH (bl). **Tony Russell:** (cl)

**Jacket images: Dorling Kindersley**

All other images © Dorling Kindersley
For further information see:
**www.dkimages.com**